TOOLS
of
VIOLENCE

GUNS, TANKS
and DIRTY BOMBS

OSPREY
PUBLISHING

TOOLS
of
VIOLENCE

GUNS, TANKS
and DIRTY BOMBS

CHRIS McNAB | HUNTER KEETER

First published in Great Britain in 2008 by Osprey Publishing
Midland House, West Way, Botley, Oxford OX2 0PH, United Kingdom.
443 Park Avenue South, New York, NY 10016, USA.
Email: info@ospreypublishing.com

Every attempt has been made by the publisher to secure the appropriate
permissions for materials reproduced in this book. If there has been any
oversight we will be happy to rectify the situation and a written submission
should be made to the Publishers.

A CIP catalog record for this book is available from the British Library

ISBN-13: 978 1 84603 225 7

Chris McNab and Hunter Keeter have asserted their right under the
Copyright, Designs and Patents Act, 1988, to be identified as the authors
of this book.

Page layout by Myriam Bell
Index by Alan Thatcher
Typeset in Sabon and Trajan
Originated by PDQ Media
Printed in China through World Print Ltd.

08 09 10 11 10 9 8 7 6 5 4 3 2 1

For a catalog of all books published by Osprey please contact:

NORTH AMERICA
Osprey Direct, c/o Random House Distribution Center
400 Hahn Road, Westminster, MD 21157, USA
E-mail: info@ospreydirect.com

ALL OTHER REGIONS
Osprey Direct UK, P.O. Box 140, Wellingborough, Northants, NN8 2FA, UK
E-mail: info@ospreydirect.co.uk

www.ospreypublishing.com
Front cover: all images © TopFoto (www.topfoto.co.uk)

CONTENTS

ACKNOWLEDGMENTS

The authors gratefully acknowledge the help and support of many who made this book possible, including Lt Cmdr Tamsin Reese of the US Navy Office of Information, East, New York; Tara Landis, Nick Bertucci, Capt Neil Stubits, Jerry LaCamera, Amy O'Donnell, Bob Kaczmarek, Joe Shannon, Ed Johnson, and Gerry Pangilinan of the US Naval Surface Warfare Center, Indian Head Division, Maryland; Landon Hutchens and Greg Maxwell of the US Naval Sea Systems Command, Washington, D.C., Kathleen Rector, Trish Hamburger, Dr Daniel Wallace, Charles Garnett, Tom Boucher, Eugene Bowie, John Elliott, Mike Pompeii and Capt Joe McGettigan of the US Naval Surface Warfare Center, Dahlgren Division, Virginia; Dr William Atwater of the US Army Ordnance Center and Museum, Aberdeen Proving Ground, Maryland; Col (ret.) Robert Work of the Center for Strategic and Budgetary Assessments; Sam Ryskind; Col (ret.) Jack E. Keeter, Jr; and Dr Tami Williams. Further thanks go to Alan James, former soldier with the Rhodesian African Rifles, for his thought-provoking interviews; Mark Lachance of the Iraq Veterans Against the War organization; Mas Ayoob of the Lethal Force Institute; firearms specialist Martin Pegler; Martin Fackler, MD, for his expertise in wound ballistics; David Willey and David Fletcher of the Tank Museum, Bovington; and Dr Amer Hameed and Professor Ian Wallace of the Defence Academy of the United Kingdom. We would also like to thank all the staff at Osprey, particularly Anita Baker for her patient support of this project from concept stage to final delivery. Finally, we extend our heartfelt thanks to family and friends, for everything they do that makes a writer's life possible.

INTRODUCTION

Any book that focuses its entire subject matter on weapons skates on thin moral ice. There are two temptations, the first of which could be labeled "data worship." Weapons are, for the most part, works of extremely advanced engineering that have a technical allure all of their own. Because of the extremity of the job they perform, they produce compelling facts and figures, ranging from muzzle velocities to explosive force, and these, when combined with the startling light and sound of their usage, can lead some to treat them with the same wide-eyed fascination as cars or space rockets, with lots of potential for dramatic trivia. For instance, eating a large chocolate bar actually generates the same energy output as that created by propellant detonating behind a 105mm field artillery shell, the key difference being that the energy of the artillery shell is released in a few milliseconds, not over half an hour or so.[1] For large chunks of the world's population, principally male, that is a fascinating fact.

The second danger of studying weapons, which can be implicit in the first, is that the users and victims of weapons are forgotten. By focusing on the abstract power of weaponry, humans are taken out of the loop and portrayed merely as servants of or helpless pawns before the might of the gun, missile, or bomb. Such is particularly true in the age of "surgical" warfare, inaugurated by the media-friendly video footage of precision-guided munitions (PGMs) striking select targets during the 1991 Gulf War. At a US Department of Defense (DoD) news briefing on March 28, 2003, in the context of a fresh conflict, Secretary of Defense Donald Rumsfeld stated that "Our military capabilities are so devastating and precise that we can destroy an Iraqi tank under a bridge without destroying the bridge." In a sense, Rumsfeld was right – the precision of some modern weapon systems is astounding, and capable of taking out pinpoint targets. Furthermore, the military is correct when it emphasizes precision as a route to minimizing the dreadfully termed "collateral damage" – history is unlikely to see a Dresden fire bombing again.

The problem with the "precision perspective" is that it devalues the experience of the human participants in the process of warfighting. From a victim's point of view, this is obvious. A surgical strike by a Joint Direct Attack Munition (JDAM), for instance, is only surgical if you are safely outside the blast radius – if you are within it, all is horror, chaos, pain, and destruction. We must never lose humility before the fact that weapons are designed ultimately to injure, kill, or destroy. Even the "cleanest" of weapons, say the copper-jacketed bullet fired from a military assault rifle, can cause either a slow, nasty death (rarely a quick death, as we shall see) or a lifetime of disability. Furthermore, like the ripples caused by stones thrown into a pond, every time a weapon strikes a human target grief spreads out into the world through mothers, fathers, children, siblings, and friends. To point to victim experience should not be interpreted necessarily as an "anti-war" message, but simply reminds us that focusing on precision is a particular form of data worship that lessens the moral gravity of what is being done.

The other side of the equation is that of the user. While this book will engage with victims, at times in depth, the user of weapons – both individual and corporate – holds a special fascination for our study. The fact is this – no matter how sophisticated or automated the weapon system, it is ultimately controlled by a human being, with all the issues of professionalism and fallibility that this entails. A soldier or police officer can be trained to perfection, but he is always going to get tired, hungry, angry, bored, and occasionally careless. We all do the same every day, but the results when you are handling weapon systems are of greater magnitude than, say, if you are operating computer spreadsheet software. The flip side of promoting the "precision" war is that we can expect weapon operators to be almost computer-like in their actions, neutral participants simply keeping the war machine fed, rather than people having to make extraordinary acts of judgment, often under pressures without comparison in the civilian world.

The purpose of this book is to bring the human fully back into the loop when thinking about weapons. In short, we will look at how weapons are actually used in the fog of war or other lethal engagements by complex human beings. Such analysis is necessary. War is on our screens every day, and over the last 20 years military systems such as Scud, Patriot, and cruise missiles, the Uzi and AK47, white phosphorus munitions, A-10 attack aircraft, and "dirty bombs" have all entered into public consciousness or media debate, but often without fully exploring the human dimension of weapon use. The result, as we shall see, is frequently a military or police frustrated by media misunderstandings, and a public misinformed.

Note that appreciating the human dimension does not mean that we will ignore technical, tactical, or strategic issues. Indeed, a central purpose of this book is to provide a comprehensive single-volume insight into modern weapon systems, a primer, as it were, on the technology of violence. We will also tackle some of the major debates in the world of military technology, such as whether Main Battle Tanks (MBTs) have a future, and what the real purpose of a navy is. Our analysis progresses from small arms, weapons that have a very intimate association with an individual user, through to air and naval power wielded within vast, complex systems of command and control. As such, later chapters will necessarily have a more strategic feel than earlier chapters. Covering so much ground also means that there will be omissions – each chapter, if explored exhaustively, would easily comprise a whole book in its own right. What we hope to achieve is to give a real sense of how weapons are used in all their technological, social, political, economic, and psychological complexity. This means looking at how people and nations really use technology to fight, from pulling a pistol to apprehend a criminal, to sending an aircraft carrier traveling to foreign seas.

1

HAND-HELD WAR – SMALL ARMS

On January 17, 1989, Patrick Purdy stepped into the playground of the Cleveland Elementary School in the city of Stockton, California. Purdy, a mentally disturbed drifter, was holding a Chinese-produced version of the AK47 assault rifle, and without hesitation he opened fire on the children. Five children were killed and another 30 wounded as Purdy fired off over 100 rounds in 60 seconds, before finally shooting himself.

The incident sent seismic ripples through the US public and government, and began the process that led to the 1994 Federal Assault Weapons Ban. Much of the media response mythologized the lethality of Purdy's firearm, and dwelt upon the terminal effects of the military rounds upon their small victims. However – and not for a second downgrading the horror of the incident – the Stockton shooting in many ways actually questions the power of modern firearms. Why was it, for example, that of the 35 victims hit by supposedly devastating rounds 30 survived, with 86 percent of those injured making full recoveries? A possible answer emerged from the world-renowned authority on wound ballistics, Martin L. Fackler, MD, in his analysis of this shooting:

> It is ironic, in this country where firearms have played such a prominent historic role, that the general knowledge of weapon effects has become so distorted. Cinema and TV accounts of shootings constantly distort and exaggerate bullet effect. When shot, people do not get knocked backwards by the bullet; nor do they become instantly incapacitated, as usually depicted. False expectations resulting from these misleading performances have confused crime scene investigators, law enforcement and military trainers, and our courts of law.[1]

Fackler highlights the dangers of misrepresenting firearms in a society where legal accountability is paramount and media analysis persistent. What this chapter will seek to do is explain small-arms technology in its real-world context, attacking some of the misconceptions that inform the daily analysis of both military and civilian engagements.

The Small-Arms Family

Modern small arms are divided into distinct groups, each group having a relatively defined purpose within military, law enforcement, and civilian contexts. A basic grasp of these family groups is a fairly dry necessity, but with some hidden controversies.

King of the firearms is the rifle. At its most basic, a rifle is simply a weapon with a rifled bore and a long barrel (when compared with handguns) which is fired from the shoulder. More fundamentally, a rifle is designed for accurate aimed shooting over range. The ranges and capabilities of rifles vary enormously according to the type of weapon, particularly its caliber. Rifle calibers extend from small rimfire hunting cartridges such as the .17 HMR up to prodigious big-game rounds like the .600 Express. While the former will function best over ranges of up to 328ft (100m) and will kill, at most, animals up to fox size, the latter will drop an unfortunate bear beyond 1,968ft (600m). In military usage, rifles have gravitated to the 7.62mm and 5.56mm calibers, the implications and politics of which are discussed below. Yet regardless of the caliber, if the sights are properly calibrated, and the user adequately trained, the rifle should produce consistent groupings of just a few inches within its accepted range.

Another level of rifle classification is according to system of operation, that is, the mechanical process by which ammunition is fed through the firearm. The simplest type of mechanism is the venerable bolt-action, in which the cartridges are loaded and empty cases ejected by the manual operation of a bolt. The principal advantage of a bolt-action rifle is reliability – the mechanism is beautifully simple and conducive to excellent accuracy (hence many sniper weapons are bolt-action types). The down-side of the bolt-action is that reloading is grindingly slow when compared to an autoloader. Best rates are around one shot every two seconds for a magazine-fed rifle, and up to 10 seconds for a single-shot rifle. Self-loading rifles are a much faster proposition, as they perform the cycle of reloading and case ejection automatically after each shot. Automatic operation offers obvious advantages to a soldier in particular. First and foremost is rapidity of fire, as the soldier is capable of firing a shot with every pull of the trigger (which is known as semi-automatic fire). The advantages of this firepower became apparent during World War II, with the development of rifles such as the US M1 Garand. The Garand shook things up during World War II. It conclusively demonstrated the combat advantage of the semi-automatic rifle, particularly in scything down mass attacks or in delivering suppressive fire, where weight of lead was more important than accuracy. The US historian Peter S. Kindsvatter quotes Lieutenant George Wilson's experience of handling a German attack in the Huertgen Forest in 1944. The attack came as his unit was digging foxholes: "We instantly dropped our shovels, lay down in the shallow beginnings of our foxholes, and fired back with all we had." The Germans, mostly armed with bolt-action rifles, "proved no match for the volleys of our Browning Automatic Rifles ... and semi-automatic M1 [rifles]. The Krauts were stopped about seventy-five yards in front of us."[2] The US experience in the Pacific theater was similar, where US infantry and marines found that one or two soldiers could decimate a couple of squads of Japanese infantry if the enemy made an open attack.

Yet for all the self-loading rifle's advantages, it also retained a number of problems. First, it fired much the same long-range ammunition as bolt-action rifles.

While a sniper, his focus centered on delivering that perfect single shot, appreciated distance capability, for the general infantryman it was largely irrelevant. German studies conducted in the 1930s into actual, as opposed to theoretical, combat ranges came to some surprising conclusions. Chief amongst these was that soldiers rarely discharged their weapons at targets more than 984ft (300m) away – a lesson still true today. The main reason for this phenomenon was that, quite simply, any human-sized target over 1,640ft (500m) away is actually hard to see, never mind shoot at. Having a range of 3,280ft+ (1,000m+) is therefore irrelevant to most. Furthermore, the shoulder-thumping recoil generated by a full-power rifle round disrupted the accuracy of follow-up shots.

The solution was the assault rifle, pioneered by the Germans during World War II. The German combat studies mentioned previously resulted in a focus on developing a new cartridge, one more powerful than a pistol cartridge but with a performance designed around a practical combat range of some 1,312ft (400m). The result was the 7.92x33mm *Kurz* (short) cartridge, an "intermediate" round with the same caliber as the 7.92mm Mauser rifle but with a case length of 1.3in (33mm) as compared to the 2.3in (56.8mm) case of the 7.92mm Mauser. The "intermediate" label gives a good idea of the cartridge's performance: a muzzle velocity of 2,296ft/sec (700m/sec) and a combat range extending up to 1,968ft (600m). Several weapons were designed for the *Kurz* round. The MKb 42(H) was the first, created by Louis Schmeisser between 1940 and 1941, but this evolved into the far more famous MP43 (later relabeled the MP44). The MP43 was fed from a curved 30-round magazine, had a cyclical rate of fire of 500rpm and delivered a 125-grain bullet at a muzzle velocity of 2,300ft/sec (701m/sec). Hitler himself gave the MP43 the title *Sturmgewehr* – assault rifle – and it laid the groundwork for the future of infantry small arms. Today, almost all professional armies are equipped with assault-type weapons such as the US M16, the Russian AK47 and the British SA80. Assault rifles offer the advantages of increased ammunition carriage (more cartridges for the same weight), controllable selective fire (because of reduced recoil) even when firing fully-automatic, and manageable dimensions, all of which have the added benefit of reducing marksmanship training times when compared to the assault rifle's hard-kicking predecessors.

At the ground floor of the small-arms family are handguns. As the name suggests, handguns are firearms that can be aimed and fired with one hand. They are subdivided according to whether they are revolvers or automatic handguns. The former puts ammunition under the gun's hammer via a revolving cylinder, the cylinder being turned from one round to the next either simply by pulling the trigger or by cocking the gun's hammer. Revolvers typically have limited ammunition capacity, usually no more than six rounds, but what they do boast is reliability. Should an automatic weapon misfire, the shooter has to remove the problematic round from the chamber manually before the gun can shoot. With a revolver, all he has to do is pull the trigger once again to move on to the next bullet (unless there is a more serious malfunction). Automatic handguns are fed not from a cylinder but from a magazine, typically inserted into the grip. The big advantage of this is capacity. For example, while a popular revolver such as the Ruger GP 100 carries the typical six rounds of .357 Magnum ammunition, the Glock 17 automatic has a magazine capacity of 17 rounds of 9mm Parabellum.

The key point when thinking about handguns is their diminutive barrel length. Handgun barrels typically range from around 2.5in (6cm) up to about 8in (20cm) for some high-power magnum guns. Effective range for such weapons is around 164ft (50m), although the practical range, as we shall see, can be much less than that. Therefore, in the family of small arms, handguns tend to be assigned as backup weapons in a military context (a firearm to use should the principal weapon fail), or as the most publicly acceptable and easily portable form of police weapon.

The next stage up from handguns in the small-arms family tree is the submachine gun. This is broadly defined as a full-auto (fully-automatic) weapon firing pistol cartridges. (The "sub" prefix in the title refers to the fact that these guns use pistol ammunition, hence they are beneath the full-caliber cartridge standards of many rifles and machine guns.) The emergence of submachine guns was governed by many of the same considerations that led to the adoption of intermediate-round rifles. The first practical submachine guns were produced during World War I in an attempt to develop a weapon suited to producing maximum firepower in the chaotic close-range actions of trench raiding or position assaults. Pistols could not entirely fulfill the brief – they emptied too quickly and were grossly inaccurate if the combat range was stretched at all. Contemporary rifles, as explored above, were too long, too powerful (in a short-range action, rifle bullets would be capable of driving through several people before coming to a stop, potentially leading to friendly-fire incidents) and too slow to fire. Submachine guns, however, ticked all the right boxes.

The Italians led the way with (arguably) the world's first submachine gun, the 9mm double-barreled Vilar-Perosa, but the "first true submachine gun"[3] was the German Bergmann MP18. This fired the 9x19mm Parabellum (still today the defining submachine gun round) at a rate of 400rpm from a 32-shot helical drum magazine, and was used to good effect by specialist German assault troops during the last major battles of World War I. Submachine guns proved themselves in concept during the war, and the 1930s and 1940s saw dozens of different models produced and adopted for military or police service. During World War II, for example, the Soviet Union made around five million 7.62x25mm PPSh-41s, while Britain equipped its forces with three million ultra-cheap 9mm Sten guns. Post-war, however, the story of the submachine gun is one of steady decline. New designs kept coming, including Uziel Gal's infamous 9mm Uzi and Heckler

& Koch's still popular MP5 series, but in a way those things that originally made the submachine gun into a blessing steadily turned into its curse. Full-auto fire at the rates of which submachine guns are capable – the Ingram Model 10, for example, will empty a 32-round magazine in less than two seconds – has its problems. Accuracy, except in the most sophisticated models, is typically wild, the violence of the burst leading to intense vibrations and often a sharp muzzle climb. Gene Weingarten, a writer for the *Washington Post*, tried out a submachine gun for the first time and noted that:

> once you start firing, your entire field of vision disappears into a gassy, smoky blur, and you are no longer really able to see your target. All you can do is wrestle desperately to keep the barrel down against a ferocious upward kick. It is as though the gun is some Satanic beast that really wants to fire directly at God.[4]

Often, the submachine gun will be "aimed" by observing the bullet impacts and then walking them onto the target. (Note that submachine guns are rarely, by professionals, fired from the hip, but are shouldered like an assault rifle.) Furthermore, the submachine gun fires pistol-caliber ammunition, with all the limitations of range and penetration that entails (although the longer barrel of the submachine gun will add additional range and muzzle velocity).

The advent and development of the assault rifle in many ways stole the submachine gun's thunder. Intermediate-power weaponry offered both full-auto capability and a far broader range spectrum, plus its accuracy tended to be better over all ranges. The result was that over the second half of the 20th century, use of submachine guns has tended to bifurcate. On the one hand, they have become weapons of choice for many counter-terrorist and SWAT- (Special Weapons and Tactics) style law enforcement agencies. For these groups, high-quality submachine guns offer the advantage of decisive firepower at very close ranges, a controlled burst of fire into the chest of a terrorist providing a quick, decisive take-down. The term "high-quality" is seminal here – with hostages possibly in close proximity, officers do not want a "spray and pray" type weapon. (Think of how accurate targeting must be in the confines of a train, bus, or airplane.) The highly accurate MP5 fulfils the specialist brief nicely, as an SAS warrior who used the gun in London's Iranian Embassy siege operation in 1980 describes: "The MP5 fires about 1,200 rounds a minute and you have a 30-round magazine. You pull the trigger and they [the bullets] have gone in about two seconds."[5]

On the other hand, submachine guns have, unfortunately, also become more common in terrorist and criminal hands. They are ideal for their purposes. Most of their actions take place at short range, so long-range rifles are unnecessary. Submachine guns, by their generalized lethality, also require little training to operate for maximum destructive pay-off, and most studies have noted that criminals rarely have any depth of firearms expertise.[6] For this reason they promote confidence amongst the inexperienced. As even Martin Pegler, a leading firearms historian and a sober judge of weapons performance, noted in interview: "Firing a submachine gun makes you feel like a god."[7]

If firing a submachine gun gives delusions of divinity, then firing a full-blown machine gun can deliver feelings of outright omnipotence, at least in the inexperienced. The purpose of a machine gun varies somewhat according to type, but generally speaking it provides suppressive fire (an intense level of firepower designed to keep enemy heads down while infantry maneuver onto their target) or the attrition of enemy personnel or material. Machine guns fire rifle rounds and larger ammunition, have fast rates of fire – anywhere between 500 and 4,000rpm – and they typically have long range and hence, with the proper mount, can be used for indirect fire. (Direct fire is where the user has line-of-sight contact with his target and fires directly at it; indirect fire is used when there is no visual contact, and the rounds are fired in a high trajectory to drop onto the target.) Feed mechanisms are typically a belt, usually of around 200–250 rounds, or a box magazine, although modern machine guns like the FN Minimi (the US Army's M249 Squad Automatic Weapon) can also take ammunition from a soft pouch or even, in an emergency, from standard infantry M16 magazines.

Machine guns are usually classified according to three basic types: light, medium and heavy. Light machine guns (LMGs) are designed to be relatively easily carried and operated by one person, although sometimes with an assistant. They are usually mounted on front bipods, although some are also placed on pintle mounts on vehicles. Light machine guns are sometimes little more than standard assault rifles with heavier/longer barrels – examples include the Russian RPK and the British Light Support Weapon (LSW) – while popular weapons such as the Minimi are sophisticated weapon systems designed to provide a considerable boost to squad firepower. (Typically, a four-man squad of infantry will carry at least one light machine gun.)

While light machine guns often take the ammunition of standard assault rifles – as with the 5.56mm Squad Automatic Weapon (SAW) and LSW – medium machine guns (MMGs) are of heavier caliber, usually 7.62mm or similar, and are more suited to sustained-fire roles. With examples including the US M240 (the US version of the popular FN MAG) or the Browning M1919, they are usually served by a two-man crew, and they can be mounted on bipods, tripods, or various vehicle mounts. Mounts, incidentally, are not just systems for controlling a machine gun's weight. The type of mount actually shapes the fire possibilities of the soldier. For example, a bipod is quick and easy to deploy, but when used by a soldier lying in a prone position it has a somewhat limited traverse and elevation/depression, hence is more suited to point targets at closer ranges. Tripods, by contrast, take longer to set up (they will usually be transported separate from the gun) but give the machine-gunner a more stable platform and, in the better models, the means to set the trajectory and arc of the fire mechanically, hence giving greater accuracy and the ability to fine-tune the shooting against long-range targets.

Heavy machine guns (HMGs) are heavy in both weight and caliber. They are always mounted on either tripods or vehicle mounts, and they boast large, extremely powerful calibers – typically .50in (12.7mm.) Heavy machine guns give enormous range and punch, and are primarily designed to be deployed against vehicles (including light armor), buildings, and bunkers, where their heavy rounds are capable of punching through structures. The violence of a .50cal M2 machine gun is vividly described by a US Vietnam veteran when interviewed for Mark Baker's book *Nam*:

> Whoa, let's think this one over, man, I am serious. A .50-caliber machine gun is not to be fucked with. Movies have done a disservice to that weapon. What they fail to convey is that a .50-caliber machine gun is big and bad enough that if you look around a city block, you will see almost no structure standing that you can hide behind safely if somebody is firing one of those things at you. It just goes through everything.[8]

This account of .50cal capabilities is borne out by scientific testing. Tungsten penetrator variants of the .50 BMG (Browning machine gun) round, when fired from an M2HB, can go through 7.87in (20cm) of reinforced concrete at 1,312ft (400m), and can smash a vehicle engine block at well over 4,921ft (1,500m). Reflect on the fact that such guns can throw out these rounds at 500rpm, and you have some idea of their power.

One last category of machine gun is the general-purpose machine gun (GPMG), typified by weapons such as the German MG3 (based on the World War II-era MG42) or the Belgian FN MAG. The GPMG, technically, can cover the roles of the other three machine gun types depending on the mount used. In World War II, for example, the MG42 was used on a bipod by infantry assault teams (as an LMG), on a tripod for sustained fire (MMG), and on heavy aircraft mounts for air defense (HMG). In reality, however, GPMGs do not adequately fulfill the HMG role, because they do not come in the heaviest of calibers.

This hasty description of the small-arms family omits some categories of weapons, but covers most of the important bases for our chapter here. One further type that requires a mention, however, is the shotgun. Shotguns are smoothbore weapons that, as the name suggests, fire shot (multiple cylindrical pellets) instead of bullets (although solid slug ammunition is available for many shotgun types). They come in a variety of configurations – principally double-barreled, semi-auto and pump-action. Shotgun caliber is denoted by gauge, this being the number of lead balls that exactly fit the gun's bore that it would take to make up 1lb (0.45kg) in weight – hence a 12-gauge shotgun would take 12 balls, a 16-gauge 16 balls and so on. Only the diminutive .410 shotgun has its caliber represented by a measurement. (Note that the word "bore" can be substituted for the word gauge.)

Shotguns have certain advantages over bullet-firing weapons. First, and central to the shotgun's capabilities, is that it fires a spread of shot that impacts over a relatively wide area. By doing so the shotgun maximizes the chances of a hit, particularly against fast-moving targets that do not allow for a precise and careful aim (hence they are classic guns for clay or game shooting). The diameter of this spread at point of impact depends on numerous variables, including the size of shot, the constriction of the muzzle (known as "choke") and the length of the barrel (the shorter the barrel the more quickly the shot spreads, hence the criminal use of sawn-off, or shorter-barreled, shotguns.)

The principal disadvantage of shotguns, however, also relates to ammunition type. Shotguns are short-range weapons when compared to rifles. A 12-gauge shotgun firing 1oz (28g) of No. 8 shot, for instance, will have an effective range against small animals of around 98ft (30m), while 00 shot can handle human targets up to 131ft (40m). Rifled slugs take the effective range out to around 328ft (100m). Compared with the 1,968ft (600m) range of an assault rifle, the shotgun appears ballistically feeble.

Yet it is precisely when used for close-quarter work that the shotgun excels. Combat shotguns such as the US Marine Corps' M1014 Joint Service Combat Shotgun are almost invariably of semi-auto or pump-action types, these typically having a magazine capacity of 5–8 rounds depending on the model. They offer a curious package of firepower properties, having target effects at close range that are far more destructive than individual bullets, yet minimizing the danger to bystanders or hostages. The US Firearms Tactical Institute describes the reasons for choosing the shotgun as a defense weapon as:

> 1) to minimize wall penetration to reduce the danger to innocent third parties in case of a missed shot, 2) to maximize wound trauma to stop a vicious assailant as quickly as possible, or 3) because a shotgun does not require as much skill as a handgun to put lead on target.[9]

Point no. 2 is the critical one here. Even at close ranges it is common to hear accounts of officers and soldiers pouring bullets into an attacker without stopping them quickly enough (see below for the sobering realities of wound ballistics). Shotguns, by contrast, deliver an instant large wound with the massive hemorrhage effects that can quickly take down an assailant. Note that in military and hostage-rescue use, the combat shotgun is actually, in many ways, a precision weapon. It is tightly choked, giving small, devastating patterns. Leroy Thompson, a hostage rescue and VIP protection specialist, states that a properly choked combat shotgun:

can actually be used to take a head shot on a hostage-taker when a hostage is nearby. This is not an advisable practice and requires great precision – normally the shooter will aim at the eye socket away from the hostage, thus keeping the spread of the pattern within the hostage-taker's head.[10]

The precision of the shotgun is something not normally appreciated. The popular media image is of a weapon that hurls out a shot spread over many feet, making accuracy on the part of the user almost negligible. Tests by Chris McNab firing 00 buck from a 28in barrel from half choke at 10 yards punched an irregular hole in the target of only 2.36in (6cm). Thompson goes on to note, however, that the principal law enforcement and counterterrorist use of combat shotguns is often simply as an entry weapon, using special ammunition designed to shatter door locks and hinges.

The Gun Criteria

What must a gun do? The question is not answered fully by the knee-jerk response "kill" – this focuses purely on the victim, not the user. Rather, a gun has to conform to a whole spectrum of human requirements if it is to achieve its end result, putting bullets on target, and some of these requirements have nothing whatsoever to do with shooting.

D.F. Allsop and M.A. Toomey, in their military firearms primer *Small Arms – General Design*, define small arms as follows:

> There are many slightly different definitions of Small Arms. In general most talk of man or crew portable, relatively flat trajectory, largely shoulder controlled weapons, in calibers up to 12.7mm, used primarily to incapacitate or suppress the enemy with bullets or fragments.[11]

This definition covers most major bases. What it emphasizes is that a firearm, even one handled by a small crew, is a personal weapon in which the user controls the relationship of the fire to the target, and makes most of the targeting decisions. (This is in contrast to, say, an artillery crew, whose targeting is usually controlled by either a forward observer, pre-agreed grid coordinates, or a designator system, rather than a member of the crew itself.)

Such a personal weapon has to fulfill some demanding criteria. First, it must be manportable. Not only must the soldier be able to carry the gun within the context of lengthy marches, but he must be able to wield it easily in combat. Second, the gun must be dependable in function, both in terms of its reliability and its user friendliness. Third, it should be accurate over its accepted range. Fourth, it must be capable of having powerful effects on the target; if that target is a person, that means creating enough damage to force a rapid incapacitation.

This snapshot list belies a world of controversy at every turn. Because firearms are the most personal of weapons with the broadest distribution, issues to do with the form and function of small arms have the widest of impacts and controversies. Looking first at issues of portability and reliability, we can start to understand some of the myriad human factors behind firearms use and design.

Portability

Standard military issue rifles today tend to weigh in around the 8.8lb (4kg) mark, with the British SA80A2 at 10.95lb (4.98kg) and the US Army's M16A2 at 8.79lb (3.99kg). Both of these weights are given with the guns loaded up with 30-round magazines – and this is crucial. Treating a firearm as a system rather than a single tool means factoring in the weight and amount of ammunition that can be carried. This is something of a political hot topic in defense circles. The lighter the round (i.e. the smaller the bullet and case) the more ammunition a person can carry. As any soldier will tell you, ammunition consumption in combat is extremely high, so maximizing the volume of rounds is always good. However, the heavier rounds have greater range and destructive effect, hence many Western soldiers still lament the replacement of the 7.62x51mm NATO (North Atlantic Treaty Organization) round with the 5.56x45mm NATO round in rifles between the 1960s and 1980s. Yet regardless of the weight of the individual round, the infantryman in a professional army will still be carrying to the limit of his capacity. James Dunnigan, a well-known writer on military tactics and technology, throws the issue into relief:

> Ammunition is heavy. Each trooper usually carries seven magazines, that's nearly twenty pounds, plus another 12–15 pounds for the rifle, bayonet, flashlight, first aid kit and some grenades. The fire teams, of four troops, are based on a light machinegun carried by one of the men, which goes into action with about a thousand rounds of ammo (70 pounds worth for a 7.62mm, half that weight for 5.56mm.) This load is split between other members of the team. So everyone is carrying 30–40 pounds worth of munitions.[12]

Dunnigan goes on to state that the weapon and ammunition are only part of the soldier's burden, with the rest of his kit pushing the total carriage through 100lb (45.5kg). This weight has significant implications for the way the soldier uses his weapon. A study conducted for *Military Medicine* magazine in 2003 discovered that upper-body muscle fatigue, particularly when concentrated around the elbows and upper arms (such as commonly occurs when carrying boxes of ammunition or antitank weapons), had an appreciably bad effect on marksmanship amongst 12 volunteer US Army soldiers. While, theoretically, the soldiers could compensate for muscle weakness by firing from the prone position or by supporting the gun on a solid external surface, the study revealed that these positions are only practically used in about 20 percent of cases – standing and kneeling were the most frequently used shooting stances. Moreover, the study also reported that the increased heart rate generated by physical exercise was a further issue:

> ... shooting accuracy was most diminished immediately after exercise when the heart rate was highest. Using a laser mounted on a rifle barrel, researchers observed increased wobble diameter as heart rate increased following exercise of rising intensity, which may affect shot group size.[13]

The study found that levels of marksmanship returned to something like normal over a 5–12-minute period, but combat conditions are rarely so forgiving as to allow recovery time. A US platoon commander in the 3rd Battalion, 4th Marines, 3rd Marine Division stationed in South Korea in the 1970s discovered such a reality when conducting an amphibious assault exercise on the South Korean coastline:

> Without describing in detail the maneuver of the battalion in the exercise, it should be sufficient to say that each marine was carrying almost 100 pounds. Those equipped with radios and crew-served weapons were carrying in excess of that weight. Movement was slow, limited in distance and the units usually worn down physically.
> I was the platoon commander for the first platoon of Company M and while it was difficult to shoulder that load and conduct a movement to contact on level ground, it was virtually impossible to do so while climbing the high, steep hills of South Korea. My marines were so fatigued from simply packing their equipment from position to position, that the enemy was not a major concern. Had this operation not been a peacetime exercise with controlled aggressors, I am certain we would have had serious problems fighting and defeating even a small enemy force.[14]

Even with modern technologies, there is little that can be done in real terms to decrease the burden. What a soldier makes in weight savings he quickly loses by taking on more equipment, hence the energy advantage is perennially lost. Nevertheless, a critical criterion for any firearm is that it is as light as possible, for the very weight of the firearm will have an impact on the soldier's battlefield handling of that weapon.

Reliability

The core of usability in terms of firearms is, above all, reliability. As soldiers the world over will acknowledge, they prefer reliable firepower over an accurate firearm any day. It should be noted that most firearms can be unreliable given the wrong environmental conditions. Mud and dust can enter through ejection ports and cocking handle slots, causing the bolt group to jam, or wearing away parts; snow and rain cause rust on any unprotected metal; icy conditions can freeze a gun up solid. Also, freshly developed firearms tend to go through a curve of reliability, encountering numerous problems on first issue, though these are (hopefully) resolved steadily in successive models.

The standard US M16 rifle is a prime example of this learning curve. While today the M16 is held up as one of the world's finest assault rifles, such has not always been the case. Its introduction into the Vietnam War, for example, caused much subsequent hand wringing. Phased into service in the mid 1960s, it was designed to replace the M14 carbine, a solid, heavy, reliable 7.62mm rifle. Dick Culver, a soldier of the 2nd Battalion, 3rd Marine Regiment, in South Vietnam, remembers being given an orientation lecture on the new rifles, in which:

> The Battalion was told that they would now be able to carry 400 rounds ashore on each operation, and were now armed with an accurate, hard hitting rifle that would tear a man's arm off if you hit him. The lecture was impressive. The interesting thing is that the Marines WANTED to like the little rifle – it was light, cute, and supposedly extremely effective! Marines are *always* in favor of a weapon that will dismember their enemy more efficiently.[15]

Despite the assurances, Culver and numerous other US soldiers quickly found that the new rifles had a shocking jam rate in combat. The key problem was that the type of propellant in the cartridges had been changed, without trials, from the Improved Military Rifle (IMR) powder to a type that increased carbon deposits around the bolt group and adversely affected the gas-operated mechanism. The result was that not only could the gun jam solid if excessive deposits had a chance to cool, but empty cartridge cases would remain stuck in the chamber instead of being extracted, with another live round crushed down on top of it.

This technical problem had very significant battlefield results. A weapon jam is a critically dangerous moment for a soldier, who is effectively rendered powerless having just alerted the enemy to his presence with his first shots. Culver highlights the terrible price paid by soldiers who operate unreliable weapons:

> On one notable occasion, a stalwart Marine crept around in a flanking movement on an enemy machine gun position. He assumed a quick kneeling position to get a clear shot over the sawgrass, and "did for" the hapless NVA [North Vietnamese Army] gunner! His second shot aimed for the assistant gunner never came, as his rifle jammed and the assistant gunner avenged his dead comrade by splattering the Marine's gray matter all over the stock of the Matty Mattel Special.[16]

The problems were gradually overcome with measures such as better powders and a chromium-lined bore (which reduces erosion and case adhesion), although in the early days many ordnance authorities were keen to pass the buck by blaming poor cleaning procedures (something that grated intensely on soldiers such as US Marines, who have a near-religious respect for weapon maintenance).

Proper cleaning is, nevertheless, vitally important to the effective operation of any gun. In fact, there are three types of behavior regarding small arms that typically distinguish poor-quality troops from professional soldiers. First, reckless waste of ammunition can occur, either through wild, inaccurate shooting in combat or, worse still, through profligate target practice to relieve boredom. (Livestock are frequently the target of this type of shooting, or unfortunate civilians who happen to wander by. One US Vietnam veteran, for instance, recounts shooting an old lady just to see what happened, while a reporter interviewed by the authors speaks of seeing Russian troops in Georgia letting off their weapons at bottles etc, but using a populated village as a backstop for their rounds.) Second, poor safety procedures (for instance lazy muzzle awareness, or not checking whether rounds are in the chamber) can lead to unusually high rates of accidental discharges and, frequently, casualties. Finally, guns may be infrequently or poorly cleaned. This last factor is critical. For all the vast improvements in powder and technology over the years, guns are still messy machines, with every single round leaving deposits in the barrel and operating system. Factor in environmental dirt and you should see a professional soldier spending in the region of 20 minutes a day cleaning his or her personal weapon. Professional soldiers will try never to make an exception to this rule; they know their lives may depend upon it.

Nevertheless, even the most diligent cleaning procedures can be defeated by extreme weather conditions. For example, despite decades of improvements and tweaks to the weapon, service personnel in Iraq still have their grumbles about the latest M16A2 and its carbine version, the M4, complaining that the guns are highly sensitive to the talcum-like dust that prevails there. This is why most armies (we will see a painful exception shortly) trial their guns in a wide variety of climate zones and conditions. Age is also an important factor in reliability, as with time and use weapon parts, particularly sensitive springs, thin firing pins, and parts of the trigger group, can become worn, rattly, and prone to failure. Complaints from Iraq concerning failures with the M249 SAW are probably in part due to the environmental conditions, but also to the fact that many of the US Army's SAW stocks are over ten years old, and are starting to feel their age.

Another serious issue is barrel heating, particularly for machine-gunners running hundreds of rounds down the barrel. Consider that modern ammunition propellant burns at a temperature of around 3,632°F (2,000°C) and can impart about half of that temperature to the surface of the rifle bore as the bullet passes down the barrel. Although the temperature of the bore drops dramatically once the bullet has left the gun, heat spreads through the depth of barrel, and keeps rising if the gun is fired repeatedly. If the gun is fired in an appropriate burst/pause manner, then the barrel heating tends to reach a steady state, but in fast-firing combat situations there is always the danger that the barrel will heat up beyond its capabilities. The critical temperature of most barrels is around 932°F (500°C) – keep the barrel at this temperature for too long, or exceed it, and problems arise. One problem is "cook off," where the temperature in the chamber becomes so extreme that it sets off ammunition without the trigger being pulled.[17] Barrels can also become so hot that their rifling is stripped off or the barrel effectively begins to melt, and droops – machine-gunners since World War I have noted that in extreme circumstances barrels have been known to go almost translucent, such is the heat.

For machine guns, barrel change is a necessity, and modern quick-change barrel systems allow barrel swapping in under five seconds. Note, however, that barrel changing is a tactical as well as a reliability consideration – firepower downtime can be potentially lethal in a firefight. Opposing soldiers attacking the machine-gun post, for instance, will often listen out for barrel-change breaks as the moment to launch their assault. Basic machine-gun training advocates firing the weapon in short bursts of roughly 6–9 rounds, with a pause of some 4–5 seconds in between, a rate of around 100rpm. This firing procedure not only extends the time between barrel changes (because cooling time is allowed between each burst), but it can also have a tactical advantage in making the machine gun less of a target. Continuous, rippling bursts of fire will clearly identify a machine gun to the enemy, who will then typically make that machine gun a priority target for his own fire. In a machine gun like the M240B, the recommended rate of fire will require a barrel change every 10 minutes. If the rate increases to 200rpm, fired in bursts of 10–13 rounds with 2–3 seconds pause between, barrel-change time drops to just 2 minutes. Should the machine-gunner simply run through entire belts without stopping, barrel change can be just 30 seconds or so. Barrels that have been changed out will be used again, and their cooling time is accelerated by placing them on a cooling surface, such as wet grass.

To see how critical reliability is in a firearm, and to get a general feel for the difference between the well-designed and poorly-designed weapon, two case studies will serve us well. They feature a gun that has attracted some of the poorest publicity in post-World War II history, and another that has literally reshaped the security status of the world.

Case study: the L85A1/SA80

The development of the British Army's SA80 rifle is an almost textbook example of how not to produce a military firearm. Produced by the Royal Small Arms Factory (RSAF), Enfield, the L85A1 (as the rifle is also known) had its launch party in 1985. The gun was to be the replacement for the 7.62mm SLR (Self-Loading Rifle), a British Army version of Fabrique Nationale's FN FAL. The SLR had reliability, accuracy, and superb long-range punch; what it didn't have was compatibility with the 5.56mm NATO ammunition adopted by the United States, plus it had no automatic fire mode and its heavy recoil stretched out training times.

The SA80 was, by comparison, incredibly compact (it measured only 785mm/30.9in in length), took the 5.56mm round, and could deliver controllable full-auto fire (something the SLR could not). It was also of a distinctive "bull-pup" design: the magazine and receiver are located behind the trigger rather than in front, allowing the gun to retain a long barrel but keep the overall dimensions short. Equipped with an optical Sight Unit, Small Arms, Trilux (SUSAT) sight as standard for combat troops (auxiliary troops made do with the rifle's open "iron" sights), the SA80 was also unusually accurate.

So far, so good. There was just one problem – the L85A1 (the first version) was despicably built and designed. In a long and politically charged saga, too complex to recite in full here, some critical mistakes were made. Development of the SA80 actually stretched back to the 1940s, when the RSAF was working on an automatic rifle known as the Experimental Model 2 (EM2). This weapon, actually a well-built 7mm firearm, was accepted under the Labour government of 1945–51, but subsequently rejected by Winston Churchill's Conservatives, who opted for the Belgian FN FAL. However, design interest in the bullpup weapon continued in the Ministry of Defence (MoD), and by the 1970s the new design – the L85A1 – was slated as the SLR replacement. Yet by this time there had been a critical change in production emphasis. Pressure to adopt more modern, far cheaper production methods of pressing, stamping, and welding rather than expensive machining forced an engineering culture change that, unfortunately, does not seem to have been backed by updated skills. James Meek, a journalist for the British *Guardian* newspaper who has published one of the most detailed studies of the SA80 saga, interviewed several designers involved in the original SA80 project who delivered some worrying admissions:

"With the move from the EM2 to the SA80, they moved from a wooden stock, and machined components, to pressed steel and plastic," says Cliff Jewell, who worked as a junior designer on the project in the mid-70s. "Although the SLR had given Enfield the opportunity to make the transition from wood to plastic, I think the pressed-steel concept was a new departure and perhaps sufficient effort wasn't invested in that." Another junior designer, who later rose to a senior position in the Royal Ordnance hierarchy, says he had become alarmed at early design meetings over the apparent failure by his bosses to understand that pressed steel and plastic parts couldn't be expected to fit together as well as machined parts: "People that were in charge were demanding tolerances from plastic moulding that could really only be achieved by the precision of being carved from solid steel. I'm talking microns [thousandths of a millimeter]. Plus or minus one or two microns is very tight."[18]

Further sources also informed Meek that a budget of around £250 was set for the SA80, even though most equivalent military standard assault rifles cost double that figure.

Problems for the SA80 designers stacked up through the late 1970s and early 1980s. NATO adopted the 5.56mm round, hence the gun (previously intended for 4.85mm cartridges) had to have all its key parts reworked, often weakening them in the process. Royal Ordnance was privatized, then bought by British Aerospace (BAe) in 1987, which subsequently closed the factory at Enfield and displaced production to Nottingham (although many of the parts were fielded out to subcontractors, rather than keeping production under one roof). Meek notes that this caused such a precipitous plunge in staff morale at Enfield in its final days that "9,000 of the last 10,000 rifles made there had their receivers, the metal core of the gun to which other parts were fitted, squeezed in a vice to make them fit."[19] Furthermore, despite the fact that production was running late and that serious issues were being raised over the gun's reliability, these concerns were quashed and the contract renewed to ensure that BAe continued its purchase of Royal Ordnance.

Suspicions that a dreadful rifle was in production go back some way. A "Small Arms Update" document published by the Infantry Trials and Development Unit (ITDU; the principal body in the British forces for developing and testing infantry weapons), dated 2000, makes an interesting observation about the SA80's trial phase:

> The saga goes back to 1978 when the General Staff Requirement (GSR) was for a rifle to fire 200rds in a 24hr period mainly single shots and for the LSW[20] to fire 800rds in the same time frame but mainly in bursts. Both weapons in their current state can do this day after day and at that time the people at ITDU could only trial a weapon in accordance with the GSR. It met that GSR and so the weapon was accepted. It had no rates of fire, stoppage criteria or mean round between failure. In fact it had no relevance to any form of firefight and was totally out of touch with the requirements of the man on the ground.

The unrealistic GSR smacks of the desire simply to push the gun through without problems, and further evidence shows that climate testing was conducted principally in laboratory conditions, rather than in field trials.

When the SA80 finally emerged in 1985, the catalog of problems was an infantryman's nightmare. They included:

- Firing pins broke easily.
- The magazine catch was easily caught, causing the magazine to drop out, and the magazine itself was poorly made (Heckler & Koch, the company subsequently charged with SA80 modifications, believed that 40 percent of stoppages came from the magazine).
- The bolt would bounce back slightly as it tried to lock the round, causing a misfire. This resulted in soldiers being taught a "forward assist" procedure – banging on the cocking handle to make sure the bolt was seated properly – that sometimes had to be performed after almost every shot.
- Empty case extraction was poor owing to a badly designed extractor and weak extractor spring. The ejection spring was also weak, and the cocking handle could also interfere with extraction.
- Bits would fall off, including such important items as selector switches (which were also loose and unreliable).
- The plastic stock could start to melt by chemical reaction when it came into contact with standard British Army facepaint camouflage.

Naturally enough, such a list of design problems began to produce disastrous press coverage of the weapon, often based on heartfelt criticisms from soldiers who felt that their lives were on the line. Paratroop forces deployed to Kosovo in the late 1990s even refused to take out the LSW, insisting instead on carrying the venerable but trustworthy GPMG, the British version of the FN MAG.[21]

Finally, after years in denial, the MoD decided that all SA80s required major overhaul, and commissioned the German company Heckler & Koch to do the work. The revision has been substantial, and has come in:

> at a cost of £92 million to sort out the 200,000 rifles and LSWs in stock: that is, £460 for each gun. The ministry asserted that this was cost-effective, as purchasing new ones would cost, apparently, £500 million, a staggering £2,500 per weapon. This is totally untrue. The American M16, as preferred by the SAS [one unit that can choose its own weaponry, hence has been spared the SA80], can be bought retail for under £400.[22]

Page is right here to point out the financial absurdities of the Heckler & Koch upgrade, which produced the SA80A2. Yet the upgrade has been done properly this time, and now we face a strange situation in the media where the SA80A2 is tarred with the same brush as its predecessor. In a parliamentary debate in July 2002 the then-Defence Secretary, Geoff Hoon, came under some very specific probing about the SA80A2:

Mr Bernard Jenkin (Member of Parliament for North Essex): If we are to make an effective contribution to the military coalition – if there is one – the soldiers whom we deploy must have 100 per cent confidence in their rifle. Can the Secretary of State confirm that the exercise in Afghanistan involving a platoon of 30, firing 90 rounds each, resulted in 20 out of the 30 rifles jamming? Can he confirm that the concern is that the cleaning regime and the handling regime of the rifle may not have been correct? Will he also confirm that unless he can restore 100 per cent confidence in the rifle, he does not rule out scrapping the SA80 and replacing it with an alternative?

Mr Hoon: I will not go into the details of what is contained in a report that is still being analysed in the Ministry of Defence, but I assure the hon. Gentleman, as I assure the House, that those matters will be properly set out before the House in due course. I want to ensure that there is confidence in the weapon. The hon. Gentleman knows, as do other right hon. and hon. Members from their own military experience, that there is no such thing as a 100 per cent successful rifle.[23]

Hoon's final statement here is one that needs to be borne in mind when assessing any report on a firearm, as it is broadly true. Although the reliability of the SA80A2 might not be as phenomenal as some official reports,[24] it was properly tested in Alaska, Brunei, and Kuwait as well as in temperate zones, and the ludicrous GSR was replaced with a proper Battle Field Mission (BFM) of 150 rounds (five magazines) in 8 minutes, mixing single shots and automatic fire under operational conditions, without jamming. Some poor reports of the M16A2, the M4 carbine, and the M249 SAW from US soldiers in Iraq show that the SA80A2 has now simply taken its place in the order of fallible modern firearms. Note, however, that with criticisms still emerging from some quarters, the SA80 family is due to be replaced in 2015.

Case study: the AK47

We now turn to a firearm with a very different history, not only military but cultural. No weapon embodies the global problem of small arms more persuasively than Mikhail Kalashnikov's AK47. The AK has achieved an iconic status seldom found in the history of weaponry. AKs appear in the national flag and coat of arms of Mozambique (and formerly in the flag of Burkina Faso), and have graced the sectarian graffiti of Northern Ireland and of the African-American ghettos of the United States. In some African countries the word "Kalash" is a slang term for boys, and a semi-ritualistic Kalashnikov purchase is often classed as a formal rite of passage to manhood. In the West rap artistes such as Snoop Dog and N.W.A have given the AK youth cache in their lyrics, the latter declaring in the controversial track "Straight Outta Compton:"

AK-47 is the tool
Don't make me act the motherfucking fool...
Not the right hand cause I'm the hand itself
every time I pull a AK off the shelf
The security is maximum and that's a law[25]

AKs are similarly vaunted in Hollywood. In Quentin Tarantino's *Jackie Brown* (1997), the gun-dealing character Ordell Robbie, played by Samuel L. Jackson, advocates the AK to Louis (Robert de Niro) on the grounds that: "AK-47, absolutely, positively the best there is ... when you got to kill every single motherfucker in the room, accept no substitutes ..."[26] The AK has, quite simply, become a popular definer of ultimate hand-held firepower.

The AK47 was the brainchild of Mikhail Timofeyevich Kalashnikov. A former engineer on the Turkestan–Siberia railroad, Kalashnikov entered the army in 1938 and, while serving as a tank commander, was injured near Bryansk during the German *Barbarossa* offensive in October 1941. It was during his six-month convalescence that he began formulating ideas for a new Soviet automatic rifle system. A protracted period of experimentation followed, but in 1947 he produced the first AK47 – a gas-operated 7.62x39mm weapon, fed from its now signature curved 30-round magazine and utilizing a highly reliable rotating bolt in its action. In 1949, after two years of testing, the AK47 was accepted as the standard firearm of the Soviet Army. Unlike the case of the SA80, little politics informed the decision – it was simply the best weapon for the job.

What followed was unparalleled in the history of firearms. Such was the AK's popularity with its users, and its ease of manufacture, that production of the AK family of weapons has to date reached an estimated 70–100 million units with a totally global distribution. No other firearm comes close to this level of output – two of the world's most common assault rifles, the US M16 and the Belgian FN FAL, have to date yielded eight million and seven million units respectively.

The reasons for the AK's notoriety and ubiquity, however, need some demythologizing. By the standards of an M16 or a British SA80, the AK is a relatively crude weapon. A standard 7.62mm AK is fairly inaccurate – it is equipped with sights that are adjustable to half a mile (a little more than half the length of a modern airport's runway); however, the AK's best performance is really confined to less than a quarter mile, like shooting along the length of a city block. (Smaller-caliber members of the AK family, such as the 5.54mm AK74, tend to have better accuracy.) Nor does the AK, to contradict Ordell, have a special claim on killing power. The 7.62x51mm NATO round used in many standard weapons such as the FN FAL and H&K G3 has a much greater penetrative power and lethal range. Indeed, almost any military-grade assault weapon with full-auto capability will boast as much lethal force as the AK at practical killing ranges.

Yet there are two aspects where the AK reigns supreme – it works and it's available. In terms of reliability, the AK is second to none. With only the occasional field strip and clean – a rudimentary process in itself – an AK will keep on working regardless of environmental conditions and usage, and its chromium-lined barrel will endure thousands of rounds of fire without complaint. (Some tests have seen individual AKs, properly cleaned and maintained, fire up to 30,000 rounds before a jam.) Plaster an M16 or SA80 in sand, snow, and mud, and it will in all likelihood jam solid upon firing. Do the same to an AK, and little more than a brush down will return it to use. Following the ban on assault weapons in Britain in the wake of the Hungerford massacre in 1987, one AK owner decided to destroy his weapon by burying its barrel in the earth and pulling the trigger from a distance with a lanyard. Normally, the overpressure created by a blocked barrel upon firing would blow the barrel apart. In this case, the firing resulted in a crater in the soil and an undamaged AK. The owner was forced to hacksaw the barrel in half.

Anyone who places his or her life in the hands of a weapon will acknowledge that reliability always trumps sophistication. The AK offers pure, rugged functionality, and this in itself is key to its popularity. In fact, during the Vietnam War Western Special Forces units often relied upon Chinese- and Russian-made AKs. Operating behind enemy lines, they found the field maintainability of the AK and the ready availability of ammunition trumped the greater accuracy and longer range of weapons like the M16 rifle, especially in close-quarters battle situations. Furthermore, the durability of the AK gives it a long shelf-life, allowing for an individual weapon manufactured in, say, the 1970s to be recycled through various hands well into the 21st century.

An anecdote will give a conclusive demonstration of the AK's tough dependability. Alan James, a young officer serving with the Rhodesian African Rifles during the brutal war in the late 1970s/early 1980s, recounts the following incident:

On the Zambesi River, they [the ZAPU insurgents] had a river crossing from Zambia. They came across in dinghies, and we had a contact with them as they hit the shoreline. Lots of them went into the water with their packs and all the rest of it, most of them couldn't swim ... but once the contact was over anything that was lost in the river obviously you couldn't see it or retrieve it. Six months later we were coming along that same stretch of river – remember it was the dry season – and we saw the butt of an AK47 sticking out of the sand ... still in the water. We pulled it out and the magazine was still in it. It was on fire and was actually on automatic. We got the magazine out, but we couldn't clear the breech [i.e. pull back the cocking handle to empty the round in the chamber]. We tried to kick it ... we kicked it several times but it was solid. So we put the magazine back in and pulled the trigger and it fired all 30 rounds.[27]

It would be unimaginable for an SA80 or M16 to perform the same feat.

This fact brings us to the issue of the AK's availability, having already noted the astonishing production figures above. In a world overshadowed by terrorist bombs and suitcase nukes, by aircraft carriers and supersonic fighters, the humble AK presents arguably the greatest current security problem faced by the modern world. Possibly 3–4 million people have been killed globally by AKs since 1947. The Small Arms Survey of 1995 estimates that 60–90 percent of all annual war deaths are caused by small arms, with the AK creating a major portion of the death toll. With an inexact but nevertheless valid calculation, that means that of the 100,000 war deaths in 2003 up to 90,000 were caused by small arms. Allowing for all other small-arms types (including mines), AKs probably accounted for some 50,000 deaths.

The AK has armed entire conventional armies, but equally it now litters the world in the hands of terrorists, factions, militias, and criminals of every continent. In Africa, for example, AKs are so common that in Rwanda and Angola one can be swapped for a chicken or bag of maize. The monetary trading price for an AK and two ammunition clips in southern Africa is around $15. By contrast, an AK bought in the United States can cost over $1,000.

The reasons for the AK's awful ubiquity are convoluted. First, there remains a highly buoyant legal trade in AK weaponry, with a large number of licensed producers outside the Commonwealth of Independent States (a confederation of former Soviet states.) Armenia, Bulgaria, China, the Czech Republic, Egypt, Finland, Hungary, Iraq, Israel, Korea, Pakistan, Poland, Romania, and Slovakia all engage in licensed production of AK-type weapons. Privatization of state arms companies often allows governments to circumvent international arms regulations and sell to any buyer. Bulgaria, for example, committed 22 military production plants – including those specializing in the production of four different models of AK – to privatization in 1997. The following year it was able to provide $1.5 million of arms to the British private military contractor Sandline International and the former president of Sierra Leone, Ahmad Tejan Kabbah.

The diversity of political interests represented in the list of AK producers ensures that almost any buyer of AKs can find a seller. Hence Texim, the Bulgarian state trading agency, sold huge volumes of AKs direct to Christian militias fighting in the Lebanon in the 1970s, while the Nicaraguan Contras groups purchased up to $3 million worth of AKs from Poland. In the 1990s the former East Germany transferred 304,000 AK rifles and 106 million rounds of ammunition to Turkey following the collapse of communism. Because of the AK's durability, once the buyer has no more need for his weapons, they can be easily transferred to other buyers, legal or illegal – Northern Ireland's IRA was hence able to purchase AKs from Mozambique in the 1980s.

More than anything, it is the illegal trade and unlicensed manufacture of AKs that creates the biggest international security problem, particularly in regions of endemic violence such as Africa and the Middle East. Access to illegal AKs is never a problem for illicit arms brokers. During the Cold War, the Soviet Union, communist Eastern Europe and China engaged in the massive transfer of AKs to fuel various proxy wars in the Middle East, South America, Africa, and Asia. Mozambique alone, just one of a total of 50 countries to accept direct Soviet military aid, received one million AKs.

The volume of AKs in circulation also enabled the United States to facilitate AK sales through CIA-sponsored brokers. At least 400,000 CIA-sold AKs went into Mujahideen hands in Afghanistan during the war against the Soviet occupation between 1979 and 1989, while the total stocks of unaccounted AKs amassed on the Pakistan–Afghan border amounted to upwards of three million weapons. In a classic post-Cold War irony, many of those CIA-traded AKs are now turned upon US forces in the "Global War on Terrorism."

The Cold War effectively ended in 1989/90, but the AKs remained in circulation. More critically, the enormous stocks of AK weaponry within the former Soviet Union and Eastern Europe lost their accounting structure. National economies tottered, and thousands of soldiers went unpaid, so illegal trade in small arms became an ideal method of increasing personal and state income. Abdel Fatau Musah and Robert Castle, consultants for the International Action Network on Small Arms, paint a terrifying picture of a trade thriving on chaos:

> When the Russian 366th Motor Rifle Regiment withdrew in 1993, it left its entire stock of weapons to Karabakh Armenians ... Throughout 1992, up to seven train loads of weapons arrive in Kalingrad each day, only to be left in an insecure compound with no accounting procedures ... A Russian news agency described most of the 70 weapons depots covering 75 hectares of land in Moscow as "built in the last century" and "sparingly guarded by three elderly men."[28]

Further sources confirm Musah and Castle's analysis. Some 3,000 Russian army officers were found guilty of illegally selling unit weapons stocks in 1993 alone. An estimated one million AKs disappeared from Albanian state arsenals with the collapse of the government in 1993. Interestingly, the inclusion of many former communist countries into NATO is exacerbating the problem; NATO small-arms standardization has fastened on 5.56mm assault rifles, so that as more previously AK-armed nations are brought into NATO, their massive stocks of AKs become surplus to requirements.

The result is that the world is awash with AKs. They are not just a problem for the developing world – 2,000 illegal AKs were seized in San Francisco in 1995. Factor in illegal unlicensed production of AK copies – AKs can be relatively easily manufactured in one-room gunsmiths – and the AK looks set to remain a critical problem for global security efforts for at least the first half of the 21st century.

Firepower – How Soldiers Shoot

On November 21, 2005, one Ahmed Kamel al-Sawamara was driving a minivan back to Baquba, north of Baghdad, after a funeral, when he approached a US roadblock. Inside the minivan were two other men, two women, and three children aged under four years old. US soldiers at the roadblock were justly nervous of any approaching vehicle – suicide vehicle bombings were, and remain, common. For reasons not altogether clear, the minivan triggered the full force of US antibomber tactics, and was saturated in blistering small-arms fire. Al-Sawamara recounts: "I slowed down and pulled off the road, but they continued firing. I saw my family killed, one after the other, and then the car caught fire. I dragged their bodies out."[29] The number of dead by the end of the attack has been reported differently by the US authorities and the Iraqi civilians, but it appears that at least two of the adult occupants and all three children were killed.

Such incidents project a certain impression into the minds of the public, that of a soldiery with a reckless use of firearms. Such a viewpoint cannot be easily dismissed, and it is arguable that many of the worst massacres of modern times – from the *Einsatzgruppen* killings of Jews at Babi Yar in September 1941 to the US killing of 500 civilians at My Lai in 1968 – might not have been prosecuted to such an extent without the psychological distance given by firearms. A powerful firearm in the hands of an 18-year-old soldier in a lawless part of the world must undoubtedly produce its moments of intoxicating power, made worse by boredom and discomfort, as is chillingly recounted by one veteran in Mark Baker's superb oral history of the Vietnam War, *Nam*. The soldier was assigned with several others to a watchtower overlooking an airbase:

> Everybody was really pissed because during the day, this fucking tower was really hot … There was a woman bent over about 500 yards away in the fields. She was just harvesting something. We're talking to each other and somebody says, "I tell you what. I betcha I can hit her." I said, "Don't be silly. Don't even bother." She was obviously not an enemy agent or anything and she was way out of range.
>
> Everybody started taking potshots at this woman, just to see if they can hit her. I was the only one who didn't … at first. But something came over me. I was pissed off. I was fucking hot. It was the second day in that fucking tower, you know. I said, "Fuck you guys. Here, watch this." I shot at her and she keeled over dead.[30]

Not all soldiers give in to such impulses, but most admit that the temptation to overstep the mark with one's personal weaponry is ever-present. In Iraq, the term "accidental-on-purpose discharge" has been coined to describe when soldiers reach for their weapon as a last-ditch attempt either to relieve boredom or to create their own "baptism of fire." Studies have shown that over a 2-hour period boredom results in a 20 percent drop in the detection of visual signals, and a 30 percent drop in auditory signals; hence the soldier's attention will tend to stray away from the suspicious to the conspicuous, with potentially lethal results.[31]

During training the infantryman often develops an intense psychological bond with his rifle. The reverential respect a soldier can have for a firearm is perfectly captured by Anthony Swofford in *Jarhead*, his account of serving as a US Marine in the 1990–91 Gulf War:

> The man fires a rifle for many years, and he goes to war, and afterwards he turns his rifle in at the armory and he believes he's finished with the rifle. But no matter what else he might do with his hands – love a woman, build a house, change his son's diaper – his hands remember the rifle and the power the rifle proffered. The cold weight, the buttstock in the shoulder, the sexy slope and fall of the trigger guard.[32]

Furthermore, until a weapon is fired in earnest the soldier lives under a question mark over the capabilities of his weapon and his own self. Only once the trigger is pulled can certain tensions be satisfied.

Battle, rather than casual sniping, is the true test of a soldier's weapon-handling skills. Here rises, potentially, a question – what dictates whether a soldier will fire his weapon or not? To get to the heart of this question we need to look back to a controversial study conducted by S. L. A. Marshall (1900–77), an official US Army combat historian during World War II and the Korean War. His most notorious work was *Men Against Fire*, a study of combat performance of US soldiers from 400 infantry companies in Europe and the Pacific during World War II, which included an evaluation of the percentage of soldiers who actually deployed their personal weapons in action. His conclusions were worrying. On average, Marshall asserted, only 15 percent of soldiers in an infantry company fired their weapons in combat situations, rising to 25–30 percent for the most highly trained and motivated companies. These figures were despite 80 percent of troops having the opportunity and range to fire.[33] When he repeated his tests in the later Korean War, the percentage of "non-firers" had dropped to only 50 percent, but nonetheless the study worried military commanders acutely.

In recent years, Marshall's conclusions and methodologies have been steadily savaged by various critics. His methodology was found to be poor, based on informal group after-action interviews rather than effective data collection, and he himself seems to have been vague about how he arrived at his figures.[34] Reaction has even been vitriolic. In Harold P. Leinbaugh's book *The Men of Company K*, his research led one war veteran to declare: "Did the SOB think that we clubbed the Germans to death?"[35] Nonetheless, while the content of Marshall's finding has been unsettled, his study has some value in raising questions about how men use their personal weapons. Anecdotal evidence can take us either way. There are plenty of historical examples where all soldiers put out a unified blistering firepower, but military historians are often less willing to quote contrasting examples. Joanna Bourke, in *An Intimate History of Killing*, brings out one such example from Lieutenant Colonel Robert G. Cole, commander of the 502nd Parachute Infantry, who wrote a report on an action on the Carentan Causeway that occurred on June 10, 1944. He noted:

> When I ordered the men who were right around me to fire, they did so. But the moment I passed on, they quit. I walked up and down the line yelling "God damn it! Start shooting!" But it did very little good. They fired only when I watched them or while some other soldier stood over them.[36]

The role of leadership in fire control has always been highly important, and works both ways. NCO (Non-Commissioned Officer) ranks in particular bear a heavy responsibility not only for getting their troops to open fire, but also for restraining the desire to fire when inappropriate, or for ceasing fire when the job is done. We must always be cautious, furthermore, about extrapolating general principles from a single anecdote, and there are numerous factors involved in assessing soldier fire rates: the difference between conscripted and volunteer soldiers, unit morale and training, command relations, and so on. What is perhaps a better line of assessment is focusing on some of the physical and emotional constraints on a soldier using firearms.

First, most firearms are line-of-sight weapons. This simply means that a soldier has to see his target to shoot it, which in turn implies that firing involves momentary exposure of himself to the enemy. Of course, if he is following his training on cover and concealment, his exposure should be kept to a minimum, but this training can be forgotten by even highly trained soldiers in the stress of a firefight. Alan James, the highly experienced combat soldier with the Rhodesian African Rifles quoted above, said that on occasions he even took cover behind light brush (which provides concealment but not cover), fully understanding in the back of his mind that it would in no way stop the 7.62mm rounds whizzing around him. Firing a weapon thus demands the courage to place your body in harm's way, and also to deliver an auditory and visual (muzzle flash) signature that announces your presence to the enemy soldiers.

This is not easy, particularly when coming under fire. Just the sound of rounds being fired can have a paralyzing effect. Recounted in Hugh McManners' perceptive work *The Scars of War*, a British Army sergeant fighting in the Falklands War was later chilled by the sounds of small-arms fire during his first engagement on the islands:

> I heard these strange sounds; one was like a dentist's drill, and the other like a very fast zip noise – lots of them. It was several years later before I realized just what danger I had been in at that time. In battle you don't get to hear the crack of the rounds being fired at you – all you get is the thump as they hit ... I then realized that Stevie Hope and I had been in the middle of the beaten zone of a machine gun – with lots of rounds very close to our heads.
>
> The drilling sound was the round entering the ground, and the zip was the displacement of air around our heads. It gave me a wave of fright to think about it – although on the night, I didn't know what it was.[37]

Such sounds can hardly be an incentive to expose the body. The point to emerge from this, however, is that the side that achieves dominance in the firepower equation usually wins. It is a critical point, especially when evaluating media reports that show soldiers seemingly blasting off at indistinguishable targets with everything they have. Firepower does not just serve to kill an enemy soldier. More importantly, heavy, continuous fire provides the opportunity for units to maneuver, the bullets of the covering fire keeping the heads of the enemy down, hence reducing their visual awareness of the situation, prohibiting their effective deployment of weaponry and inflicting attrition on both personnel and equipment. The side that establishes the dominant firepower is likely to win the engagement. Maintaining that firepower is also critical – any momentary pause in the volume of fire gives the enemy an opportunity to engage with their own weapons.

This demand for continuity of fire is the essence of many fundamental infantry tactics. The classic infantry fireteam is composed of four men, comprising a careful balance of firepower. Taking the typical US Army fireteam as an example, one man is armed with an M249 SAW, two men with standard-issue M16A2 or M4 rifles, and one with an M16A2 fitted with an underbarrel M203 grenade launcher. The tactical thinking behind this configuration runs as follows. When the squad executes an offensive or defensive action, the SAW gunner can lay down a "base of fire" that suppresses enemy personnel, and permits the rest of the squad to maneuver themselves against the enemy. The M203 increases the firepower against enemy who are emplaced in bunkers, inside buildings, behind walls etc., although all infantrymen will have personal supplies of hand grenades to give them close-range explosive capability (see Chapter 2). To ensure that the squad does not suffer breaks in its firepower, its soldiers will move in a "bounding overwatch." One soldier will move between points of cover while the other provides covering fire. After about 3–5 seconds – any longer gives the enemy more opportunity to get an accurate aim on the soldier – the running soldier will drop behind cover, and take over the covering-fire role while the other soldier moves forward or backwards. This maneuver can be scaled up to squad, platoon, or even company level. It should be noted that a modern, well-equipped platoon or company will often have additional support fire from HMGs, mortars, artillery, armor, and even air assets.

To see some of the complexities of firefights in action, and also to appreciate the principle of dominance of fire, here is a description of an engagement on Tumbledown Mountain on the Falkland Islands in 1982. Sergeant McCollum of 3 Para describes the confusion as two British machine-gun teams remained stuck in their positions after their platoon had temporarily pulled back:

> They were under heavy fire, which was breaking down the rocks in front of them ... I was reluctant to give covering fire, for fear of drawing enemy artillery. I shouted down, asking how much cover they had, and would it last until nightfall ... By the time it got dark, they'd been under fire for over three hours. The Harriers [an air strike had been called in] took about 45 minutes to do their attack, then finally the HE [high explosive] came down and the platoon opened fire against the enemy positions. I've never seen people move so quickly.[38]

There are several factors to note about this engagement. First is the point made earlier, that using weapons attracts attention; in this case support fire is not delivered, to prevent attracting enemy artillery fire. Second, only once the British air strike rolls in with a high-explosive bombing run, thus switching the fire advantage to the British, does the platoon open up with all its weapons against the enemy. Third, the sergeant's question as to the durability of the rocks raises the issue of adequate cover.

This last point deserves some consideration. A common misrepresentation in the movies – noted by the US soldier earlier talking about the .50cal machine gun – is that if the soldier (or police officer for that matter) positions himself behind a wall or vehicle, then he is adequately protected. This is a long way from the truth. Most rifle rounds, for example, will quite happily cut straight through wall partitions and a vehicle's bodywork. It is common in the movies to see a police officer take cover behind the side windows of a patrol car or behind the vehicle's open door, his weapon rested on either the car roof or the door frame. In reality, such cover would present no obstacle to a high-power rifle, particularly those that fire heavy rounds not prone to fragmentation, although passing through any medium heavier than air will alter the trajectory of the bullet.

When it comes to heavy and persistent fire, such as from a machine gun, bullets will eat their way through cover. For example, standard 5.56mm ball ammunition fired from an M16A2 will penetrate the following structures at almost any part of the round's effective range: plasterboard, wood paneling, wooden building frames, and furniture. Heavier structures will stop individual rounds, but not indefinitely. The US Army's Field Manual FM 3-06.11, *Combined Arms Operations in Urban Terrain*, provides the following data on the numbers of 5.56mm rounds required to penetrate the urban structures. The figures represent the numbers of rounds producing either simple penetration, a loophole about 7in (18cm) in diameter (here denoted with *), or a breachhole through which a person could wriggle (**):

	simple penetration	loophole / breachhole
8in (20cm) reinforced concrete	35	250*
12in (30.5cm) cinder block with single-brick veneer	60	250**
16in (40.6cm) tree trunk or log wall	1–3	
24in (61cm) double sandbag wall		220**
³⁄₈in (1 cm) mild steel door	1	

From these figures, we get an initial sense of the fragility of cover against small arms. The loophole or breechhole figures might sound excessive – indeed they are for one rifle-armed soldier – but on considering that a fireteam or squad could easily put out 100rpm on a target it becomes apparent that a soldier behind cover must always be preparing to move. Furthermore, logs or tree trunks provide a poor form of protection, while sandbags rank as one of the best.

When we examine medium or heavy machine guns, the problem of finding adequate cover becomes more alarming. At 656ft (200m) a 7.62mm ball round – the standard round of machine guns such as the M240 – will penetrate 41in (104cm) of pine board, 8in (20cm) of cinder block and 2in (5cm) of concrete. This means that a single six-round burst of 7.62mm machine-gun fire would, allowing for a spread of rounds rather than every one hitting in the same place, smash through about 4–6in (10–15cm) of concrete wall. For a .50cal machine gun the figures are even more pronounced, and the Field Manual notes that "The caliber .50 round can penetrate all the commonly found urban barriers except a sand-filled 55-gallon drum."

The points discussed above about penetration and volume of fire have important implications for the sensitive issue of collateral damage. No matter how well a soldier controls his or her weapon, the danger to bystanders is very real, particularly in a developing-country urban environment where low-resilience structures predominate. Events in Iraq have proved particularly distressing in this regard. *Guardian* journalist Jason Burke talks of an incident in the Shia town of Majar al-Kabir in 2003, when a protest against British weapons search policies degenerated into a horrific firefight:

> By about 10am an angry crowd had gathered in the bazaar. What happened next is unclear ... Most agree that a local man, possibly a former Ba'ath party official, started shooting with a handgun. The British then opened fire.
> "It was about 10.15 and the market was very crowded," said Mr Younis. "I threw myself on the ground and shouted to everybody to run away or get down. The shooting lasted for about five minutes but there were bullets going everywhere. They were firing on automatic." ... At least 17 people were hit. They included a 13-year-old girl caught by a ricochet in the shoulder and a nine-year-old boy. Several other casualties have spinal injuries and multiple fractures. In all, five men have died from their wounds.[39]

The dynamics of this engagement are hard to piece together. From the soldiers' point of view, being engaged by enemy fire provoked a trained response – the attempt to gain dominance in the exchange of fire. Yet, as the example of the 13-year-old girl shows, bullets have a life of their own once they are fired. Striking any oblique surface will usually cause a bullet to ricochet, and this round will retain in some cases as much lethal energy as the bullet during unobstructed flight. Bearing in mind the penetration figures given above, bullets would easily pass through light cover and intended human targets, a factor that undoubtedly contributes to the high percentage of civilian casualties in modern urban war zones.

This incident raises further questions about how soldiers shoot, particularly in the high-stress, maximum-confusion urban settings that seem to characterize much of modern warfare. Marksmanship training varies greatly between armies. During the initial stages of Operation *Iraqi Freedom*, for example, it became rapidly clear that there was an enormous discrepancy between the standards of US marksmanship and those of the opposing Iraqi forces, a discrepancy explained by Dr Stephen Biddle before the US Committee on Armed Services:

> Iraqi training was radically substandard in important respects, and especially in weapon employment. Most Iraqi fighters had fired little or no live ammunition in the year prior to the war; some had never fired their weapons at all. The 2nd division of the Iraqi Regular Army, for example, had no live fire training in the twelve months prior to the war. The 3rd division held a single live fire exercise

in which each soldier fired four rounds of ammunition. None of the soldiers in the 11th division's 3rd battalion had fired their weapons in the past year. Even the Baghdad Republican Guard division held only a single live fire exercise with just ten rounds for every soldier in the year leading up to the war. By contrast, a typical US infantry unit might fire 2,500 rounds or more of ammunition per soldier in an average year; for units preparing to enter combat that figure would be much higher. The typical American infantryman thus had over 250 times as much target practice as even the best Iraqis.[40]

Volume training with weapons is essential if a soldier is to become fully proficient in firing. It allows the soldier to become truly accustomed to every aspect of the rifle's operation and dimensions, its handling second nature. A soldier who has fired thousands of rounds will move through jam-clearance procedures with automatic speed, and have an instinctive feel for the weapon's shooting characteristics.

The type of training a soldier receives is also important. For at least the first half of the 20th century, and beyond for many less professional armies, marksmanship training often consisted of little more than range qualification. While this produced some excellent shots, it was lacking one crucial element – realism. Exclusively range-based practice only prepared a soldier to shoot at static targets from comfortable firing positions. Actual combat, however, sees target presentations lasting only a few seconds – often while the target is moving between positions of cover – with the shooter having insufficient time to adopt a model shooting position.

Some prescient commanders and organizations recognized this earlier than others. During World War II, the Special Operations Executive (SOE) and the Office of Strategic Services (OSS) were training in various forms of "instinctive shooting" or "point shooting," whereby new recruits were taught to shoot without considered aim, relying instead on the faster target acquisition produced by a reflexive instinct to point accurately. Furthermore, these organizations also introduced stress-based training scenarios, teaching the recruits how to control their weapons even when their bodies were flooded with adrenaline. Second Lieutenant Rex Applegate, an American commando instructor and author of the greatly respected book *Kill or Get Killed*[41], was employed by the OSS during World War II to put its agents through realism-based combat training. To stress-test his recruits, Applegate constructed a "House of Horrors" training complex, in which inadequate lighting, blank cartridge detonations, blasts of sound, "bodies" lying on the floor, and other phenomena ramped up the anxiety levels of the recruits, while also testing the point shooting method against pop-up targets. The SOE also recognized the crucial part that pressure testing would play in combat training, observing the role of "visualization" decades before it became a commonly accepted training tool:

... it is possible to teach the Pistol successfully by acquiring a thorough knowledge of the principles involved and applying them in a practical way. The principles are based on natural body movements not unique to gun fighting and for that reason the instruction is simple, providing the imagination is used to the fullest extent to visualize the circumstances of Gun-fighting [sic], to provide a background. Particular attention must be paid to instinctive body movements combined with the speed upon which depends survival.[42]

The emphasis on imagination is critical, for it acknowledges that the shooter's conditioned response to combat (not their theoretical appreciation of it) will in many ways dictate the efficiency of that person's weapon handling. The document goes on to indicate that the traditional method of firing against targets alone is "no good" even if some of the recruits have previously "achieved considerable success using the pistol as a defensive weapon or in competition shooting."

From the 1960s to the present day most of the world's modern armies have steadily appreciated the need for realism as the cornerstone of firearms training. Current US Army marksmanship training, for example, teaches "reflexive fire," which has its ancestry back in the techniques of Applegate and his peers. Reflexive fire teaches fast target acquisition and rapid shot taking, all of which have been thoroughly tested in combat conditions in Iraq. Of particular importance is that the soldier can handle his weapon with total confidence, that he exercises correct physical balance and gun mounting (a gun incorrectly mounted, or incorrectly fitted for that matter, can cause an accuracy-knocking flinch when firing), and an aiming strategy appropriate to the target. (The gun-ready posture so often seen in soldiers in Iraq or Afghanistan, with the stock tucked under the armpit and the gun held up or down at a 45-degree angle, is part of the reflexive-shooting training, as from this position the rifle requires minimal movement to slip up into a firing position. Note that clay shooters, who have to perfect the art of very rapid target acquisition and instinctive shooting, often use a similar hold.) New technologies have increasingly allowed soldiers to experience the dynamism and stress of combat during their training phase. Rifles can be fitted with laser-firing adapters, a "hit" on another soldier being registered by sensors on the soldier's clothing. Simunition® ammunition is used, which has similar flight properties to standard rifle rounds over short distance, but without lethal terminal effects (although the sickening pain of being hit gives a very real incentive to be realistic about cover and concealment). Three-dimensional combat simulators allow soldiers to experience the pressure of target selection in tactically realistic scenarios. Targets have become more human and realistic, some manikin-like figures being filled with a blood-like liquid that bursts out when struck, helping the soldier acclimatize to the visceral sights of killing.

Another fundamental consideration for the combat soldier is the type of fire he uses. A series of 1968 studies by the US Army concluded that semi-automatic and automatic fire produced different hit ratios at different ranges within a set time period.[43] Surprisingly, at more than 164ft (50m) but within comfortable visual range, semi-automatic aimed fire (one shot per trigger pull) gave the most target hits. The semi-auto mode encourages aimed shooting while, as we have already observed, the muzzle-shuddering characteristics of full-auto fire tend to throw off the aim. Below 82ft (25m), however, full-auto fire produced more hits, reflecting the fact that at close range a single swept burst was likely to include multiple hits. Beyond comfortable visual range (say above 2,624ft/800m), and excluding professional sniping, full-auto machine-gun fire gave the greatest likelihood of target strike, this creating a generally destructive "beaten zone" (the elliptical pattern on the ground where the bullets strike) in which a target was unlikely to survive unscathed. Furthermore, between 164 and 984ft (50 and 300m) semi-auto fire was always the quicker in terms of time elapsing from first pull of the trigger to a target hit, proving that at practical combat ranges well-aimed fire is generally the most effective, even if it uses fewer rounds than full-auto fire. These results are important for the infantryman. As Peter Watson points out:

> in real war, so as to give the enemy as little information as possible about your own position, the number of trigger pulls to first hit are very important ... In other words, automatic fire may kill the enemy quicker, but only at greater distances (200 metres plus) is this not offset by the risk of giving away your own position.[44]

Our study of soldier fire control here is absolutely critical to judging media assessments of firefights. Hard, repetitive training will ingrain good fire control in a professional soldier, and this will stand out particularly when the professional faces the amateur. Amateur soldiers tend to rely heavily on full-auto fire, consuming their ammunition excessively, and often substitute noise and light for accurate aimed fire. Combined with a poor appreciation of maneuver, cover, and concealment, this is partly why, in many "limited war" scenarios against poorly trained insurgents, the combat losses are disproportionately in favor of the modern army. As a dark example, during the infamous "Black Hawk Down" engagement between around 160 US troops, mostly US Army Rangers, and several thousand Somali fighters in Mogadishu in October 1993, final US casualties were 18 killed and 84 wounded. By contrast, the Somalis lost anywhere up to, and possibly exceeding, 800 fatalities. Casualty figures for combat between US soldiers and the Viet Cong/NVA insurgents during the Vietnam War were equally imbalanced in favor of the Western troops, although many of the communist dead were caused by artillery or air strikes.

Yet coming back to our issue of volume of fire, it has to be recognized that the enormous firepower available to professional armies can predispose over-enthusiastic firing. In mid 2005 a story broke in the media that British defense chiefs had expressed concerns to their US equivalents about excessive firepower. Their argument was that an easy willingness to open up with maximum firepower massively raised the prospect of civilian casualties, and hence of losing the "hearts and minds" war and creating new generations of hate-filled insurgents. A British officer interviewed by Sean Rayment of the *Daily Telegraph* stated that the US Rules of Engagement (RoE) lead to firepower as a "first resort" in force protection:

> US troops have the attitude of shoot first and ask questions later. They simply won't take any risk. It has been explained to US commanders that we made mistakes in Northern Ireland, namely Bloody Sunday, and paid the price. I explained that their tactics were alienating the civil population and could lengthen the insurgency by a decade. Unfortunately, when we explained our rules of engagement which are based around the principle of minimum force, the US troops just laughed.[45]

Unpacking this judgment would take more space than we have here, but suffice it to say that while the volume of fire doctrine is a perfectly valid one for open combat situations, in complex insurgency environments the effects can be horribly problematic, particularly when unleashed by soldiers suffering chronic stress from daily IED (improvised explosive device), RPG (rocket-propelled grenade), and sniping attacks. Accounts of the 2003 invasion of Iraq chart worryingly high civilian casualty levels, partly incurred by overwhelming coalition fire responses. Evan Wright, in his eye-opening account of his time embedded with the US Marine First Recon unit in 2003, recounts an incident outside of Ash Shatrah in which a mass of US armored vehicles and troops is parked near a hamlet of three or four buildings. One soldier spots a mother and two children "nervously peeping out" from behind a house. The next moment, however, a US armored car opens up on the buildings with its 25mm cannon, precipitating a headlong rush for dozens of other soldiers to join in, despite observers screaming the presence of civilians and commanders issuing ceasefire orders:

> Now a dozen or more rifles and machine guns in the nearby armored units come alive, crackling and sending red streaks of tracer rounds into the entire hamlet. Marines with mortars jump off a track vehicle in front of us, yelling and cursing. They're in such a rush to attack the village, one Marine falls off the vehicle, landing on his ass.[46]

The woman and her children, it was noted, "disappeared in a cloud of dust." Such incidents highlight the absolute requirement for firm command and control at a local level, and sage RoE when soldiers have such an awesome firepower advantage.

Except in the case of snipers, who strive for a perfect kill with a single shot, soldiers are accustomed to letting off many, many rounds before hitting a human target. In World War II, it was estimated that about 15,000 rounds of small-arms ammunition were fired for every kill (in terms of total ammunition expenditure). During the Vietnam era, that figure climbed to an astonishing 50,000 rounds. Detailed figures for the Iraq conflict are not available, but there have been some worrying trends. Lieutenant Colonel Dean Mengel of the US Army conducted a study of ammunition shortages in Iraq, and discovered some worrying conclusions:

> During the spring and summer of 2004, reports and news articles began to surface that highlighted the ammunition problem in OIF [Operation *Iraqi Freedom*]. In one article it was noted that the Army estimated it would need 1.5 billion small arms rounds per year, which was three times the amount produced just three years earlier. In another, it was noted by the Associated Press that soldiers were shooting bullets faster than they could be produced by the manufacturer.[47]

Putting aside the issue of industrial output, the situation Mengel describes perfectly demonstrates how intense ammunition expenditure is in a combat situation. What we have seen so far is that shooting, rather than being a clinical process of target selection and accurate fire, is a far less controllable, dynamic reality in which volumes of fire often take precedence in an armed engagement.

Ammunition and Terminal Effects

Any understanding of firearms must acknowledge that guns are just delivery systems – in actual fact it is ammunition that is the part that does all the damage.

Furthermore, ammunition types have to be used according to the objective in mind. Some grim examples from the world of hunting will illuminate this. For rabbiting, hunters tend to prefer either shotguns firing a small size of shot (Nos 5 or 6) or a relatively low-power .22 rimfire round that minimizes damage to the meat. Hit a rabbit with, say, a high-velocity .30 deer-hunting round and all you will be left with is unappetizing tufts of fur floating on the air. Conversely, for hunting the largest of game, the .22 rimfire, and even many larger calibers, would do little more than create some nasty localized injuries on the animal. Alan James, the RAR (Rhodesian African Rifles) soldier mentioned above, told the author in interview of coming across an elephant that had trodden on a landmine, devastating one of its feet. Even with a military spec FN FAL rifle firing 7.62x51mm NATO – a round respected for its power – James had to empty the best part of a 30-round magazine into the unfortunate creature before it collapsed to the ground. (It should be mentioned that James was also, at this time, an experienced elephant hunter – this was no haphazard spraying.)

Taking this train of thought into the world of military and law enforcement work, you would think that as adult human beings are fairly consistent in size and shape, designing ammunition to stop them would be a non-contentious issue by now. Nothing could be further from the truth. The arguments over the best combat cartridges are still ongoing and frequently vitriolic, being an arcane mix of combat anecdotes and frequently misunderstood science.

The best means to feel our way into these arguments is first to note the basic types of ammunition in military/security use. In current military rifles and light–medium machine guns, the principal standard-issue ammunition types (with examples of relevant weapons) are the 5.56x45mm NATO (M16, M4, SA80, M249), the 7.62x51mm NATO (FN MAG, M60, many sniper rifles), the 7.62x39mm (AK47 and variants) and the 5.45x39.5mm (AK74 and variants). Three types of bullet are typically fired; ball, armor-piercing, and tracer bullets. "Ball" is the generic name for standard, non-expanding type ammunition, and usually consists of a lead or similar heavy core wrapped in a copper-jacket to reduce leading of the barrel, to prevent the bullet stripping itself against the rifling, and to improve penetration. Ball is also the standard type of round fired from military handguns. Armor-piercing bullets feature a penetrator core, made of a tough material such as hardened steel or tungsten carbide, which provides better penetration against protected targets, such as combatants wearing body armor. Tracer bullets feature a pyrotechnic element in the base of the bullet, which is ignited when the cartridge is fired and allows the user to observe bullet flight. Note that tracers tend only to be used in machine guns, in a ratio of one tracer to every 3–4 ball rounds, to allow the soldier to steer the cone of fire onto the target.[48] An extension of the tracer round is the incendiary round, used for igniting fires against flammable targets.

Within the law enforcement world, the picture is more varied, mainly because it is permitted to use expanding ammunition in its rifles and handguns. Expanding bullets, as the name suggests, "mushroom" out on impact, for several reasons that are useful to law enforcement agencies. First, they tend to arrest quickly inside the target, thereby reducing the dangers to bystanders of over-penetration. Second, they generally deform more easily on impact with solid surfaces, reducing the lethality of ricochets. Third, the widened diameter of the expanded bullet, combined with the expanded round's sharp "petals" of metal, increase the damage inflicted inside the target, hence producing a greater likelihood of quick incapacitation. The expanding round itself can take several configurations, from a cavity drilled or slits cut into the nose of the bullet to a metal jacket that does not extend to cover the bullet tip, which is made of a softer material and therefore deforms upon impact.

Almost every hunter will use expanding ammunition in his rifle, so why doesn't the military? The answer goes back to an arcane point of legality. By the late 1800s, the invention of more powerful smokeless propellants and the introduction of smaller-caliber jacketed rifle rounds led some soldiers to feel that their bullets were no longer having the potent effect of the early large-caliber soft-lead rounds. In British India, staff of the Dum Dum Arsenal near Calcutta came up with a solution. They removed the jacketing around the nose of the bullet, exposing the lead core and effectively making the round an expanding bullet. Three subsequent marks of expanding round were produced for the British Army.

However, at the Hague Convention of 1899, the international community attempted to impose some morals upon the essentially immoral experience of war. The international gathering cast its eye back to an earlier convention, the Declaration of St Petersburg of 1868, which amongst its statutes declared:

> That the only legitimate object which States should endeavor to accomplish during war is to weaken the military forces of the enemy;
> That for this purpose it is sufficient to disable the greatest possible number of men;
> That this object would be exceeded by the employment of arms which uselessly aggravate the sufferings of disabled men, or render their death inevitable;
> That the employment of such arms would, therefore, be contrary to the laws of humanity;
> The Contracting Parties engage mutually to renounce, in case of war among themselves, the employment by their military or naval troops of any projectile of a weight below 400 grammes, which is either explosive or charged with fulminating or inflammable substances.[49]

Apart from the restriction upon exploding munitions, the declaration was usefully vague over what arms "uselessly aggravate the sufferings of disabled men." However, the 1899 Hague Convention, which stated that it was "inspired" by the St Petersburg declarations, became far more prescriptive:

> The Contracting Parties agree to abstain from the use of bullets which expand or flatten easily in the human body, such as bullets with a hard envelope which does not entirely cover the core, or is pierced with incisions.[50]

The result of the Hague Convention was that from then on ball ammunition became the only legally acceptable type for military service. The word "military" should always be remembered, especially as every so often there are controversies about "dum dum" bullets where, in fact, there should be none. Such an example came from a particularly sad shooting that occurred in London in July 2005.

On the morning of July 22, 2005, in Tulse Hill, London, a Brazilian-born electrician left his flat for work, heading out for a job in the northwest of the city. In an experience familiar to all Londoners, his journey was soon convoluted by line closures on the Tube system, but after two bus journeys he found his way to the Stockwell tube station. There he passed through the barriers, swiping his travel pass, went down to the Northern Line platform, and waited. At this point Jean Charles de Menezes was wrapped in normality, and had no idea that his violent death was literally minutes away.

The train finally drew up to the platform at 10.05am, and Menezes boarded, took a seat, and began reading a paper. At that moment his world caved in. A group of plain clothes police officers burst into the carriage (their action was initiated by another plain clothes officer within the carriage itself), dragged Menezes from his seat and forced him onto the floor of the train. Then one of the officers deployed his issue handgun and emptied seven rounds into the back of Menezes' head, killing him instantly.

The killing of Jean Charles de Menezes took place in the feverish aftermath of the July 7, 2005 Tube and bus bombings, in which 52 people had been killed and around 700 injured. Nevertheless, the brutal shooting of what turned out to be an entirely innocent man was politically disastrous for both police and government. What it highlighted in particular were seminal issues about the police deployment of handguns. While this chapter will in no way attempt to unpack the procedural and investigative issues surrounding the Menezes case, much of the public reaction fastened on the seeming brutality of the firearms deployment. The official Jean Charles de Menezes Family Campaign web site (www.justice4jean.com) includes in its list of critical issues the following:

- The application of shoot-to-kill policy and the political and legal implications of this.
- The use of dum dum bullets to kill Jean, a type of bullet that is illegal in international warfare.

While in no way diminishing the tragedy of the Stockwell shooting with technicalities (the British police indeed seem to have hard questions to answer about the day's incidents, but mostly about intelligence and procedural issues), these statements do hint at a yawning gulf between public perceptions of how the police should deploy firearms, and the technical, legal and psychological realities. The British *Daily Telegraph* newspaper, for example, stated in an article that:

> The Brazilian man shot dead by police in the mistaken belief that he was a suicide bomber was killed with a type of bullet banned in warfare under international convention, the *Daily Telegraph* has learned. The firing of hollow point ammunition into the head of Jean Charles de Menezes, 27, is believed to be the first use of the bullets by British police.[51]

The BBC also followed up on the story, interviewing the cousin of de Menezes, Alex Peirera, who said of the ammunition revelations:

> I am shocked and angry. I had no idea ... If they [police] break international law they should be punished. How can the police in the UK use bullets that the army is not allowed to use? The police need to be open about what they are doing and if they act illegally they should be punished.[52]

While both the BBC and the *Daily Telegraph* admitted, well down in the articles, that the use of hollow-point rounds by the police was not necessarily illegal, the overwhelming tone was one of condemnation for resorting to seemingly "barbarous" ammunition. As the *Telegraph* further clarified regarding the issue of the ammunition:

> It is believed the decision was influenced by the tactics used by air marshals on passenger jets – where such bullets are designed to splinter in the body and not burst the fuselage. They have been assessed as posing less risk to people around the suicide bomber than conventional bullets but the effect on victims is devastating.[53]

The statement about the influence of air marshals in the post-9/11 world is misleading. The advantages of hollow-point ammunition for close-quarters security use have been known for decades. Furthermore, the debate amongst air marshals about the right type of ammunition has been surprisingly vigorous. While some authorities have advocated hollow-point rounds, others have promoted "frangible" ammunition – bullets purposely designed to break up into fragments upon hitting the target, the fragments having little penetrative power of their own and therefore posing little danger to the aircraft fuselage. However, Martin Pegler told the authors that many air marshals are now advocating the use of ball ammunition with good penetrative capability, the reasoning being that the huge numbers of seating and bulkhead structures on an aircraft mean that an officer will most likely have to shoot through such structures to reach the hijacker or terrorist. Even if the bullets penetrated the fuselage, the chances of aircraft decompression would be minimal.

To drop the whole debate into context, we need to clarify how bullets do their work. When they hit a person, bullets perform their damage through two principal effects – the permanent cavity and the temporary cavity. The permanent cavity is the really important one. This is the actual track through the flesh created by the bullet. The size and seriousness of the permanent cavity vary according to the caliber of the bullet, but also depend on how the bullet behaves as it passes through the body. Some rounds might "yaw" around their axis (present themselves sideways), enlarging a ragged cavity, while expanding bullets will open up and create a large cavity, albeit one that stops more quickly than a non-expanding round. Regarding yaw, it is worth noting that when traveling through tissue all bullets that do not deform will attempt to present their base first, though different bullets do this in different distances.

The second mechanism, temporary cavity, has itself a major history of scientific and popular mishandling. The temporary cavity is a displacement of tissue lasting a fraction of a second, the diameter of the displacement being many times greater than that of the bullet. It is caused basically by the "splash" effect of the bullet smacking into the tissue – the flesh recoils away from the impact. Large temporary cavitation has traditionally been associated with high-velocity rounds, but this association has bred a world of myth. Dr Martin Fackler, mentioned at the beginning of this chapter, one of the world's leading authorities on wound ballistics and president of the International Wound Ballistics Association, describes some of the background to this controversy:

> In 1967, a group reported the wounds caused by M-16 rifle bullets in Vietnam as "massively destructive" and possessing "devastating wounding power ... tremendous wounding and killing power." Because the 3,100 foot/second (945 m/sec) muzzle velocity of the M-16 bullet was higher than that of previous military bullets, "high-velocity" became synonymous with "devastating wounding power."
>
> These subjective descriptions attracted the attention of Swedish researchers. In 1974, a Swedish wound-ballistics researcher claimed that the tissues surrounding wounds caused by "high-velocity" projectiles were "subjected to the formation of the temporary cavity [which was] 30 times the diameter of the projectile" and that these tissues "will not survive." Implicit in this claim was that in the treatment of any wound caused by a "high-velocity" projectile the surgeon must excise a cylinder of tissue at least 30 times the diameter of that projectile: To treat a wound caused by a 30-caliber bullet (such as that fired by the AK-47 "assault rifle"), a surgeon would have to carve out a cylinder of tissue at least 9 inches [23 cm] in diameter. This procedure equates to performing amputation for practically any wound of the arm or leg.[54]

The alarming result of this history, as Fackler stated to Chris McNab in interview, is that some surgeons, and many military/law enforcement officers, still equate high velocity with destruction, and this can lead to inappropriate acquisition of both ammunition and firearms and to misguided clinical practice.[55] The temporary cavity is a wounding mechanism, but in many cases the tissue is simply, albeit vigorously, pushed aside before returning to its normal configuration. Certain, more inelastic body structures – particularly the bowel and liver – are vulnerable to serious damage from the temporary cavity, and a temporary cavity impinging on the spinal column, or created within the skull cavity, will also have serious effects. But the most important point is that any wound should be treated on the basis of what damage actually exists. (In interview Fackler recommended that police officers receiving treatment for firearms injuries do not tell the surgeon what sort of firearm fired the bullet, to avoid unnecessary tissue excision.) Furthermore, ballistic tests with low-velocity bullets of 19th-century type show that they produce just as much temporary cavity as the modern high-velocity types.

The arguments about the best ammunition type for military use are still ongoing, and have a turbulent political history. They revolve principally around debates about the relative effectiveness of the 5.56x45mm vs 7.62x51mm cartridges. From the moment of its introduction in the 1960s, many soldiers have reported less than satisfactory performance from the 5.56mm round, despite its "high-velocity" mythologies. Indeed, reports of inadequate penetration and take-down power are still emerging from Iraq, and many old soldiers wistfully look back to the days when the 7.62mm was the standard round.

Comparative examination of the two types of round helps clear up some, but not all, of the issues. Against many expectations, the penetration of the 5.56mm round is actually greater over many ranges than that of the 7.62mm. For example, a test in 1986 concluded that:

> The SS109 [a 5.56mm round] can penetrate the 3.45mm standard NATO steel plate to 640 meters [2,100ft], while the 7.62mm ball can only penetrate it to 620 meters [2,034ft]. The US steel helmet penetration results are even more impressive as the SS109 can penetrate it up to 1,300 meters [4,265ft], while the 7.62mm ball cannot penetrate it beyond 800 meters [2,624ft].[56]

Add the facts that recoil is more controllable with the 5.56mm, particularly for full-auto fire, and that the soldier can carry more ammunition, and the balance seems weighted toward the smaller round. And yet, the report quoted actually concludes that "the older 7.62mm NATO is a better standard cartridge." Why? The first, most important, factor comes from its damage capabilities. At ranges of under 656ft (200m), the SS109 5.56mm fired from a standard M16A2 rifle with a 20in (508mm) barrel will indeed have devastating effects. With a muzzle velocity of 2800ft (853m), the 5.56mm round tends to fragment upon impact, the individual fragments cutting their own paths through the flesh. The temporary cavity can then unite all these fragment paths into one large injury, accounting for the "explosive" effects sometimes noted by combatants and surgeons. One US Vietnam soldier, for example, said that when he first hit a Viet Cong soldier with an M16 round he "wasn't prepared for what I saw. As the bullet slammed into him, it ripped the whole arm and shoulder from his body, spun him around, and rammed him into the ground so hard that he bounced."[57]

Persuasive testimony indeed, but at 656ft (200m) the velocity drops and with that drop goes the bullet's fragmentation effect. Hence if it strikes someone at longer range it tends to go through the target in an uncomplicated fashion, greatly increasing the chance of the victim surviving. This problem has been made more acute by the widespread adoption of the M4 Carbine version of the M16 amongst US forces. The M4's much shorter barrel dimensions – 14.5in (368mm) – cause a consequent drop in muzzle velocity, with the result that the 5.56mm round loses its all-important fragmentation effect much sooner, hence the reports of inadequate performance in Iraq.

The 7.62mm bullet tends to cause its damage effects via a yaw after a penetration of around 4.7in (12cm), the round flipping over to display its base first while generating a fairly large permanent cavity. The advantage with the 7.62mm round is that it tends to do this consistently over its range, thereby delivering greater terminal effects at distance than the 5.56mm round. Furthermore, the West German 7.62mm NATO round, which actually has a different jacket material from the US version, not only begins its yaw after about 3.1in (8cm) of point-forward penetration, but also breaks at the cannelure (the narrowed point at which the front of the cartridge case grips the bullet), with the remaining rear portion fragmenting and producing a similar fragmentation/cavitation effect as the SS109, but over longer ranges.[58] The greater weight of the 7.62mm round also gives it a superior long-range accuracy and resistance to weather conditions:

> For example, at 400 meters [1,312ft] the required windage adjustment for a 10 mph [17km/h] crosswind for the SS109 is approximately 9 clicks into the wind using the M16A2. Under the same conditions, the required windage adjustment for the 7.62mm NATO cartridge is only 4 clicks using the M14 sights.[59]

Ballistically, the 7.62mm round seems to win out. Yet the reduced training times for the low-recoil 5.56mm and its increased ammunition capacity mean that there is little chance that the 7.62mm bullet will make a resurgence. As an aside, the ballistic performance of the AK-47's 7.62x39mm ball round is often little different from a standard handgun firing ball rounds. It tends to yaw after about 10.2in (26cm) of point-forward penetration – meaning that it often goes straight though someone with a narrow permanent cavity – and neither deforms nor fragments in soft tissue. The 5.45x49mm Russian round has a 5mm air gap in the tip of the bullet that, by keeping the bullet's weight heavily to the rear, increases the tendency for an early yaw and maximum damage. Note that in all the examples above, yaw can begin both before or after the average distance quoted.

Interestingly, current research on the best NATO round is fastened on rebarreling the M16 for new cartridges between 5.56mm and 7.62mm, mainly 6.5mm and 6.8mm. These new rounds demand minimal changes to the SS109 case design – hence the M16 will not have to be radically redesigned – but offer greater caliber and weight, and thus range and terminal energy. The wisdom of this move is being violently debated, with experts on both sides of the argument for and against the new round. Suffice it to say that in many ways there is no such thing as a perfect rifle round, or a perfect gun for that matter.

Hitting the Target – Police Engagements

An abiding misconception regarding firearms and ammunition is that a person struck by a bullet dies, or at least drops, instantly. Much of the blame for this idea lies at the door of Hollywood. When someone is hit by a bullet on the big screen, typically that person gives a loud scream then immediately drops to the floor unconscious. Real life is somewhat different, and much darker.

The fact is that in a large percentage of cases, human beings who are shot neither die nor collapse immediately to the ground. There are three main ways in which a subject is decisively stopped by bullets:

1) The central nervous system is hit through a strike either directly to the brain or to the upper spinal cord, resulting in the shutdown of conscious and/or autonomic functions.
2) There is a massive loss of blood volume, leading to the catastrophic onset of circulatory shock and unconsciousness.
3) The psychological effects of pain and shock cause the subject to go into complete mental shutdown.

None of this is as straightforward as it sounds. Urey W. Patrick and John C. Hall have spent much of their professional careers studying the mechanics of lethal engagements, and have some sobering analysis. They state that point 1 above is the only circumstance in which a person will be dropped immediately, and strikes on those points – when the target is moving and resisting – are extremely difficult to achieve. Bullets anywhere else have far less predictable consequences:

> In a healthy standing adult, adequate blood pressure can be maintained until at least a 20% loss of blood volume occurs at which point the effects of decreased blood pressure begin to be felt. Healthy young people can tolerate a sudden loss of approximately 25% of their blood volume without significant effect or permanent injury, if laying flat on their back.[60]

Patrick and Hall continue their analysis by showing how the body's compensatory mechanisms also help an injured person cope with the sudden blood loss well, hence the effects of volume reduction are not felt until the 25 percent point is reached. Even a catastrophic injury can leave plenty of time for the victim to act:

Assuming that the thoracic artery is severed (the largest artery), it will take almost five seconds at a minimum for a 20% blood loss to occur in an average-sized male. But:

> Most wounds will not bleed at this rate because:
> 1) bullets usually do not transect (completely sever) blood vessels;
> 2) as blood pressure falls, the bleeding slows;
> 3) surrounding tissue acts as a barrier to blood loss;
> 4) the bullet may only penetrate smaller blood vessels;
> 5) bullets can disrupt tissue without hitting any major blood vessel resulting in a slow ooze rather than rapid bleeding.

This analysis does not account for oxygen contained in the blood already in the brain. Even in cases where the heart stops beating and blood flow to the brain ceases, there is enough residual oxygen in the brain to support wilful, voluntary action for 10 to 15 seconds.[61]

As this analysis cogently proves, human beings are hard things to stop with bullets. Sometimes people do go straight down after they have been shot in a non-incapacitating point, but this is mostly down to psychological reaction. In many people, however, particularly those fueled by adrenaline, drink, or alcohol, they may not even have an awareness of being shot, and may continue in their behavior until incapacitation kicks in. The time lag between being shot and going down, moreover, can have critical significance for law enforcement officers and soldiers. On April 11, 1986, for example, an FBI squad in Miami engaged two well-armed criminals in a shootout. One of the assailants, William Matix, was quickly killed, but the other, Michael Platt, continued shooting even after being struck by several bullets. It was the first bullet that hit him, however, that would result in his death – a 9mm round went into his chest cavity and stopped just short of his heart. Despite this being the death shot, in the time he remained functional he killed two agents and wounded several others.

Here we come up against another media myth – that of a person being thrown across a room or hurled to the ground by the "energy transfer" of a bullet. Basic physics is enough to tell us that the energy transfer of a bullet hitting a target can never be more than the force of recoil felt by the shooter, and in most cases is comfortably handled. Martin Fackler conducted tests with a bulletproof-vest-clad associate in which military 7.62mm NATO rounds were fired at close range into the vest. Even when the recipient of the fire stood on one leg, at no point was he in danger of being knocked over. The Firearms Tactical Institute, a Washington DC-based firearms research group, notes that when someone wearing body armor is struck by a bullet, the armor prevents penetration but it does not stop the officer experiencing the full impact of energy transfer from the round. Nevertheless:

There's not one documented incident in which an officer was knocked unconscious or physically incapacitated or in any way rendered unable to perform willful activity after his soft armor stopped such a projectile. These officers absorbed nearly 100 percent kinetic energy transfer, yet none were incapacitated by the blunt trauma "shock" of projectile impact or temporary displacement of underlying soft tissues.[62]

The upshot of all these points, first of all, is that target placement is vital. A hit on the arm just isn't going to do the job when multiple torso strikes are required. Many other authorities concur, and real-life illustrations are dramatic. Dave Spaulding, a former law enforcement officer and writer on firearms engagements, noted after his research into 200 real-life shooting incidents:

> Truly, the most important thing in all this is where you hit your opponent. I have spoken with a little old lady who severed the aorta of a home invader with a FMJ .32 [a small, non-expanding round] while, at the same time, talking to a police officer that could not stop a knife-wielding assailant with five rounds of .45 ACP hollow-point [a large-caliber expanding combat round]. As a matter of fact, many of the people that I spoke with continued to fire until the threat was no longer in front of their gun. Think about the time it takes for gravity to pull a 200-pound male to the ground. As a matter of fact, time it for yourself.[63]

The fact is, a hit in the right place is worth much more than a hit in the wrong place. Hence most police forces operate a simple formula for "shoot to stop":

1) Aim for the center mass of the assailant (essentially the solar plexus), thus maximizing the possibilities for strikes on vital organs.
2) Deliver multiple quick shots into the target until the assailant is completely incapacitated.

British police guidelines recommend that the officer evaluate the target status after each shot, but in split-second engagements, Spaulding's "fire until the threat disappears" appears more practically realistic. This need to keep firing until the threat is stopped is a primary reason why some police and military shootings can appear excessive in ammunition consumption and the number of hits on the target. In the case of Jean Charles de Menezes, while details of the shooting may throw up procedural problems, the targeting of the head with multiple shots is a standard tactical procedure for dealing with potential suicide bombers, who only require a fraction of a second to detonate a device. By destroying the brain, the chances of a reflexive flick of a detonator switch are dramatically reduced.

Another major consideration in police shootings is the practical limitation of accuracy. In February 2006, Senator David Paterson of Albany, New York, made a second attempt at trying to push through a bill obliging US police officers to "shoot to wound" during firearms engagements. The bill, which exposed police officers to charges of second-degree manslaughter if they unnecessarily killed rather than wounded a criminal suspect, was handled vociferously by the police community and failed, but it is symptomatic of the widespread misunderstanding of weapons usage in police engagements.

Hollywood movies have commonly depicted officers making phenomenally accurate handgun shots at ranges of 164ft (50m) plus – think of *Die Hard* and the *Dirty Harry* films. Although such accuracy is achievable (though rarely) only under controlled and peaceful range conditions, the damage is done. Firearms officers around the world conduct their duties under the constant threat of major litigation and possible imprisonment. Yet controversial shootings can only be judged fairly if the public truly understands the technical capabilities and limitations of police weaponry and related tactics.

When opening fire on an assailant, a police officer typically has no direct intention to kill the opponent, purely to render him/her physically unable to prosecute an attack on either the officers or third parties. This goal is put more forcefully by Clint Smith, a former US police officer and Vietnam veteran:

> Officers don't care about the suspect's clothing color, skin color, ethnic background, religious preference, if he comes from a broken home, or if his dog was killed by a car when he was a child. They just want him to drop the knife, by verbal compliance or compliance by gunfire and it's the threat's choice.[64]

Smith makes the important point that the police officer's objective is the nullification of threat, not the death of the subject nor the interpretation of the subject's psychological background. Yet "shooting to stop" invites controversy by its very nature, particularly when using handguns.

Handguns require special consideration when studying police shootings, because they are by far the most commonly distributed official weapons. However, handguns have little to recommend them as law enforcement tools. Accuracy with these guns, even in trained hands, is limited to well below 98ft (30m) for aimed shots, curtailed by the handgun's short barrel length, low-power ammunition and the instability intrinsic of grip.

Even with a two-handed support grip, a pistol has only one major point of contact (the palm of the shooting hand) between gun and user, whereas a rifle has forward hand, rear grip hand, shoulder weld and cheek weld. The principal advantages of a handgun, however, are its portability (hence it can be rapidly deployed) and its public acceptability – it is less threatening to see an officer with a small gun contained in a holster than carrying a large, potent-looking longarm.

In the lightning-fast dynamics of a real-life engagement, we must never think that the handgun is a tool for precision shooting. (Engagements between pistol-armed officers and assailants have taken place at distances of only a few yards, but in many instances neither side has registered a hit.) Post-action analysis of police handgun engagements has shown that sight-awareness is minimal or non-existent in the split-second blur of a shooting – the officer will resort to point shooting, where the gun is pointed like a finger rather than aimed using the sight. Some researchers have noted that officers using revolvers can be slightly more aware of a sight picture than those using auto handguns, the former usually having more elevated front post sights than the low-profile sights typical of automatic weapons. Annual reports from the US Department of Justice show that most police engagements took place under 21ft (6.4m) range, with some interesting variables. Engagements by police in the confines of New York City generally took place at 10ft (3m), while those of officers from sheriffs' departments, highway patrol, and border patrol units generally exceeded 21ft (6.4m) and extended up to 65ft (20m), although the latter group of officers tends to rely more on longarms. At the average short ranges, in a dynamic situation, the handgun will be in a state of rapid motion. A shift of only 1–2in (2.5–5cm) from the centerline of aim will translate into a shift of 2–4ft (0.6–1.2m) at typical combat ranges – a crucial fact considering that a human torso is typically less than 2ft (0.6m) wide and will be moving, presenting itself in shifting angular profiles during a shootout. With these facts in mind, the idea that police should attempt to shoot guns out of hands or aim at only non-critical areas of the body is simply not credible. As a further consideration, the fact that the target is moving while the officer is shooting frequently produces injuries to the back – which in court can be presented as if the assailant was shot while fleeing or cowering.

Nevertheless the torso, packed with vital circulatory and respiratory organs, is by necessity the target of choice in a police firefight. When wielding an inaccurate handgun in a high-stress situation that occurs over 1 or 2 seconds, and with no guarantee of a one-hit takedown, multiple shots at the center mass at least raise the officer's chances of hitting something vital and achieving the shoot to stop goal. This is more important the closer the range.

Police officers, and indeed soldiers, have today become more accountable for their actions than ever before. The problem with this scrutiny is often that their actions are assessed within the slow forensic luxuries of a courtroom, where the prosecutor has had possibly months to come up with his analysis of a situation that was over in seconds. Once someone has to deploy a firearm in a life-or-death situation, they enter a strange mental state that can be unfairly unpacked in court. For a start, they have to make a split-second decision about whether the situation demands the application of lethal force. Should they try to make sure of their decision 100 percent, their weapon deployment and shooting will often be too slow to be effective and could result in their own death. Even in some controlled decision-oriented tests conducted with the gun drawn and held at the ready, over a second lapsed for the officers to fire their guns. In a street situation, allowing for the effects of stress (which can double decision-making time), the time from first spotting the threat to drawing, targeting, and firing the gun is typically around 3–5 seconds. An assailant, by contrast, will often have the advantage that he is already prepared for violence, so the policeman must act with great speed to achieve any advantage.

During a firearms engagement, an individual will experience the full force of "fight or flight" physiological changes in brain and body chemistry, regardless of how well trained he or she is. One key effect of this is to limit the awareness and retention of non-essential events. After a lethal engagement, officers will usually have only fleeting glimpses of what actually happened because of the stress of the encounter and the speed with which it occurred. Unfortunately, in the courtroom they are often required to unpack the events second by second, and the forensic pressure can lead many to fill in the blanks with their imagination, hence making them appear as untrustworthy witnesses.

One final issue also needs to be laid to rest, that of the perceived advantage of a gun over a knife. The lethality of a knife must not be underestimated. It requires no loading, reloading, or firing procedure, can produce lethal injuries with every single thrust, retraction, and slash, and is often better than bullets at generating injuries producing critical blood loss. Patrick and Hall make note of tests done at the Firearms Training Unit (FTU), and the FBI Academy in Quantico, Virginia, where a rubber-knife armed instructor would charge and attack a fellow officer, armed with a blank-firing pistol, from a variety of ranges:

> Beyond a distance of 21 feet [6.4m], the agent with the handgun had time to evade the initial attack and shoot, if the gun were already in hand. Inside 21 feet, most of the agents could still fire a shot by the time the attacker reached them with the knife, as the attacker concurrently was able to stab or slash the agent. The harsh reality in such circumstance is that unless the shot happens to hit the attacker in the central nervous system, the attack will succeed ... At closer ranges, the attack was successful before the agent could raise his weapon and fire a shot. When the agent started from a holstered position, he was successfully stabbed/slashed every time when the attack commenced inside 21 feet.[65]

Such tests demonstrate that knives should never take second place to guns in a notional scale-of-force. In a video seen by the authors, four Brazilian police officers – all armed with guns – surrounded a deranged assailant armed with a kitchen knife. The knife-wielding man subsequently managed to wound three of the four officers before he was finally brought to ground by gunfire.

This chapter has taken a long journey through the world of guns and shooting. What is clear is that if we ever take human imperfections out of the equation when analyzing lethal engagements of any kind, or neglect to understand tactical realities, the unfortunate result can be condemnation of those who face situations that for most of us, thankfully, will be just the stuff of nightmares.

On a final note, at the time of writing the United States has just witnessed its worst mass shooting incident in history, the killing of 32 people and wounding of 25 more by a lone gunman (Seung-Hui Cho) at the Virginia Tech Institute in Blacksburg, Virginia. This truly awful event stands as a counterpoint to the Stockton shooting with which we opened the chapter – here was someone armed only with a 9mm Glock 19 and .22 Walther P22 who nevertheless was able to kill more than 30 people. Full analysis of this event is impossible here, as details are still emerging. The unusually high death toll seems, on first assessment, a product of extremely high volumes of fire (the gunman fired over 170 rounds) combined with execution-style tactics, trapping the terrified students in classrooms with the doors chained and padlocked, and firing at extremely close quarters. Cho brought the killing to an end when he shot himself, but the massacre reminds us that guns, while bringing out discipline and control in some, can facilitate dark ambitions and fantasies of power in others.

2

PERFECT DESTRUCTION – EXPLOSIVES

On the evening of March 14, 1941, the town of Wakefield, in North Yorkshire, was typically quiet. Although Britain was in the midst of the Blitz, Wakefield was not a principal target – the Germans had far more temptation in regional large-scale industrial centers, such as Sheffield and Manchester. There had been a handful of opportunistic raids, in August, September, and December 1940, but no one had been killed and damage was mercifully light. That night, however, would be quite different.

Although Wakefield was not in the bombers' sights, all the usual air raid precautions were followed. So it was on March 14 that Brian McNab, a 12-year-old boy living on Thornes Road (and the father of the author Chris McNab), went with his mother and sister (his father was on duty as an Air Raid Precaution warden) to his next door neighbor's house as the air raid sirens sounded yet again. The neighbor, a Mrs Clegg, had a deep cellar beneath the house, in which the Cleggs and McNabs sat out interminable boredom and chilly discomfort. At around 10.45pm, however, the two families had had enough. The only heat in the shelter was from candles placed under upturned plantpots (the plantpots served to shield the light and warmed up themselves as primitive central heating). Hours had passed with neither the distant sound of bombs nor that of antiaircraft guns. Quietly, everyone ascended the stairs into the living room for a good cup of tea.

Unbeknown to all the families of Thornes Road, many of whom had made the same choice to come out of hiding, up high a single German Heinkel He 111, laboring with two 2,000lb (909kg) bombs, was lost. British radar-jamming efforts had thrown off the bomber's navigation, and it was now attempting to head back to its home bases across the North Sea. Running low on fuel, the aircraft would also have to lighten its load. Brian continues the story:

> She [Mrs Clegg] came out with the tea ... and we were saying how it had all been very quiet tonight when we heard a slow drone in the sky. It was just a gentle hum. And we wondered whether we ought to go down into the cellar again, but nothing happened so we stayed put. Then as we were sat there the droning got nearer and nearer. We felt at this point that we should go back down into the cellar, but we suddenly heard a whistle in the sky, getting louder and louder. It started off right in the distance but built up to a crescendo ... we seemed to be listening to this, absolutely transfixed, for ages. Then it seemed as if all the heavens had opened, an unbelievable roar. The windows came out. The blast threw us all forward out of the sofa into the fireplace, then hurled us back while at the same time soot came

rushing out of the chimney and covered us. I would have sworn that the bomb was on our house next door ...

Scared witless, everyone flew back down the cellar, the McNabs wondering whether they still had a home to go to.

The next morning revealed that just two bombs had completely transformed the life of an entire community. Eight residents were killed, including a woman decapitated and two twin infants killed in their beds from the blast, with not a mark on them. Four people were injured and dozens of residents left homeless. Brian's experience of the devastation left a powerful impression of the devastating potential of high explosive. Several houses were entirely gutted by the blast, with one completely shorn in half at an angle. Inches of soot covered the road, sucked out of dozens of chimneys by the inrush of air feeding the blast. Brian found that a large piece of shrapnel had punched through the side of his garage, cut right through the car inside, smashed out of the opposite wall and embedded itself in a fence. When Brian touched it, about 12 hours after the bomb had gone off, it was still warm to the hand.

The devastation wrought by just two bombs on the street draws out many of the issues this chapter will confront. Regardless of how precisely an explosive device is deployed, the violence of its detonation is blindly indiscriminate. Anyone – man, woman, or child – within the effective blast or fragmentation radius of the bomb, unless they are behind effective cover, is likely to die instantly or suffer horrible mutilation. For professional armies, this capacity presents both an opportunity and a problem. The opportunity is for a single device to take out numerous enemy personnel or materiel assets at a stroke. The problem is that the explosion will not choose between military personnel and bystanders, potentially generating the "collateral damage" that can blacken an entire military campaign in the eyes of the world.

The focus of this chapter is on the use of land-warfare explosive devices, such as grenades, landmines, and demolitions, while also evaluating the brutal mechanics of any explosion.

The Explosive Mix

Visiting an explosives-producing center can be a curious experience for those not familiar with such establishments. A recent visit by Chris McNab to the US Naval Surface Warfare Center's Indian Head Division, a major producer of military explosives and energetics based in Maryland, revealed an industrial complex spread, cautiously, over many acres. Huge explosive mixer vats stood ready to blend explosive compounds; the vats were actually modeled directly on domestic food mixers, with huge paddles inside for churning the lethal mix together. The friendly, professional staff, high-tech laboratories, and stark surroundings seemed light years removed from the chaotic violence that would be unleashed, somewhere in the world, by the products. Nevertheless, the production and development of explosives is not simply a case of making a substance that explodes. As I was frequently reminded, explosive devices are developed to do a job of work, which might stretch from simply unearthing an awkward tree stump to vaporizing everything within hundreds of yards. Achieving this is a technically and practically complex job.

If one includes everything from nuclear explosions to pyrotechnic flares, tying down the definition of an explosive is difficult. In essence, the British Explosives Act of 1875 came up with the most open-ended definition, an explosive being "a substance used or manufactured with a view to produce a practical effect by explosion."[1] The Global Security organization attempts to be a little more specific:

> An explosive is defined as a material (chemical or nuclear) that can be initiated to undergo very rapid, self-propagating decomposition that results in the formation of more stable material, the liberation of heat, or the development of a sudden pressure effect through the action of heat on produced or adjacent gases. All of these outcomes produce energy; a weapon's effectiveness is measured by the quantity of energy – or damage potential – it delivers to the target.[2]

Making a subsequent, and relatively crude, division of the above, explosives basically break down into low explosives or high explosives. Low explosives are substances that "deflagrate" (break down) very rapidly when ignited, burning at rates of up to 3,300ft/sec (1,000m/sec) rather than exploding. Good examples of this are black powder and chemicals used in pyrotechnics. Note that although most low explosives do not produce a damaging explosion in their loose state, when confined they can be surprisingly destructive. For example, empty the powder charge from a 12-gauge shotgun shell, spread it over a length of around 6in (15cm), and light it, and it will methodically burn through at a rate of roughly 1in (2.5cm) per second. Confined within the shotgun shell, however, the whole load will burn almost instantaneously, its burn rate accelerated dramatically by the pressure produced in the chamber.

Gunpowder is an interesting substance for discussion. Confined gunpowder has produced some of history's most spectacular blasts. For example, on October 12, 1654 a powder magazine in Delft, Netherlands, containing 95,000lb (43,200kg) of black powder, blew up and destroyed a quarter of the city, killing 100 people. Although it tends to be associated with pre-20th century warfare, gunpowder still has a 21st century terrorist potential. In the United States, a citizen can own up to 50lb (22.7kg) of black powder without having to register that possession with the Bureau of Alcohol, Tobacco and Firearms (ATF), so long as the powder is "used solely for sporting, recreational, or cultural purposes in antique firearms or in antique devices."[3] This easy availability of black powder and also more powerful smokeless propellants means that gunpowder still finds explosive use in terrorist pipe bombs – such a device was detonated at the Atlanta Olympics in 1996, killing one person and wounding 11 others.[4] Further back, in 1988, a terrorist from the Japanese Red Army was caught heading for New York with the intention of carrying out a terrorist attack. His weaponry consisted of hollowed-out fire extinguishers, gunpowder, and a quantity of roofing nails to form a deadly shrapnel.[5] Terrorist attacks continue to be planned and executed through the means of gunpowder, its limitations as an explosive perhaps offset by its easy availability and the social disruption generated by any level of explosion. (Note also that gunpowder still finds military use in some types of time fuse, detonators, and blasting caps.)

Low explosives, although dangerous in their own right, pale into insignificance when compared to high explosives; hence high-explosive applications in military demolitions and warheads. High explosives erupt at rates of up to 29,500ft/sec (9,000m/sec), producing enormous shock waves and blast effects, and are customarily separated out into primary and secondary categories. Primary explosives are highly sensitive to detonation by impact, friction, or heat, and include lead azide, lead styphnate, pentaerythritol tetranitrate (PETN), and diazodinitrophenol (DDNP). They are too lively in themselves to be used in large quantities, but are useful in tiny quantities in primers (to ignite the main charge by setting up the initiation train) and detonators – the mechanisms used to trigger a main explosive charge, hence primary explosives are also known as "initiating explosives." Often there is what is known as a "booster charge" between the initiating explosive and the main charge, which in some cases can be gunpowder (particularly in propelling charges) but in high-explosive weapons is typically an explosive such as tetryl, CH-6, PETN, or Composition A-5.

Main explosive charges are generally secondary explosives. These are fairly resistant to shock and heat, and usually require initiation via a detonator. The list of explosives that fall into this category is dauntingly long, and includes: TNT, RDX (cyclotrimethylenetrinitramine), Amatol, Composition A/B/B-3/C-3/C-4, dynamite, HBX (high brissance explosives), PBX (polymer bonded explosive), pentolite, Semtex, and Torpex.

To analyze the properties and performance of each of these explosives, and the many others available, is simply not feasible here. A choice selection of one or two, however, can illuminate some interesting issues.

TNT

Trinitrotoluene (TNT) is a secondary explosive used as a demolition charge, a booster or bursting charge within shells and bombs, and as a composite ingredient of other explosives, such as Amatol and pentolite. Its detonating velocity is a respectably powerful 22,600ft/sec (6,900m/sec), but its real value for weapons designers is its stability and its ease of handling in the production stages. TNT can be safely melted at only 176°F (80°C), and in this state can be conveniently poured into warheads. It also does not react with metal, making it further suited to warhead applications. Very importantly for soldiers, TNT is enormously resistant to impact:

> In order to detonate, TNT must be confined in a casing or shell and subjected to severe pressures and/or temperatures (936 degrees Fahrenheit) such as from a blasting cap or detonator. In fact, US Army tests on pure TNT show that when struck by a rifle bullet TNT failed to detonate 96% of the time and when dropped from an altitude of 4,000 feet onto concrete, a TNT-filled bomb failed to explode 92% of the time.[6]

Such qualities must be refreshing should you be, say, a battlefield engineer transporting packs of TNT around a live war zone. TNT was actually developed by the German scientist Joseph Wilbrand in 1863, and achieved its first major military use with the German Army's adoption of it as a shell filling in 1902. During World War I, the British also made a rapid shift over to TNT as their standard warhead filling, but even though 238,000 tons of the explosive were manufactured in Britain during the conflict, it still wasn't enough to meet demand – hence TNT was mixed with ammonium nitrate to create a new explosive, Amatol.[7] Since then, TNT has frequently been used as a component in many other explosives such as Baratol, Composition B, HDX, Octol, and pentolite.

Not everything about TNT is user friendly. Most explosives, somewhere along the line, can have adverse effects on health if you are in contact with them long enough. Ageing TNT can produce exudate – a leaking of some of its chemical contents. The exudate is flammable and mildly explosive, and as such is one of the reasons the US Navy no longer has TNT in its munitions. Handled with frequency, the explosive also has toxic effects which, depending on the length and type of exposure, can include headaches, anemia, sickness, respiratory problems, impaired liver function, reduced male fertility, depleted immune system function, eczema, irregular heartbeat, and yellowed skin.

In both production and storage, these problems have been largely eradicated through effective health and safety measures, but such was not always the case. During World War I, the predominantly female workers employed in explosive production in Britain came to acquire the nickname "canary girls," owing to the dramatic yellowing of their skin. Skin color change was just the tip of the health issues. Of female workers at the Royal Arsenal, Woolwich, 37 percent suffered muscular pains and constipation and 34 percent had disrupted menstrual cycles from their explosives handling. The employees of a new armament factory at Chilwell (established because of the shell shortage scandals of 1915), soon experienced similar symptoms and hence a critical article in *The Lancet* that finally brought about more health-aware procedures.[8] It is worth noting that for all TNT's stability, accidents with it have happened. In July 1918, 8 tons of TNT exploded at the Chilwell plant, killing 134 workers and injuring a further 250. (There were rumors that possible sabotage could have been behind the explosion.)

Semtex

On December 21, 1988, Pan Am Flight 103, a transatlantic Boeing 747 flying out of Heathrow, was destroyed by a terrorist bomb over Scotland, much of its flaming remains crashing down upon the small town of Lockerbie in Dumfries. A total of 270 people died. Subsequent investigations of the "Lockerbie bombing," as it became known, revealed that the source of the explosion was just 12–16oz (340–450g) of Semtex plastic explosive contained within a Toshiba radio cassette player, which was stored in a case and deposited in the luggage hold.

The Lockerbie bombing, and a handful of other terrorist incidents, helped make Semtex an unusually high-profile explosive, particularly during the late 1980s and the 1990s. The name still has currency, often being used by pop culture enterprises to label, amongst other things, soft drinks (specifically a soft drink produced by the Czech Pinelli company), DJs, and music channels. There are reports that the pop star Madonna has even recently established a British limited company called Semtex Girls. At the time of writing there is some confusion as to what Semtex Girls actually does, but it appears to refer to Madonna's female assistants, as she states: "The Semtex Girl is a girl who is dynamic, a girl who explodes, who doesn't know the meaning of nine to five, a girl who is unstoppable and who doesn't take no for an answer. And has excellent taste. Guys can be Semtex Girls too."[9]

Amongst the explosives family, only "dynamite" has a similar public name cache, so how has a modern plastic explosive gained such street credibility? The origins of the explosive reach back to the 1960s when a Czech explosives scientist, Stanislav Brebera, received a commission from the communist government to produce a plastic explosive similar to the US C-4, which at that time was being used to powerful effect in the Vietnam War (particularly in the M18A1 Claymore mine – see below). What he produced was Semtex, the name being a fusion of Semtin, the East Bohemian village where Semtex was developed, and the first two letters of the word "explosive." In strictly dispassionate terms, Semtex was an excellent product. It had an incredible power to weight ratio (just 3lb/1.4kg of Semtex will destroy a two-storey building), can be molded readily into almost any shape, is stable to use and is completely odorless. This last design achievement was to prove especially important in the explosive's future terrorist use, as it meant that it could evade even the sensitive noses of sniffer dogs. However, we must not ascribe any mythical properties to Semtex. Explosia a.s., the current producer of Semtex, is quick to point out that many other countries in the world have similar products:

SEMTEX is by no means the only plastic explosive throughout the world, similar types of explosives are produced by a number of producers. Out of the most known producers it is possible to mention:

USA	C 4 (Composition 4)
Great Britain	DEMEX, ROWANEX, PE 4
France	PE 4, PLASTRITE (FORMEX P 1)
Poland	PWM, NETROLIT
Germany	Spreng Körper DM 12
Yugoslavia	PP – 01 (C 4)
Slovakia	CHEMEX (C 4), TVAREX 4 A
Austria	KNAUERIT
Sweden	Sprängdeg m/46[10]

A similar defense of the product has been made by the creator in an interview for the *Christian Science Monitor*:

> Brebera says that with so much Semtex already in the hands of terrorists, and similar explosives being produced in other countries, the Czech Republic can no longer control it. "Semtex is no worse an explosive than any other," he says, defensive at the sight of accusatory headlines in Western newspapers. "The American explosive C4 is just as invisible to airport X-rays, but they don't like to mention that."[11]

It is its history, rather than its chemical properties, that has given Semtex its notoriety. Having been developed for North Vietnamese use, its distribution rapidly broadened following the Soviet takeover of Czechoslovakia in 1968. Through official state sales, and some less than official trafficking, Semtex went global. Cambodia, Iran, Iraq, Libya, North Korea, and Syria all took hefty deliveries, and from there Semtex could be easily channeled into terrorist hands. For example, between 1985 and 1986 at least 1 ton of Semtex was moved, via Libya, to the Irish Republican Army (IRA) in Northern Ireland. The writer Peter Taylor has commented on the impact of this transfer:

> Although the IRA's four shipments from Libya contained a few spectacular additions to its armoury like SAM 7 surface-to-air missiles, the most lethal donation from Colonel Gaddafi was a large quantity of Semtex high explosive. This could be used on its own to devastating effect or as a booster for the IRA's huge fertilizer-based bombs. Nineteen eighty-eight was the year of Semtex, and there was little the "Brits" could do to counter it beyond warning the security forces to be vigilant and look under their cars before they got in... Largely due to Semtex, thirty-four soldiers died in 1988, more than in any other year since 1982.[12]

Taylor goes on to list a string of Semtex-related atrocities. The worst was the bombing of a coachload of Light Infantry Regiment soldiers on the A5 trunk road near the village of Ballygawley. A command-detonated explosive device containing around 30lb (14kg) of Semtex and sited by the side of the road demolished the bus entirely, killing eight soldiers and injuring 27.

The end of the Cold War, and the seeming resolution of conflicts such as that in Northern Ireland, has brought no end to illegal Semtex use. Indeed, the aftermath of the break-up of Czechoslovakia in 1989, and the economic problems that event unleashed, meant that the illegal trade in Semtex increased. For example, around 1,980lb (900kg) of Semtex and 2,000 detonators were stolen in Slovakia in October 1993.[13] A series of export bans has not prevented the build up of an estimated stockpile of 40,000 tons of Semtex worldwide, much of that stockpile subject to poor regulatory control. (It should be noted that Explosia a.s., the current producer of Semtex, is a full signatory to international conventions on the control of Semtex. It also states "that new production of SEMTEX is minimal. Primarily rework and marking is carried out at present, or disposal of demilitarized plastic explosives from the Czech Army stock. Supplies of newly produced explosive are predominantly assigned to military purposes."[14])

The Explosive Effect

Before moving on to the weaponized use of high explosives, some groundwork is required on how high explosives actually work, and the effects that they have. This takes us into numerous, frequently unpleasant, areas including wound effects, building destruction, and battlefield handling.

When a high-explosive device is detonated there is a rapid release of energy in four forms: shock wave (created by the production of large volumes of gas), heat, sound, and light. It is the first two on this list that really do the damage. The shock wave is a compression of the air surrounding the explosion, or "overpressure." A large, military-grade high-explosive weapon will in its initial phase of detonation develop an overpressure of some 385 kilobars (385 times the normal atmospheric pressure) and then return to atmospheric pressure, all in the space of thousandths of a second.[15] The shockwave slams into anything within its reach, generating enormous destructive pressures. Just how destructive is illustrated by information presented in a document on building security design by the American Institute of Architects, which considers the effects of various terrorist vehicle explosions:

> The following is a list of vehicles, their general capabilities (in pounds of TNT), and the amount of atmospheric overpressure such charges would create 30 feet [9.1m] and 100 feet [30.5m] from the blast's point of origin:

Vehicle Type	Charge in lb	psi at 30 feet	psi at 100 feet
Compact car trunk	250	182	9.5
Large car trunk	500	367	15
Panel van	1,500	1,063	33
Box truck	5,000	2,900	100
Single tractor-trailer	30,000	9,290	593
Double tractor-trailer	60,000	13,760	1,150[16]

The destructive force suggested by such figures is enormous, although it is worth bearing in mind that the duration of the shock is extremely short, less than a second. Hence if a structure can survive the brevity of the blast, it might survive relatively intact. Also, the further the shock wave gets from the source of the explosion, the weaker is its effect. (The practical area affected by the explosion is often referred to as the blast radius.)

After the overpressure phase of an explosion (known as the positive phase), the vacuum created by the blast creates a "negative phase" where the air pressure drops to sub-atmospheric levels. The air consequently rushes in at speed to fill the void, causing damage in its own right – large-volume targets such as spacious buildings can literally implode during the negative phase owing to the internal pressure and the wind drag on already weakened surfaces. The positive/negative phases of an explosion create a push-pull effect – see the description of the Wakefield bombing above for a practical illustration of the effects of this phenomenon. Airburst detonations – explosives detonated above the ground – have enhanced blast effects, owing to the original shock wave combining with the blast reflected from the ground to form a third wave called a "Mach Wave" or "Mach Stem." The Mach Stem rushes outwards at enormous velocity on a plane nearly perpendicular to the ground, and maintains its force for longer than the original shock wave. An Indian Head Division briefing document notes that:

> Using the phenomenon of Mach reflections, it is possible to increase considerably the radius of effectiveness of a bomb. By detonating a warhead at the proper height above the ground, the maximum radius at which a given pressure or impulse is exerted can be increased, in some cases by almost 50%, over that for the same bomb detonated at ground level. The area of the effectiveness, or damage volume, may thereby be increased by as much as 100%.[17]

Regarding blast, note also that certain explosive devices can extend the duration of the blast, particularly fuel-air explosives (FAE) and thermobaric bombs. Fuel-air explosives work by dispensing a flammable aerosol gas over a wide area then igniting it. Their effects can be little short of small nuclear bombs, with a blast radius of several hundred meters and massive incendiary effects. On humans, according to the Defense Intelligence Agency, the effects are ugly:

> The [blast] kill mechanism against living targets is unique – and unpleasant ... What kills is the pressure wave, and more importantly, the subsequent rarefaction [vacuum], which ruptures the lungs ... If the fuel deflagrates but does not detonate, victims will be severely burned and will probably also inhale the burning fuel. Since the most common FAE fuels, ethylene oxide and propylene oxide, are highly toxic, undetonated FAE should prove as lethal to personnel caught within the cloud as most chemical agents.[18]

FAEs were first used by US forces in Vietnam, but the above effects have meant that in Western armies they have seen little use since. Russian forces, however, have applied FAEs in Chechnya, vaporizing entire villages or burning fields of crops.

Thermobaric weapons are often confused with FAEs, but work on a different principle. They utilize a dispersed metalized explosive that acts with atmospheric oxygen to extend the duration of the blast, with similar effects to FAEs. Thermobaric weapons jumped into focus during operations in Afghanistan from 2002, where air-dropped thermobaric weapons were used against Taliban hiding out in deep mountain caves. Dropped at the entrance to the cave, the explosive blast worked its way deep into the cave system, sucking out oxygen and suffocating or blowing apart anyone inside.

Accompanying all phases of an explosive detonation are the particles thrown out at lethal velocities by the blast. Fragments come from two sources: the warhead itself and the detritus picked up and thrown by the shock wave (glass, stones, pieces of metal) etc. As the blast energy transfers into the kinetic energy of the fragmenting shell, these fragments can achieve velocities well in excess of rifle bullets, and they carry their lethality much further than the effects of the blast wave. More about the technicalities of warheads is discussed in the chapters on armor, artillery, and air power, but suffice it here to say that the warhead's fragmentation is to a large degree, especially in modern warheads, controlled by the warhead design. Warhead cases are often pre-scored to optimize the size (and therefore velocity and flight properties) of fragments, or fragmentation materials such as metal balls or rods are packed inside. The fragments can either radiate outwards in a uniform spread from the warhead or be directed to strike a relatively small "footprint." High-explosive fragmentation warheads have their fragmentation content usually designed to defeat a specific target type. (Note also that specific fragmentation warheads might have only 10–20 percent of their weight accounted for by actual explosive.) For example, splinters weighing 0.003–0.035oz (0.1–1g) are best suited to antipersonnel (AP) targets, while those from 0.035–0.35oz (1–10g) can destroy light vehicles, missiles, and air assets. Heavy 0.35–3.5oz (10–100g) fragments can puncture light armor.[19]

Having explored explosions themselves, we now switch our focus to the effect of explosions on targets – people, structures, vehicles. This shift is not just grisly fascination – the military spends a great deal of time, research and development funds attempting to match the explosive device to the job of work. Get this match wrong, and the result can be unacceptable collateral damage or, conversely, a surviving target.

People are obviously vulnerable to explosions, and the closer they are to one the worse their situation becomes. At the most extreme, individuals right next to very powerful explosions can be completely vaporized – at pressures of 5,000psi there may well be no trace of the person left at all.[20] Outside this level of destruction is a horrendous list of injuries associated with blast and fragmentation. We will take blast first.

Blast waves can and do produce violent disintegration, but it is not uncommon to find people killed by explosions with almost no outward damage. Air-filled organs and cavities are acutely vulnerable to overpressure. Lungs, for example, can collapse at overpressures of 35psi upwards, with death a virtual certainty at pressures above 100psi; often the lung damage only emerges about 12–36 hours after the explosion, when respiratory failure sets in (this condition is known as "blast lung"). Other blast effects include perforated eardrums, bowel perforations, internal bleeding, bleeding of the brain, and death from embolism (air emboli formed in the pulmonary and coronary vessels).[21] Just being thrown through the air by an explosion can result in a grim catalog of injuries, typically blunt trauma from hitting hard objects, damage to internal organs from rapid acceleration and deceleration, and limbs being whipped against posts or walls.

Added to blast are the effects of heat and fragmentation. The amount of heat generated by an explosion varies according to the type of warhead, and the full spectrum of burn injuries can be seen in explosion victims, including severe burns to the lungs resulting from breathing in superheated gases and flesh burns from heat and fire. Fragmentation injuries range from a few minor puncture wounds caused by flying stones and glass to multiple, devastating ballistic injuries that can almost tear a person apart. Of course, there are the accompanying problems of infection that result from the penetration of so much unclean matter. For soldiers, the wearing of body armor has significantly reduced the number of deaths from fragmentation injuries. However, a study by S.G. Mellor and G.J. Cooper for the *British Journal of Surgery*, which analyzed the deaths or injuries of 828 British servicemen caught in terrorist explosions in Northern Ireland, found that body armor had little appreciable effect in reducing the number of deaths when blast was the major mortality factor.[22]

A victim's chances of surviving a bomb blast often depend on the location in which the explosion occurs. The chances plunge dramatically if a person is caught by a blast that detonates in an enclosed space, such as a room or a bus. In enclosed spaces blast is reflected off the surrounding surfaces, rather than dispersing outwards as in an outdoor explosion, intensifying the effects on those within the space, as Yoram Kluger explains:

> Indoor explosions are characterized by increased immediate and late mortality. The high incidence of blast lung explains why mortality is so high in indoor explosions. In a confined space the blast is bounced off the walls, increasing mortality and morbidity. In ultra-confined space like buses, the localized area of overpressure from the explosion is instantly amplified by reflections from the enclosing bus walls. The high mortality in such explosions can be only partly attributed to the proximity of the victims to the explosion site, because the intense overpressure is the immediate cause of many deaths.[23]

Kluger goes on to evaluate the mortality figures incurred in open space, enclosed space and bus explosions. For example, a bomb detonated in an open space creates on average a 2.8 percent mortality rate amongst those involved. In an enclosed space, however, the figure rises to 15.8 percent, while on a bus the number is 20 percent. Kluger notes that:

> While in-hospital mortality from gunshot wounds from acts of terrorism was [according to figures from the Israel Center for Disease Control] 22.8% that of bomb explosion victims was 4%, probably because immediate mortality of explosion victims is very high and could reach 29% for explosions in enclosed spaces.[24]

Such data indicates why terrorist bombings, which frequently target enclosed areas, produce such horribly high casualty figures.

Two of the key factors in surviving a bomb blast are "stand-off distance" and the type of cover between an individual and the detonation. The first issue is of critical importance in the development of new explosives by the military, aware as it is that "collateral damage" increases media criticism and, in turn, bolsters support for an enemy. During North Vietnam's Tet Offensive in 1968, for example, the exchange of firepower destroyed around 50 percent of the city of Hue, with US ground-attack aircraft dropping unguided high-explosive ordnance directly into the heart of the citadel. The extreme firepower, while swinging the battle in the US favor, provided cruel photo-imagery of destruction and death within middle-class areas of the city, and contributed to the international impression that the US had no concern over civilian casualties.

The problem with explosive ordnance is that it does not discriminate between enemy and civilian – only targeting can do that. Furthermore, innocent/friendly parties have to be a good distance away from a blast to ensure their safety. For example, a 2,000lb (909kg) high-explosive JDAM bomb, a standard US military air-dropped munition, will almost certainly kill everyone within 110ft (33m) of the point of impact (PoI). However, realistically a person should be over 1,312ft (400m) away from the PoI to have a good chance of surviving the blast unscathed (under that distance there may be a 50 percent mortality). Even if they survive the blast, fragments could kill up to 1.9 miles (3km) away. This problem is mitigated somewhat by the high level of accuracy with JDAM munitions – they typically strike within 43–98ft (13–30m) of the point of aim (POA) – but consequences of any targeting errors can be harrowing. (See Chapter 5 for more on aerial weapons.) For example, on December 4, 2001 soldiers from the 3rd Battalion, 5th Special Forces Group, were conducting operations alongside units of anti-Taliban forces north of Kandahar, Afghanistan. At around 10:00am local time a B-52 began a strike on nearby Taliban positions, but a 2,000lb (909kg) JDAM landed within around 328ft (100m) of the soldiers, the blast killing three US servicemen, five anti-Taliban fighters and wounding 20 others. This level of devastation occurred within an open area of operations, so it is obvious how difficult it is to apply explosive munitions within an urban setting, where there is almost certainly a high concentration of civilians within the immediate area of the blast. Such a problem has been exercising the minds of the weapons designers, and there are some solutions emerging. One approach is the Small Diameter Bomb (SDB). This in itself can provide a smaller blast footprint on the target, and through the use of a composite casing dramatically cuts down on lethal fragmentation. Ordnance specialists have also been looking at incorporating Dense Inert Metal Explosive (DIME) as the warhead fill. DIME mixes the explosive content with a heavy metallic dust. The dust itself does not contribute to the force of the blast (hence the word "inert"), but instead forms a lethal cloud of "microshrapnel" that causes intense slicing injuries to its victims. The key point about the DIME munition, however, is that the tiny fragments lose their velocity extremely quickly, reducing the zone of lethality to around 12ft (4m). Incorporated into the SDB the DIME explosive forms the Focused Lethality Munition (FLM), and combined with precision guidance this could well be a system for dramatically reducing collateral damage.

Turning to buildings, the issues surrounding the relationship of building design and terrorist-generated explosions are obviously hot topics following such incidents as the bombing of the Murrah Federal Building in Oklahoma City in 1995 and the 9/11 attacks of 2001. This relationship is also an issue for military weapons designers, not only from the point of view of destruction but also, as we have seen, from the need to limit that destruction. Weapons can have unpredictable results. For example, US soldiers in Iraq and Afghanistan have been using the Shoulder-Launched Multipurpose Assault Weapon (SMAW), a rocket launcher that fires a thermobaric missile for use against building and armor. A US Marine Corps report records some diverse combat effects from experience in Iraq:

[On the] SMAW thermobaric ... [Marines] only received reports of two shots [April 2003]. One unit disintegrated a large one-story masonry type building with one round from 100m (328ft). They were extremely impressed. However, another unit tried to breach a wall of a similar masonry building after being unsuccessful at trying to mechanically breach a door. "The round just bounced off the wall." They were not so impressed.[25]

As with people, buildings are most vulnerable to the blast part of an explosion. The shockwave of an external explosion first impacts upon the exterior wall, driving in windows and any weak points in the wall's structure, and also lifting floor structures. As the shock wave expands outwards in a radial pattern, it wraps itself around the building, pushing inwards from multiple directions and even downwards. These intense inward pressures can result in total building collapse, as floors, walls and columns give way. However, complete and immediate building collapse from an explosion is relatively rare. The shock wave exists for such a fraction of a second that it has only a very short time to mobilize the movement of the heavy structures. Nevertheless, a complete face of a building may be ripped off and multiple floors collapse or resultant fires can weaken primary supporting girders and later result in building disintegration (as happened in the World Trade Center towers on 9/11). Glass, both falling and propelled, is a major wounding factor in building explosions, and indeed 40 percent of the survivors of the Murrah building in the Oklahoma bombing suffered from glass lacerations.

Explosive Weapons

For the remainder of this chapter we will turn our attention to specific types of explosive weaponry. Many such weapons and warheads are considered in other chapters of this book, so here we will focus on a fairly narrow band of static or hand-launched explosive devices. Before doing so, a word about safety. It is an irrevocable fact of life that soldiers are a rough-handed bunch, and will be rough-handed in climates ranging from the arctic to the tropical. Any explosives transported into battle, therefore, have to be resistant not only to mishandling – the frequency of which will increase with the stress of combat – but also to the conditions in which they will be stored and transported.

Accidents with explosive munitions are common enough in peacetime, never mind in warfighting conditions. Between 1996 and 2000, for example, there were 285 explosives accidents within the US Army, which in total killed 14 people and wounded 274.[26] An article on these figures in the *Ground Warrior* magazine noted that human error was the "leading cause" of these accidents, with some of the most common causes being:

- Tampering with pyrotechnic devices.
- Misusing a pyrotechnic device, or placing it improperly.
- Throwing or activating a pyrotechnic device too close to people.
- Prematurely clearing a stopped or jammed weapon.
- Failing to identify a target, failing to safe a weapon, or improperly handling weapons.
- Losing track of dud grenades.
- Grenades not being fully in a bunker.
- Personnel in the "back blast" area.
- Failing to tie down or secure munitions while transporting them.[27]

Note that the primary causes of soldier injury revolve mainly around fairly low-power explosive devices or pyrotechnics, those of types almost every soldier can come into contact with. (Soldiers issued with demolition explosives or who are charged with handling powerful warheads are typically specialist engineers or weapons officers, and so have the advanced training that maximizes safety.) In combat the soldier adds to the perils of mishandling the dangers of enemy action, particularly munitions being detonated by enemy projectile strikes. There is little apart from training that can be done to reduce the numbers of accidents, and weapons can only have so many safety devices fitted before they become impractical to use. Note, however, that in the field of explosive warheads much expenditure is being poured into so-called "Insensitive Munitions" (IM). In DoD terminology, these are munitions that are "are safe throughout development and fielding when subjected to unplanned stimuli."[28] Since 1999, the Department of Defense has been legally obliged to ensure that all its newly acquired munitions comply with IM criteria.

The key benefit of the shift to IM munitions (in modern Western armies anyway) is that we are unlikely to witness some of the hideous ordnance disasters that were commonplace until fairly recently in military history, such as some of the devastating accidental explosions on US aircraft carriers during the Vietnam War. As Neil Gibson and Rupert Pengelley stated in 2005 in *Jane's Defence Weekly*:

> The safety benefits of IM are by now reasonably well understood: there being a reduced risk of response to accident or combat stimuli; a reduction in collateral damage to personnel and equipment; and a reduced prospect of a minor incident escalating into a catastrophic event. The perceived battlefield payoffs of IM technology range from an increased possibility of retaining some or all of a weapon platform's combat capability even if its own munitions are triggered; a reduction in the loss of key assets and personnel; greater flexibility for commanders, who can safely have more munitions where and when they are needed, thanks to IM's

reduced quantity/separation-distance requirements; speedier out-loading, since greater quantities can be handled at the dockside, easing berthing constraints and increasing ship availability; to enhanced interoperability through adherence to internationally agreed standards.[29]

Insensitive munitions are beneficial at every level, except that of cost in some cases. In fact, the extra cost per unit of insensitive rounds has led to some resistance from the artillery community, but generally that concern has been allayed through the greater efficiencies accompanying IMs.

Now we turn to specific explosive weapons of interest, separating them into those that belong to the conventional military and, turning to the dark side, those utilized by terrorists and insurgency forces. We will see that what makes these individual weapons distinctive is not so much their explosive power, but their mode of deployment. Note also that weaponry designed specifically for antiarmor effects is considered in Chapter 3.

Grenades

In effect, grenades are a soldier's own personal artillery. Although each grenade delivers tiny explosive power when compared to an artillery shell or air-dropped munition, they can be deployed immediately on the battlefield at localized targets. Furthermore, whereas in World War II soldiers were generally armed with either hand grenades or rifle grenades – the latter being laborious to load and use – today's infantryman might have fully-automatic grenade launchers at his disposal, capable of significant area destruction.

First, hand grenades. Within the many categories of hand grenade (which are summarized below), the fragmentation grenade is the principal infantryman's type. As the name suggests, a fragmentation grenade does its nasty job primarily by its lethal fragmentation. As an example, the US M67 fragmentation grenade is essentially a metal sphere 2.5in (6.35cm) in diameter, capped by a fuse mechanism that gives the grenade a total length of 3.53in (8.9cm). The explosive content is a mere 6.5oz (25g) of Composition B, but this is enough to give the fragments – produced by the casing – a lethal radius of 16.25ft (5m) and a significant injury-producing radius of 49ft (15m).

Hand grenades come in all shapes, sizes, and types, and give the soldier a versatility beyond the simple destruction of enemy personnel. The gas grenade is the only one commonly in civilian security use. Gas grenades operate in the same way as their smoke cousins, but instead pump out irritant or incapacitating gas, typically CS gas. The typical effects of CS are coughing, watering and painful eyes, stinging skins, and sometimes dizziness, these effects kicking in after about 10 seconds and taking 20–30 minutes to wear off. The problem with CS gas, and smoke for that matter, is that it can work both ways. Police trials showed that up to 78 percent of officers using CS gas were themselves partially affected by the gas; furthermore, up to 10 percent of people aren't affected by the gas at all, the reasons for this ranging from sheer adrenaline to the use of intoxicants.[30]

Regardless of their type, hand grenades generally have a similar method of deployment. The safety pin is pulled, while at the same time the soldier holds down the spring-loaded lever at the side of the grenade. (Some grenades also require a thumb-operated safety lever to be pushed in before the pin can be extracted.) Releasing the lever ignites a delay fuse, which will typically give 3–5 seconds before the grenade explodes. Managing the time delay is important, as it is far from uncommon for enemy soldiers to pick up a grenade and throw it back at its user while the fuse is still burning. To prevent this, or if the soldier is deploying the grenade up a slope and does not want it tumbling merrily back at him, the soldier might release the lever and count 1 or 2 seconds off before throwing the grenade, thereby shortening the time to explosion.

The hand grenade's hand-held launch is both its strength and its weakness. On the credit side, a hand grenade has complete immediacy for the soldier, giving him or her the ability to deploy explosive firepower in seconds. Grenades are critical tools in urban combat warfighting and in bunker/trench clearance operations, as the soldier can quickly deposit one through a doorway or window, get back under cover and let the grenade partially or completely neutralize any threats in the room before entering. Grenades, of course, can be thrown further – up to 131ft (40m) by a soldier armed with a fragmentation grenade and a muscular throwing arm. Grenades also have the advantage of being deployable from behind cover. Throwing grenades, however, has its dangers. For a start, in combat the soldier will not be throwing with the studied concentration of a baseball pitcher, but will be in a hurry and probably under the restrictions of enemy fire. The soldier has to make a decent snap judgment about range – if his target is less than 49ft (15m) away then he must ensure that his own cover will stand up to the grenade fragments. Furthermore, a grenade can quickly alter its trajectory if, say, it clips the rim of a trench or bounces off a nearby building.

The dangers of grenades are frequently impressed upon recruits, sometimes unfortunately through terrible accidents. For example, a US infantry live-ammunition night training exercise at Schofield Barracks, Wahiawa, USA on April 14, 2002 saw troops attacking a mock-up trench system. An accident with an M67 grenade during one of the assaults resulted in the death of one soldier and the wounding of three others. Grenades can also be bad news for civilians, as is demonstrated in this dramatic incident recounted by Alan James of the Rhodesian African Rifles, who was sent to interdict insurgents in a local Rhodesian village:

We went in to clear a village one morning. That night on patrol we had seen gooks [the insurgents] in this village. Now, I had a senior officer with us, we were actually heading off somewhere else. I wanted to go in at 5 o'clock in the morning, just before sunrise, because I knew what time the gooks would be leaving. They'd moved into the village at night, and they would go out and lie up somewhere during the day – it was standard procedure for them. But he [the senior officer] outranked me and told me to go in at first light – I thought that first light was too late anyhow ... I said I would take the house that looked like to me the one the [rebel] commander had gone into ... So I had another soldier who was covering me. I banged on the door and had a grenade in my hand. My rifle was leaning against the wall, so you can imagine how vulnerable you must feel when you haven't got your rifle in your hand. A grenade takes three to five seconds to go off and that kind of time spell ... it's amazing what can happen in five seconds. So I banged on the door and a woman came to the door. I grabbed her, pulled her out, said "Who else is in there?" She said there was another woman in there. I threw her to one side and called for the other woman to come out. She came out and I grabbed her ... I say to her "Anybody else?", and she says "no." I chucked the grenade in and she tries to run back in. I stop her and she says "My kids." And there were two babies lying on the floor, and don't ask me to this day – it was a brick-built house, concrete floor. They were lying on the floor there and the grenade went off, and other than burst eardrums not a single fragment hit them. And I said "Why didn't you tell me, I asked you?" And she said, "I didn't think that you meant children."[31]

This incident provides a chilling insight into how battlefield confusion and collateral damage walk hand in hand. It also illustrates something of the limitations of grenades – even a modern fragmentation grenade is not guaranteed to neutralize every individual in a room (in this case, thankfully).

Aside from hand-thrown grenades, there is a whole range of mechanically-propelled grenade weapons. The most popular of these are underbarrel launchers, which are an enormous improvement over the muzzle-attached rifle grenades that were used in World War II. Most armies have their own varieties, but it is the US Army that has the greatest commitment to the system with the M203, which fits beneath the barrel of the M16 series weapons. The M203 was introduced in the 1970s as a replacement for the Vietnam-era M79 "Blooper" gun, a robust standalone grenade launcher that many soldiers still lament losing. The M203 is basically a single-shot 40mm grenade-launcher tube that fits beneath the fore-end of the rifle, the separate trigger for the unit sitting just in front of the magazine (the magazine acts as a grip). The great advantage of a system such as the M203 is its range – the soldier can fire a grenade up to 1148ft (350m). At ranges of over 492ft (150m), however, the soldier will use the weapon in an indirect-fire mode, lobbing the bomb upwards in a manner reminiscent of mortar fire, and shouldering the weapon under his armpit because the straight-line flight of the grenade is very short (the muzzle velocity of the large grenade is only around 250ft/sec [76m/sec]). There is no doubt that the M203 and underbarrel launchers in general add an invaluable component to squad firepower. In the US forces, there is one "grenadier" – an M203-armed soldier – in every squad of four soldiers. In Iraq and Afghanistan the weapon has found good use, its point-shooting capabilities under 492ft (150m) enabling the user to put a grenade through a window while remaining at reasonable range, or drop grenades onto an area target well beyond the reach of a hand-thrown bomb. Smoke grenades fired from the M203 have also proved useful in handling road blocks. During the advance into Iraq in 2003, some lead US Marine units became troubled with the number of Iraqi civilians being killed in their vehicles at roadblocks, the result of confusion over stop procedures designed to counter suicide bombers. Soldiers of the First Recon unit, and others, tried to clarify their stop message using M203 launchers firing smoke grenades, with mixed results. Evan Wright was a journalist emplaced with a First Recon company during the initial Iraq conflict, and witnessed the new policy first hand:

Now, when the first vehicle, a white pickup truck, approaches, Colbert [Sergeant Brad Colbert] strides into the road, ahead of the Humvees.
"Do not engage this truck!" he shouts to his men.
He fires a grenade from his 203 launcher. It makes a plunking sound almost like a champagne cork popping, then bounces into the road, spewing green smoke. Three or four hundred meters down the road, the white pickup truck turns around and drives off.[32]

The range advantage of the M203 here is clear – such a security measure would be far more difficult with a hand-thrown grenade. Wright, however, subsequently witnesses two more incidents of smoke grenade traffic control. In one, it takes two smoke grenades to stop the driver of a speeding car, and in another, for reasons unclear, a Marine fires a burst from an SAW just after launching the smoke grenade, fatally injuring the car's apparently unarmed driver.

For all the M203's practicality, it is far from a perfect weapon. It takes skill to master and is known to be quite inaccurate, the grenade being easily knocked off trajectory by wind or heavy rain. The system is slated to be replaced by the Heckler & Koch M320, which is of the same caliber but offers better accuracy over similar ranges and greater safety in operation. There are also some formidable standalone launchers available. The Milkor MGL 40mm launcher (known amongst US forces as the M32), for example, can release grenades at two rounds per second to devastate an area of 66x197ft (20x60m). The extremely low recoil impulse generated by the gun allows the user to keep his eye on the target while shooting, allowing him to make quick visual adjustments to put the rounds on target. The MGL/M32 can also take a collection of new rounds with a nasty lethality. The 40mm Hellhound high-explosive round, for example, has a maximum range of 1,312ft (400m) and twice the explosive fill of the standard M433 projectile, giving it a lethal fragmentation radius of 33ft (10m) and a mild steel penetration of 3.5in (90mm). The "Hellhound" name, incidentally, is a contraction of the almost comical "High Order Unbelievably Nasty Destructive Series" (HOUNDS) title.

Looking much further ahead, however, the capabilities of soldier-carried grenade launchers could become far more potent. The US experimental Objective Individual Combat Weapon (OICW), for example, combined a 5.56mm assault rifle and a 25mm magazine-fed grenade launcher in one unit. Although the 25mm grenades were nearly half the size of those fired by the M203, the rounds could be automatically programmed to explode as airburst. A laser range-finder mounted on the weapon calculated the distance to the target, then, via its own fire-control system, the OICW preprogrammed the fuse of the grenade about to be fired. Once the grenade was launched, the fuse detonated the grenade directly over the heads of the enemy, obviating their frontal cover. Recent testing has resulted in the cancellation of the OICW program, however, mainly on account of technical problems and the re-evaluation of priorities from combat experience in Iraq, but its principle could well inform the future.

Mines

Of all the explosive devices we could discuss, few carry as much controversy as mines. Although, as we shall see, landmines can include self-destruction features, most do not, and once buried in the ground they remain active and indiscriminate for years. This lengthy lifespan, combined with the fact that literally millions of mines have been sown worldwide since 1945, means that mine warfare is a profound global problem.[33]

Some basic statistics clarify the issue. Around 90 countries worldwide are affected by landmines, and active and emplaced landmines number some 60–70 million. Every year between 15,000 and 20,000 people are landmine casualties, which equates to one person killed or injured every 30 minutes. Well over 90 percent of these casualties are civilians, and one third are children – children tend to explore their landscape without the caution of adults, and they also tend to play with unfamiliar objects.[34] Most antipersonnel landmines (APMs) are designed to injure rather than kill, which results in a chronic drain on both society and medical resources, especially as landmines are a particular problem in developing countries, often with already shaky medical care. (For example, in Africa it takes on average 12 hours for a landmine victim, often hideously injured, to reach formal medical care.) Furthermore, even if landmines are known and avoided, their presence negates the use of valuable land that could be used for crop-growing or pasture.

Even if a single landmine is suspected, the area becomes psychologically a minefield, a fact that some military forces have utilized to their advantage, marking out minefields that do not in fact exist.

For all those in a landmine-free West (apart from the territories of the former Yugoslavia), it is hard to imagine the grim, daily reality of the landmine problem elsewhere. Grassy verges by the sides of roads, playing fields, woodland, dirt tracks, cropland, derelict buildings – all might harbor landmines. To take an example of an enduring landmine problem, we need look no further than Cambodia. Set at the heart of the Cold War's Southeast Asian battleground, Cambodia has endured several decades of indiscriminate landmine sowing. Not only were mines emplaced during the Vietnam War by US-backed forces (there are also an estimated 50,000 tons of US unexploded ordnance (UXO) scattered across the country), but during the 1970s the Khmer Rouge, both as insurgents and as a government, relied heavily on minefields to secure the borders with Vietnam and Thailand, to control the movement of peoples within its borders, and to enforce a climate of fear. Mine expert Norman Youngblood describes how the problem persisted after the Khmer Rouge was thrown out of power by Vietnam in 1979, and resumed an insurgency that lasted into the 1990s:

> All sides in the war relied heavily on landmines to secure their defensive positions and territory. In 1985, the Vietnamese began work on the K5 barrier belt, a 600-kilometer-long [372-mile-long] mine belt running along the Cambodian-Thai border, designed to prevent incursions by Khmer forces based in Thailand. The K5 belt contained as many as three million landmines and was built by forced labor. The belt effectively closed off the Cambodian border with Thailand, making it as difficult for Cambodians to leave the country as it was for Khmer forces to enter the country. The Vietnamese kept few if any records of the location of individual mines, and their allies and enemies were no better.[35]

The K5 belt continues to pose an immense problem for Cambodia, although today its territorial coverage and location is at least well marked. In 2004 alone over 900 civilians were killed or injured by mine/UXO detonations. There are some positives – mines are being cleared at a fast rate, with 71,475 antipersonnel and 1,742 antivehicle mines (AVMs) being cleared in 2004.[36] The monthly casualty figures have dropped by around 60 percent since the mid 1990s. Nevertheless, potentially four million active landmines lie out there in the Cambodian fields, putting over five million Cambodians in nearly 6,000 villages at risk of death and injury. Similar stories are repeated around the world. Afghanistan is one of the most heavily mined countries in the world (many of the mines are air-scattered devices deployed by the Soviets during their occupation from 1979–89). In Bosnia and Herzegovina, there were a total of 18,319 mined areas in 2005.[37] Peru is blighted by an estimated one million landmines. Even the Falkland Islands remain contaminated, with a total of 100 minefields containing up to 16,000 mines.

The sheer scale of the landmine problem has led, unusually, to meaningful international action. In 1992 the International Committee to Ban Landmines (ICBL) was formed as a pressure group to ban both the use and production of APMs and to promote mine-clearance operations. Through their leverage, and other sources of pressure, increasing numbers of governments started to implement landmine restriction policies, leading to the 1997 Convention on the Prohibition of the Use, Stockpiling, Production and Transfer of AntiPersonnel Mines and on their Destruction (also referred to as the Ottawa Convention). A total of 122 countries signed the treaty, the main clauses being as follows:

1. Each State undertakes never under any circumstances:
– To use antipersonnel mines;
– To develop, produce, otherwise acquire, stockpile, retain, or transfer to anyone, directly or indirectly, antipersonnel mines;
– To assist, encourage or induce, in any way, anyone to engage in any activity prohibited to a State Party in this Convention.
2. Each State Party undertakes to destroy or ensure the destruction of all antipersonnel mines in accordance with the Provisions of this Convention.

By the end of 2006 more than 150 countries were signatories to the Convention, signaling a sea-change in attitudes to the use of landmines. However, in February 2007 40 countries remained outside the Convention. They included some big names, such as China, the Russian Federation and the United States. Why, in the face of such powerful international condemnation of landmine use, do so many countries hold out?

The short answer, but the one most commonly overlooked, is that in harsh tactical terms mines are really very useful. Killing and injuring enemy personnel and damaging their vehicles is only part of what landmines achieve, and not necessarily the most important part. A minefield is effectively a tool for controlling the enemy's tactical options and tempo. Once an enemy force hits a minefield, it has to stop, figure out the extent of the minefield and the types of mines employed, and then either find a way around it or commit itself to the lengthy procedure of clearing a path through. In effect, the area-denial created by the minefield allows a force to dictate how the enemy forces maneuver, slowing them down (and hence giving the mine-laying side time to retreat, advance, or emplace defenses) or channeling them into kill zones. More basically, minefields can also act simply as barriers, functioning as a lethal type of fence to protect borders, demilitarized zones, and perimeters. (The heavy US-sponsored mining of the border between North and South Korea was one key reason for the United States holding back from signing the Ottawa Convention.) Even if mines are not laid in a systematic field (such as occurs in the use of air-deployed mines), their presence can have a critical effect on force movement, especially at the small unit level. Soldiers have to move with considered caution, any relaxation of security procedures often leading to casualties. With the very landscape being a threat, the presence of mines dramatically increases operational stress. Hugh McManners, in his book *The Scars of War*, recounts the experience of Corporal Kelly, a soldier of the British Army's 3 Para, during the night attack on Mount Longdon in the Falklands War. Kelly takes over the story:

> Everything was going to be so simple. As the initial assault platoon we were going to take the first part of Mount Longdon, and then the other two platoons were going around to clear another bit. However, after 50 metres we walked into a minefield, which changed everything ... We knew we were in a minefield because Corporal Milne (One Section Commander) stood on one. The noise wasn't so bad – just the very bright flash. He started screaming about the pain in his leg. We all went down, then someone crawled forward to give him first aid and morphine. (He lost the leg all the way to the top of his thigh.) The Argentine sentries opened fire ...[38]

The functions of the minefield are here graphically illustrated. First, the mine takes out a member of the attacking force, in this case a section commander, whose role will then have to be adopted by another individual. Other soldiers are diverted to give treatment and evacuation. Second, the detonation alerts the defenders, initiating small-arms fire. Third, the explosion forces the attackers to drop to the ground, although only temporarily, disrupting the momentum of the attack and increasing battlefield chaos. All the above effects of mines are achieved without the employing force actually having to be present, giving mines the insidiously catchy benefit of being "force multipliers."

Mines are generally separated out into two types: APMs and AVMs. APMs are usually triggered via a pressure plate, exposed prongs or tiltrods, tripwires, breakwires, or infrared beams. AVMs, because of the different signatures of their targets, add acoustic-, seismic- (vibration) and magnetic-activated mechanisms to the list, along with "scratch wires," which scrape along a vehicle chassis or body and provide the necessary signals to trigger the fuse. Two other systems of mine initiation are command detonation – the user detonates the device remotely – or time delay. The former is useful for synchronizing mines within an ambush plan, while the latter serves to hamper mine-clearance efforts. Time-delay devices have also been one way in which countries have negotiated the unpopularity of mines, by making the weapons "self-sterilizing." The US Area-Denial AntiPersonnel Mine (ADAM), for example, comes in two formats. The M692 long-destruct variety will self-destruct within 48 hours of being deployed, while the M731 will self-destruct after only 4 hours. Self-sterilizing mines can be useful to the employing force, as they give it the knowledge that after a certain period of time the mines will no longer be a danger, hence they can move safely through the area.

Note that how a mine is detonated generates its own set of political considerations, particularly in relation to the Ottawa Convention. Pressure-plate activated AVMs, for example, will usually have a pressure-detonation requirement greatly exceeding the weight of a typical human being. However, some AVMs can be detonated with pressures of less than 330lb (150kg), and research conducted by the Landmine Action Group in 2001 discovered that a human was capable of generating 330lb of pressure if he was running or jumping down from a vehicle. Worse still, any AVM detonated by tripwire will just as easily be triggered by a human. Many antimine organizations note that if AVMs are triggered by tripwire, breakwire, tilt rod, and scratch wires then they are just as likely to detonate through human contact; and even magnetic influence, acoustic and seismic mines might be triggered by people and hand-held equipment rather than vehicles. They further query whether an AVM fitted with an antihandling device (AHD) actually constitutes a *de facto* APM, and therefore should fall under the prohibitions of the Convention. An AHD is part of the mine itself, or an external fitment (such as an APM placed beneath an AVM) that detonates the main mine if someone attempts to defuse it. The Human Rights Watch organization notes that some AVMs have particularly worrying antihandling mechanisms:

> Certain AVM are factory equipped with an AHD called a "ball in cage" mechanism. Detonation of the mine occurs when the mine is moved and a metal ball bearing inside a metal housing (cage) moves to complete a simple electrical circuit. This mechanism is dependent on a battery to provide power and will become inert once the battery expires. AVM reported to have a "ball in cage" antihandling mechanism include the SB-81/SB-81AR [Portugal, Spain] and the AT2 [Germany, Italy, Norway and UK].[39]

The sensitivity of such antihandling devices raises the concern that the mine as a total system will endanger humans as much as vehicles, and it serves well to show how difficult it is to legislate against APMs in a watertight fashion.

There are three principal types of APM, none of them pleasant. Blast mines do their damage via explosive force – typically just enough to wreck someone's leg or foot (usually with 3.5–7oz /100–200g of explosive content). Injuries from these mines tend to be traumatic amputations of the lower limb to varying heights up the leg. The worst injuries result when a person places his or her heel directly onto the mine, as the force of the detonation is sent directly up the bones of the leg, shattering them.

Once activated, bounding mines work by throwing their explosive component into the air – usually to a height of around 1m (3ft 3in) – before detonating. (A time-delay fuse, or activation by tripwire, ensures that the victim is not standing on the mine when it launches.) They will usually have a higher dedicated fragmentation component than blast mines, and these fragments will blast out in a high-velocity arc into the head and chest of whoever is standing nearby. Unlike blast mines, bounding mines are designed to kill, and their "advantage" is that they can take out more people than the one who tripped the device.

The final mine type is the directional mine, one that is designed to fire a concentrated spread of fragments in a chosen direction. The best, but far from the only, example of this type of mine is the US M18 Claymore. The Claymore is essentially a convex plastic pack containing explosive and 700 steel spheres, each ball weighing just 0.03oz (0.75g). It is bedded in the ground using two sets of attached metal prongs, with the instruction "FRONT TOWARD ENEMY" indicating the direction of employment. When detonated, either by command or tripwire, the Claymore will blast out the metal balls in a 60-degree arc to a height of 6½ft (2m), the horizontal arc fanning out to 165ft (50m) wide at 165ft range. Directional mines such as the Claymore are best used to cover possible routes of enemy attack, or as ambush devices in conjunction with other weaponry, and their effects on exposed infantry are devastating. In interview with the authors, Professor Dr William Atwater, curator of the Aberdeen Proving Ground museum in Maryland and a US Marine Corps Vietnam veteran, told of an ambush set up for Viet Cong insurgents moving along a jungle trail. Several Claymores were placed with interlocking fields of fire at a point where the trail bent around. However, the trail was at this point raised above the surrounding floor level, and there were concerns that the survivors of the Claymores could simply hide behind the bank and return fire. To allow for this, the Marines buried det-cord – an explosive-filled cord used for linking together multiple explosive devices – into the ground behind the trail. The unfortunate Viet Cong patrol, when it did turn up, was massacred either by the Claymores or from the det-cord exploding beneath their feet as they sought cover. None survived.

Mines are only as effective as their method of emplacement, and here, yet again, we unearth more controversies. Minefields are best laid in a systematic mix of APMs and AVMs, the latter destroying enemy armored vehicles while the former attrites their infantry support and the ability to clear the mines. Laying such fields, however, takes time. The two basic categories of mine-laying are manual and mechanical. Manual involves hand-emplacing each mine, something that is time-consuming but, in the hands of experts, will produce the best results in terms of device concealment, distribution pattern and detonation. Far faster, and still with decent results, is mine-laying using a dedicated mine-laying vehicle or trailer. These devices are essentially like plowing machines – they cut a furrow to the required depth, "plant" a mine into it and then cover the mine over again. They are also fast – the Ranger mine-laying trailer used by the British Army (towed behind a AFV 432 or Warrior IFV) can put down 600 AVMs in only one hour, using just a three-man crew.

Scatterable mines (scatmines) are by far the fastest way of putting down a minefield – an entire field can be laid in the time it takes for a munition-dispensing shell to explode. Scatmines are dispensed from either aircraft bombs, artillery munitions or special dispensing packs, and they effectively spray a minefield out over a wide area in a matter of seconds. The mines then sit on the ground (they are generally well camouflaged so they don't stand out against their background), to be detonated by various forms of disturbance.

Scatmines have impressive capabilities. Take the ADAM mine, for example. A single 155mm artillery shell contains 36 mines, which are distributed over a wide area when the shell breaks open around 1,968ft (600m) over the target area. Each mine, once deployed, throws out up to seven ultra-sensitive trip lines (very fine camouflage thread). If anything touches one of these lines, the mine is triggered, throwing its explosive kill mechanism up a short distance from the ground, and producing a lethal blast radius of 15ft (4.5m). Remember that the minefield just described is produced by only one shell – a battery of three guns would be able to lay a blanket of over 500 mines in much less than a minute – and can be done at a range of up to 17 miles (27km).

Another system of scatmine deployment currently available to US forces is the M131 Modular Pack Mine System (MOPMS). This consists of a pack that contains 17 AVMs and four APMs, which is emplaced wherever soldiers feel their perimeter is threatened, or in areas where the enemy is likely to pass. Using a remote command system, a soldier can initiate the deployment of the mines (or multiple MOPMS), which individually use a similar system of tripwires to the ADAM. Other dispensers in the US inventory include the fearsome Volcano system, a vehicle- or helicopter-carried dispenser that carries 960 mixed AVMs/APMs and can lay a field 3,608 x 656ft (1,100m x 200m) in a matter of seconds, and also air-deployed systems such as the Wide Area AntiPersonnel Mine (WAAPM) and the Gator mine system.

Scatmines could seem like a commander's dream – an instantly and remotely deployable minefield that, unlike conventional buried mines, will typically self-destruct and save the protests of human rights activists. However, they are not the wonder weapons they might purport to be, mainly because of the human and tactical realities involved in suddenly transforming a large area of ground into a lethal space. Such issues arose out of a US Government Accountability Office (GAO) report to the House of Representatives, which studied US mine warfare techniques during Operation *Desert Storm* of 1991.[40] In total, approximately 117,634 scatterable mines were deployed during the conflict, these being Gator,

Remote Anti Armor Munition (RAAM), and ADAM types, all of self-destruct varieties. The report admits that the records about such deployments are scant:

> Department of Defense records on the Gulf War provided us include little detail on why land mines were used. Available records indicate that US forces employed land mines both offensively and defensively when fighting in Iraqi controlled Kuwait. For example, US aircraft offensively employed concentrations of surface-laid Gator land mines to deny Iraqi use of Al Jaber airbase in Kuwait and to hamper the movement of Iraqi forces. In addition, Gator land mines were used extensively with the intent to inhibit free movement in and around possible staging and launch areas for enemy Scud missiles. In a defensive mode, Gator land mines were employed along the flanks of US forces. In addition, US Marines defensively employed concentrations of artillery-fired ADAM and RAAM land mines to supplement defenses against potential attacks by enemy forces north of Al Jaber airbase in southern Kuwait.[41]

The report highlights instances of perfectly sound use of scatmines, principally to protect US troops or to break up the movement of Iraqi forces. However, it then goes on to conclude that:

> The services reported no evidence of enemy casualties, either killed or injured; enemy equipment losses, either destroyed or damaged; or enemy maneuver limitations resulting, directly or indirectly, from its employment of surface-laid scatterable Gator, ADAM, and RAAM land mines during the Gulf War.[42]

Why this is so is hard to fathom. One distinct possibility (apart from issues of data collection) is that while scatmines are theoretically useful, their application in fast-moving tactical situations – where friendly forces might unexpectedly have to move through areas recently mined – could have restricted them to areas of small tactical importance. This conclusion is embellished by later findings in the report, in which feedback gathered from battlefield commanders expressed concern that fratricide and a reduction in battlefield mobility could result from the use of scatmines, leading "to the reluctance of some US commanders to use landmines in areas that US and allied forces might have to traverse."

Related issues now emerge, the first being a general concern about safety issues with US mine ordnance. The same report noted that the Department of Defense figures for the reliable self-deactivation of its mines was in the order of 99.99 percent, if the 120 days battery run-down was included. However, in the aftermath of the Gulf War various mine-clearance contractors were employed throughout Kuwait to clear up ordnance and mines. One of them, Conventional Munitions Systems (CMS) Inc., was put to work around the Al Jaber airbase mentioned in the quotation above. The subsequent CMS report noted that in this sector 1,977 scatmine duds were found, these being munitions that had failed to self-destruct. Note that these were in addition to 118,000 unexploded US submunitions from cluster bombs.

The GAO report shows concern over such data:

> DOD reports that it employed in the Gulf War a total of about 118,000 self-destruct land mines ... and that their self-destruct failure, or dud, rate is 0.01 percent (1 in 10,000). However, if, as DOD reported, about 118,000 of these self-destruct land mines were employed and they produced duds at the DOD-claimed rate of 0.01 percent, there should have been about 12 duds produced, not 1,977 as CMS reported finding in one of seven Kuwaiti battlefield sectors. Thus, a substantial inconsistency exists between the DOD-reported reliability rate and the dud rate implied by the number of mines that CMS reported finding from actual battlefield use.[43]

Department of Defense tests conducted in 2002 with scatmines revised its reliability figures somewhat more in line with the CMS report. Tests were conducted on eight different scatmine self-sterilizing systems, and in some cases the dud rates reached 10 percent.[44] In one test of the Volcano system "66 out of 564 land mines failed the test. Among the failures were 1 hazardous dud (meaning that it could explode), 24 nonhazardous duds (meaning that they had not armed), 6 mines that detonated early, and 1 mine that detonated late."[45]

These figures show that there is frequently a yawning gulf between the conceptual application of a weapon system and its battlefield use. They also demonstrate how even the most modern of mine technologies can present a long-term threat. One particular concern surrounds minefield reporting. All minefields require diligent mapping, and that information needs to be passed through central command and then distributed to all relevant units. The data file also needs to be kept open, sometimes for years, and disseminated to civilian organizations where relevant. The very speed with which scatmines can be deployed, in some cases in a one-shot fire mission, makes their reporting in time-critical combat situations difficult. GAO researchers found that:

> Shortly after the Gulf War, one DOD fact sheet reported that DoD's joint procedures for coordinating the use of air-delivered mines had not been widely disseminated. Further, according to the fact sheet, the procedures were outdated with respect to the rapid mobility of the modern Army. Thus, the warning information – such as the locations and self-destruct timing durations – "was next to impossible to obtain and pass to ground component commanders."[46]

Further alarming conclusions from the Department of Defense included Navy and Air Force Gator raids having no recording system in place, with one Army report stating that the US Air Force "flew over 35 GATOR missions (the exact number is not known) without reporting or recording the missions."[47] As a consequence of inexact scatmine recording, both of air- and land-deployed varieties, fatalities and injuries were suffered amongst US forces. The report acknowledges that the numbers are impossible to pin down, but of 81 casualties ascribed to land mines and 142 to "unexplained explosions," the possibility of a significant proportion having come from US scatmines is very real. Data about the effects on the civilian populations of mined areas is not available. Moreover, during the UXO cleanup operation in Kuwait, a total of 84 UXO technicians were killed.[48]

This lengthy discussion of scatmines must not skew our minds to the fact that the vast bulk of mines laid in the world are simple, crude explosive devices with no self-sterilizing features. Nevertheless, it alerts us to the fact that however sophisticated mine warfare might become, equipment failure seems to keep track at some level and will render all mine usage problematic. And mine warfare could become very sophisticated indeed. Minefields of the future will be switched off or on at will by the operator, allowing his forces to move through safely but rearming the minefield for the enemy. One possible future is the "self-healing" minefield, a development of the Defense Advanced Research Projects Agency (DARPA). Here the mines communicate with one another in a wireless network and will literally move themselves in relation to one another to form a consistent minefield. Furthermore, should a path be cleared through the minefield, the mines will sense the gap and reposition themselves – "hopping" up to 30ft (9m) at a time – to close off any pathway. Mine-clearance soldiers within the field must literally fight each mine as it repositions itself.

In the meantime, the long, slow business of mine clearance goes on. There are military methods of fast clearance, such as the M58 Mine Clearing Line Charge (MCLC), which fires a cable of explosive into a minefield and, once detonated, instantly clears a path 328ft (100m) long by 26ft (8m) wide. In most cases, however, demining is a methodical business that involves four basic stages:

1) Locating the minefield and mapping its extent.
2) Preparing the minefield for clearance – a dangerous job in itself that involves tasks such as removing obstructions and cutting back vegetation.
3) Detecting the location of each mine and marking it.
4) Disposing of the mine through removal and/or detonation.

Mine detection is often the really tricky part. The makers of mines deliberately design their products to defeat mine countermeasures, hence many mines have almost no metal components within them, frustrating the metal detectors (battlegrounds are also typically sprayed with metal fragments, meaning that on average only one contact in 1,000 is actually a mine). Some mines are also "hardened" to resist the effects of tools such as the MCLC.

Canine detection is one of the best detection methods, for reasons noted by the engineering scientist and mine-clearance expert Maki K. Habib:

> So far, dogs are considered the best detectors of explosives. Their sensitivity to this kind of substance is estimated to be 10,000 times higher than that of a man-made detector. Specially trained dogs are used to detect the characteristic smell of explosive residue that emanates from mines regardless of their composition or how long they have been implanted. This enables dogs to detect mines with low metal content that are undetectable by metal detectors ... Mine detection dogs can work in almost all types of terrain. They are also easy to transport and highly reliable, and they can screen land up to five times faster than manual deminers.[49]

Habib notes that dogs do have their limitations, mainly on account of fatigue (the animals need regular rest) and confusion when there are multiple detections within a limited area. Several organizations are experimenting with rats (particularly African pouched rats) as mine detection creatures, and results are promising. Rats are drawn on leashes behind a bar that moves slowly across the minefield. They have been conditioned through a detect-and-reward system to respond to explosive odors – their nasal sensitivity is equal to a dog's – and when they scent a mine they scratch at the ground. Rats also have the advantage of being light – their weight will not trigger even the most sensitive APMs. Field trials in Africa showed that the rats could be used to search an area of around 1,614 sq ft (150 sq m) in only half an hour. Furthermore, a single rat can be trained for around $2,000, compared to $10,000 for a dog. However, rats have a demining competitor in honeybees, whose use in mine clearance has been pioneered by the University of Montana. During their "training," the bees are conditioned to swarm over areas of explosive residue, their reward being food from a sugar-water feeder. Tests have shown that the training period can be as little as 2 hours, the cost of a hive around $100, and the accuracy rates approaching 98 percent, all these factors holding out great promise for developing nations to possess their own mine detection systems.

Beyond living systems of detection, there are mechanized methods of mine clearance, including vehicles fitted with special flails or plows that detonate mines on contact. These demine at a far faster rate than manual techniques, and do not suffer from the rate-reducing fatigue issues. As with most mine-clearance technologies, however, mine vehicles have their limitations. Sometimes they can simply displace mines rather than detonate them, and complicated terrain can be challenging. Nevertheless, mechanical demining offers significant time and cost savings over manual demining, particularly when demining large areas of farmland.

Dr Peter Schoeck, a world expert in ordnance engineering and disposal, calculates that demining European agricultural land is financially self-sustaining at 40 cents/sq m – beyond that point demining becomes a humanitarian project. Schoeck points out that the "global average cost per deminer" is approximately $10,000, with a clearance rate of 43–75 sq ft (4–7 sq m) per man hour and, depending on local safety restrictions on daily hours, an annual clearance rate of 64,583–193,750 sq ft (6,000–18,000 sq m) per year. This equation means that manual demining costs $1.70 per sq m, hence Schoeck concludes that manual demining is necessarily a "humanitarian undertaking."[50] Using mechanical demining, however, gives clearance rates of 32,291–58,819 sq ft (3,000–5,000 sq m) per hour. Furthermore, the design of the mechanical deminers can actually leave the ground in a ready-to-cultivate state, and fulfills the 40 cents optimum noted. (Obviously, these figures are subject to wide changes based on movements and effects within global economies and agriculture.)

Regardless of such figures, it would obviously be better were the mines not there in the first place; but the combat advantages they offer mean that they will always remain part of the global arsenal.

Improvised Explosive Devices

At the time of writing, the problem of Improvised Explosive Devices (IEDs) is at the forefront of governmental and media consciousness. Around 90 percent of US and British casualties in Iraq since 2003 have been the result of explosive devices, mostly in the form of roadside bombs. For the global terrorist and insurgent community, IEDs quite simply constitute the most practical and effective campaign tool.

IEDs have a considerable ancestry. For example, around midday on September 16, 1920 a horse-drawn wagon drew down Wall Street, New York City, and stopped outside the J.P. Morgan building. Inside the wagon was 100lb (45kg) of TNT with 500lb (230kg) of cast-iron bolts packed around the explosive. At 12.01pm the explosives were detonated via a timer, killing 38 people and wounding 400 others – the streets were thronged with workers on their lunchtime break. Italian anarchists perpetrated the attack.

Apart from the sophistication of transport, there is almost nothing to separate this incident from the vehicle-borne explosions occurring on an almost daily basis in Iraq. Space does not allow for a lengthy consideration of the evolution of terrorist bombings between these two points, but we need to acknowledge that the September 11, 2001 attacks were part of a continuity of terrorist methods, rather than a new beginning. What was distinctive about the 2001 attacks was the fact that the IED was the delivery mechanism itself – the four aircraft with their combination of heavy fuel load and high velocity obviated the need for explosives.

Almost any group dedicated to constructing explosive devices will find the tools to do so, and hence IEDs range from the egregiously crude to devices of military-grade sophistication. In the Northern Ireland of the 1960s and 1970s, for example, rioters quickly found that a home-made fragmentation grenade could be produced by dipping a standard firecracker in glue and then coating it with BB pellets. By contrast, bombmakers in Iraq are emplacing multiple artillery shells linked, or "daisy-chained," by det-cord, and command detonated via a mobile phone. What distinguishes the IED from, say, mines are basically its "homemade" characteristics, which as we shall see are both the IED's strength and its weakness.

To make any bomb, the bombmaker requires three basic elements: the explosive itself, a detonator (with power supply) and a delivery mechanism.[51] In terms of sourcing explosives, the bombmaker can either obtain pre-made explosives or make them himself. The former option is preferable in terms of device efficiency, and explosives are not altogether difficult to source with the right contacts. Commercial mining provides an important source of IED explosives. The United States, for example, uses around 3 million tons of explosive every year for commercial purposes and Russia 600,000 tons. Restrictions on access to these explosives and the associated detonators and boosters are typically tight, but such are the volumes that even small percentages of theft pose a credible security threat, as Bronislav V. Matseevich of the Krasnoarmeisk Scientific Research Institute of Mechanization points out:

> This multimillion-ton genie has been let out of the bottle, and there is no way of putting it back. It would seem that getting hold of 0.01 or 0.001 percent of this amount would not present any difficulty. Nevertheless, even those percentages would amount to tons, and furthermore the terrorists' manuals have long included methods for producing simple explosives themselves.[52]

The problem of commercial explosives entering the wrong hands is more acute in developing countries and those with internal security issues. Figures from the ATF in the United States, by contrast, have shown that high-quality commercial and military explosives figure little in terrorist attacks. Taking the decade 1987–97, the ATF found that only 3 percent of bombings within the United States used high explosives. By contrast, 32 percent used smokeless or black powder, 29 percent chemical mixtures (simply retasking household chemicals), 16 percent fireworks or similar pyrotechnics, 1 percent homemade explosives and 14 percent were either not identified or not reported.[53]

Note the significantly high use of black powder and smokeless propellants in US attacks/explosions – societies will use the materials most available to them. (The author Hunter Keeter notes that a delivery of 10lb/4.5kg of black powder was once simply left all day on his front porch with a delivery note.) The types of explosive used can also have some demographic implications. Around 79 percent of people arrested in the United States for explosives offenses are juveniles, most of them pursuing nothing more serious than thrill-seeking, which the easy availability of gun propellants and fireworks makes perfectly feasible. However, apply availability issues to a country like Iraq and you have a different level of problem. In the aftermath of the 2003 invasion, an estimated 250,000 tons of military-grade munitions disappeared into the population. For example, during the looting of a military college at Baquba, north of Baghdad, several hundred missile warheads were taken, with each warhead containing around 57lb (26kg) of high-grade commercial explosives. The unaccounted-for stockpiles of explosives and warheads in Iraq are sufficient to maintain an ordnance-based insurgency for decades to come, even without external resupply.

For those who cannot acquire professionally produced explosives through either theft or illegal supply (there are plenty of countries worldwide that are quite prepared to sell explosives openly on the black market), there is always the option of making their own. This is a tricky business – an estimated 60 percent of casualties from homemade explosives are the bombmakers themselves. Nevertheless, the dividends for the terrorist can be impressive. On April 19, 1995, homegrown terrorist Timothy McVeigh detonated a huge truck bomb outside the Murrah Federal Building in Oklahoma City, comprehensively wrecking the north face of the building and killing 168 people. The explosive used was 4,800lb (2,181kg) of ammonium nitrate fertilizer. Ammonium nitrate is one of the world's most commonly used fertilizers, and is readily available through agricultural wholesalers. Once saturated with a hydrocarbon such as diesel fuel, it is effectively transformed into a powerful explosive. Ammonium nitrate has a high detonation point, hence the tricky parts for the bombmaker are lowering the detonation threshold – a process that can be accomplished with chemicals such as aluminum, zinc, or potassium sulphate – and obtaining initiating mechanisms, such as professional detonators and TNT (McVeigh stole these parts from a local quarry).

Ammonium nitrate has been a primary explosive in numerous terrorist attacks worldwide, ranging from Northern Ireland in the 1970s through to the Bali nightclub bombing in 2002. Consequently, many countries are putting in place measures to control the sale of the fertilizer, or producing it in a form that makes it more difficult to weaponize. Yet the popularity of ammonium nitrate worldwide will ensure that it continues to crop up in terrorist hands for many years to come. And if the home-grown bomber can't make fertilizer explosive, there are plenty of other options to choose from, many of which can be produced from common household chemicals such as ammonia, peroxide, and solvents. A cursory scan of the internet yields dozens of web sites with explosives-making instructions, the explosive recipes including those for nitro-glycerine, acetone peroxide, HMTD (hexamethylene triperoxide diamine), nitrated milk powder, and nitrogen trichloride. The great problem, thankfully, with a high percentage of homemade explosives is their instability, with many easily detonating with heat or friction. Yet determined individuals, especially those with a decent background in chemistry, will continue to manufacture some high-grade explosives. Richard Reid – the infamous "shoe bomber" – used a plasticized form of acetone peroxide (also called triacetone peroxide, TATP) in his attempt to blow up an airliner in 2001. All that is required for the manufacture of TATP is acetone, concentrated hydrogen peroxide, and sulfuric acid. Once these ingredients are mixed, crystals form, and these are filtered out as an extremely powerful explosive, producing violent blast effects with little heat. TATP has found applications in Middle Eastern suicide bombings and some other terrorist attempts, but its use is limited by its sensitivity – it is extremely shock sensitive and becomes more so over time, and is also liable to blow up the bombmaker at many stages of its production, storage, and handling.

The tactical advantages of IEDs are easy to appreciate. They give the insurgent "standoff" distance, thereby reducing the risks of casualties from an enemy that usually has superior firepower resources in direct- or indirect-fire engagements. Large IEDs maximize the potential to inflict heavy casualties within a short window of time, and provide one of the few resources for tackling heavy armor or protected installations/buildings. The opportunities and locations for emplacing IEDs are almost limitless; therefore target selection and timing are precisely controlled.

More intangible, but just as important, are the psychological and social effects of IEDs. The expectation of encountering IEDs, for example, breeds caution and the need for modified tactics. For example, in Iraq vehicle convoys have to be staggered, with vehicles moving in a variable, elastic relation to each other to disrupt the timing of bombers using command detonation systems. Every suspected IED must be investigated and neutralized by Explosive Ordnance Disposal (EOD) officers, resulting in frequent halts in convoy or troop movements. The cumulative effect of these stops is to deprive a force of control over operational tempo, typically one of the decisive elements of maneuver warfare. Note also that just the suspicion of an IED has a retarding effect, a fact that insurgents have been quick to exploit. In Northern Ireland, IRA operators would weigh down the trunk of a car with blocks of concrete and park the vehicle in a suspicious location. The security forces, fearing the vehicle contained a major car bomb, would have to go through full EOD procedures, putting a drain on their finances and planning. Furthermore, the enforced stop would give the bombers plenty of time to observe EOD operations, and design countermeasures.

IEDs also have a major effect on the morale of troops. The levels of combat stress they induce are profound. Mark Lachance, a US Army Iraq veteran interviewed for this book, drew an analogy to illustrate the profound anxiety caused by IEDs:

It's what they do psychologically is what makes them an effective tool. You can take your most war-hardened veteran from any country and put him in a Humvee and have him go driving down a road and just have IEDs blow up randomly and it's going to slowly start to affect him after a while. I myself was in many IED strikes, and had to blow up many IEDs that were discovered before they could be used against us ... Imagine this – next time you are driving down the road and you are going to work or home, look at every guard rail, every trash can, every cement kerb and all those things could blow up at any moment ... just think about that ... Everything that is there is prospectively your enemy ... My Staff Sergeant said it best, "It's like playing the lottery, if you play it long enough eventually you are going to win. That's how it is with roadside bombs. No-one's protected, no amount of armour can save you. Although the first ten times you might survive, all it takes is once and you're dead."[54]

Lachance vividly summarizes the tension of living in an IED environment, and emphasizes the relative impotence of countermeasures. Veterans have noted some indicators of a possible IED attack. Middle Eastern societies have an extremely high percentage of children, so an absence of children can mean they have been cleared from an ambush zone. Vegetation and kerbing stones might appear disturbed, and isolated parked vehicles can act as choke points to funnel vehicles into a kill zone (or may contain the bomb themselves). IEDs are more likely to be detonated at places where vehicles are forced to slow and bunch up – such as bridges and river fords – hence soldiers have to be vigilant for any bombers (isolated individuals watching a convoy from high ground or cover could be the bomb operators). Mark Lachance also noted that most civilians in Iraq wear sandals, which are not suited to fast movement. People wearing training shoes arouse suspicion, indicating that they might want to make a quick getaway on foot.

In the civilian world, the effects of IEDs are just as profound. Civilian movement is hampered by the security measures put in place to counter IEDs, or the fear of encountering IEDs, which in turn has a detrimental impact upon trade. In Israel, for example, amidst the wave of suicide bombings during the 1990s and early 2000s, restaurant custom plummeted after bombers repeatedly targeted such establishments, people choosing to eat at each other's homes rather than venture out. The restaurants had to incur the further costs of employing door security to screen all customers, thus squeezing their profit margins even further. Such knock-on effects are duplicated across thousands of businesses, having a critical effect on the national economy. An Australian report in 2004, for example, estimated that terrorist attacks in East Asia would reduce economic growth in the region by 6 percent over the next decade.

A further problem for those facing IED situations is that they are tremendously difficult to counter. Advanced technologies do exist for detecting

IEDs, but the enemy that uses such weapons is almost infinitely adaptable within the three primary methods by which an IED is deployed: package, vehicle, or human (suicide bomber). Packaged devices include not only parcel and letter bombs, but any static IED. The variety of these devices, and how they are deployed, can be endlessly diverse. In special forces hands, of course, packaged bombs can be tools of precision killing. Such was the case during the infamous Israeli Operation *Wrath of God*, a series of Israeli reprisal actions for the Munich massacre. The PLO (Palestine Liberation Organization) representative in France, Dr Mahmoud Hamshari, was mortally injured on December 8, 1972 in his Paris apartment by a bomb installed in his desk telephone – the bomb was command detonated by Israeli agents who telephoned Hamshari and got him to confirm his identity. In Cyprus a month later, the Fatah representative Hussein Al Bashir was killed in Nicosia, Cyprus, by a bomb detonated beneath his bed. In Iraq, the targets are more generalized and the need to limit collateral damage almost non-existent, hence the most common type of explosive device is an artillery or mortar shell, typically of 120mm or greater, with its impact fuse or shipping cap replaced by a conventional detonator. How these devices are used, however, shows an ingenuity equal to that of Mossad. Multiple shells are linked together to create kill zones several hundred meters long. Shells are encased in plaster of Paris to appear as kerb stones, or have been inserted into the corpses of animals lying on the roads. Bombs have been strapped to the backs of donkeys, the extra elevation directing more of the blast against vulnerable vehicle windscreens. Mobile phones and cheap remote-control doorbell systems provide command-detonation capabilities. The power of such devices is terrifying. A video widely distributed on the YouTube network shows a large IED detonating directly beneath an M1 Abrams tank – the entire 68-ton vehicle is bodily thrown into the air. Moreover, in around 60 percent of cases, IEDs are the trigger mechanisms for ambushes.

Vehicle-borne IEDs (VBIEDs) have also had a devastating effect on Iraq's security situation. The key advantages of a VBIED are the precision and speed of deployment, plus the weight of explosives that can be carried. In our vehicle-centered world, cars and trucks have all the anonymity of people, but when converted to bomb carriers their destructive potential is enormous. The ATF has ranked vehicles according to their size, explosive capacity, and potential destructive effect. At the bottom of the scale is the "Compact Sedan," with a maximum explosives capacity of 500lb (227kg), creating lethal air blast range of 100ft (30m) and a minimum evacuation distance of 1,500ft (457m). Jump to the opposite end of the scale and we have semi-trailer trucks with maximum capacities of 60,000lb (27,273kg), which if detonated creates a lethal air blast of 600ft (183m) and a minimum evacuation distance of 7,000ft (2,134m). Although bombings rarely ever approach the upper limit of this scale, even a mid-sized box van has enough capacity to create enormous destruction. On March 27, 2007, a truck containing an estimated 2 tons of explosives was detonated in the northern Iraqi city of Tal Afar. The truck also contained flour, which was used to lure out large crowds suffering from the deprivations of war. Once the crowds had gathered, the explosives inside were command detonated, killing 152 people and wounding 347 others. The crater from the blast measured 76ft (23m) across and 100 homes in the vicinity were either destroyed or severely damaged. In a stark illustration of how IEDs breed a cycle of violence, nearly 40 people were killed in reprisal attacks.

Countermeasures for VBIEDs typically involve road obstacles that prevent vehicles approaching at any speed. Suspicious approaching vehicles, should they ignore warnings, are usually shot to pieces. In a country such as Iraq, with its thousands of vehicles and poor foreign-language skills amongst Western forces, the consequences are that checkpoints become places where the innocent as well as the guilty die, all of which furthers the insurgent cause.

Another form of IED delivery is the suicide bomber. Suicide bombing is principally a component of Islamic terrorism and insurgencies, although it has been used in conflicts such as the Vietnam War and, between 1987 and 2001, by the Tamil Tigers group in Sri Lanka and India. In the Middle East, the tactic emerged in earnest in the Lebanon in the early 1980s, pioneered by the Hezbollah (Party of God) organization. Since then, groups that have taken up the suicide bomb tactic include al Qaeda, the al Aqsa Martyrs, Amal, Hamas, Kurdistan Workers Party, and Palestine Islamic Jihad.

Suicide bombings tend to take two physical forms. The first involves the bomber wearing an explosive vest wrapped around the torso and abdomen, which is self-detonated by a plunger or button or command detonated by a handler (see below). Second, suicide vehicle bombs enable the bomber to deliver larger amounts of explosive at speed. Typically, the vest-wearing bomber will attack "soft" targets such as shops, crowds, and buses, while vehicles are used for "harder" targets with either better physical protection or more security elements. (An advantage of a vehicle bomb is that once it is rolling it takes considerable resources to stop; even if the driver is killed, which of course is an ultimate goal in suicide bombings, the vehicle can continue rolling and be detonated by a third party.)

Moral considerations aside, it is relatively simple to understand the attraction of the suicide bomb on a tactical level. First, it is the ultimate "smart" weapon. The bomber can take the device directly to the target, adapting the approach constantly to deal with problems. If his or her primary target proves inaccessible, then others can be selected at will. In April 2002, for example, a female suicide bomber attempted to attack the Mahane Yehuda open-air market in Israel, but was unable to enter because of security screenings. In response, she walked into a nearby packed bus stop and detonated her explosives, killing six people and wounding 73. In case the suicide bomber has a sudden attack of nerves, many handlers often have the ability to detonate the bomb remotely. (In some cases, the suicide bomber has no control over the device he or she is wearing; the handler simply observes him or her walking or driving around the target area and chooses the moment of detonation.) In any case, the suicide bomber can consciously maximize the results of the detonation, as Bruce Hoffman graphically illustrates in his 2003 article "The Logic of Suicide Terrorism," which deals specifically with Israel:

> Such are the weapons of war in Israel today: nuts and bolts, screws and ball bearings, any metal shards or odd bits of broken machinery that can be packed together with homemade explosive and then strapped to the body of a terrorist dispatched to any place where people gather – bus, train, restaurant, café, supermarket, shopping mall, street corner, promenade. These attacks probably cost no more than $150 to mount, and they need no escape plan – often the most difficult aspect of a terrorist operation. And they are reliably deadly. According to data from the Rand Corporation's chronology of international terrorism incidents, suicide attacks on average kill four times as many people as other terrorist acts. Perhaps it is not surprising, then, that this means of terror has become increasingly popular. The tactic first emerged in Lebanon, in 1983; a decade later it came to Israel, and it has been a regular security problem ever since. Fully two thirds of all such incidents in Israel have occurred in the past two and a half years – that is, since the start of the second intifada, in September of 2000. Indeed, suicide bombers are responsible for almost half of the approximately 750 deaths in terrorist attacks since then.[55]

Hoffman outlines further advantages of the suicide tactic, including the fact that the planning phase is simplified by the lack of need for an escape plan. (Moreover, the death of the bomber means that there is no one left for interrogation, and no wounded comrades to tend.[56]) The attacks can be cheap to execute, but the precision of the bomb placement and the control over detonation timing ensures maximum destructive effect. Hoffman goes on to point out that buses have been popular targets for suicide bombers, particularly during the winter and summer when the windows are closed for heating or air-conditioning respectively. The confinement of the bus – which as we have seen intensifies explosive force – plus the high number of people on it produces "a significant return on a relatively modest investment. Two or three kilograms of explosive on a bus can kill as many people as twenty to thirty kilograms left on a street or in a mall or a restaurant."[57] Hoffman further notes that when security improved on Israel's buses, the suicide bombers simply switched their focus to other targets – the method is ever flexible, hence it is difficult to predict and counter.

Countering suicide bombers, and IEDs in general, requires a maturity of approach often overlooked in the history of counterinsurgency. The first point to recognize is that although IED attacks can seem like acts of casual improvisation, they usually take place within a relatively sophisticated network of expertise and organization. In Iraq, for example, IED bombings will be executed by a cell typically numbering six to eight people.[58] The cell leader is responsible for planning and financing the attack, and tends to be an educated individual with prior government or military service. The device itself is produced by an expert bombmaker, likely to be someone who learnt his skills in the army, particularly the Iraqi Republican Guard, or from the Mukhabarat, the Iraqi Intelligence Service (IIS). Over time, and with the external support of groups like Hezbollah and countries like Iran, and the all-informing internet (most bomb attacks are videoed for propaganda and training purposes), the skills of bombmaking have spread to a wider base.

The two other key individuals in the IED cell are the emplacer and the triggerman. Greg Grant makes the following notes on the emplacer:

> This person usually has some military expertise and is skilled at moving unnoticed into and out of an area while transporting an IED ... He is familiar with American patrolling tactics and techniques and is often supported by lookouts armed with cell phones who will tip him when a patrol nears. The emplacer's primary motivation is money. He is a foot soldier, is often paid as little as $50, and told to place an IED in a specific location at a specific time. A common technique is to pull a car over to the side of the road to change a tire or appear as if it's broken down. He places the IED – 75 percent of IEDs are placed in a hole previously used for the same purpose – covers it up with something, turns the switch on and drives away. Often they don't even stop, as insurgents use cars with a hole cut in the floor so they only have to slow down and drop the device onto the road. Of all the members of the IED cell, the emplacer's skills are the most difficult to replace. When taken out, an IED cell's activity is at least temporarily disrupted as a replacement is sought.[59]

If the IED is going to be delivered by suicide means, the emplacer will be replaced by a handler, someone who will guide the bomber from recruitment stage through to final execution. The triggerman is the individual who simply detonates the device, although he will require training and/or military experience to initiate bombs properly. For example, the time it takes for the first vehicle in a convoy to pass between two points will give the triggerman his interval before detonating to hit the second vehicle in the convoy.

This neat description belies several complexities. First, the bombers are completely absorbed within civilian society, hence they in no way stand out. This is a particular problem with suicide attacks. Whereas in the 1980s suicide bombers used to fit some neat demographics – typically male, educated, and aged in their 20s – today they cross all ages and both genders. Second, in Iraq the IED cells are highly decentralized and tend to be autonomous, forming and disbanding fluidly, merging with other groups or starting up splinter cells, and even hiring themselves out to other groups on a mercenary basis. Such mutability challenges the efforts of systematic intelligence gathering.

Nevertheless, intelligence and "hearts and minds" operations do seem to be the key to countering IEDs, regardless of some of the advanced technologies entering the marketplace. Many of these, such as the US Warlock system, function by jamming the radio signals used to detonate IEDs or predetonating the devices. They have proved to be useful, but the point of IED deployment is that the cells learn to counter the countermeasures – underestimating the ingenuity of the enemy is a critical mistake. By far the most important level of counter-IED operation is aggressive intelligence and sweep operations against the IED cells and their infrastructure. For example, Israel's response to the suicide bombings was Operation *Defensive Shield*, launched in March 2002. Israel deployed thousands of troops and intelligence personnel into the occupied territories, radically controlling the movement of the population through curfews, roadblocks, and other measures – and hence limiting the freedom of the bombers to move. Intensive intelligence-gathering amongst the local population interdicted terrorist cells during their planning stages, or at least made it problematic for them to organize bombings. Bruce Hoffman described the objectives of the operation:

> The goal of the IDF [Israel Defense Forces], though, is not simply to fight in a manner that plays to its strength; the goal is to actively shrink the time and space in which the suicide bombers and their operational commanders, logisticians, and handlers function – to stop them before they can cross the Green Line, by threatening their personal safety and putting them on the defensive.[60]

The main problem with *Defensive Shield* is that some of its more heavy-handed measures – particularly the Israeli destruction of the refugee camp at Jenin – generated international condemnation, and arguably fueled the incentives for future generations to become bombers. Thus the aggressive approach requires an almost indefinite deployment, with repression building a militancy that requires further repression and so on. The real challenge for those wishing to counter IEDs, therefore, is to alter the culture that encourages the creation of the bomber. As Dr Amer Hameed, Senior Lecturer at the British Defence Academy, told the authors in interview: "Perhaps we can do more to stop IEDs with David Beckham and a couple of football fields than with all the technology we can design."[61]

3

MECHANIZED MUSCLE – BATTLEFIELD ARMOR

Armor is the supreme symbol of land warfare. It is a motif both of victory and of oppression – one of the most publicly memorable images of armor is that of the young man standing in front of a Chinese tank in Tiananmen Square in 1989. As with all weapons systems, the nature of the beast depends on which end of the barrel you are.

Armored Basics

An Armored Fighting Vehicle (AFV) is really distinguished by its armored protection. This varies tremendously between vehicles, from an inch or so of simple steel plate, sufficient to stop light small-arms fire, through to massive MBT (Main Battle Tank) armor that can halt tank rounds and missiles. Where we make our first major division in the AFV family, however, is over mobility. AFVs run on one of two systems – wheels or tracks. The choice of which is used has kept technicians and tacticians in argument for decades. The critical starting point is that AFVs are off-road vehicles, and as the weight of the vehicle increases so does the risk that the vehicle will sink into soft ground, or at least lose traction on it. The challenge, therefore, is to lower the vehicle's ground pressure by spreading the weight, at its point of contact with the ground, over as wide an area as possible.

Tracks are good for this on account of their broad "footprint." The US Army formula applied is that if a vehicle spends more than 60 percent of its time off-road, and weighs over 10 tons, then tracks are best.[1] Note that a tracked vehicle cannot just go anywhere – the driver of a 68-ton Abrams tank, for example, will diligently avoid soft, boggy ground, very deep snow, or steep crumbling earth. Nevertheless, the off-road capability of tracks is excellent, and tracked vehicles can do useful things such as neutral steer – turning around on the spot within the length of the vehicle, something that can be very handy in urban zones or other confined terrains. Tracked vehicles also offer a host of other advantages, including a low profile, greater internal space, and greater armor protection (tracked vehicles can carry the increased weight more easily).

Tracks seem to win the argument, therefore; well, not necessarily. What wheeled vehicles offer above anything is speed. Take two comparable US systems. The Bradley Infantry Fighting Vehicle or IFV (tracked) travels at a maximum road speed of 38mph (61km/h), while the eight-wheel Stryker combat vehicle (derived from the MOWAG Piranha III) can move along at just shy of 62mph (100km/h). Such speed offers faster deployment potential – very appealing in the modern rapid-reaction ethos – and also a much better fuel economy over tracks.

Wheels can also compensate for lighter armor in terms of survivability – a vehicle is harder to hit the faster it moves. On modern vehicles, run-flat inserts inside the tires mean the vehicle can keep going if a tire is destroyed, and some vehicles even offer the ability to control the tire pressure from the driver's cab, thereby giving control over ground pressure.

The wheels/tracks debate continues in some quarters, but seems to have been largely settled by simply having both types of vehicle within the make-up of the armored forces. Leaving self-propelled artillery for the next chapter, we can separate AFVs into three basic categories: tanks, armored personnel carriers (APCs), and infantry fighting vehicles (IFVs). Of tanks, we shall say much more below. APCs, however, are essentially "battle taxis," lightly armored wheeled or tracked vehicles used to transport one or two squads of infantry to the battlefront. Fitted weaponry tends to be light, typically a pintle-mounted machine gun, but some of the Soviet varieties (such as the BMP series) feature antitank guided missile (ATGM) launchers and turret-mounted cannon. APCs were particularly popular during the Cold War era, and they included the US M113 series, the British FV432, the aforementioned Soviet BMP series and the Chinese Norinco YW 531C. They offer the advantage of a protected environment for infantry, the ability to deploy the infantry at the same speed as other armor, and special mobility characteristics – most APCs have some amphibious capabilities for crossing rivers etc. Note also that the basic APC platform can be adapted for a variety of purposes. Adapted APC roles have included command-and-control, medevac, ATGM carrier, vehicle recovery, bulldozer, fire support, air-defense system, minelayer, and many, many more.

IFVs retain the battle taxi role but are usually more heavily armed than APCs, having turret-mounted firepower, and typically have much greater ballistic protection. Their role is to deploy infantry into the combat zone – IFVs usually carry around 6–10 infantrymen in a compartment at the rear – but also to provide heavy firepower support. IFVs have become tactically central to professional modern armies, in many ways threatening the role of the tank. The US Bradley, for example, has a turret-mounted 25mm M242 chain gun, a coaxial 7.62mm M240 and a twin-launcher on the left side of the turret for seven TOW (tube-launched, optically tracked, wire-guided missile) ATGMs, these having a range of 12,303ft (3,750m). Firing ports allow the infantry contingent to fire their weapons from the vehicle and explosive reactive armor (ERA) fittings improve the survivability of many Bradleys. The vehicle is also fully amphibious. Other notable modern IFVs include the British Warrior, Japan's Type 89, Germany's Marder 1, and the Russian BMP-2. As with the APCs, IFVs can switch through a multitude of different roles.

In modern, integrated armies, tanks and IFVs typically work hand in hand, complementing each other with their different fire capabilities, although some units will exclusively operate one particular type of vehicle to give it a fast-deployment capability – the US Stryker Brigade Combat Teams are good examples of this principle. The picture for the future may be complicated by initiatives such as the US Future Combat System (FCS), where one vehicle platform will take over multiple roles through different turret fitment, theoretically replacing the Abrams, Bradley, Paladin self-propelled gun, and other vehicles in one fell swoop. The FCS is studied in greater detail in the next chapter, but we can explore some of the issues by looking at the future of the greatest AFV type – the MBT. Before doing so, however, it is worth reflecting on what life is like for those who work and fight from within an armored vehicle.

Life Under Armor

There is a danger when studying any impressive weapon system of treating it almost as an autonomous beast, whose mass and power operate independently of the humans manning the interior. Such is particularly true of armored vehicles, especially the mighty MBT. Yet an AFV is simply a massive static roadblock without the crew to animate it, and focusing on them rather than the technology illuminates some oft-overlooked issues of armored warfighting.

There can be no claustrophobics amongst AFV crews. The interior of an AFV is cramped and dark, with hard metal edges wrapping around the crew and passengers. Visibility is provided through a mixture of periscopes, vision slits and TV monitors, depending on the vehicle. Even with the most advanced systems, the crew will have a distinct sense that there are things going on out there that might harm them and that they cannot see. A video posted on YouTube, for example, shows an Iraqi insurgent methodically creeping around a parked Bradley IFV, and dragging two IED weapons directly under the hull of the vehicle. This "mission" goes on for around 5 minutes, the insurgent diligently avoiding all vision blocks, before he retreats to a safe distance and the IED is detonated.

One response to this vulnerability in the past has been for the tank's commander to direct combat standing up from an open turret. This has its advantages – the commander gains a complete perspective of the battlefield, being cognizant of all threats, including those from the air. He can also spot enemy infantry attempting to creep up on his tank. The Israeli Armored Corps (IAC) was particularly fond of this approach, until its experience during the Yom Kippur War. The losses amongst the exposed tank commanders were horrific, and too many crews had the ghastly experience of speaking to their commander one second, then seeing a headless body drop into the interior of the vehicle the next. This tactical lesson has required relearning in Iraq, with many vehicle commanders being seriously injured by small-arms fire, RPGs, or IEDs while observing from their turrets, or simply taking a breather from the terrible heat down inside the vehicle.

The "iron coffin" sensation of being in an AFV is very strong, particularly during the horrifying intensity of combat. This experience is well conveyed by Ken Tout, an author and ex-World War II tanker for the 1st Northamptonshire Yeomanry and King's Dragoon Guards. During a briefing speech given on November 27, 1986, Tout outlined some of the anxieties of manning a tank in action:

> The tank is a home and a workshop and a social club and a transport. Only when the first real explosions sound and only when the first comrade tank explodes into flame and only when a visible enemy gun turns in one's direction does the tank become a potential tomb, a place of terrifying enclosure.[2]

Tout acknowledges that the experience of this "terrifying enclosure" rarely leads to anyone actually abandoning his tank, but can result in a tortured mental and physical paralysis:

> As far as I can ascertain the only remedy for such enclosure paralysis is, in training, a constant repetition of a drill, almost as a Catholic learns and recites the Rosary – insisting until the lesson is etched into the substance of the mind: "the protective value of the armour, the escape drill in the moment of emergency, the need to keep alert and active, if you shoot first and straight you're safe, yes, it's bad inside the tank but, my God it's a damned sight worse outside."[3]

Training does, of course, save lives and minds. In a combat situation a well-trained crew should be able to function and fight despite their inner turmoil. The problems can arise when an armored crew has to maintain the tension of living with mortal threat for day after day. In Iraq, for example, the fact that vehicles are being used at around five times their normal peacetime rate has become a clear issue in terms of logistics and vehicle maintenance, but it is also a problem for the crews who have to operate them. Precise branch-of-service breakdowns of post-traumatic stress disorder (PTSD) casualties in Iraq are not available, but psychiatric casualties are traditionally high for armor. During World War II the highest rates of physical casualties amongst the Allies were suffered by aircrew, then infantry, then armor. In terms of psychiatric casualties, however, the reverse was true. Brigadier General Vorvolakos Nicolaos, a former commandant of the Greek Army Armor Training Center, wrote of how the modern battlefield is unlikely to reduce the nature of the mental pressure:

> The crewman in the contemporary operational environment has to move through deadly antitank long range weapons, to confront enemy helicopters and air crafts [sic] with antitank abilities, advanced enemy tanks, scattered mines, supermodern radars and night vision and aiming instruments that will inflict the continuance of the fight during the night. All these will increase the fears, the stress and the exhaustion of the crewmen, while at the same time will decrease the time for his sleep, food and relaxation.[4]

With the hindsight of operations in Iraq, Nicolaos might have added IEDs to his list of the tanker's nightmares. For although AFVs have improved tremendously in terms of their survivability, the threats arrayed against them have likewise increased. Furthermore, a tanker will have to live with the knowledge of the terrible deaths suffered by comrades, particularly those who died trapped inside a tank on fire. During the battles in North Africa during World War II, such was the horror of having to listen to friends burn to death over the radio that many tankers went into battle with pistols on their laps, with which to commit suicide in case their tank "brewed up." Ben Shephard, in his book *A War of Nerves – Soldiers and Psychiatrists 1914–1994*, one of the best complete studies of military psychology, found plentiful evidence of how the horrors of armored warfare corroded morale and well-being:

> The sight and sound of another tank's death throes as it "brewed up" was not something easily put behind you. For Robert Maughan watching two Cruiser tanks burning was "the bitterest moment of my life": he had felt great affection for their commanders. Days later he "could [still] hear the screamings of men trapped to death." Even more awful was the decision, sometimes forced on a tank commander, to abandon his own crew, the men he had lived with so intimately, to their fiery fate inside a doomed tank; riding in the turret, he could get out and they could not. That left a nasty aftertaste and, for some, terrible incapacitating depression.[5]

Of course, with the widespread mechanization of modern armies, and the fact that infantry now spend a significant portion of time being transported around in IFVs, tankers aren't the only ones to experience the disquieting effects of armored life. A Warrior AFV, for example, will take seven infantry personnel in its rear compartment, and during a prolonged advance they may spend several hours in there, suffering heat or cold (depending on the climate) and aching discomfort. Furthermore, the IFV's role as a battle taxi can lead to grim experiences. A British soldier in Iraq remembered that the Warrior duties included "fire support, assault, casevac, relay, extracting, escorts, VCPs [vehicle checkpoints], intimate support – everything."[6] This multiplicity of duties could lead to extra pressures on the crews, as exemplified by one incident described in Richard Holmes' study of British warfare in Iraq, *Dusty Warriors*. After one engagement with Iraqi insurgents, Private Stuart Taylor of the Princess of Wales' Royal Regiment (PWRR), under orders that all Iraqi dead be brought back to base for identification, found that his Warrior was packed with ten badly mutilated bodies. Once he got to camp:

> The medics were waiting to take the bodies out of the back. Unfortunately the rear door failed to open and being the driver of the Warrior I had to climb through the

turret and over the bodies to open the door. The experience was bad and I still have nightmares on a nightly basis.[7]

One other aspect of being an armored crew member is that you have to share your life at intimate close quarters with a group of other soldiers. Almost every behavior and character trait is exposed, and during prolonged operations there is absolutely no privacy. Ken Tout observed that there were many times when the most pressing emergency was not issues of mortal danger, but of conflicts within the tank crew:

> The immediate crisis turned upon a crewman's sanitary, or insanitary habits, within the noisome den of the tank closed up for six hours without respite. It turned upon the gunner's asinine humour at inappropriate moments. It turned upon the driver's habit of incessantly singing doleful hymns, or simply upon the fact that the cockney commander spoke with an assumed Oxbridge accent.[8]

A breakdown in crew relations can have very serious consequences, as communication and smooth, united responses are the keys to AFV survivability in battle. For example, a typical MBT either has a four-man crew: commander, driver, loader, and gunner; or in those tanks fitted with auto-loaders (typically Russian-built vehicles) the loader is dropped to create a three-man crew. In a combat situation, each man has his own discrete field of responsibility. The driver must competently negotiate the terrain and obstacles with his monstrous charge, while also taking his orders directly from the commander and placing the vehicle to assist effective gunnery and find cover and concealment. The gunner has to have lightning reactions to targets of opportunity, and to those designated by his commander, while also making judgment calls about range, ammunition, target type etc. In addition, it will usually be the gunner who takes over from the tank commander (TC) should the TC be wounded or killed. The loader has to keep the gun fed with the correct type of shells according to the gunner's/TC's instructions, and when not in combat must contribute to the endless series of tasks all tankers perform to keep their vehicles running well. The TC, naturally, has to coordinate the whole enterprise, not only within the tank but also with surrounding infantry, air, artillery, and other armor assets. Such a job is a demanding one, even with modern networked battlefield systems that allow the TC to see the real-time positions of all proximate friendly forces.

Should any one member of this team not fulfill his duties perfectly, the integrity and relevance of a 60–70-ton MBT can be jeopardized. Hence it is no surprise that armor unit commanders spend much time in consultation with their NCOs making up the best crews, in which personalities and talents are most in harmony. Captain Jason Conroy, a US tank commander discussed in more detail below, gives one of the most revealing insights into this process:

TC-gunner combination is the most crucial on the tank. If those two do not get along or communicate well, the tank can end up being more of a liability than an asset ... In my gunners I was looking for soldiers who, despite their relative youth and lack of time in the Army, had the maturity to deal with stress and responsibility ... We looked at personalities, background, experience, and ability to deal with subordinates on the crew, particularly the loader and driver ... Working with the first sergeant and the platoon leaders, we tried to put the less experienced gunners with more experienced tank commanders, and vice versa.[9]

Conroy's method is not to find the best individuals and pack them all into one vehicle, but to create the best teams, aware that individualism (as opposed to individual initiative) is not a valued trait in a tank crewman. Interestingly, he also goes on to address the language issues of a modern army, particularly a US Army in which a high percentage of soldiers have Spanish as their first language. His policy in many cases was to concentrate Spanish speakers within individual tanks; this was no doubt a wise move, as under times of stress, such as in combat, bilingual people will tend to revert to their mother tongue.

Not only do armor crews have to contend, or harmonize, with each other, they also have to handle the environment of the tank itself. In many ways, even modern tanks are unwholesome places to occupy. One of the first problems is the close proximity of so many unyielding metal surfaces, inviting serious impact injuries as the vehicle buckets along rough ground. This issue is particularly acute in IFVs, where accompanying infantrymen are often not as securely strapped in as crewmen. In both tanks and IFVs, blunt trauma is a leading cause of injury and death when the vehicle has hit an IED/mine, even if the integrity of the crew compartment has not been compromised. Adding to this danger of impact can be the effects of constant vibration emitted by the motors. The vibrations are transmitted into the body through the floor and any other surfaces with which the crewman has contact. In 2003, military physician Jorg Sandmann conducted interviews with 64 German Federal Army tank commanders to assess health problems arising from a 199-mile (320km) armored march. The results were troubling:

> After 36 hours, one-half of the soldiers indicated feeling some pain, which consisted primarily of knee and back troubles. In addition to the marked disturbances after 24 hours, 50% of the soldiers indicated suffering from at least one health disturbance, and after 36 hours, 80% of the soldiers suffered at least one health disturbance. The disturbances appear faster and more frequently the longer the soldiers are on the battle tank as commanding officer. There is also a subjective increase in troubles with the years of service. Our results show that the vibration load on the battle tank can cause health disturbances.[10]

Sandmann's exploration of the health problems becomes more concerning as it expands. Physical problems included lower leg swellings, ankle joint edema (excessive build up of fluid in the ankles), pain in the knee joints and back, and Raynaud's syndrome (a circulatory problem in the hands and feet). Sandmann also noted that "we found a Yugoslavian report on the degenerative dystrophy syndrome [weakness or wasting of muscles] of the spinal cord and one Russian report about the radiculitis [inflammation of nerve roots] of the spinal column of tank crews." (Russian/Eastern Bloc AFVs of the Cold War era are renowned for their high vibration levels, particularly the T-54, T-62 and the BMP range.) The study also found that after 8 hours of exposure to the vibrations those officers who had been longest in the service suffered more health issues, suggesting vibration injuries also have an accumulative effect over time. The principal safeguards against such injuries are, naturally, reducing vibrations from the engine, padding seats and other relevant surfaces, and limiting the amount of time spent in the vehicle.

Vibration health threats are just the tip of the iceberg. Noise levels, mainly from the engine but also from the weapons, can be deafening. Research by the US Army Center for Health Promotion and Preventative Medicine concluded that for steady-state noise (constant noise, like a vehicle engine) anything over 85 decibels could cause hearing damage, and likewise for impulse noise (like a gun blast) over 140 decibels. Now bear in mind that an Abrams tank under way generates around 117 decibels (rising to nearly 200 at speed) and a TOW 2 missile launch comes in at 179 decibels and you see the problem. Up to 60 percent of soldiers returning from combat duty in Iraq and Afghanistan have reported some hearing impairment (particularly reduced acuity or tinnitus); a significant percentage of these is from impulse noise, but vehicle noise is also taking its toll.

The effect of having hearing-impaired soldiers aboard a tank is serious. A 1990 US Army report into the issue found, amongst other things, that such troops:

- Experienced a delay of up to 50 seconds when identifying a target, and only (in the case of a gunner) hit the target 41 percent of the time, compared to the normal 94 percent.
- Were 36 percent more likely to mishear a command.
- Were 21 percent more likely to have "their entire crew killed by the enemy."[11]

Such alarming conclusions have led many health and safety officials to recommend mandatory use of earplugs by armor crews, but many soldiers find these impractical, uncomfortable, and somehow unmanly.

The other great bane of life under armor is heat. Tanks generate enough heat by themselves, but place them under a baking sun and they effectively turn into iron cookers. Crews in everything from Humvees to Abrams in Iraq have commonly reported internal temperatures of 100°F+ (37°C), the discomfort of which is compounded by the crew's bulky clothing, which may include armored vests and full NBC (Nuclear, Biological, Chemical) gear. A November 2004 newsletter from the US Army Research, Development and Engineering Command noted that, in the case of the Humvee, "Soldiers could not properly complete missions due to the extreme heat and humid conditions."[12] Even with the most modern tanks' air conditioning systems, the consequences can be dehydration, rapid fatigue, headaches, and, in the worse cases, heat stroke. Current research in the West is focusing on supplying armor crews with cooling vests to wear, it being easier to cool them than the tank.

Compounding heat issues is the build up of carbon monoxide from the engine and from burnt munitions propellant. This is not typically a problem if the hatches are open and the vehicle is well ventilated (fume extractors usually pull out most of the propellant fumes), but when "buttoned down" the build up of gas can affect even the most modern tanks. (US Army training, for example, recommends that the Abrams' NBC system be switched on every 5 minutes when the tank's hatches are closed to evacuate carbon monoxide.) Those operating inside much of the older Soviet-era machinery can experience significant carbon monoxide poisoning after just a few hours.

On top of the challenges just outlined, there remain literally hundreds of minor and major health hazards to do with armored vehicles. Arms and shoulders can be smashed by recoiling gun breeches. Bystanders can be crushed to death when a tank suddenly starts up and surges forward. Icy or wet conditions make it easy to slip when climbing up on the vehicle. Ammunition or fuel can explode if not handled correctly, or crew can be burnt by hot radio antennae or exhaust pipes. A US Army *M1 Abrams Tank Safety Guide* lists over 200 individual points regarding tank safety, which include:

• Always use safety pin and install the antirecoil plug before removing fire extinguisher bottles. Bottles can take off like a rocket if they become activated.

• Turbine engine exhaust gases are very hot. Under the right conditions, they can ignite dry vegetation or other combustible materials. When operating in dry conditions, pay attention to the material around the rear of the tank during halts.

• If time permits, the driver should warn the crew if he applies the brakes hard. Crew personnel could be thrown into parts of the tank causing severe injuries.

• Do not use the tank to push over trees. Such practices are unsafe. The tank can be lifted off the ground, and the main gun hung up on a limb.

- Soft drink, beer, fruit juices, vinegar, and cleaner lube can corrode 120mm rounds. Corrosion may cause premature detonation of rounds.
- Personnel can be blinded if they look directly into a laser beam without wearing laser protection goggles. Treat the laser rangefinder as a direct-fire weapon with a hazardous range of 8,000 meters [26,250ft].[13]

Such a list reminds us that the life of an armor crewman, regardless of what force he belongs to, is a tough one. To take into account the dangers and complexities of the vehicle itself, while also using the vehicle effectively as a combat tool, requires nerves, intelligence, and teamwork.

The End of the Tank

When we think of armor, the defining image is that of the Main Battle Tank. Nothing seems to represent the power of an army better, whether the tank is squatting ominously on a street corner, engine idling and turret turning, or churning across a battlefield in an earth-shaking formation. Yet the irony is that its demise has been predicted with generous frequency.

The tank's threatened existence is capably summed up by Rupert Smith in his searching study of modern warfare, *The Utility of Force*. Smith points out that the Yom Kippur War in 1973 was actually the last time when "the armoured formations of two armies manoeuvred against each other supported by artillery and air forces" and the last time in which "tanks in formation were the deciding force."[14] Although Smith acknowledges that most professional global armies still have huge numbers of tanks in their inventories, and that they have been deployed frequently in infantry-support operations, he still sees a declining rationale for these monstrous vehicles:

> [The] use of the tank as a machine of war organized in formation, designed to do battle and attain a definitive result, has not occurred during three decades. Nor, for that matter, is it ever likely to occur again, for the wars in which armoured formations could or should be used are no longer practical. This does not mean a big fight with large groups of forces and weapons is no longer possible, but does mean that it will not be an industrial one in either intent or prosecution; industrial war no longer exists.[15]

So are we seeing the last days of the tank? Certainly, development of new MBTs on the world market has virtually ceased – most armored warfare investment has gone into upgrading existing tanks or towards other projects. Yet few large-scale armies seem to be seriously contemplating letting go of their MBTs. Setting aside for the moment Smith's claim that "industrial war no longer exists," the tank's applications in the war in Iraq from 2003 seem, if anything, to have confirmed its place in the ranks of armies. To work out why, we have to start with a basic assessment of the tank itself.

Sitting Heavy

MBTs are essentially tracked, heavily armored fighting vehicles equipped with a long-range, turret-mounted gun designed mainly for destroying other armored vehicles. A British idea, they made their first combat appearance on the Western Front during World War I, when a Mark I ground its way across the battlefield in September 1916 at Flers-Courcellette, holding a solidly British walking pace and sending more alarm through the enemy than damage. Against much early resistance, the tank gained ground, aided by inter-war theoreticians of armor such as J.F.C. Fuller and Heinz Guderian and justified in the competent displays of mechanized warfare unleashed by the Germans during the *Blitzkrieg* of 1939 and 1940.

In a sense, much of the conceptual groundwork of armor's application changed little over the next 50 years. During that time tanks were principally conceived of as "battlefield muscle," relying on their firepower, speed, and armored protection to smash through enemy positions and exploit weaknesses. Tank vs tank engagements also became the primary tactical and training focus, spawned from the mass armor engagements of World War II and the Cold War fears of huge tank battles on the plains of Germany and Eastern Europe. At both strategic and tactical levels, the MBT's status seemed assured.

Then came 1973 and the awesome tank battles of the Yom Kippur War. Egypt and Syria, aware that the Israeli Armored Corps (IAC) constituted its greatest land combat threat, underwent a massive Soviet-fueled rearmament program during the early 1970s that included purchasing plentiful amounts of 9M14 Malyutka – better known by the NATO reporting name AT-3 Sagger – and RPG-7 antitank weapons. The wire-guided Sagger could destroy an Israeli Centurion or M48 Magach at a range of up to 9,842ft (3,000m). RPG-7s were unguided weapons designed for close-range use, but which still had a real tank-destroying potential when handled sensibly. The devastation wrought upon Israeli armor by these weapons was shocking to the IAC, as is apparent in the words of one Israeli officer who faced Egyptian antiarmor infantry during a brigade-strength assault against Egyptian positions east of the Suez Canal:

> In the distance I saw specks dotted on the sand dunes. I couldn't make out what they were. As we got closer, I thought they looked like tree stumps. They were motionless and scattered across the terrain ahead of us. I got on the intercom and asked the tanks ahead what they made of it. One of my tank commanders radioed back, "My God, they're not tree stumps. They're men!" For a moment I couldn't quite understand. What were men doing out there – quite still – when we were advancing our tanks toward them? Suddenly all hell broke loose. A barrage of missiles was being fired at us. Many of our tanks were hit. We had never come up against anything like this before.[16]

The trauma experienced by this tanker is as much to do with the size of his enemy as the nature of his weapons. The power contrast between the tree-stump-sized soldiers and the rolling Israeli armor is turned on its head by the antitank technology. Similar stories were repeated across the Sinai and on the Golan Heights. The lesson should not have been entirely new. During the latter stages of World War II, for example, German infantry fighting in Berlin inflicted a heavy toll on Russian T-34s using Panzerfaust shaped-charge missile launchers, and the US Bazooka could be similarly effective. Such weapons were undoubtedly close-range tools, as is the RPG-7, but the Sagger and its ilk suddenly gave the foot soldier the means to engage tanks with precision at virtually the same ranges as the tank gun. Moreover, there were hundreds of them.

Having suffered critical losses – over 400 IAC tanks were lost in the Sinai alone – the Israelis rearranged their tactics and turned the tide of the war. Once the tanks moved up fully protected by infantry and artillery the casualties dropped dramatically. One disadvantage of the Sagger was that it was a Manual Command to Line of Sight (MCLOS) weapon, requiring the operator to "fly" the missile via a joystick for the entire duration of its flight to target. The Israelis quickly discovered that saturating the firing position with small-arms or mortar fire chronically disrupted the aim of the operator or killed him. In short, keep the antitank team worried about the presence of ground troops and shelling, and they have less time and mental space to engage tanks.

Nevertheless, the implications of Yom Kippur have resonated to this day, especially as guided antitank weapons have improved beyond recognition since their early days. Infantry armor-threatening slogans have developed, such as the Marine Corps' well-known "Killing tanks is easy and fun." Such certainly seemed the case during the 1991 Gulf War, when the massive destruction unleashed on Iraqi armored forces by ground-attack air power augured the end of tank vs tank engagements, which in many ways was the raison d'être of the tank's existence. Captain Mark Schulte, a pilot on a Bronco control aircraft during the conflict, seems to highlight the emerging impotence of the tank in his account of a US air attack by TOW-armed US Marine Cobra helicopters on an Iraqi armored brigade:

> We finally found the Iraqi tank brigade, maybe 40 tanks ... At about that time, the tanks started spreading out into an attack formation. Finally, they sent a round down range, which pretty much started the engagement ... The four Cobras used TOW missiles. They took out at least eight tanks. After they'd expended their TOWs they went back behind friendly troops. We flew high over our own line and started calling up air support. As soon as we got the jets in we'd fly back out there and take out the rear elements. We got a pair of Harriers each time, and each Harrier would make two runs. As they finished, we'd fly back and try to call up some more. We did that three times. After about two-and-a-half hours, the engagement was just about over.[17]

Allowing for the terseness of the language, there still seems an almost insouciant ease about the destruction of a force of 40 tanks. Similar stories abound. In one day alone A-10 tankbuster aircraft of the 76th TFS/23rd TFW destroyed 23 T-62 or T-72 tanks with fire from their 30mm cannon or AGM-65 (Air-to-Ground Missile) Maverick missiles. Yet it was the superb performance of attack helicopters such as the Cobra and Apache, kitted out with the new Hellfire missiles, that put the biggest question mark over the tank's future. Many military authorities felt, quite simply, that attack helicopters would take over the antitank role previously occupied by tanks themselves. The figures from the Gulf War seemed to provide ample proof – some 4,000 Iraqi tanks were lost in Operation *Desert Storm*.

The voices against the tank are therefore multiple, from inside and outside the military, and are often informed by huge shifts of perspective in military acquisition. In the United States, the announcement of the FCS program by General Eric Shinseki, US Army Chief of Staff between 1999 and 2003, seemed to sound the death knell for the MBT. Proponents of FCS predicted armored vehicles with the same survivability and firepower, but at a third of the weight they would be rolling straight out the back of transport aircraft into the fight. The threat to heavy armor is clear from a testimony presented to the House of Representatives' Subcommittee on Tactical Air and Land Forces in April 2004 by J. Michael Gilmore, assistant director of the FCS program:

> The FCS program would, according to the Army, greatly enhance the capability and agility of its heavy units and also make them less reliant on support from other units. It would do so by developing new systems to replace most of the combat vehicles in the service's heavy units and by developing and buying several types of unmanned air and ground vehicles to provide remote – and sometimes autonomous – surveillance and protection. Specifically, the FCS program would develop eight new types of armored vehicles, four classes of unmanned air vehicles (UAVs), three types of unmanned ground vehicles, unattended ground sensors, a missile launcher, and improved munitions, all of which would be linked by advanced communications networks into an integrated combat system.[18]

The next chapter contains a more detailed study of the FCS, but the sense that "heavy units" are laborious, logistically intensive entities is clear. Indeed, Gilmore throws out a few specific examples, such as: "The FCS vehicles are also being developed to be more fuel-efficient than the Army's current armored vehicles, some of which – notably the Abrams tank and Bradley fighting vehicle – go less than two miles on a gallon of fuel."

The feeling that the tank has had its day also spreads out well beyond the United States. Even in Israel, which still relies heavily on its armored forces, production of the Merkava Mk IV MBT is being (at the time of writing) wrapped up, with defense budget allocation shifting more towards aviation, autonomous combat systems and networked, lighter land vehicles. And yet, in the midst of all this, we just keep using tanks. In the post-2003 conflict in Iraq, tanks have been in constant demand despite operating in the most asymmetric of settings. Will the troops on the ground, those who have to do the fighting, regret the demise of the tank, if that is the course taken?

The Case Against the Tank

A major headache associated with the MBT is cost. MBTs are extremely expensive systems to develop, build, acquire and maintain. One country that has discovered the cost of a new-build tank first hand is India. In the early 1970s, India decided to move away from the licensed production of British-type MBTs and the purchase of Russian models to a home-grown design, one that reflected some of the latest developments in fire control and armor. The first Arjun prototype appeared in 1984, which had an expected price tag per tank of US$1.6 million. However, as the project continued, the problems escalated in everything from electronics to armor systems – with a consequent 500 percent increase in development costs.[19] By 2001, when production was approved, the Arjun's cost had risen to US$5.6 million per unit. Consequently, and for reasons of acquisition re-evaluations, fewer than 130 tanks have been ordered.

Of course, the Arjun is not, by a long way, the only defense procurement that has gone wildly over budget. However, in a world where defense budgets are typically the first port of call for a government looking to trim its fiscal sails, investment in MBT technology can look excessive, especially if there is a doctrinal question mark hanging over that system. Even once a tank has been developed, the requisite upgrade programs that keep the tank relevant cost huge sums. Each year, US Army budget requests for Abrams upgrades and improvements come in at about US$300 million. The resistance to such investments varies, of course, with the exigencies of the situation. For example, House Report 106–371 for the Fiscal Year (FY) ending September 30, 2000 contains the following thoughts on Abrams upgrades:

> With some reluctance, the conferees have approved the Army's request to renew multi-year procurement authority to continue the M1A2 Abrams tank upgrade program subject to the condition described below. The conferees seriously question the Army's proposal to enter a new follow-on multi-year agreement that would increase the average unit cost of a tank upgrade (M1 to M1A2 SEP) from $5.6 million per tank in FY 1999 to $6.7 million per tank starting in FY 2001. The conferees note that, in general, the trend throughout the Department has been that follow-on multi-year agreements show significant unit price decreases as production efficiencies improve and mature. While much of the cost increase for this program can be

attributed to lower planned production rates, the conferees remain puzzled why greater efforts have not been made to lower unit costs, especially when the cost of this upgrade now threatens to equal the cost of procuring a new tank.[20]

Similar concerns plague British armored forces. Lewis Page, in his book *Lions, Donkeys and Dinosaurs – Waste and Blundering in the Armed Forces*, places the British Challenger II MBT squarely within the remit of his subheading, noting that the "whole Challenger II project is reckoned to have cost the government $2.2 billion for 386 tanks."

Crude development costs wouldn't be so bad if the tanks weren't subsequently so expensive to run. The costs stem from two main areas – fuel and maintenance. Regarding fuel, tanks are truly thirsty creatures. Take one of the more fuel-efficient vehicles, such as the Russian T-90: its 263-gallon (1,200-liter) fuel tank will give about 342 miles (550km) of maximum road range. This sounds decent enough, but road range is very different from the fuel consumption of operational conditions, when the tank will be constantly revving, accelerating, and decelerating. Even when standing stock still with its engine ticking over, the tank will be using up several gallons an hour. Some of the modern Western tanks fare much worse in the fuel consumption stakes. Returning to the Abrams again (the Abrams is always a useful example, as it stands at the apogee of MBT technology), the problem becomes critical. Bruce I. Gudmundsson, in his book *On Armor*, has looked at some of the logistical problems of the Abrams when the US Army brought it into service, replacing the old M60 tanks, and took it into combat in the 1991 Gulf War:

> Where the M60 tank could move three miles [4.8km] for each gallon of fuel consumed, the Abrams required somewhere in the vicinity of two gallons of gasoline for each mile [1.6km] traveled and ten to twelve gallons for each hour spent sitting still with its combat systems turned on. Put another way, each of the nearly 2,000 Abrams tanks involved in the ground war needed to fill its 500-gallon fuel tank about once per day. Among other things, this greatly complicated the effort to complete the victory of coalition forces by preventing the escape of all the Republican Guard divisions that were retreating out of Kuwait. In simpler terms, US forces could not complete the planned encirclement of the Republican Guard because many American units had (quite literally) run out of gas. This happened, moreover, despite a Herculean effort to make an adequate supply of fuel available to coalition ground forces. (This effort began with the accumulation of a stockpile of some 39,000,000 gallons of gasoline and diesel fuel during the six months prior to the start of the ground war.)[21]

Gudmundsson highlights in striking fashion a simple truth – tanks are a huge drain on resources, and if the fuel does not keeping flowing the MBT will essentially turn into a 70-ton static position. Moreover, all that fuel has to be bought and paid for. On paper, vehicle fuel costs around $1 per gallon to purchase, which sounds cheap enough. However, the actual cost of the fuel varies enormously based on the cost of storing it and delivering it to the battlefield. These extra costs are often ignored in Department of Defense accounting, mainly because once the fuel is bought it is no easy matter to track its subsequent cost. Sherri W. Goodman, a former deputy undersecretary of defense for environmental security who was part of a Defense Science Board panel investigating military fuel consumption, stated that "the cost in the accounting system is $1 or so a gallon, but the true cost of fuel delivered to the battlefield is closer to $17."[22] General Paul Kern, the head of the US Army's Materiel Command, however, acknowledged to the panel that in some circumstances the cost of a gallon of fuel could rise to $400. In light of these figures, gas-guzzling MBTs look like a serious drain on resources.

This situation is worsened by the sheer amount of maintenance required to keep a tank, or indeed any armored vehicle, running smoothly. For all their mass and strength, tanks need constant care. They cannot drive long distances on their own treads without serious malfunction. Typically, a tank will break down every 155–186 miles (250–300km), the breakdown requiring a few hours of maintenance work to get the vehicle going again.[23] Within combat conditions, and with the increasing age of an armor fleet, the frequency of the breakdowns and the seriousness of the malfunctions can increase dramatically, so much so that a unit might experience a 50 percent loss of armor simply to failed mechanics. The classic problems are damage to the track links and rollers, hydraulic failures, engine component failure (due to the high operating stresses of a modern tank engine) and breakdowns in electronics, wiring, and computers – in short, pretty much everything except the inert armor is prone to breakdown.

The environment can severely exacerbate the mechanical problems. Probably the most dramatic example of this occurred in the winter of 1941/42 on the Eastern Front, when the onset of the Russian winter paralyzed the German armored force; the Panzers sat silent with engines frozen solid. Nor has modern development solved the problem of environment. Western tanks, when deployed to the Middle East in 1990–91, discovered that while air filters in the European theater were good for one or two days, under the talcum-like desert dust the filters needed replacing about every two hours. Furthermore, as the filters became clogged up, engine power was lost. The intense heat of the desert also affected wiring and computer systems. All these problems mean that every tank must have a dedicated maintenance crew who will be constantly employed keeping the vehicles running.

Adding to the cost of the MBT is the sheer problem of getting it to the battlefield in the first place. To deploy large numbers of MBTs to a distant war zone usually requires transportation by large, and very slow, transport ships – not ideal when you want a rapid reaction force on the ground within a matter of days. The weight and dimensions of a typical MBT means that it has extremely limited airlift options. For example, in the US arsenal a C-5A transport aircraft can carry four LAV IIIs, and a C-17A can take two. However, both are capable of carrying only one Abrams tank. Furthermore, once in the battlezone the LAVs can be locally airlifted by helicopters such as the Sikorsky CH-53E; there is currently no helicopter in existence that is capable of lifting an MBT.[24]

In terms of land transport, tanks are usually carried on dedicated transporters and, when approaching the operational area, take to their own tracks. However, at every stage of the journey there can be problems. While tanks can cover many terrain types, soft, watery ground presents a real danger for getting stuck fast. A great many bridges cannot take the weight of an MBT, and roads are frequently damaged by the grinding effect of the tracks. All of these factors can make the MBT a liability in peacetime operations – "hearts and minds" are quickly lost in traffic jams caused by unwieldy MBTs. In combat, when there is frequently not time to check the solidity of a structure before moving across it, the effects can be disastrous. During combat operations in Iraq in 2003, for example, a convoy of the 7th Cavalry Regiment, 3rd Infantry Division was advancing along the western bank of the Euphrates when it came under heavy fire from Iraqi Army forces. The convoy attempted to make its escape across a bridge, but after five vehicles had crossed an Abrams tank overwhelmed the bridge's structure. The tank crashed into the river, destroying the bridge and forcing some 500 vehicles to find another escape route.

Another major cost of MBTs is training time. The differences between well-trained and poorly-trained crews can be startling. Nowhere was this more obvious than in the 1991 Operation *Desert Storm* and the 2003 Operation *Iraqi Freedom*. In both instances, the Iraqi armor crews handled themselves appallingly, and paid for it heavily in lives. In many cases, Iraqi crews simply adopted dug-in positions, the tanks set in holes with just their turrets over the parapet. Hence they deprived themselves of the mobility that is a key part of MBT survivability, and were destroyed by the thousand at the leisure of strike aircraft and accurate coalition tank gunnery. Such poor tactical decision making, bred in part by the chronic centralization of Iraqi command and control procedures, combined with some of the coalition's technical advantages, had a devastating effect. Lieutenant Colonel E.L. Dyer, commander of the 1st Battalion, 37th Armor during Operation *Desert Storm*, here recounts the overwhelming superiority achieved by US tank formations when they met armored units of the Iraqi Republican Guard:

> Lead elements of our brigade made contact just prior to 1830 hrs, it was completely dark by now and the weather was deteriorating rapidly – wind, driving rain and blowing sand ... At 2000, D Company TF 1-37 made initial contact with enemy

tanks and a long-range gun duel ensued with TF 1-37 and TF 7-6 standing off at approximately 3000 m, destroying enemy vehicles with long-range tank fire and TOW missiles from the Bradley Fighting Vehicles. When the enemy tried to return fire they were totally ineffective since they had limited night vision capability and did not have the range of the M1A1 and TOW. While we were unsure of the size of the enemy force, by 2015 the B Company commander reported that he could see eleven enemy vehicles burning and there were other reports of enemy vehicles attempting to withdraw.[25]

Even allowing for the Iraqis' technological inferiority, the fact remained that they were pitted against crews that were proficiently destroying their vehicles at a range of 1.8 miles (3km). Another example of this from *Desert Storm* occurred when an M1A1 tank, stuck fast in mud and waiting for recovery vehicles, was attacked by no less than three Iraqi T-72s. All three Iraqi tanks fired and scored hits on the Abrams, although the outstanding quality of the armor prevented the shells from doing any significant damage to either tank or crew. By contrast, the well-trained US crew, relying purely on turret mobility, engaged the Iraqi vehicles and destroyed all of them. In one instance the Abrams gunner even put a sabot round through a sand dune to strike the tank that had been hiding behind it.[26]

Such feats show the pay-off for training up crews well, but doing so takes time and money, both of which are in short supply when a country faces high operational demands, such as in a time of conflict. At the time of writing, an article by defense journalist Michael Smith in the British *Times* newspaper is quoting a leaked British Army report that lists a chronic shortage of military equipment because of the drain of fighting in Iraq and Afghanistan. Of armor, the leak notes that:

Only 28 Challenger tanks are available to train troops for Iraq, sufficient for just two squadrons, or 400 men. There are not enough Warriors or Scimitar light tanks, such as those used by Prince Harry's regiment, to give units even the reduced numbers they are now supposed to be allocated. At least one regiment, the 9th/12th Royal Lancers based in Bergen in Germany, has spent long periods with no Scimitars at all except for when they were on operations in Iraq.[27]

Taken together, all the above costs make MBTs egregiously expensive systems to use, and hence they are vulnerable to all the traditional cutbacks. Furthermore, MBTs are vulnerable to certain types of attack. We shall explore the issue of antitank weapons and tactics in some depth below, but current experience in Iraq is worrying. Note that during the 1991 Gulf War the United States lost only 18 Abrams tanks, even though there were indeed some major tank vs tank engagements. Since March 2003, however, over 80 tanks have been so severely damaged in Iraq, principally by IEDs, that they have required either shipping back to the United States or scrapping. Such losses, added to a climate of skepticism, provide a recipe for the end of the MBT.

Power and Survival

So the MBT's future looks decidedly troubled. And yet, it is hanging on, possibly even clawing its way back, and from an unexpected source. We will come to the reason for this in due course, but to give full context it is worth reminding ourselves of some of the MBT's battle-winning capabilities.

MBTs have two critical values: firepower and survivability. The firepower element is fundamentally about the main gun and the sophistication of its accompanying fire-control system. Modern tanks have a first-round hit rate of around 95 percent – an exceptional level of accuracy. To see how such precision is achieved, we look again to the US Abrams. From the M1A1 version onwards, the Abrams tank has been fitted with the smoothbore M256A1 120mm gun. Its ideal range is around 9,842ft (3,000m), but with the latest fire-control systems some gunners can engage targets out past 13,123ft (4,000m). The sheer power of this gun is perfectly described in Michael Green and Greg Stewart's book *M1 Abrams at War*:

> When an Abrams gunner or TC [tank commander] identifies a suitable target and fires the main gun with his firing switch, an electrical current flows through a firing pin, setting off the electrical primer of the cartridge in the firing chamber, just in front of the breechblock; an explosion (really a rapid burning of the propellant within the cartridge case) then takes place. In fewer than 16.4 feet (5 meters) and in less than a hundredth of a second, the projectile reaches an average of 26,000 Gs as it accelerates to Mach 5 (3,580 miles per hour or 1,600 meters per second). The pressure in the chamber approaches 100,000 pounds per square inch for some types of ammunition.[28]

The violence of this detonation is extreme, and the velocity of the round – flying at around 2,297ft/sec (700m/sec) faster than an assault rifle bullet – translates into truly devastating target impact. But such velocity is unimportant if the gun is not accurate.

The field of fire control has seen one of the true revolutions in tank technology. In the Abrams, two people can operate the gun – the gunner and the tank commander. (This duplication allows the tank commander to respond quickly to threats that he has spotted but which would take time for the gunner to acquire visually.) The gunner sights his target through the gunner's primary sight (GPS), while the tank commander can take manual control and use the gunner's primary sight extension (GPSE) to aim. A conventional optical sight sits by the side of the gun in case of GPS failure. For night-fighting, but also with utility in daytime combat, there is a thermal imaging sight (TIS) that identifies targets by heat signatures. The TCs of M1A2s and System Enhancement Program (SEP) vehicles also have a commander's independent thermal viewer (CITV). This can act as a backup gun sight, but is primarily used by the commander to designate targets for the gunner.

Of course, visually acquiring a target far from ensures a hit, and it is here that the Abrams' onboard digital fire-control computer does much of the work. A laser range-finder precisely calculates the distance to the target, displays the distance on the GPS and GPSE, then makes automatic adjustments to the barrel angle based on factors such as drop, air resistance, gravity, and ammunition (certain types of ammunition have a slower velocity, so require more elevation). Furthermore:

> The fire-control system on the Abrams tank series also accounts for propellant temperature, tube wear, air temperature, wind speed and direction, cant, and angle of site, in addition to motion imparted by a moving target and/or the moving Abrams. The resulting ballistic solution makes the Abrams tank more accurate than a sniper rifle at ranges greater than about 1,313 yards (1,200 meters).[29]

The rapid calculations made by the fire-control system (FCS), combined with a fully stabilized gun system, mean that the Abrams can fire accurately even when crashing up and down over rough terrain. Manual overrides and setting controls are built in, so the Abrams does not suddenly become impotent if the FCS fails.

So what of its ammunition, the bit that actually does the grim business of destruction? Three basic types of round are carried by the Abrams, and they are typical of tank shells worldwide. The first is the M829A1 Armor-Piercing Fin-Stabilized Discarding-Sabot Tracer (APFSDS-T) round. To understand this ammunition, bear in mind that the Abrams gun is smoothbore – it has no rifling to spin-stabilize the shell, such as is found in British Challenger tank guns. The advantages of a smoothbore gun are that the shells can be fired at much higher pressures than those of rifled weapons (in turn creating higher velocities), the barrels don't wear out as fast, and penetration against target armor is actually better. The APFSDS-T consists of a slim sub-caliber depleted uranium (DU) dart encased in an aluminum sabot that fits the bore of the gun. Once the shell is fired, the sabot peels away, leaving the dart – made from one of the densest substances known – to fly onwards at incredible velocity, with fins acting like the flights on an arrow. Note that there is no explosive content whatsoever – the APFSDS-T simply does all its damage by kinetic energy alone, slamming through the target with the force of an 11-ton truck hitting a wall at 70mph (112km/h), but with the impact concentrated over an area of less than an inch square. Having punched through a tank's armor, the pyrophyric (heat) properties of the round can ignite fuel and ammunition. Pieces of fragmented armor and other objects violently fly around the tank interior (lethal detritus such as this is called "spall," and can occur from shockwaves alone, even if the rod has not penetrated). Occupants can literally be vaporized.

Another type of kinetic energy (KE) round uses a tungsten dart that has phenomenal armor-penetrating properties. While enormously destructive against armor, however, the tungsten shell is little suited to anything else – fired at a light vehicle it might only make small entry and exit holes. Two other shells offer wider applications: the M830A1 MultiPurpose AntiTank (MPAT) round and the M830 High-Explosive AntiTank MultiPurpose Tracer (HEAT-MP-T). Both are shaped-charge rounds – a form of warhead consisting of explosives packed behind a cone of metal (typically copper), the base of the cone pointing in the direction of the target. When the shaped-charge shell hits the target, the explosive detonates and turns the cone into a thin, ultra-high-velocity jet of molten metal that punches through armor or any other obstacle. More about shaped charges will be said below, but for the Abrams the explosive content of its two HEAT (High-Explosive AntiTank) shells enables it to engage light armored vehicles, bunkers, buildings, and people more successfully (they are also used to finish off tanks already hit by sabot rounds). The difference between the two is that the MPAT has a proximity fuse option (the shell can be set to explode in the vicinity of the target), which means that the Abrams can also engage helicopters.

Our discussion of Abrams tank shells may have a slightly dry feel to it for civilians, but for "tankers" the distinctions are crucial. In battle, with possibly multiple targets presenting themselves every few seconds, shell selection and gunnery speed are life-or-death issues. In contemporary writings, nowhere is this better illustrated than by Captain Jason Conroy in his study of armored warfare in Iraq, *Heavy Metal*. As commander of Charlie Company, Task Force 1-64, 2nd Brigade Combat Team, 3rd Infantry Division, Conroy was at one point engaged in a close-quarters battle with Iraqi T-72 tanks in Mahmudiyah. The issue of shell selection and effects comes to the fore in this edited extract:

> Stewart's first shot hit the back slope of the T-72 sitting on the right side of the street. The extra fuel drums on the back exploded, sending flames and black smoke shooting high into the late afternoon sky. The tank's turret popped off, and the engine was knocked to the other side of the street.
>
> The brass AFCAP [the metallic base of the 120mm round] of the M1A1 HEAT round [the HEAT-MP-T] was ejected from the tube, hit the deflector with a clang, and fell into the catch on the floor. Lopez [the loader] quickly called for another round. But instead of the SABOT that Pinkston [the tank commander] called for, it was a HEAT.

The SABOT with its depleted uranium penetrator is the round of choice for killing tanks. We started the mission that day with many of the tanks battle-carrying SABOT because we anticipated fighting tanks. When we encountered trucks and bunkers, many tank commanders shifted to HEAT rounds, which are more effective against those targets because of the high explosives content. Now facing tanks, Pinkston's tank had HEAT more easily accessible in the ready rack [a quick-access ammunition rack] than SABOT.

Pinkston saw the round go into the main gun's breech but decided to let it go rather than have Lopez try to remove it and try to dig up a SABOT. There was a second tank to be killed and he did not want to waste any time ...

Stewart fired another HEAT round at the second Iraqi tank. It hit the turret, but there was no massive explosion like the first.

England's tank pulled up close to Pinkston's.

"Alpha section! One round SABOT! Move out and fire!" England ordered.

Sgt. Chris Freeman, the gunner on England's tank, squeezed the trigger and the SABOT round sliced into the second T-72. It exploded in a flash of fire and smoke, sending fragments of steel clattering down the street.[30]

This dramatic account shows the clear distinction between the HEAT and SABOT rounds when engaging armor, and viscerally conveys the sheer potency of the latter.

If we broaden our study beyond the Abrams, we discover a whole range of other warhead types. High-Explosive Squash Head (HESH), for instance, basically splatters high explosive on the outside of the target before detonation, the shockwaves creating a lethal spall effect on the other side of the armor. For antipersonnel applications, some tanks can fire the particularly nasty "beehive" round, each shell containing thousands of flechettes – basically steel darts – that are blasted out in the manner of a massive shotgun. These recently saw operational use in the hands of the Israel Defense Forces (IDF) in their engagements with Palestinian fighters in the West Bank and Gaza Strip. On May 22, 2001, *Jane's Defence Weekly* reported that IDF armor was "using a modified version of the M494 105mm APERS-T (AntiPersonnel – Tracer) round provided by the USA in the 1970s," each shell releasing 5,000 flechettes, which form a killing cone 984ft (300m) long and 308ft (94m) wide.[31] The United States also has flechette shells for its 105mm Abrams, but is bringing in a new round, the M1028, which fires a canister containing many thousands of tungsten metal balls, each leaving the barrel at a muzzle velocity of 4,593ft/sec (1,400m/sec) and killing out to 1,640ft (500m).

Such rounds are already attracting the attention of human rights organizations, mainly because their wide and imprecise kill radius obviously has serious implications for any unlucky civilians in the area, especially as the beehive rounds seem to have most relevance in urban settings. In early 2003, the

Palestinian Center for Human Rights and the Physicians for Human Rights brought a case to the Israeli Supreme Court arguing that the IDF should cease using flechette rounds in their operations in the Gaza Strip. The catalyst for the petition was the firing of flechette shells on June 9, 2001, in which three civilian women were killed. Three children died in a similar incident in December 2001. The judgment on the petition, delivered on April 27, 2003, predictably held out against the Palestinian arguments. While acknowledging that the flechette rounds had to be used with discipline and caution, the Court asserted that flechette submunitions were in no way prohibited by UN conventions:

> The Court held that, since the use of flechette shells was not prohibited by international conventions, it could not grant the petition. The Court noted that it had previously held that it would not intervene in the IDF's choice of military weapons, which it employs in order to prevent terrorist attacks. The Court further held that it believed that the IDF had properly set out the conditions under which the use of flechettes was authorized. Of course, the question of whether the use of flechettes is justified under individual circumstances is given to the discretion of the authorized commander. This commander will act according to the military directives, which are intended to prevent casualties among residents who do not endanger the IDF forces or Israeli civilians.[32]

The wording here gives flechette rounds full legal status, and such ammunition continues to be used or held in storage by forces worldwide. Depleted uranium shells have also attracted their fair share of political heat, but that issue is explored in more depth in Chapter 5.

We now turn to the second key ingredient of the tank – survivability. While the Marines might state that "Killing tanks is fun and easy," without the right weapons and training soldiers will actually find MBTs incredibly tough things to kill – remember the incident described above when the Abrams tank took three hits from T-72 shells at close range without its function being affected.

One of the qualities that defines a tank is the density, weight, and type of armor. The most basic type of armor is homogenous steel plate. Such plate lacks sophistication, but at several inches thick it will still comfortably stop all small-arms rounds and many larger-caliber shells. The effectiveness of such armor, indeed any armor, is multiplied by angling the plate – the angle increases the depth of armor confronting the projectile without increasing the actual depth of the plate, and it also ups the possibility of shot deflection. Yet with the post-war proliferation of shaped-charged antitank warheads, steel plate became inadequate. One partial solution to this problem was already in existence – spaced armor, which had its origins back in the days of World War II. Spaced armor consists of two or more plates of armor set with a gap between them. The gap serves to disperse energy after a shot or explosion has already done its work smashing through the first layer of plate. A shell, for example, is thoroughly deformed by the time it reaches the inner plate, hence has lost much of its penetrative power. The lava-hot jet of molten steel produced by a shaped-charge warhead also weakens as it crosses the gap. Spaced armor has found integral use in tanks such as the Leopard 1, but armored vehicles of all descriptions have used the principle through improvisation. There are photographs of Russian T-34s on the streets of Berlin in 1945 with wire meshes bolted on to trigger the detonation of Panzerfaust warheads before they strike the main armor. Similarly, in Iraq Stryker combat vehicles are typically seen cocooned in "slat armor," a framework of steel pipe weighing 5,200lb (2,364kg) that wraps around the vehicle's hull and turret, its purpose being to thwart RPGs. In this role it is surprisingly effective. In one incident a slat-armored Stryker was hit by nine RPGs in an ambush, but both vehicle and crew survived and escaped. (Similar cage armor systems are also fitted to Bradley and Warrior vehicles.) Note that many other improvised measures are used to create a "stand-off" against shaped-charge warheads. These include strapping logs, sandbags, crude iron plate, and indeed anything else that comes to hand to the outside of the vehicle.

Another type of armor, one which came into widespread use from the 1960s, is composite armor. Today, composite is the principal form of armor fitted to many MBTs. Composite armor is, as its name suggests, made up of layers of contrasting materials. During the 1950s, military trials revealed that ceramic armor offered a strong resistance to shaped-charge warheads, being around four times tougher than hardened steel. Hence in the 1960s the British created an armor "sandwich" of multiple layers of steel and ceramic plate (later forms of composite armor would also include plastics and other synthetic materials). This evolved into the most famous type of composite armor, known as Chobham, which in its varieties and updates has graced the British Chieftain and Challenger main battle tanks and informed the armor on the US Abrams tank. As intended, Chobham-type armor works extremely well against shaped-charge warheads – the ceramic plate in the "sandwich" tends to shatter and, in so doing, draws away the force of the molten jet to make further penetrations. In fact, although a shape-charge warhead might be capable of penetrating 39in (1,000mm) of standard armor, it will generally be defeated by the 24in (600mm) of Chobham-type armor on an Abrams.[33] Further additions to composite armor have also come in the form of DU plates (Abrams), these being added to provide protection against KE (kinetic energy) rounds. Note that composite armor is found not only on MBTs, but on many other lighter armored vehicles.

A further key type of armor is explosive reactive armor (ERA). Simply put, ERA consists of explosive panels on the vehicle, panels that detonate outwards if struck by a shell and – hopefully – cancel out the penetrative force. Note that ERA is fitted in separate panels over inert armor, as the panels have to be easily replaced once detonated. While it was the Israelis who combat-proved ERA on Centurions and M60s during the 1970s, it was the Russians who became particularly fond of ERA during the 1980s. Then again, the Russian Army has never been noted for care of its infantry, and herein lies one of the problems with ERA. The detonation of an ERA panel can be just as dangerous to nearby friendly troops as the impact of the enemy shell, so troops need to maintain a decent stand-off. Also, ERA has traditionally been effective against HEAT rounds – less so against modern KE rounds. Yet science never stands still, and new types of ERA are constantly emerging that use less explosive force, which create no lethal fragments for proximate troops, and which can adjust the amount of blast delivered by sensing the type of projectile that has just struck.

Looking to the future, armor is about to get very smart. Electrically charged armor is one avenue of development. Here a strong electrical current runs through the armor, and when struck by a HEAT projectile the armor delivers a massive electrical current to the impact site. The current charges the molten jet, which disrupts its integrity and therefore its penetration. Other systems – known as Active Protection Systems (APS) – actually focus on destroying the enemy projectile even before it strikes the tank, by sensing the incoming projectile and launching a lightning-fast counter-strike. Israel, for example, has developed the Trophy APS, which fires shotgun-like blasts of small metal pellets at the projectile from dispensers mounted on the sides of the vehicle. Its companion APS, known as Iron Fist, is fitted to light AFVs and instead of pellets throws out an explosively formed penetrator (EFP) to handle large KE and HEAT projectiles. Other systems include the US Army's Full Spectrum Active Protection (FSAP) system, the countermeasures ranging from EFPs and metal bar projectiles to "birdcatcher" nets designed to defeat top-attack munitions. The FSAP system may even initiate automatic tactical decisions based on threat detection. In addition to "hard kill" technologies, many modern tanks are also receiving "soft kill" systems, which are designed to defeat enemy missile guidance systems. Abrams tanks, for example, are often fitted with the Missile Countermeasure Device (MCD), which detects and jams the guidance mechanisms of ATGMs. Note, however, that in light of the IED attacks in Iraq many people are questioning the reliance upon active protection systems. Military analyst Scott Boston noted in *Parameters* magazine:

> As of 2002, active defenses under testing had effectively engaged antitank guided missiles and rockets (despite requiring a 50–100 [164–328ft] meter stand-off range) with designers anticipating a 90-percent hit probability by 2006. Impressive as that is, for an active defense system to be a true replacement for armor plate it will need to be even more capable than this; a ten-percent failure rate in the face of massed enemy fires would still result in high US casualties against a skilled and determined opponent.[34]

Whatever the future of armor, the fact remains that MBTs are, while far from invulnerable, extremely well protected. Fire from small arms, cannon, and even RPGs tends to be shrugged off, and even if hit by major explosions the crew has good odds of surviving. The following narrative illustrates this point aptly. It is given by Captain Neil Prakash, a US armor officer, who witnessed the toughness of the Abrams tank at first hand during battles for Fallujah, Iraq, in 2004, when his unit came under mortar fire:

> I told Mewborn [the driver] to back it up and, just as I said that, a round exploded right in front of my tank. My loader and I were sitting up on the turret with our butts on the hatches and I'm looking backwards and start screaming, "Go back, go back!" He floors it and we go in reverse, and I'm just waiting for the next round to hit us. All of a sudden, the whole left side of the tank explodes, the tank goes up a little, and both my loader and I fall into the hatches. So I'm on the turret floor, my feet are on my gunner and I'm reaching for the hand mike to tell them I'm okay, which I was finally able to do. I was cussing up a storm thinking we'd just been hit by friendly artillery. I get on the ground and look in front of me and my tank isn't even facing west anymore; it's facing north. The whole left side of the track had been blown off. I walk around the track and call my wingman forward. He tied his ratchet strap from his gun tube to the track. He was trying to lift the track up to try and drag it back to the tank so we can line it back up and fix it. At this moment, the recovery has already started, an M88 is about to come out to my location and then my wingman calls me over and says, "Hey sir, what the hell is this?" I walked over to him and there was a giant, yellow-beige doggie dish-sized disk under the track and there were two more under the track that he hadn't even raised yet. I was like, "That's a f------ tank mine!" He kicks it, the top pops off and you can see the explosives underneath and the pressure plate. He was like, "Holy shit!" I said, "Man, that's a tank mine. I think we're in a minefield!"[35]

Here the tank has been hit by a mine specifically designed to destroy tanks, a device strong enough to slew a 68-ton vehicle round 45 degrees. Not once, however, is the survivability of the crew threatened. Such personnel benefit from other safety features in the vehicle. An internal Kevlar liner, for example, protects against spalling, and fuel and ammunition are kept in armored compartments that, if ignited, actually direct any explosion away from the crew compartment via blow-off panels.

But despite the toughness of tanks and AFVs, the fact remains that they do get destroyed. Before moving to a final evaluation of the MBT's role, and that of armor in general, it is worth looking at the threats arrayed against AFVs, and at how armored protection has become a deeply human and political issue.

The Antiarmor Threat

Apart from other tanks, there are five main threats facing armor on the battlefield: airpower, artillery, mines, IEDs, and antiarmor missiles. The armor-killing potential of airpower and artillery is covered in the dedicated chapters, and the general principles of mines and IEDs are studied in Chapter 2. However, of antiarmor mines and IEDs we need to say a little more here, based in part on the traumatic experiences of coalition forces in Iraq.

The key point to note about antiarmor devices is that they can achieve varying degrees of kill. First is the Mobility Kill (M-Kill), which denotes the destruction of the AFV's tracks or wheels, rendering it immobile. An M-Kill vehicle may still be able to fight, but the loss of mobility renders its survivability precarious. Antivehicle mines (AVMs) are the classic mechanism for an M-Kill, some "tankbuster" types being designed with only enough explosive to achieve that result. An M-Kill, like a wounded soldier, is also a greater drain on logistics than a completely destroyed vehicle – it needs to be recovered and repaired, often in a major security operation, and the crew rescued. A different challenge is the F-Kill, standing for Firepower Kill. Here the AFV's primary weapon system is destroyed, often through a missile impact that jams the turret, damages the gun barrel, and/or impairs the fire-control system. The third type of kill is the Catastrophic Kill, denoted by K-Kill. This occurs where the AFV is totally wiped out, usually through the devastating ignition of fuel and ammunition. Note that only one of these categories involves the total destruction of the tank, yet the other two remain classified as "kills." The reason for this is simple – the AFV exists to move and fight, and if it can't do one of those then it can make little significant battlefield contribution.

Experience in Iraq since 2003 has provided a sobering insight into AFV vulnerability. Approximate figures for US AFV combat losses between 2003 and late 2006, compiled by the *Army Times*, break down as follows:

M1 Abrams tanks	20
Bradley Fighting Vehicles	50
Stryker Wheeled Combat Vehicles	20
M113 APCs	20
Humvees	250
Fox wheeled reconnaissance vehicles, mine clearing vehicles, heavy and medium trucks	over 500[36]

These losses reflect K-Kills; the actual number of vehicles hit by enemy weapons is far higher, but many are returned to service. By far the biggest problem is huge roadside IEDs. All the bomber needs to do is link up several large-caliber artillery shells using det-cord and he can destroy almost any vehicle, even the heaviest MBTs.

IEDs and large antitank mines can create devastating injuries to those inside a vehicle. Although armored vehicle crews suffer a lower percentage of combat injuries, when they do occur the severity of injury and mortality is up to 50 percent greater.[37] The detonations of antitank mines and IEDs, even if the blast does not penetrate the crew compartment, can cause very severe injuries as a result of the crew being hurled around the interior. (A study of fracture injuries amongst the crew of a Soviet AFV that had struck a land mine showed that 83.7 percent of the injuries were concentrated in the limbs and shoulders.) Should an explosion compromise the armor, whether from an IED or other antiarmor weapon, the injuries range from chronic burns and damaged lungs to massive spinal injuries and multiple flesh wounds from spall. Alan James, the Rhodesian African Rifles soldier encountered in the previous chapter, gives some idea of what it is like to hit an IED in a vehicle:

> Seven times I've actually hit land mines. They [the insurgents] used to boost the landmines ... but our vehicles were pretty good: they were all armour plated and in the backs we used to put conveyor belting down, sandbags on top of that, and conveyor belt on top of that ... They used to boost these landmines so much that sometimes lorries used to fly 30–40ft without touching the ground ... they used to put five or six landmines into one hole, and maybe a slab of cordite as well. The lorries would just literally take off, and just fly in the air. Afterwards, underneath your legs, you'd get like pimples, and you'd squeeze these spots underneath your legs and stones would come out, where the pores of your skin had opened up and ... the stones on the conveyor belt or on the sandbags would actually fly up and penetrate the skin. One time I hit one [a mine] with the front wheel and my arm and the side of my face went black from the cordite going into the pores of my skin.[38]

The scale of the problem has in no way receded in the three decades since James' combat experience. The problem is that no amount of armor can compensate for the totally enveloping crushing pressures of a large detonation, and that the insurgents can keep ratcheting up the explosive force until it exceeds the protection of the armored vehicle. A US government report recently noted that:

> Insurgents have constructed IEDs powerful enough to kill soldiers inside 22-ton Bradley Fighting Vehicles. In one incident in 2004, after a Bradley ran over a large IED, the armored bottom plate of the vehicle was reportedly found some 60 yards from the site of the explosion.[39]

An additional element to the IED threat that has recently caught the headlines, although the technology is far from new, is the explosively formed penetrator (EFP).

EFPs are similar to shaped-charge warheads, in that they work by detonating explosives behind a metal liner. However, the EFPs turn the liner into a solid metal rod or slug traveling at speeds of Mach 6, capable of punching through the thickest armor. The advantage of an EFP is stand-off – a shaped-charge must detonate against the target, while an EFP can deliver its attack at up to 164ft (50m) and beyond. This stand-off capability opens whole new avenues for attacking armor. Many modern ATGM systems utilize EFPs and overflight patterns to make lethal top attacks. The Predator Light Antiarmor Missile (known in the UK as the Kestrel) or the TOW IIB, for example, guides itself to the target and flies directly above the selected impact point – typically the thinner top armor of the vehicle. At precisely the right moment, laser and magnetic sensors trigger an EFP, which is fired down onto the impact point.

Similar technologies are now installed in certain air-dropped submunitions and in some of the latest antitank mines. EFPs rose to public prominence, however, in 2006, when the media began to receive reports of coalition military vehicles being destroyed by remotely activated EFP devices allegedly supplied to Iraqi insurgents by Iran. There is no doubt that EFPs are causing genuine concern amongst defense experts. Armor technology exists to counter these devices, but the problem arises when armor has to accommodate multiple threats – the armor for a shaped-charge might not handle an EFP or other IED, for example. Furthermore, reports have also been received of multislug EFPs, a problem noted in an article in April 2007 in the *Army Times*:

> Some improvised explosive devices are now being built with multiple explosively formed penetrators that can fire several slugs of molten metal at a single aim point. "A multi-slug causes a lot of problems," said Vernon Joynt, lead scientist for Force Protection, the South Carolina-based vehicle maker known for the improvised-explosive-device-stopping Buffalo and Cougar. "It shoots all the slugs like a machine gun in line. Problems arise with certain kinds of ceramics. They defeat the threat but do not remain in place. They are brittle. If you have one slug hitting them it will defeat the slug but shatter in the process, so if you have a multi-slug the rest [of the slugs] will come flying through like through a tunnel."[40]

The article goes on to quote defense sources as saying that the fitting of ERA tiles to Abrams, Bradleys, and Strykers, bolstering their existing armor, has provided a sufficient counter to any antiarmor projectile, including EFPs, although the principal reason behind installing ERA was to counter RPG attacks. This remains to be seen, as it is acknowledged that even simple dual-warhead shaped-charged missiles can overcome ERA.

Despite improved armor systems, in terms of human-operated direct-fire weapons, it is currently the now infamous RPG that is the greatest threat to forces engaged in insurgency warfare, principally the RPG-7. The RPG-7 is one of a broad class of unguided antitank rocket launchers (ATRLs) whose ancestry stretches back to the Bazooka and Panzerfaust of World War II. It is little more than a tube for the recoilless firing of a variety of HEAT, thermobaric, and fragmentation warheads. Firing one requires no more skill than sticking the missile in the end of the tube, flicking up the sights, pressing the arming button, then aiming and pulling the trigger. On firing, a booster charge pushes the missile out to a distance of 32ft (10m) then the rocket motor ignites, driving the missile onwards to a range of around 1,640ft (500m) before the motor cuts out, leaving the rocket to fly on, potentially, for another 1,968ft (600m) – although the round usually self-destructs after 4.5 seconds of flight. Armor penetration from the best rounds is up to 24in (600mm) of rolled homogenous armor (RHA). One of its more advanced rounds, the PG-7VR, is also designed to defeat ERA by featuring a dual charge: the first part of the missile detonates the ERA panel, then the HEAT warhead goes off to cut through once the outward explosion has spent its force.

There are many other weapons like the RPG-7. The United States has the M136 AT4, the Shoulder-Launched Multipurpose Assault Weapon (SMAW) and, making a comeback (in an improved form) from the Vietnam War era, the M72A7 Light Antitank Weapon (LAW). The Russians have not stood still either since they developed the RPG-7 back in the late 1950s – one of their latest AT (antitank) weapons, the RPG-29, has a reputed RHA penetration of up to 29.5in (750mm).

While the movies can portray such weapons as real battle-winners, their use is much more problematic than might appear. First, armor penetration against better-protected AFVs is far from assured, particularly if the user targets thick frontal armor. Better-trained users will target a vehicle's weak points, traditionally the engine compartment and the lower sides, both less well protected than the turret and frontal slope. RPG users in Iraq also adopted another tactic to maximize chances of a kill – simply opening up with multiple RPGs in a mass close-quarters volley. Second, most ATGMs generate an enormous backblast on launch and the propellant gases vent out of the back of the launcher to balance out the recoil. This creates two problems, practical and tactical. On the practical level, the user has to leave enough space behind the launcher for the gas, or it will endanger him and his comrades through burn or blast effects. Typically this means several meters of linear space behind the launch tube, a requirement that creates problems for soldiers/insurgents fighting in claustrophobic urban environments. The tactical problem is that the backblast also creates a swirling patch of dust behind the launcher, clearly indicating the operator's location and instantly attracting every opposing firearm in the neighborhood – this was one of the factors that undid the Egyptian and Syrian antitank teams during the Yom Kippur War.

As an aside, note that many of the most modern antitank missile systems, mainly the sophisticated ATGMs such as the MBT LAW, Predator, and Javelin, have a "soft launch" capability. Here a small charge propels the missile with just enough power to reach a distance of around 32ft (10m) from the user before the main engine starts. This system creates a very small backblast, allowing the missile to be fired from inside confined buildings, while also generating little dust signature. In addition, many antiarmor missile systems have multiple combat roles apart from engaging AFVs, also being much used to engage enemy positions and personnel. With thermobaric and fragmentation warheads available, they are, in effect, multipurpose, manportable, direct-fire artillery for the infantryman.

In terms of more conventional army vs army engagements, the major threat to armor comes from ATGMs. Until recently, most ATGM systems were of the MCLOS variety – the operator would, once the missile was fired, literally fly the missile to the target using a joystick, the tracking information sent to the missile via fiber-optic wires unraveling from the operator's console. These could be very accurate in well-trained hands, but as we have seen the attentions of enemy infantry could disrupt the accuracy of the operator while the missile was winding its way to the target (at ranges of, say, 1.2 miles/2km, this flight could take 10–15 seconds). The new generation of missiles is, by contrast, of the "fire and forget" type. Here the operator is responsible for the initial targeting and launch, but once the missile is off it will track itself to the target. The advantage of this system is obvious – the ATGM operator does not have to hang around once the missile is fired, which improves both his survivability and the chances of the missile striking home. These ATGMs are becoming very, very good at their job. Take, for example, the US Javelin system. The missile is mounted on a Command Launch Unit (CLU) and readied for action in less than 30 seconds. Through his sight, the operator places a cursor box over the target and initiates the automatic tracking system. Next he simply gives the command to launch and the missile flies fairly unerringly towards its target, which can be up to 8,202ft (2,500m) away. The really clever part of the system is that the user can select between direct-fire and top-attack modes. In the latter, the missile climbs to a peak altitude of 492ft (150m) before plunging straight down on the target, attacking the thinner top armor. Its tandem-warhead, consisting of two HEAT charges, can defeat almost any armor out there.

Combat testing has more than proven the values of the Javelin, as Roy Adams, Raytheon Business Development Manager for the Javelin joint venture, confirmed in an interview for *Army* magazine:

Javelin's significant combat lessons learned included the April 2003 Battle of Debecka Pass in Northern Iraq, where the Javelin missile played a decisive role in enabling a Special Forces unit to stop and neutralize an attacking Iraqi armor formation.

"Debecka Pass basically had two Special Forces 'A' Teams facing a battalion-sized enemy force that had 12 tanks, 24 armored personnel carriers, three howitzers, a multiple rocket launcher, an anti-aircraft gun, 150 soldiers and probably another 18 to 20 light vehicles and trucks," Adams said.

"The American force ended up destroying two tanks, eight personnel carriers and four cargo trucks. More important, they were able to hold off that enemy force until the 173rd Airborne Brigade could relieve them and assume ownership of that pass."[41]

For a relatively small unit of infantry to destroy 14 enemy vehicles could suggest that the Marine Corps' axiom about hunting tanks is correct. Factor in the even greater threat to AFVs – air power, examined in Chapter 5 – and we see that armor has something of a problem. It's time to return to the question posed much earlier on: Has the MBT had its day? The answer has implications for the people inside all AFVs and comes from an unexpected source – urban warfare.

Urban Warfare and the Return of the MBT

Urban warfare is traditionally, and rightly, regarded as an AFV's nightmare. For proof of that, ask the Russians. In 1994 Russia invaded Chechnya, a breakaway republic previously part of the former Soviet Union, and so began one of the most protracted and bloody conflicts in post-World War II history. One of the first objectives for the mechanized Soviet-style divisions was Grozny, the Chechen capital. Despite having an obvious firepower superiority over their Chechen opponents (at one point the Russians were putting 4,000 artillery shells an hour into the city) they didn't have a decent grasp of urban warfare. Between November and January, the Russians experienced a level of slaughter not encountered since 1945. Chechen fighters, often working in dedicated antiarmor killing teams, would draw armored vehicles into dead-end streets where they were destroyed by RPGs and Molotov cocktails deployed from overhead windows – the Russian tank guns couldn't elevate enough to engage their attackers. Chechen machine-gunners would suppress Russian infantry, while multiple antiarmor teams assaulted a single vehicle, targeting the AFV's vulnerable points.[42] (As in Iraq, RPG volley fire was used – some destroyed vehicles had more than 20 individual RPG strikes.) The results were devastating. One of the first Russian units to enter Grozny, the 131st Maikop Brigade, lost 20 of 26 tanks and 102 of its other 120 armored vehicles.[43] In only the first month of the invasion, the Russians lost 225 vehicles, over 10 percent of the AFVs committed to the campaign.

The Russian experience in Chechnya was, undoubtedly, greatly the product of poor tactics, training, intelligence, and morale. Yet from the streets of Stalingrad

Royal Marine Commandos undergo training with the SA80 rifle. While the SA80 is undoubtedly an accurate weapon, chronic problems with its reliability have plagued its time in service, and have only been remedied by a comprehensive update programme that has resulted in the more effective SA80A2. (Sean Clee © Crown Copyright/MOD, www.photos.mod.uk)

Islamic Jihad fighters display their AK assault rifles during a rally in Gaza in 2003. Millions of lives have been lost to Kalashnikov's AK47 and its derivatives, and with up to 100 million produced it is the most successful individual weapon type in history. (© Fabrizio Bensch/Reuters/Corbis)

A soldier from the US 25th Infantry Division engages insurgents in Mosul in 2004 with his M249 squad automatic weapon (SAW). Any insurgents hiding behind the vehicle in the street below would have little protection from the 5.56mm high-velocity rounds. (Sgt Jeremiah Johnson: courtesy US Army)

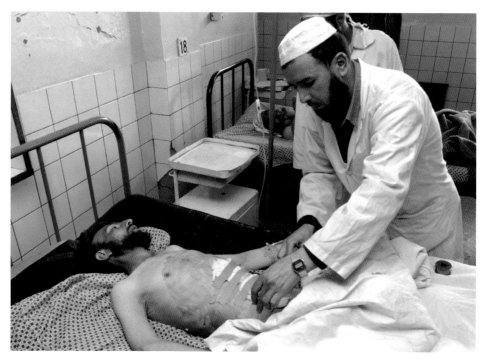

A gunshot victim is treated in hospital in Afghanistan. Even high-velocity bullets will wound far more often than they kill, leaving the victim to cope for the rest of his or her life with disability and psychological trauma. (© Boris Roessler/dpa/Corbis)

A police marksman of the German security forces scans the urban landscape of Berlin during a visit by the Israeli president. Although snipers can and do take shots out past 3,280ft (1,000m), the typical range of engagement in urban settings is 984–1,968ft (300–600m). (© Fabrizio Bensch/Reuters/Corbis)

Fertilizer-based explosives, although crude compared to professionally manufactured high-explosives, are still capable of devastating results. Here is the Alfred P. Murrah Federal Building in Oklahoma after some 4,800lb (2,181kg) of ammonium nitrate fertilizer ripped through it in 1995, the worst terrorist bombing in the United States until 9/11. Timothy McVeigh's attack gave a grim illustration of the opportunistic power of terrorist tactics. The method of bomb delivery – a large van – allowed precision placement of a large amount of explosives (the driver of such a weapon is effectively a low-cost precision guidance system), while the civilian, low-security context of Oklahoma meant that McVeigh had minimal counter-terrorist concerns. Our civilization's dependency on vehicles, plus the relative ease with which explosives can be obtained or manufactured by determined individuals, means that car and truck bombs will remain a security problem worldwide for the foreseeable future. (© 2003 Topham/AP, TopFoto.co.uk)

The attacks of July 7, 2005 brought the phenomenon of suicide bombings to London. One of the four bombs detonated was on a double-decker bus, killing 13 passengers; the destruction was intensified by the explosion's containment within the confines of the vehicle. (© Photonews/TopFoto.co.uk)

An insurgent throws rocks at a car destroyed by an improvised explosive device (IED) in Iraq. The IED had been planted in a parked car and was detonated as a convoy passed by, wrecking this vehicle. IEDs have emerged as the greatest challenge for conventional forces since 9/11. (© Namir Noor-Eldeen/Reuters/Corbis)

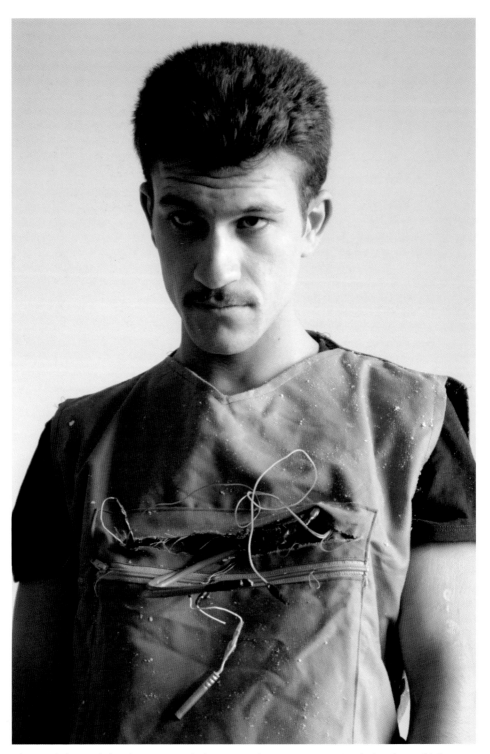

This Kurdish suicide bomber was caught by security forces in Iraq in 2002 before he could detonate his weapon. Here he is seen in interview, wearing his explosive vest. Suicide bombing is extremely hard to counter militarily, as placing physical restrictions on a people tends to generate recruits for the suicide units. (© Reuters/Corbis)

One of the thousands of Iraqi armored vehicles destroyed during Operation *Desert Storm* in 1991 sits on a highway just south of Kuwait City. The ease with which the coalition mopped up the Iraqi armor led many strategists to predict the end of the MBT. (© Roger-Viollet/Topfoto)

Palestinian children play a dangerous cat-and-mouse game with an Israeli Merkava tank in Gaza. In today's world, the main battle tank (MBT) is far more likely to find itself deployed in urban security roles than in tank-vs-tank combat, leading some to question the relevance of the MBT in modern warfare. (© Mohammed Saber/epa/Corbis)

A US M1A1 Abrams tank drives through snow-covered mountains in Germany while on exercise in 2005. The 120mm gun can kill enemy armored targets at ranges of over 9,842ft (3,000m), its depleted uranium rounds chopping through even the heaviest armor plate. (Richard Bumgardner: courtesy US Army)

The infantry of modern armies, particularly in urban warfare, now tends to ride into battle inside armored vehicles, disembarking only when contact with the enemy is made. Here US troops exit a Bradley infantry fighting vehicle (IFV) on the streets of Fallujah, Iraq, in 2004. (© Stefan Zaklin/epa/Corbis)

Israeli artillery troops open up with a 175mm howitzer, part of a bombardment of Syrian forces during the battle for the Golan Heights in 1973. Self-propelled artillery has greater survivability than towed artillery, as it can move at a moment's notice to avoid enemy troops and counter-battery fire. (© Bettmann/Corbis)

The scourge of armor today is antiarmor missile systems such as this US Javelin. The Javelin is a 'fire and forget' type weapon – it locks onto the target before launch and guides itself to the target once fired from its launcher unit. (Courtesy US Army)

A Hamas militant fires a rocket-propelled grenade during clashes with Fatah forces in Gaza city. The Russian RPG series of weapons has huge international distribution, and has given hundreds of thousands of developing-world fighters a genuine antiarmor capability. (© Mohammed Saber/epa/Corbis)

Allied troops inspect the catastrophic damage inflicted on German forces trapped in the Falaise Pocket in France in 1944 by Allied artillery. Depending on the terrain, up to 75 percent of casualties during battle in World War II were inflicted by artillery, although artillery fire rarely won an action by itself. (IWM CL909)

The German Panzerhaubitze 2000 is the ultimate in mobile firepower. Using its multiple simultaneous round impact (MSRI) capability, it can drop four shells at the same time on a single target, with a fire-control system that obviates the need for ranging shots. (© TopFoto)

Multiple launch rocket systems (MLRSs), such as this Brazilian ASTROS, are designed to deliver enormous area destruction using airburst submunitions. The vehicle here can deliver 32 high-explosive fragmentation warheads to targets 19 miles (30km) away, destroying almost everything within an area the size of a soccer pitch. (© Topham/Photri: TopFoto)

Largely forgotten by the outside world, the war in Chechnya witnessed area artillery bombardments on a scale not seen since World War II. Here the Chechen capital city of Grozny burns under a torrent of shellfire in 1995, artillery being a blunt tool to smash the insurgency. (© Patrick Chauvel/Sygma/Corbis)

A Scud missile is here seen in the firing position on its transporter-erector-launcher (TEL) vehicle. During the 1990–91 Gulf War, aging Iraqi Scuds were primarily weapons of terror, used against Israel and Saudi Arabia with the intention of bringing political results rather than militarily significant destruction. (© Reuters/Corbis)

A US infantry mortar team open fire against insurgent targets in Iraq. Mortar technology has advanced greatly over the last ten years, so much so that some claim it may take over the role of much short- and medium-range artillery in the future. (Courtesy US Army)

to those of Baghdad, it has been widely recognized that AFVs are at a critical disadvantage in urban warfare. For this reason, bizarrely, even Western armored forces have tended to neglect urban warfare training for armor until very recently – if cities weren't suited for armor, then why train for them? And yet, military forces cannot escape the fact that the bulk of the world's future wars will be fought largely in cities (75 percent of the world's population will be living within cities by 2016). The question is, how does armor fit into this landscape?

The detractors of MBTs can often fall into the trap of looking at the vehicles as isolated systems, rather than as one element in the make-up of a combined arms force. The fact is that any AFV that maneuvers through a hostile urban landscape largely unsupported is heading for disaster. Air, artillery, other armor, and infantry assets must together create a broad spectrum of offensive and defensive response, multiplying the concerns of the enemy so that they are unable to fasten their attention solely on the AFV. The infantry/armor balance is particularly critical, and has been the source of debate ever since armor took to the field. Armor cannot survive without infantry support and vice versa, the infantry tackling the enemy antitank teams while the armor protects the infantry by delivering heavy firepower. In a grossly simplified nutshell, the question of the right balance revolves around whether the infantry advances in front of the tanks, attracting enemy fire to which the armor then responds, or whether the armor goes up front, and attracts fire to which the infantry responds.

In Iraq, this balance has become somewhat of a moot point, as when deploying into the most hostile areas the infantry will typically ride within IFVs such as the Bradley, Stryker, and Warrior. Putting infantry on foot in the worst areas, particularly where there is a high threat of IEDs, is a short route to major casualties. The question returns, therefore, to survivability – which vehicles are best acclimatized to survive?

Armor survivability has become a political hot topic in the post-9/11 world. For the United States, the issue is focused most acutely on the Humvee, its ubiquitous mode of light infantry transport. Concerns about its poor level of armor protection date back to the early 1990s, and resulted in the creation of the Up-armored Humvee (UAH), which featured 2,000lb (909kg) of additional ballistic protection to the bodywork and doors. As compared to the standard Humvee, the UAH proved its worth in US deployments in Bosnia, where it gave decent protection against small-arms fire and proximate explosions. However, by the time of the deployment to Iraq in 2003, the Army and Marine Corps were still several thousand UAHs short, the majority of troops relying on the standard Humvee models. The result was terrible casualties amongst Humvee personnel and political embarrassment for the US government. US soldiers were forced to scrabble around for any bits of improvised armor they could find, from dangling body armor out of windows through to piling their vehicles up with sandbags.

In December 2004, the then-US Secretary of Defense Donald Rumsfeld, while conducting a meeting with US troops in Kuwait, was challenged during a question session by Specialist Thomas Wilson of the Tennessee National Guard:

> **SPC THOMAS WILSON:** We're digging pieces of rusted scrap metal and compromised ballistic glass that has already been shot up, dropped, busted – picking the best out of this scrap to put on our vehicles go into combat. We do not have proper armament vehicles to carry with us North.
>
> **DONALD RUMSFELD:** As you know, you go to war with the army you have, not the army you might want or wish to have at a later time. You can have all the armor in the world on a tank, and a tank can be blown up. And you can have an up-armored Humvee, and it can be blown up.[44]

Rumsfeld was right on one point here, namely that any vehicle of any size can be blown up. However, he was missing the vital issue – you are less likely to die in a well-armored vehicle, even if that vehicle is destroyed. Captain Mark Chung, a US Army reservist, discovered some of the benefits of the UAH when his vehicle was hit by an IED during a patrol. Here is Chung talking with Paula Zahn of CNN:

> **ZAHN:** So describe to us tonight what it's all like when the bomb hit and how it was that this armor on your vehicle saved your life?
>
> **CHUNG:** Well, when the IED exploded about three feet off the front right tire of our vehicle, it was, obviously, pretty traumatic. You basically go blank for 3 to 5 seconds or so. There is smoke everywhere. Even the vents inside the Humvee blew out and once everything sort of cleared up, I could see that the windshield was just shattered. But nothing came through the windshield. It's about, I don't know, three or four inches thick and that really stopped a lot or all of the shrapnel to come through that I'm sure would have hit myself in the face, as well as the driver.
>
> **ZAHN:** So without that, you think you probably would have died?
>
> **CHUNG:** Oh, you know, it's hard to say if I would have died or not but I can tell you shrapnel was coming right at the windshield. A big huge chunk of metal or something went through the right front tire. It nearly sheared the chassis in half and the whole hood was blown off.[45]

The improved survivability of the UAH seems clear from such accounts. The US forces also began to receive up-armor kits to apply to their existing Humvees, but even by the time of writing in 2007 there is a definite sense that light armored vehicles, which a UAH remains, are not suited to an IED-rich setting. On May 10, 2007, Defense Secretary Robert Gates announced that the Department of Defense was looking at augmenting, then replacing, its Humvee fleet in Iraq and Afghanistan with the new Mine Resistant Ambush Protected (MRAP) vehicles, these being AFVs purposely designed to cope with the types of threats faced in Iraq. (Features include a V-shaped hull floor to deflect the blast of mines outwards.)

Other vehicles also have question marks over them. The Stryker, initially hailed as one of the more survivable AFVs in Iraq on account of its good firepower, maneuverability, and respectable armor, has started to suffer heavy casualties from IEDs. In one week alone in May 2007 one infantry company lost six Strykers, and AP (Associated Press) journalists Robert H. Reid and Anne Flaherty took the following comment from Michael O'Hanlon, an analyst with the Brookings Institute: "It is indeed open to question if the Stryker is right for this type of warfare ... I am inclined to think that the concept works better for peacekeeping."[46] The British have also had intense political problems with the armor, or lack of it, on Army Land Rovers.

Here we start to find a return to the reason that we have MBTs. MBTs are not invulnerable, as we have seen, but with sensible tactics, plentiful infantry support, good intelligence and, of course, their copious armor protection, they could well be the best vanguard for urban warfare alongside other well-protected AFVs. An unclassified after action report from Iraq from the TM C/3-15 Infantry, Task Force 1-64 Armor, dated April 24, 2003, provides an illustration of how this works. It is worth quoting at length:

> Discussion: The current doctrinal manuals on Urban Operations do not address how best to utilize armored forces in an urban environment. The enemy faced by this unit hid his tanks and vehicles under camouflaged covers, beneath bridge overpasses, inside of buildings on narrow streets, and under low trees. These enemy systems were not seen until they were only meters away. No degree of IPB (Intelligence Preparation of the Battlefield) could compensate, alert, or prepare any US force for the massive numbers of RPGs (Rocket Propelled Grenades) stored in houses, shacks, lockers, and cars. The only way to counter RPGs fired from covered and concealed positions was to absorb the hit, identify the source of the fire, and respond with massive overwhelming firepower.
>
> Tanks and Bradleys repeatedly sustained hits from RPGs and ground directed anti aircraft fire that dismounted infantrymen, HMMWVs and other light skinned vehicles could not sustain. Bradleys successfully protected the infantrymen inside while at the same time delivering a massive volume of fire against dismounted enemy, trucks, tanks, and armored vehicles. The firepower and shock generated by tanks and Bradleys could never have been matched by dismounted infantry. Without the use of these systems initially, the enemy would have caused many more casualties.
>
> The current doctrine recommends clearing the built up area with dismounted troops prior to any armored vehicles entering. This Task Force proved that this is not a requirement and is not necessarily the best initial course of action. By moving armored vehicles along a pre determined route and destroying any enemy forces

whether dug in, in buildings, or on roof tops with massive overwhelming fires from M1A1 tanks and M2A2 fighting vehicles, an entire line of communication can be opened up allowing access not only into the built up area but through it also. Once the line of communication is open, clearing operations with dismounted forces are much easier. A key to this is the overwhelming psychological effect the firepower of these weapon systems have on the enemy once the initial raid is conducted, almost all remaining enemy forces will withdraw from the initial shock. This initial shock of overwhelming firepower facilitates the attacks of dismounted infantrymen into the built up area.

Recommendation: The BCT [Brigade Combat Team] submit to the United States Army Infantry School and the United States Armor School an update to the current urban operations doctrine. Additionally, send only vehicles that can sustain RPG hits into urban combat zones.[47]

The final recommendation here is crucial. If we recognize that survivability is the key to deploying armor when it is not safe to lead with dismounted infantry, vehicles such as MBTs fulfill the brief perfectly. Furthermore, their awesome firepower proves surprisingly useful in urban warfare, enabling forces to pinpoint targets with tank guns, 25mm cannon and TOW missiles with precision, minimizing the "collateral damage." John Gordon, author of a tellingly titled article " 'Everybody Wanted Tanks': heavy forces in Operation *Iraqi Freedom*," noted that "high praise for heavy forces appears throughout the written reports and interviews on *Iraqi Freedom*," noting of MBTs that:

In summary, the tank was the single most important ground combat weapon in the war. Tanks led the advance, compensated for poor situational awareness [by attracting fire], survived hostile fire, and terrorized the enemy. These attributes contributed much to the rapid rate of advance from Kuwait to Baghdad. A senior Marine Corps infantry officer offered an appropriate summation of what the authors repeatedly heard: "Everybody wanted tanks."[48]

Gordon also points out another key feature of the MBT – its ability to inspire terror. Tanks undoubtedly create an impressive psychological effect. Infantry veterans of World War II commonly report the sickening sensation of fear triggered purely by the grinding, squeaking sound of tank tracks approaching from a distance. In mass and at the right proximity, they can also make the ground shake. Mark Lachance, an Iraq war veteran interviewed by Chris McNab, noted that just the emergence of an MBT could be enough to cause a previously committed enemy to stop firing and make a rapid retreat. Nevertheless, the momentum towards replacing the MBT may be too great to stop. As ever, soldiers on the front lines will pay for any poor decisions.

4

DEATH FROM A DISTANCE – ARTILLERY

> Russian shells were coming over in profusion. For a moment we watched the storm
> closing in. Then, with a cry of despair and a prayer for mercy, we dived to the bottom
> of our hole, trembling as the earth shook and the intensity of our fear grew. The
> shocks, whose centre seemed closer every time, were of an extraordinary violence.
> Torrents of snow and frozen earth poured down on us. A white flash, accompanied
> by an extraordinary displacement of air, and an intensity of noise which deafened
> us, lifted the side of the trench. None of us immediately grasped what had happened.
> We were thrown in a heap against the far wall of the hole, wounded and intact
> together. Then, with a roar, the earth poured in and covered us. In that moment, so
> close to death, I was seized by a rush of terror so powerful that I felt my mind was
> cracking. Trapped by the weight of earth, I began to howl like a madman ...[1]

Few accounts in military literature give a more horrifying impression of what it means to be under heavy shellfire. The author, Guy Sajer, was a young soldier in the German Grossdeutschland regiment on the Eastern Front during World War II, one of the millions who had to endure the terror of mass Soviet artillery bombardments. The defining sense is one of utter powerlessness under the onslaught, and it is for this reason that artillery has traditionally been held to be the infantryman's greatest fear.

The Psychology of Artillery

Although studies into the psychological effects of weapons on their human targets were conducted during World War I and the Spanish Civil War, it was in World War II that the investigation took a more comprehensive approach. Out of these studies one consistent fact emerged – soldiers traditionally fear artillery the most, at least with the insight gained from combat experience. Peter Watson collated much data from such studies, and found that during World War II 50 percent of soldiers feared air attack the most at the beginning of their combat experience, with only 20 percent most afraid of artillery fire. However, with duration of time spent in combat the proportions started to switch, and after only 12 days in combat they were completely reversed.[2] Furthermore, other studies Watson analyzes state that 24 percent of the survey participants said that over time they grew more afraid of machine guns, as compared to 43 percent who grew less afraid. With artillery (specifically mortars), in comparison, 31 per were less afraid over time, compared to 40 percent more afraid.[3]

The lesson seems clear – artillery is actually more dangerous than at first believed. It isn't hard to find reasons for this. Indeed, Watson's tabular data from World War II, relating to "percentage of men's reasons for fear of weapons," indicates the following for German mortars and 88mm flak guns:[4]

	Mortar	88s
Accuracy	37	31
Lack of warning	19	11
Rapidity of fire	8	7
Noise	11	19
No defense	1	2
Other	24	3

It is interesting that in both of these cases, noise – a non-lethal event – features quite highly in the fear factor. By itself, the noise of continual explosions can have a severe effect on mental well-being. The intense blasts produce mental trauma, chronic fatigue, and sleep deprivation with a consequent erosion of reasoning skills. Noise can also, as we saw in the previous chapter on armor, have physiological effects. A high-explosive artillery shell, on detonation, can generate well over 140 decibels of impulse noise, easily enough to create temporary hearing loss. In Iraq a total of 1,550 soldiers treated by audiologists for hearing damage between the spring and fall of 2004 had their injuries caused by acoustic blast trauma, with 72 percent of those suffering from hearing loss.[5] Note too, in balance, that acoustic damage is also a very real danger to the operators of artillery – the firing noise of a modern howitzer is around 185 decibels.

It is the top two categories of the list, however – "accuracy" and "lack of warning" – that cut to the heart of the reason that soldiers and civilians alike fear shellfire. Taken together they create a sense of impotence, a feeling that one's existence is in the hands of some remorseless, precise, distant machine. A vivid description of what this sensation is like comes from Lieutenant Anthony Alfands, a British officer who came under heavy shellfire in the trenches of the Western Front in August 1915:

> I must say that it is a devilish affair altogether. You sit like rabbits in a burrow and just wait for something to come and blow you to hell. You don't see the enemy and you kill very few of them ... It gets on one's nerves always waiting for the next bang. If one or two land unpleasantly near one's fore trench the usual effect is that you imagine every other shell is coming around and about the same place. If they do you lie flat on the trench and trust to luck. If they don't come near you well and good. Nerves seem to be the one vital thing for a soldier, nerves good and strong and better still no nerves.[6]

World War I opened society's eyes to the phenomenon of "shell shock," the complete mental breakdown of an individual from the effects of enduring explosion concussions while feeling the acute tension of waiting for the next one to hit. Indeed, psychologists were so alarmed at the symptoms of shell shock – which included everything from stammering to complete catatonia – that at first the symptoms were ascribed to physical effects caused by being in the proximity of detonation. (This perspective was useful in terms of propaganda, as it suggested no mental weakness on the part of the sufferer.) By 1916, however, the psychological community had come to the growing realization that it was the conditions of modern warfare, which included the effects of prolonged industrial-scale bombardment, that literally overwhelmed the mental stability of those men who suffered them.

The crippling psychological impact of shellfire has by no means changed with the passage of time and the transformed technologies of warfare. During the Yom Kippur War in 1973, for example, of 1,323 Israeli soldiers referred for psychological evaluation following the conflict, 277 were diagnosed with post-traumatic stress disorder (PTSD). Of this subset, 122 individuals, constituting 44 percent of the group, gave exposure to shellfire as the primary stressor behind their condition.[7] (The next largest group was 50 soldiers/20.9 percent, whose primary cause of stress was the result of witnessing the death of a fellow soldier.)

Taking an alternative perspective, to be on the side delivering a crushing artillery bombardment can be as empowering as it is terrible for the enemy. Although history has shown that massive bombardments rarely completely subdue an enemy, the sight of rippling explosions and the feel of the concussions can provide a huge morale boost and something akin to religious awe in those witnessing it. Take the account of Captain Gregory McCrum, a medical officer present at the US incursion into Fallujah in 2004:

> I believe it was around 2100 to 2200 when the Army and Marine elements started using 155 millimeter artillery and our own 120 millimeter mortar platoon started engaging targets in the city to soften up the initial breach point on the northern side of the city ... they started about a two-and-a-half to three-hour artillery barrage and smoke screen. That was a significant life-changing event you could say. The sheer power and intensity that goes into that type of conflict is something truly to be awed. I don't think you can go through something like that and really think of the 4th of July the same way again. It just pales in comparison.[8]

While there is undoubtedly a certain horror underlying Captain McCrum's comments, there is equally a reverence in the presence of perfect, dominant destruction. Such awe is common in soldiers witnessing a bombardment, even in seasoned veterans, and empowers the soldier with the feeling that he is part of some colossal machine released upon the enemy with the force of the gods of antiquity. McCrum's account is mirrored in that of a soldier who witnessed a breathtaking Allied artillery bombardment of Monte Cassino in 1944, on which he remarked:

> With a hoarse, exultant scream four-hundred shells sped low over our heads to tear into the ground less than five hundred yards in front, bursting with a mighty antiphonal crash that echoed the challenge of the guns. It was Wagnerian ... The fury of it was elemental, yet precise. It was a controlled cyclone. It was splendid to hear, as the moment of actual combat approached.[9]

Acknowledging the psychological effects of bombardment is critical to comprehending the role of artillery. The British military historian Chris Bellamy summed it up capably when he said that "artillery oppresses, jars, stuns and disorientates the enemy and lifts the morale of its own troops."[10] While artillery is undoubtedly capable of delivering massive physical destruction, as we shall see, it also has a critical effect on enemy morale and the ability to conduct military operations. Once artillery fire has been experienced, the soldier and civilian remain ever fearful of this terrible weapon. Nevertheless, the place it occupies on the modern battlefield is in the process of transformation.

The "King of Battles"

Most studies of artillery quote the widely accepted label of artillery being the "king of battles." This is primarily applied on account of artillery's formidable history of producing the bulk of battlefield casualties, at least in the context of warfare from the early 20th century onwards. James Dunnigan explains the statistics in his book *How to Make War*:

> During World War II, artillery caused nearly 60 percent of all casualties. World War II still holds the record for the most artillery fire thrown at the most troops. During World War II, it was found that artillery's effects varied by terrain type. In open plains and deserts, about 75 percent of the casualties were from artillery, and in forests and built-up areas it was 50 percent or less.[11]

Furthermore, when an artillery shell goes off, everyone in the unprotected vicinity will die, soldiers and civilians. A highly controversial study of civilian mortality during the first 18 months of Operation *Iraqi Freedom*, published in the British medical journal *The Lancet* and conducted by Johns Hopkins Bloomberg School of Public Health, Columbia University School of Nursing and Al-Mustansiriya University in Baghdad, concluded that upwards of 100,000 violent civilian deaths had occurred (excluding exceptional casualty figures from Fallujah). The research further argued that 84 percent of those deaths were at the hands of coalition forces, and 95 percent of those deaths were the result of air strikes and artillery fire.[12] Estimations for the percentage split between air strikes and artillery fire are weighted towards the former, but the study still indicates that in terms of land weapons artillery remains the chief form of casualty creation.

Although artillery fire might seem like wanton destruction, the actual degree of devastation is usually split into four levels, with some variation. The first level is *harassment,* which consists of light but regular shellfire designed to interfere with the enemy's movement, efficiency, morale, and sleep, and aims for up to 10 percent destruction of the enemy's capability. Up from that is *neutralization,* with the level of destruction raised to 30 percent. Neutralization's goal is to cause a temporary loss of function in the target unit, dictating its maneuver options and degrading or cutting its communications. *Demolition* involves damaging the enemy unit's infrastructure (roads, buildings etc) so it is effectively unable to use those assets, and would only be able to restore them with major engineering and financial investment. The most extreme level, however, is *annihilation* or its equally frank alternative, *destruction.* For a single target this means a 70–90 percent probability of a complete kill, and for an area target the destruction of 50–60 percent of the enemy assets within the area. In short, the target is pulverized beyond existence.

When talking about artillery fire from the point of view of targeting, we also distinguish between two fundamental forms of fire – direct and indirect fire. Direct fire is used when the gun crew themselves can see the target, and they literally aim the gun in a flat or near-flat trajectory to hit it. With indirect fire, by contrast, the crew cannot see the target, which is usually at long distances (although mortars can make indirect fire missions at relatively close ranges), and they lob the shell in a high arc to drop onto the target from above. Although direct-fire artillery weapons are still found and used throughout the world, particularly by the Russians and similarly equipped forces, in more advanced armies today direct-fire work has been almost entirely supplanted by guided missiles – the principal form of direct-fire gun was the antitank gun, and antitank work is now mainly covered by tank guns and by missiles launched from ground and air.

Artillery systems can be crudely split into two categories – tube and rocket. Tube artillery is any artillery piece that fires a shell from a barrel, such as mortars and howitzers. Rocket artillery is exactly what it says, powered missiles propelled by rocket motors. Taking tube artillery first, field guns come in two basic forms – towed and self-propelled. A towed artillery piece is transported by a third-party machine and has to be manually emplaced by its crew before firing. Towed artillery is rather like the MBT – its demise is regularly predicted but it doggedly hangs on in there. The principal threat for towed artillery is its comparison to the advantages of self-propelled artillery, to which we shall turn shortly. Admittedly, towed artillery has some shortcomings. It can take as long as 30 minutes to emplace a towed gun and configure it for firing – not helpful for a spontaneous forward observer (FO) who wants to bring down fire on a fleeting target. Furthermore, once emplaced it takes just as long to pack up and move, a quality that makes it especially vulnerable to counter-battery fire or air attack. Towed guns are also pulled by tractors and trucks; these vehicles are not only slower than the armored spearhead of an army, but are also vulnerable to even the lightest types of enemy fire. For that matter, because a towed crew stands out in the open (not within the protective hull of a self-propelled, or SP, gun), they themselves are also particularly exposed.

For all these black marks, there are enough positives to keep the towed guns in business. One excellent reason is that they are cheap to buy – SP guns cost about three times as much – with an extremely buoyant second-hand market. Thousands of vintage US 105mm M101 Howitzers, for example, litter the world, and many are now receiving extended barrel conversions to lengthen their lives as well as their ranges. The cheapness and availability of towed guns makes them ideal weapons for any financially challenged country looking to bulk out its artillery forces. Hence many of the old Soviet-era models are popular on the world market, including pieces such as the 122mm D-30 and the 130mm M-46, both which have widespread licensed manufacture. Nor are such guns second-rate performers. The D-30 can throw a shell accurately out to 50,196ft (15,300m), while the M-46, with the right ammunition and configuration, can reach 121,390ft (37,000m).

There are many other practical reasons for purchasing towed guns. First, towed artillery is light. Not only can you sling several British 105mm Light Guns, for instance, into the hold of a C-130 and fly them to the battlefield, you can also sling one under a suitable helicopter (a Puma or Chinook, for instance) and fly it to a position inaccessible to even an SP gun, such as a mountaintop or jungle clearing. The light weight also means that the gun can be pulled by a medium-weight vehicle, such as a Pinzgauer TUM/HD or Hagglund BV206, which reduces the dangers of destroying rickety bridges with the huge bulk of an SP weapon.

For the above reasons, towed artillery will stay with the world's armies for the long-term future. Yet in advanced armies there is an undeniable psychological swing towards SP guns. The core reasons for this move are speed, mobility, and survivability. With modern auto gunlaying systems, an SP gun such as a US Paladin or British AS90 can halt, load, and fire within 30 seconds of receiving a GPS-directed fire order. Furthermore, while most towed guns require manual loading, a relatively slow procedure that gets even slower as the loader and crew tire, most good SP guns have autoloading systems that can tirelessly ram home shells every few seconds. Such speed loading equates to devastating barrage effects downrange. The AS90, for example, has a burst-fire rate of three rounds in

10 seconds, and during trials two of these guns put 574lb (261kg) of ordnance onto a single target within that time frame. Autoloading, combined with sophisticated fire-control systems, can, on some guns such as the German Panzerhaubitze 2000 and the future Non Line of Sight (NLOS) cannon, deliver a crushing effect known as Multiple Round Simultaneous Impact (MRSI). Here the gun rapid fires a series of shells, reducing the arc of trajectory with each shot and thereby reducing the flight time of each shell. The net result is that a barrage of around five shells will land on the target simultaneously, maximizing the impact of the all-important first strike, when enemy troops and vehicles are least prepared and most exposed.

SP guns also offer a ground mobility unavailable to most towed guns. They can go wherever tanks and other armored vehicles can and will maintain good speed on rough cross-country terrain that would have towed guns flying around wildly. Once they have fired, they can move almost immediately, giving them the "shoot and scoot" capability that protects them from counterbattery fire and air attack. Note that while SP guns typically ride on tracks, a whole new generation of wheeled SP guns is steadily coming into service. The wheels give the advantage of wheeled armored vehicles discussed in the previous chapter – very fast road speed for rapid deployment. While some of these guns, the South African 155mm G6 being a good example, follow the traditional turreted lines of SP systems, others are emerging that consist of the gun system strapped to the flat bed of a military truck.[13] The French Giat 155mm Caesar, for example, mounts a 155mm howitzer on the back of a Mercedes-Benz Unimog 2450 6x6 lorry. Speed on its wheels is 62mph (100km/h) on the road, which is over twice the speed of most tracked SP vehicles. Its combat weight is 38,896lb (17,680kg), light enough to transport inside a C-130. Compare this to the weight of an AS90 (also SP), which stands on the scales at 99,000lb (45,000kg). Although the truck has an armored cab, the survivability of such a vehicle is obviously much less than a fully armored SP gun. But this is not the point. Unlike tanks, which have to get close to the enemy, modern artillery has phenomenal stand-off. The Caesar, for example, can fire at targets nearly 25 miles (40km) away. Such stand-off alone offers survivability, as long as air supremacy is established and rear-area security is good.

Rocketry

Modern battlefield rocket artillery is almost entirely self-propelled. Rockets aren't easy things to set up and launch, so having them ready mounted into vehicle-transported launchers is the best option. Rocket artillery emerged in earnest during World War II, and was principally used to provide rippling mass barrages. Accuracy was shocking, but what the rockets lacked in precision they more than made up for by sheer volume of explosive force and by their nerve-jangling psychological effect. The supreme exponents of battlefield rocketry (as opposed to naval systems) were the Russians with their Katyusha truck-mounted launchers (the BM-8, BM-13 and BM-31) that terrorized German ranks on the Eastern Front. Such was their effect that after the war the Russians kept faith with rocketry, bringing out an increasingly potent series of BM vehicles with greater degrees of accuracy and power. The BM-21, for example, was introduced in 1963 and has gone on to see worldwide service. Mounted on the back of a Ural-375D truck chassis, the rocket launcher can launch 40 122mm rockets in one fearsome 6-second barrage, each rocket carrying a frag-HE, incendiary, chemical, or cargo (submunition) warhead out to ranges of 12–19 miles (20–30km). Although the accuracy of the rockets, compared to the old Katyusha, has been improved by spin-stabilization, it is still not precise. However, a battalion of these systems will fire 720 missiles in one go, so in terms of circular error probable (CEP – the radius of a circle into which a missile, bomb, or projectile will land at least half the time), accuracy is less important.

Nevertheless, as with tube weapons, rockets have bought into the accuracy revolution of the last 20–30 years. Modern Multiple Launch Rocket Systems (MLRSs), such as the US MLRS and the Russian BM-30 Smerch, can now send guided missiles out to ranges of 43 miles (70km) and land within 328ft (100m) of the target. Submunition effects have also been radically improved so that single rockets can wreck an area roughly the size of a football pitch (see below). In fact, the two central advantages rocket weaponry offers over tube artillery in open warfare are extended range and better cargo-munition carrying capability – even the largest artillery shells will carry under 100 submunitions, whereas an MLRS rocket can transport over 600. Note, however, that this capability is best in "clean" conventional battlefield conditions, hence MLRS technology gave excellent performance in the 1991 Gulf War. If, by contrast, you want to deliver a pinpoint strike against an urban target surrounded by lots of civilians, use something else.

That is, unless your purpose is terror, of course. Rocket weapons have long been used both by insurgents and by states as tools of persuasion, even if the military damage they do is slight. A good example is the use of Scud Tactical Ballistic Missiles (TBMs) by Iraq during the 1991 Gulf War. TBMs are at the big end of artillery, some versions being capable of carrying a nuclear warhead well over 621 miles (1,000km). History's greatest and most well-documented TBM was Germany's V2 launched against Britain and Western Europe in 1944 and 1945, which killed over 2,500 people in London alone, injured over 20,000 and destroyed 29,000 homes. The SS-1 Scud was a Soviet development of the late 1950s, but its main operational service was to be in the Middle East. Fired, as with most TBMs, from its own transporter-erector-launcher (TEL) vehicle, the Scud steadily cranked up its range throughout its development history, from 81 miles (130km) with the Scud A through to 435 miles (700km) for the Scud D.

At the same time its CEP went from a dismal 13,123ft (4,000m) to just 164ft (50m). In 1990–91, the Scud was a useful tool for Saddam Hussein, especially as the rest of his armed forces was hideously outclassed. He already had experience of using these weapons – during the Iran–Iraq War (1980–88), Iraq fired some 190 Scuds at urban targets in Iran, principally Tehran, in an attempt to break the stalemate into which the land war had descended.[14] Although by 1991 the stockpile of Scuds was ageing and inaccurate, they still had the capability to hit targets in Saudi Arabia and Israel. A total of 130 were launched, but the damage they caused was, in the context of the whole war, minimal. In Israel, two people died and 230 were injured.[15] The worst incident in Saudi Arabia occurred on February 25, 1991, when a Scud hit a US Army barracks at Dhahran, killing 28 American soldiers.

What was potentially far more troubling about the Scud attacks was their psychological effect. TBMs attack at supersonic speeds from extremely high altitudes, so apart from radar contact give no warning of their arrival. Furthermore, until they detonate no one knows what the missile contains – gas, chemical agents, nuclear warhead, or "just" conventional explosive. As it turns out, Saddam's Scuds contained purely the last of these, but for Israelis in particular the donning of gas masks disinterred some historical nightmares for a nation born out of the Holocaust. Furthermore, the fact that almost all the Scud attacks occurred between 11:00pm and 4:00am, guaranteeing maximum disruption to sleep, enhanced the fear.

Ultimately, Saddam was aware that Israel would never be militarily defeated by Scuds; his intention was to provoke an Israeli military response that would in turn lead, in Saddam's logic, to other Arab nations making an active military contribution to his campaign. The plan stumbled on Israeli restraint. The coalition's effort to control the media landscape, and keep Israel reassured, lay in its use of Patriot air-defense artillery.

Air-defense artillery comes in two principal forms – guns and missiles. On the gun side of things, antiaircraft artillery (AAA) ranges from a humble 20mm cannon equipped with an optical sight through to self-propelled multibarrel guns systems such as the Russian ZSU-23-4 Shilka, with four radar-controlled 23mm cannon that can pump out a lethally accurate stream of shells at a combined cyclical rate of 4,000rpm. Missile defense (depending on the system), however, has far better capabilities to hit aircraft at high altitude and speed. The MIM-104 Patriot was developed in the 1970s, its first deployment coming in 1984. In its first incarnation it could travel at speeds of up to Mach 3 and hit fast-moving targets 43 miles (70km) away. The subsequent Patriot Advanced Capability (PAC) upgrades in the late 1980s supposedly gave the Patriot the capability to intercept ballistic missiles, a talent put to the test when several Patriot batteries were deployed to Israel and Saudi Arabia in 1990 to provide air defense against the Scuds.

The Patriots were soon streaking up into the skies over places such as Tel Aviv and Riyadh, and the results were apparently impressive – the US Army claimed an 80 percent interception rate over Saudi Arabia and a 50 percent rate over Israel, later revised to 70 percent and 40 percent respectively. Writers for the British paper *The Sunday Times* captured the public and media enthusiasm over the Patriot:

> Israel now has the new wonder weapon of the war, the Patriot ... The Patriot became a talisman for allied forces; in one hotel lobby a chunk of the anti-missile missile had a place of honor and inscription reading "We love you." After the drama of the air raids over Baghdad, the worldwide television audience was being treated to a new video game: Missile Wars. Night after night, the skies over Israel and Saudi Arabia were lit by streaks of light as Patriots soared off to intercept Scuds. People gave up hiding in bunkers and went on to the rooftoops to enjoy the spectacle.[16]

The likening of the "missile wars" to a "new video game" is apt; the images provided a sense both of drama yet also of clinical control that fitted in well with the idea of "surgical" warfare that was promoted at many levels. The problem was that, quite simply, the success figures were deeply questionable. Suggestions that the success rate figures were wide of the mark prompted official investigation in Washington, plus troubling testimony from defense experts such as Professor Theodore Postol, who stated that "The results of these studies are disturbing. They suggest that the Patriot's intercept rate during the Gulf War was very low. The evidence from these preliminary studies indicates that Patriot's intercept rate could be much lower than ten percent, possibly even zero."[17]

Postol's conclusions were, needless to say, vigorously contested, and with some justification. A commonly proclaimed figure of only 9 percent successful engagements was attacked by Raytheon (the corporation that produces the Patriot) as a misrepresentation of Government Accountability Office (GAO) statistics from the following statement:

> About 9 percent of the Patriot's Operation *Desert Storm* engagements are supported by the strongest evidence that an engagement resulted in a warhead kill – engagements during which observable evidence indicates a Scud was destroyed or disabled after a Patriot detonated close to the Scud. For example, the strongest evidence that a warhead kill occurred would be provided by (1) a disabled Scud with Patriot fragments or fragment holes in its guidance and fuzing section or (2) radar data showing evidence of Scud debris in the air following a Patriot detonation. The other 16 percent of the engagements the Army is highly confident resulted in warhead kills are not supported by such evidence. In these cases, however, radar

tracking data collected proves that in some cases the Patriots came close to the Scuds, but it does not prove or disprove whether the Patriots came close enough to have a high probability of destroying, disabling, or diverting them.[18]

One of the problems that emerged in the analysis was that the Scud Bs used by Iraq had been modified to achieve greater speed, but the result was that they frequently broke apart during re-entry to the earth's atmosphere. This would cause a loss of Patriot lock-on, with the result that the warhead section would frequently tumble through to the ground. Furthermore, an average of 3–4 Patriots were fired at each Scud, hence the percentage of misses would not necessarily tally with the number of events classified as a mission success.[19]

A definitive conclusion as to the outcome of the missile wars is unlikely, primarily because of problems of gathering accurate data. Nevertheless, and accepting the fact that the destruction of any Scud by the Patriot means the system was performing a militarily useful service, the fact remains that during the war itself these missiles had an extremely important effect on morale in the targeted territories. Rockets are as much about light and noise as they are about destruction. The Islamic group Hezbollah has discovered this truth from within its Lebanese border territories. Rockets, at their most basic, are one of the cheapest forms of field artillery for an insurgent force. Simple rockets with a couple of miles range can be home built – as a quick search on the internet for rocket enthusiast groups demonstrates. Combine such a rocket with a crude warhead and give it direction by firing it from a rail or pipe, and you have an excellent "shoot and scoot" weapon ideal for inflicting a politically useful anxiety upon a more powerful neighbor. Palestinian insurgent groups, for example, have created a surprisingly sophisticated range of rocket weapons, despite having little manufacturing base to draw upon. (Components are smuggled into the Palestinian territories from across the Middle East.) Hamas, for example, has developed its Qassam range of rockets, with ranges extending from 2.8 miles (4.5km) for Qassam-1 up to 10.5 miles (17km) for Qassam-4, and warheads from 11–44lb (5–20kg) of TNT; reports of missile attacks in 2006 confirm that improvements in range and firepower are occurring constantly. Other rockets produced by Palestinian groups include the Al-Batar antitank missile and even a purported antiaircraft missile based on the Russian SA-7.

Hezbollah has taken its rocketry to a more sophisticated level than most militant groups. Its regional popularity in its war against Israel has enabled it to access the lively market in military surplus rocketry, particularly unwanted Soviet-era weaponry or Iranian technology. Its most basic weapon is the BM-21 Grad missile, which gives it the ability to reach up to 15.5 miles (25km) into northern Israel. Its other acquisitions, however, extend the range much further: Fajr-3 missile – 28 miles (45km); Fajr-5 – 47 miles (75km); Zelzal-1 – 62 miles (100km); and Zelzal-2 – up to 124 miles (200km).[20]

Typically, the gross inaccuracy of insurgent rockets, usually without any form of guidance system and using erratic propellants, makes them primarily a nuisance to the enemy and morale-boosting to the home side. However, on July 12, 2006 a barrage of rockets provided a necessary diversion to allow a Hezbollah unit to cross into Israel territory, kill three Israeli soldiers and kidnap two more. The incident provoked an all-out war between Israel and Hezbollah that ran for a month. Ground fighting between the two sides in southern Lebanon was fierce, but in many ways the conflict was defined by its exchange of artillery. Between July 12 and August 14 Hezbollah fired up to 4,300 rockets, mostly Katyusha types. On August 3 alone, a one-hour barrage sent 230 rockets into Israel to a depth of 27 miles (43km). In total the attacks killed 53 people and wounded 2,250 (although only 250 were serious injuries), and displaced over a quarter of a million. Israel responded in kind: in addition to the Israeli Air Force flying 12,000 air combat missions, the Israeli Navy fired 2,000 artillery shells and the Israeli Army over 100,000 shells back into Lebanese positions. Between 800 and 2,000 Lebanese civilians were killed and over 4,000 wounded.

Note how, in what remains very much an asymmetric conflict, artillery of one kind or another played a critical role. Neither side could aim to "win" by artillery alone, but the strategic implications of Hezbollah's rocketry are clear from a statement by the Jerusalem Center for Public Affairs:

> Rockets and rocket launchers emerged as one of the defining weapons of the second Lebanon War and will remain so in the foreseeable future. This impacts on the security of US and Western interests in the Middle East. Effective response measures must be devised and deployed as soon as possible. Two objectives should be pursued: first, to reduce the "Flash to Bang" (Hizballah rocket launch to Israeli response) cycle time to a few seconds from the time of launcher location pinpointing; and second, to develop and deploy effective and affordable active defense against rockets to protect vital civilian and military installations.[21]

As a "defining weapon," rocket weaponry has the power to shape Middle Eastern politics, despite groups like Hezbollah having much in quantity and little in quality. Should the sophistication of guidance and warhead technologies improve amongst insurgent groups, then the future of conflict in the Middle East could be very different.

Munitions and the "Clean War"

An artilleryman of World War II would look on the modern array of artillery ammunition as if it were something from science fiction. Of course, the bulk of what artillery forces worldwide throw out remains conventional high-explosive shells, but for those that can afford them there are Improved Conventional Munitions (ICMs) that heighten range, accuracy and explosive effects.

Range

Apart from increasing the amount of propellant behind an artillery shell and lengthening a gun barrel, both of which have practical limits, there are other ways in which shells can be flung further and further. Base-bleed shells work by pushing out gas from the base of the shell, not to provide thrust but to reduce the aerodynamic drag on the base of the shell, which is one of the primary factors limiting a shell's range. Typically, a base-bleed ICM will add around 30 percent more range over a conventional shell, and howitzers firing such shells can usually attack targets out to 19–25 miles (30–40km). Up to 50 percent more range can be achieved by Rocket-Assisted Projectiles (RAPs). As their name suggests, RAPs have additional thrust provided by a rocket motor installed in the base of the shell. A supreme example of this type of shell is to be found in the US Navy's experimental Extended Range Guided Munition (ERGM). Designed to be fired from the Mk 45 Mod 4.5in gun, ERGM's rocket drives it to high altitude before the shell "flies" onto its target, steered by a Global Positioning System (GPS) guidance system in the nose. Its range is an undeniably impressive 60nm (110km), enough to give the Navy secure stand-off while retaining its shore-bombardment role. (More about naval gunfire systems can be found in Chapter 6.) However, RAPs have also percolated down through the military to mortar level. A typical 120mm mortar firing conventional shells will have a range of around 4.3 miles (7km), but firing an RAP can take its range up to 11 miles (17km). Furthermore, munition designers are looking to incorporate ramjet technologies to give artillery shells even greater depth. A ramjet-assisted 120mm mortar, for example, could have a range of 22 miles (35km), giving the frontline infantryman the capability to rival large-caliber tube artillery for range. The continuous advances in artillery range may, ultimately, strip away some of the advantages air power has in terms of reach, at least within a tactical, if not a strategic, scenario.

Accuracy

Putting aside the issue of fire control, which we will deal with below, ICMs are now exhibiting accuracy to rival anything that is dropped from the sky or flies its own way to a target. The seminal factor in artillery guidance has been the miniaturization of GPS units, making them small enough to fit into shells. A good example of a modern GPS shell is the US Army's M982 Excalibur. Excalibur is a 155mm GPS-guided shell with a range of some 22–25 miles (35–40km), which can be fired from a variety of gun platforms, including the M109 Paladin and the M198 Howitzer. Bear in mind that a conventional unguided shell can, at extreme range, land anywhere within about 1,312ft (400m) of the intended target, depending on factors ranging from the skill of the gun crew through to weather conditions, although 246ft (75m) is much more likely with a modern gun and professional crew. This broad CEP is one of the reasons why artillery has struggled to find a place within asymmetric urban warfare – 1,312ft from the intended target is likely, after all, to be a residential area packed with unfortunate civilians. Excalibur, however, has a remarkable CEP of only 32ft (10m) across its full range spectrum. During range tests the performance even exceeded these limits, with two test firings at Yuma Proving Ground, Arizona, in 2004 landing 11ft (3.4m) and 22.5ft (6.9m) from the target point 12.4 miles (20km) away.[22] Considering that the kill/injury radius of the Excalibur explosion is up to 492ft (150m) from point of impact (PoI), then you have a truly effective method of pinpoint destruction.

The big problem with Excalibur is that each shell costs around $80,000. Furthermore, some argue that Excalibur isn't that relevant in light of the USAF's new 250lb (114kg) Small Diameter Bomb (SDB), which is just as accurate and provides an even bigger bang. Yet the comparison is unfair, not least because the SDB costs over $100,000 and requires all the sophistication needed to bring in an air strike.[23] Furthermore, destroying the intended target with any expensive advanced precision munition still works out cheaper, especially once the reduced logistics are factored in, than using multiple conventional munitions to find the target, even if each of those shells costs much less.[24] Also, the problem of expense is being solved, in US forces anyway, by the introduction of the Precision Guidance Kit (PGK). Like the JDAM kit used by air forces, the PGK is simply a fuse-sized module that attaches to the nose of an artillery shell and gives that shell GPS guidance capabilities. At the time of writing the PGK's CEP is around 164ft (50m), but planned improvements will probably decrease that figure to 98ft (30m) and better. Best of all, the PGK costs about half the amount of Excalibur.

GPS guidance isn't the only way precision artillery fire is being brought down upon the enemy. Laser guidance is another method, in which the shell homes in on a laser beam "designating" the target. The US used the Copperhead laser-guided shell during the 1991 Gulf War, primarily against enemy armor, but it fell from production as its thunder was stolen by air-dropped munitions. The Russians have the Krasnopol, and this proved useful in Indian hands when deployed against Pakistani forces in the Himalayas in 1999. Not everyone is a believer in ICMs, citing the great improvements in the accuracy of conventional munitions delivery and also the obvious fact that not every ICM works as it should. The latter point is always a concern with GPS-guided shells – if a GPS projectile loses the signal in flight, then it could be far more inaccurate than the most casually fired conventional round. Yet such concerns always accompany new technology, and battlefield experience is likely to show the value of ICMs in the hands of professional armies that are as concerned about media effects as battlefield results. (There remain plenty of armies around the world that are perfectly happy to pound away with hundreds of conventional rounds, quite oblivious to civilian casualties.) Furthermore, ICMs undoubtedly increase the ability of artillery to engage pinpoint targets, such as individual buildings and vehicles. In the antiarmor field, we now have fearsome munitions such as M898 SADARM, the acronym standing for Sense and Destroy Armor. SADARM is a 155mm artillery shell that airbursts 3,280ft (1,000m) above the target area, and deploys two submunitions on parachutes. The submunitions descend over the battlefield, spiraling round at about 30 degrees from the vertical. Sensors in the nose of the submunition scan the battlefield as it descends slowly. As soon as the sensors detect an armored vehicle, the submunition fires an EFP straight down onto the target's vulnerable top armor. SADARM had its first operational airing in Iraq in 2003, in the hands of the US 3rd Infantry Division. One of their after action reports conveyed enthusiasm for the new munition:

> The SADARM exceeded expectations and became the preferred precision munitions for field artillery (FA) battalions and their supported maneuver commanders. Out of 121 SADARM rounds fired, 48 pieces of enemy equipment were destroyed. Units also found they could fire substantially less than the doctrinal 24 rounds to achieve effects on target ... The SADARM truly added a quick-kill ability to the artillery of the 3ID (M).[25]

Such data shows that SADARM is an effective antiarmor weapon, although there remains the question of what happened to the 73 weapons that did not destroy vehicles, potentially answered by the probable firing of SADARMs in barrage effects, and not as single hunter munitions.

More about the precision of artillery fire, and the role that human beings play in the loop, will be discussed in the section on fire control below. Yet the precision of ICMs must never obscure the fact that they are designed for destruction, for with advances in accuracy have come equal advances in firepower.

Explosive Effects

Within technical data about ICMs there lies a trap for the unwary, the notion of the "clean war." Paul Rogers, Professor of Peace Studies at Bradford University, attacks the supposed cleanliness of precision weapons in his article "The myth of the clean war – and its real motive." One of the problems, he notes, is that the warheads inside precision munitions are anything but clean:

> But in parallel with the "precision revolution," new generations of a class of weapon known as Area Impact Munitions (AIMs) have been developed. These are specifically conceived, designed, and used to kill and injure as many people, and over a wide an area, as possible. The euphemism of "soft targeting" can smoothly distinguish these from the "hard" targeting of tank, other armoured vehicles and bunkers by precision-guided weapons; but the reality is that most AIMs are planned specifically to kill and maim on a very large scale.[26]

AIMs are indeed formidable weapons. Take the M26 rocket, for example, the standard munition fired from the MLRS. The basic M26 contains within it 644 M77 Dual-Purpose Improved Conventional Munition (DPICM) submunitions, mixing antipersonnel and antiarmor effects. These submunitions are dispersed by air burst above the target, blanketing an area of around 1,640ft (500m) square before detonating. The MLRS system has 12 such rockets, meaning that it can put down 7,728 submunitions in a one-minute barrage.

For those facing such a lethal storm, there are few places to hide. Iraqi commanders during the 1991 Gulf War nicknamed the MLRS "steel rain" because of its horrifying effects. One officer, when later interviewed, said that after one MLRS strike only seven men were left alive out of a company of 270. An Iraqi artillery commander noted that while air attacks destroyed 20 of his 100 guns available, an MLRS attack destroyed 73.[27] A new missile, the M39 Army Tactical Missile System (ATACMS), promises even greater antipersonnel lethality. Its Block I version contains about 950 M74 bomblets, and each of these blows out showers of razor-sharp shrapnel that have a kill radius of 49ft (15m). It is not only rockets that have bought into such "cargo munitions." Several standard howitzer rounds can take DPICMs, or release a variety of antipersonnel and antiarmor submunitions. Professor Rogers focuses on such AIMs, but even with unitary warhead ICMs it has to be remembered that the blast radius will be greater than the CEP – once the warhead goes off, devastation not precision is the goal.

Rogers is right to challenge the notion of the clean war, though you rarely come across actual soldiers who believe in such a concept or say that it is possible. Commanders of most armies will emphasize publicly that every effort is being made to minimize collateral damage, and most will mean it, but they recognize that hurling around tons of explosive and steel, whatever the precision of the weapon, is going to have unintended effects. Furthermore, a weapon may be precise but that in itself is a purely passive fact; the targeting is the active part of the equation. Civilians can be just as easily targeted with ICMs as soldiers, although those countries who can afford ICMs in bulk tend to have the most media accountability and hence refrain from such targeting. But not always. Controversy has raged over Israeli use of artillery-launched cluster munitions against urban areas in southern Lebanon in 2006. A conference report from the Human Rights Watch organization noted that 155mm artillery and MLRS strikes were the main Israeli delivery systems for submunitions, and raised major issues over targeting:

> During parts of six days immediately following the cease-fire, Human Rights Watch researchers documented approximately 50 Israeli cluster strikes, including strikes in about 30 towns and villages. Many strikes hit in the middle of and throughout

these urban areas, indicating deliberate targeting of the areas. Large urban areas such as Tibnine and Nabatiyah were hit. The town of Yahmor was hit especially hard, as were Tibnine, Ain Ibel, Yaroun, Bint Jabael, and Qfar Tibnit. Often, the targeted towns and villages had been largely or completely abandoned by the Lebanese people, as they heeded Israel's warnings to depart before an attack. But civilians are encountering large numbers of submunition duds as they return to populated areas. Many strikes were targeted at olive groves and tobacco fields, which would have been likely locations for Hezbollah to launch rocket attacks at Israel.[28]

The issues surrounding the accusations from Human Rights Watch are a moral minefield, and unpacking them would require a book of their own. However, one consideration that military planners and officers always need to consider is that the remoteness of weapons such as artillery and air power can create a distance between launching firepower and understanding its effects. By not being close to the consequences of targeting decisions, there may well be the tendency to select munitions inappropriate to the target, or to use excessive volumes of firepower. Sometimes, of course, the root problem is quite simply that the sides in a conflict just don't care about civilian casualties, or actually want to impose them. Such an occasion is described in Jefferson D. Reynolds' impressive article "Collateral Damage on the 21st Century Battlefield," where he highlights the humanitarian gap in the Russian use of artillery during the grim war in Chechnya:

> In Chechnya, Russian forces were indifferent to enemy forces attempting to invite or fabricate collateral damage. When advancing on the city of Grozny in 1999, Russian forces were challenged by Mujahedin forces deployed in surrounding villages to attract Russian fire on the civilian population. When villagers protested, they were sometimes beaten or fired at by Mujahedin. Russian forces ignored the attempts to use the villages as a shield and directed "heavy fire – tube and rocket artillery as well as aerial bombing – in order to subdue the centers of resistance." The number of civilian fatalities was estimated from hundreds to thousands in 1999.[29]

The bitter ethnic tensions at the heart of the Chechen war, replicated in countless other conflicts from the Congo to the former Yugoslavia, make, in an unpleasant fashion, artillery targeting decisions far easier for the combatants. Furthermore, by destroying civilian and military targets alike, they can impose a wider degree of political influence, and support their own social or territorial engineering programs.

For armies who do purport to care for civilian casualties, targeting is much more problematic, and is governed by protocols on what constitutes a military target and the effects that the target destruction will have within the context of overall operations. When the conflict is of an asymmetric type, the difficulties multiply accordingly. Here, more than ever, targeting is crucial.

Precision Fires

Artillery munitions will only go where they are told to, and that is the job of targeting. Targeting artillery is an advanced technical and mathematical activity conducted amidst the heat and frenzy of war, and any lapses in judgment or accuracy on the part of the targeting procedure can result in dreadful consequences – inaccurate shells will just as happily kill civilians or friendly troops as enemy soldiers.

Up until the last couple of decades of the 20th century, artillery control rested fairly squarely in the hands of the Forward Observer (FO – also known by various other names, such as Fire Support Officer), an individual trained in guiding artillery fire to its goal. The FO, who would have visual acquisition of the target, would communicate directly with the Fire Direction Center (FDC) as follows:

1) *Observer identification*
The FO identifies himself to the FDC.

2) *Warning order*
Here the FO calls for the fire mission, identifying the type of mission and force of artillery required, and the method of target location.

3) *Target location*
The FO gives the target location, supplying either the grid reference or a location description (typically a "shift from a known position").

4) *Target description*
The target is described, including details such as the area it covers, the type of vehicles, whether there are personnel in the open, how much cover the enemy has etc.

5) *Type of fire required*
The FO describes the nature of the firepower required, such as whether precision or area fire is needed, and also informs the FDC whether "danger close" conditions prevail.[30]

6) *Method of fire and control*
The FO describes how the fire would be controlled in terms of its timing and aiming adjustment. In the US Army, two major commands are "At

My Command," meaning the guns should open fire when the FO tells them to, and "Time on Target," at which the FO gives a specific time for the artillery to engage.

After all this information had been transferred, the FDC would relay the information back to the FO to check, and following confirmation the firing would commence. (Note that the above elements of a call for fire could vary in their order and nature depending on the nationality and branch of service of an army.) Should the first shells miss, which was more than likely, the FO would radio back adjustments, walking the shells onto the target through angular and distance corrections. All elements of the call for fire would be passed from the FDC to the gun battery commander, who would then pass the details onto his gunners, who in turn would lay the guns and fire.

Such calls for fire are still commonplace today, and most well-trained infantry will have a decent idea of how to bring in artillery. Yet within this seemingly clinical process lies a whole myriad of lethal possibilities for error. Fratricide from artillery fire has been all too common throughout history. For example, on February 17, 1970 a US Army communication unit, Company A44, 36th Signal Battalion, was hit on its hilltop position in Vietnam by two artillery strikes, separated by a four-hour interval. The experience of the attacks was captured by Phillip Coleman, a member of the unit, who here describes some of the heart-stopping moments under the second barrage:

> Just as I turned I could see Jimmie execute a perfect roll-out. He was responding as I should have. Suddenly, the shock wave hit. Tossing the front end of my cot off the floor, I quickly leaned forward using my weight to force it back down. As it crashed to the floor my grip broke loose. My body swayed uncontrollably. I reached down and grabbed the rails of the cot again. Looking up toward the window the bright red fireball rose high into the sky creating distorted shadows on the 2-by-fours lining the windows of the hootch next door. Its heat burned my chin then slowly moved up my face. I turned my head down toward my cot to keep it from burning my eyes... An instant later I went completely deaf. Every sound around me vanished as if someone in outer space had turned a dial shutting off the volume all over the world. I closed my eyes to make sure I wasn't imagining my deafness. I had never experienced complete silence before. I tried to remember the last sounds I heard but my mind was a blank. It was like trying to imagine seeing something I'd never seen. Squinting over at Jimmie's cot a few feet away, his limp body appeared unconscious.[31]

By the time the last attack stopped, six soldiers were dead and 30 wounded. At first, the authorities of Military Assistance Command, Vietnam (MACV), blamed insurgent activity, but later, under journalistic investigation, confessed that the attacks were actually friendly fire incidents. Such incidents were unfortunately common in Vietnam, where a frequently confused battlefield situation and high levels of fatigue amongst the troops led to common errors in fire-mission handling.

As artillery control is a skill requiring precision handling of coordinates of both friendly and enemy positions, it is one often quickly degraded by stress and fatigue. Colonel Kenneth K. Steinweg, a military physician, has studied how physiological symptoms affect incidents of fratricide and notes that:

> sleep deprivation effects are uneven. Purely manual tasks are the least affected, while skills requiring complex mental tasks are first to decline. Such critical functions as command and control, fire control, awareness of orientation to friendly and enemy troops, and target designation and tracking are some of the first skills to be affected ... In short, weapons can still be loaded and fired efficiently over time, but the ability to exercise good judgment and employ the weapon correctly deteriorates rapidly.[32]

Arguably, the risks of this type of fratricide are now lessening, at least in terms of artillery usage, on account of new precision fire-control technologies entering service. Fire control has now firmly entered the "netcentric" realm. Whereas previously the artillery relied mainly on FOs to provide target information, today the data is streaming in from multiple platforms – footsoldiers, vehicles, UAVs and drones, satellite, ships, and aircraft, and can be centrally processed in real-time to provide cross-service pictures of both friendly and enemy forces. Targeting data is now acquired by the platform or personnel using GPS designators such as the Ground/Vehicular Laser Locator Designator (G/VLLD) or Long-Range Scout Surveillance System (LRAS3), which provide highly accurate ten-digit grid references that can be transmitted straight back to the FDC. The battery commander then transmits the information directly to the guns, which will lay themselves using their own fire-control computers that calculate everything that will affect trajectory, from windspeed to wear and tear on the barrel. In effect, the gun crews are simply there to keep the guns fed with ammunition and functioning properly. Combined with battlefield fire-planning systems such as the US Advanced Field Artillery Tactical Data System (AFATDF), which coordinates the use of all theater fire assets, such advances in fire control have resulted in a major drop in artillery fratricide incidents in Iraq, even during the initial highly mobile open-combat phase.

Of course, not every artillery piece or fire-control system fielded is so sophisticated, and when networks go down, which they do from time to time, traditional FO skills are required. Nor must we think that somehow the precision of modern artillery control diminishes the skill and judgment required by artillerymen and those who do the targeting. A good example of the complexities of a modern call for fire is given below – an account by Captain James T. Cobb who, during the battle for Fallujah in 2004 (Operation *Phantom Fury*), was the Fire Support Officer (FSO) for 2nd Battalion, 2nd Infantry Regiment, or Task Force 2-2:

I think it was an unmanned aerial vehicle (UAV) from the Marines that saw a bunch of insurgents running in and out of this building, using it as a headquarters or a weapons cache. We tried to call close air support (CAS) on it but they had trouble identifying the target. It took a long time and I don't know what the problems were; but while we were waiting I went ahead and called the mission to the artillery, to our platoon, and had them working on the data just in case. When CAS finally could do it – and the target had been dwelling a long time; and when you do that, you start losing effects. The people you want to kill in that target are going to filter out, so you have to hit it pretty quickly. Lieutenant Colonel Peter Newell looked at me and told me to fire the artillery. We had a grid from the UAV but we didn't have an observer on it, so I called BRT [Brigade Reconnaissance Team] and asked them to send somebody down there. I think it was Lieutenant Neil Prakash from the BRT – great kid. He went on to win the Silver Star in Ba'qubah [sic] later on. He got his tank with his wingman and drove across boundary [sic] – way behind enemy lines – so he could lase the target, verify the grid and then observe for me about 800 meters [2,625ft] away. After I was satisfied that we had a good accurate location – because we're firing next to a mosque and I wanted to limit the collateral damage as much as we could. And by the way, CNN had a camera stuck about 12 inches away from my head watching me do all this. So, no pressure, right? I sent a platoon, a 20 rounds fire-for-effect mission – which if you had two guns shooting and you ask for 20 rounds, that's 40 rounds of high explosive (HE) coming down. I asked for a converging sheaf. Usually when you fire artillery you want to get a large dispersion area and the computer will plot the aim points so you can cover more area with your impact and your blast. I asked for a converging sheaf which had one aim point for both tubes, so it would be more accurate and I would have less dispersion of the rounds. The lieutenant called back and told me we had multiple target hits, building's been hit multiple times, there's dust and it's smoking. But there were still some people moving so he asked to repeat the mission, we shot it again, and after that we had no more problems out of that building. I think that was around November 9th. We weren't sleeping a whole lot. The first three days sort of all blended together there.[33]

Note that even though the insurgents are observed and the target data acquired by a UAV, Cobb still sends a human to observe the target, based on his consciousness of collateral damage dangers and, in a perfect image of the media/military relationship, "a camera stuck about 12 inches from my head." There is also a clear sense of computerization at every stage in the process, from the laser designator on the tank through to the computer plotting the spread pattern on the guns. In this technological landscape, the role of the FO appears more as an arbiter of firepower, someone who makes judgment calls about whether to put in train the process that leads to an artillery barrage.

The upshot of this is that whatever the technological advances in artillery fire, humans are still very much in the loop, whether it is on the front line or at much higher headquarters. Indeed, because of the precision of artillery fire it is arguable that the pressures of those who deploy artillery are greater – every shell, in a sense, has to be justified.

Reaching the Horizon – Relevance and Reality

Times are changing in the world of defense technology. In terms of procurement, fast and light are the watchwords for future defense spending, meaning that future weapon systems, including artillery, have to be light enough to transport quickly and easily to a distant battlefield, and fast in terms of their maneuverability and their comparative lack of dependence on a heavy logistical trail.

In the United States all eyes are on the Future Combat System (FCS) program, one of the most revolutionary plans for redeveloping military technology in the last 100 years. One of the best summaries of the FCS program runs as follows:

> Planned to enter service from 2014 hence, the FCS project will completely equip approximately 43 active and reserve brigades with a "system of systems" comprising manned ground vehicles, unmanned ground vehicles, unmanned air vehicles and unattended munitions. Senior service officials have summarized the aim of the FCS project as combining "the lethality and survivability of the heavy force with the deployability of the light force."[34]

This entire system, from the humble infantryman through to the heaviest of the armored vehicles, would be networked through a common information architecture designed to give each element of the system complete battlefield awareness. Of particular relevance to our study of artillery, and that of armor in the previous chapter, is the plan to replace the Abrams tank and Bradley IFV, the Paladin howitzer, the M113 APC, and the M88A2 recovery vehicles, plus several other vehicle types, with a range of eight manned ground vehicles. Each vehicle will be based on a common armored chassis and hull structure, and all will have a top speed of 56mph (90km/h) and range of 466 miles (750km). No FCS vehicle will weigh more than 24 tonnes (26.455 tons), this allowing three to be transported comfortably in a C-17 aircraft. The Abrams, for example, will be replaced by the Mounted Combat System (MCS), which has a turreted 120mm gun main armament. The Bradley will yield to the Infantry Combat Vehicle (ICV). In the case of artillery there are two systems proposed. The Non Line of Sight Cannon (NLOS-C), which will replace the Paladin, has an M776 155mm gun, MRSI capability and a faster rate of fire than the Paladin, and is showing up well in trials. For lighter fires, the Non Line of Sight Mortar (NLOS-M) has a 120mm mortar mounted on its chassis, and the capacity to fire ICMs.

FCS is attracting its fair amount of controversy, particularly in terms of issues of survivability for the MCS and ICV vehicles. This is possibly why the British version of FCS, the Future Rapid Effects System (FRES), is also aimed at re-equipping with a new generation of lighter vehicles, but alongside the retention of Challenger 2 tanks, Warrior IFVs, and AS90 155mm howitzers.[35] Nevertheless, artillery's future may be facing dramatic change.

Like tanks, one of the things that field artillery periodically has to do is justify its existence when air power is taking out many of the long-range targets, or when asymmetric urban warfare questions the value of being able to blast acres of ground into oblivion. Furthermore, artillery is enormously heavy on logistics – for every gun there is a snaking trail of other vehicles and support personnel, providing everything from ammunition carriage to maintenance. The point is vigorously put by Lewis Page, who unfavorably compares the effort of delivering an artillery shell with that of an air-launched weapon:

> The shells ... must normally be driven across hundreds of miles of perhaps inadequately pacified country, at some effort and likely some risk to hundreds of our people. Then we require many hundreds more artillery soldiers, who must get to within a few tens of miles of the target on the ground, to actually carry out final delivery. These soldiers and their very heavy equipment were none too easy to get there in the first place – compared to the strike jets – and have the same massive requirements for fuel, water, food and other supplies as their infantry and cavalry colleagues.[36]

In his analysis Page seems to overlook the cruel logistical chain behind a modern combat aircraft, but even so his attack on artillery carries some weight. From a different perspective, an article by US Army field artillery battalion commander Steven A. Sliwa, published in 2005, poses questions for artillery based on the limited opportunities for artillery deployment in the Iraq war:

> In 2003 as units attacked north from Kuwait into Iraq, they relied on the firepower of all weapons at their disposal and did so with realistic rules of engagement. This allowed the FA [Field Artillery] to impact many battles significantly until the fall

of Baghdad. From DS [direct support] 105-mm to GS [general support] ATACMS [Army Tactical Missile System] fires, all fires were responsive and, from the reports I read, quite devastating. However, with a relatively short campaign at the higher end of the spectrum of warfare, this opportunity to employ our trade was short compared to the current operational pace and intensity in Iraq.[37]

Sliwa goes on to point out that at the end of conventional operations in Iraq, much of artillery's operational requirement ended also. Hence Sliwa recommends that artillery soldiers, for whom "serving as infantry is the reality on the ground in Iraq," take their place amongst other infantry ranks as maneuver troops. (Note that this is nothing new; artillery personnel have a long history of multitasking in everything from transport roles to combat infantrymen.)

Sliwa is not questioning the relevance of artillery *per se*, just the proper use of its troops. Furthermore, our main concern here is not whether Sliwa is correct – such decisions should rightly be made by troops on the ground – but whether, once conventional warfighting is over, the artillery effectively runs out of a job. More seriously, the fact that air power does have a reach beyond anything artillery can accomplish, and can deliver precision close-air support, seems to threaten artillery's long-range raison d'être.

US studies of the use of artillery in Military Operations Other Than War (MOOTW) have indeed raised some serious questions over artillery applications. One major study came in the document "Field Artillery in Military Operations Other Than War – An Overview of the US Experience," published by the Combat Studies Institute Press. Looking at the "Global War on Terrorism", the report makes an important note about the forces initially deployed to Afghanistan:

Of the numerous and diverse weapon systems employed, one was conspicuously missing: field artillery pieces. The omission was deliberate, a decision made by General Tommy Franks, commander of the US Central Command. Taking issue with Chief of Staff of the Army Eric Shinseki, who wanted the Army's Crusader howitzer deployed, Franks argued that the airlift was not available to move artillery pieces into position and that artillery pieces would be affected adversely by the altitudes involved. As a result, howitzer crews who did deploy with the 10th Mountain and 101st Airborne were trained to fire 120-mm mortars, a more mobile weapon than the 4,400-pound M119 105-mm howitzer but one that trailed the M119 in range and accuracy. As the battle in the Shah-e-Kot mountains unfolded, therefore, mortars and air power provided close support for the infantry units committed. The results only fueled the debate that started with the decision to keep the field artillery pieces at home.[38]

The statements contained here were subsequently supported by testimony from Major General Franklin Hagenback, the commander of the 10th Mountain Division, who specifically stated that he did not need 105mm howitzers to accomplish his mission during Operation *Anaconda*. In such operations, mortars were preferable on account of their easy portability and their much smaller logistical trail. Another problem was that while Firefinder counterbattery radars could detect the source of enemy artillery fire, counterfire was limited by the fact that the RoE (Rules of Engagement) needed to confirm that no civilian targets were in the area. Hence the "usual response to hostile fire, therefore, was to launch a patrol or attack helicopter in the area pinpointed by the radar and hope to catch the enemy still in place. The ability of artillery to locate but not dispatch the enemy again raised the issue of artillery's relevance on a low-intensity battlefield." The result was, amongst artillery crews, "disappointment and frustration, triggered in part by doubts as to whether the artillery was accomplishing any good against the hit-and-run tactics of the insurgents."[39]

Although this report might seem to be leading to the conclusion that field artillery has had its day, it also discusses the battle of Fallujah (2004). Here field artillery was used in earnest, including Paladins and towed pieces, and in "most cases, the rounds landed within 5 yards of their target." Paladin SP guns plus a variety of other tube artillery pieces fired over 2,000 rounds into the city. Proximity-fused munitions created precision airbursts to take out targets on rooftops. White phosphorus and smoke were used for screening operations. A US Munitions Executive Summit lecture delivered on February 10, 2005 also noted that "the 155mm and 120mm fires routinely were within 200 meters [656ft] of friendly forces."

We must never think that the only job that artillery performs is destruction: destruction is always required, but its primary purpose might be to provide some effect other than wrecking the infantry's positions or vehicles or killing personnel. Often, the artillery is used to provide an accompaniment to ground-forces maneuvers, such as when a barrage of high explosive or smoke is laid down to mask infantry or armor movements from the enemy. Note that an occasional complaint of artillerymen is that not only do the general public misunderstand the tactical capabilities of artillery, but non-artillery land forces can do likewise. One artilleryman from the US Army, Captain Christopher Lacour, an assistant fire support officer (FSO) for 2nd Battalion, 2nd Infantry Regiment during Operation *Phantom Fury* in Fallujah in late 2004, noted in post-operation interview:

> I don't think the way the infantry trains, say, at the National Training Center (NTC) ever prepares them for how effective artillery really is, so they don't really think in terms of cannon shells. They think in terms of stabbing and shooting and blowing things up with direct fire. They employ mortars but they didn't really understand it at the battalion or brigade level.[40]

Because indirect fire is now king amongst artillery, the humble infantryman at the front line is often physically and therefore mentally more distant from artillery than in previous generations, and it requires education and confidence to get him used to the fact that awesome fire support is often simply a radio call away. Such an attitude can also mask the amount that highly mobile Western forces still rely upon artillery fire to accomplish their conventional missions, and not just on the more media-spectacular air power (which in a sense acts as a form of "flying artillery").

Of course, artillery is still used as a blunt instrument to batter and smash enemy targets, but those armies with the most modern equipment have, as we have seen, experienced a quantum leap in accuracy and proficiency that is every bit as great as the equivalent leap experienced by air power. That quality, combined with the fact that field artillery can respond with fires far more quickly than an air strike and can operate in all weathers, gives artillery a very real battlefield utility. The war in Iraq has shaken up many ideas in the military community, but one danger could be that professional armies are reconfigured principally for MOOTW. Soldiers who fight on the ground must be confident that if the nature of a conflict takes a turn for the unexpected, their combat systems can cope with the demands. Furthermore, they must also be assured that any apparently revolutionary combat systems are not simply driven by their government's account books.

5

POWER FROM ABOVE – MILITARY AVIATION

At 18:00 local time (Greenwich Mean Time plus 4 hours), June 8, 2006, a pair of US Air Force F-16C Fighting Falcon jets were patrolling above Hibhib village, which lay about 33nm (61km) north of Baghdad, near Baquba, in Iraq's Diyala district. The weather was clear and the sky still bright with summer sun. Near the village was a house belonging to Abd al-Rahman, who was alleged to have been the spiritual advisor for the Iraqi branch of the militant group, al Qaeda. Al-Rahman's house among the tall palms was the hiding place of "al Qaeda in Iraq's" self-styled leader, 36-year-old Jordanian criminal Abu Musab al-Zarqawi.

Under the bronze-tinted canopy of one F-16C, the roar of the jet's engine was muffled by the pilot's padded helmet and the hiss of air forced through his oxygen mask. The pilot glanced through his tinted visor at the head up display, or HUD, an angled slab of glass that showed a pattern of green hash marks, lines, arcs, and digits that summarized his navigational heading, altitude, his plane's attitude, and his airspeed. Beneath and to the left of the HUD, a glass panel multifunction display showed data from the plane's engine, hydraulic, and electrical systems. To the right, another screen showed the pilot's flight plan as a series of connected way-points. With a green Nomex-gloved finger, the pilot switched this display to "air-to-ground mode." A light showed, "master arm on," indicating that the weapon system was now active. The pilot flicked another switch and brought up a television image of the ground, wired up to the display from a camera in the fighter's targeting pod.

The pod was a gray cylinder mounted beneath the jet's fuselage. It housed camera optics and other electronics, including a laser range-finder that could reach out to detect the range and bearing of a target from a distance up to 40,000ft (12,192m) away. The laser designator could then "paint" the target with a spot of reflected light, on which laser-guided weapons could home in. On pylons beneath its wings, the F-16C carried a mixed load of 500lb (227kg) Guided Bomb Unit (GBU)-12 laser-guided bombs, and GBU-38 Joint Direct Attack Munition (JDAM) bombs, which were guided by electronics that used data from the Global Positioning System, or GPS, satellites.[1]

The F-16Cs weren't alone. Humming along with them above Hibhib – at north latitude 33 degrees, 46 minutes, 53 seconds; east longitude 44 degrees, 29 minutes, 58 seconds – a turboprop-powered MQ-1 Predator unmanned aerial vehicle, or UAV, kept its all-seeing eye trained upon the house. Prior to the attack, Predator UAVs had had the house under surveillance for more than 600 hours. [2]

In fact, a great many eyes were on the house at Hibhib. The Predators were controlled by pilots and intelligence analysts from the 15th Reconnaissance Squadron at Nellis Air Force Base, Las Vegas, Nevada, thousands of miles from the scene of the action. Also taking part, the US Air Force's 50th Space Wing, at Schriever Air Force Base, Colorado – more than 6,098nm (11,293km) from Baghdad – provided satellite transmission bandwidth that moved crucial information among the F-16Cs, the Predator UAVs, and a command staff directing the action.

Back in the cockpit, the pilot's display screen showed a TV image of al-Rahman's house and the grounds surrounding it. A five-digit counter in the lower right corner of the TV image ticked off the seconds – 000:03 ... 000:02 ... 000:01. Quietly, but for the clicking of its airfoils, a laser-guided bomb plunged down, homing in upon a spot of light reflected from the house. The bomb struck with a brutal shock wave that gutted the breeze-block structure. In a few heartbeats, a second weapon, a JDAM, thundered down, collapsing what remained of the structure and tearing open a great hole in the ground. 500lb bombs are bad news. The house was obliterated. Spat about the crater were a few shattered palm trees and domestic debris – broken furniture, the odd shower shoe.

The intended target, al-Zarqawi, was killed, as were six other occupants of the house, including his wife and child. From a public relations standpoint, the attack was a success, having brought retribution to a person associated with horrific crimes (in 2004 al-Zarqawi had decapitated kidnapped Briton Kenneth Bigley, and was alleged to have been responsible for similar acts of violence). It is perhaps more questionable whether the other occupants of that house, especially the child, warranted death from above.

To be fair, the desire to avoid collateral damage is precisely why so many billions of dollars and so much effort have been expended on technological innovation in weaponry, and on training to enhance the professionalism of modern combat pilots. The image of a sky swarming with bombers, raining down explosive steel on helpless cities, is exactly what air forces are trying to avoid today. Mass destruction has increasingly become politically, strategically, and morally unacceptable. The developed world's defense establishments have found it is often more effective to apply deadly force with precision nearer the bull's-eye of a target, than to flatten a city block to take out a single structure, or even a room within that structure.

The cult of precision may have sold itself too well, however. A perhaps overly credulous perception of infallibility has arisen around the capabilities of modern aircraft and high-tech weapons. While technology has demonstrated amazing feats of pin-point accuracy, there are dark consequences from its use, written in the blood of accidental victims. This is why the attack at Hibhib is interesting: it seems to show both sides of the story. On the one hand, from the point of view

A US Air Force F-16C Fighting Falcon jet, from the 20th Fighter Wing at Shaw Air Force Base, South Carolina, is shown armed with radar and infrared guided air-to-air missiles, targeting pods and carrying two large external fuel tanks for increased range and endurance. (Staff Sgt Suzanne Day: courtesy US Air Force)

An aerial view of the compound where Abu Musab al Zarqawi and six companions were killed in 2006 by laser- and GPS-guided bombs released by F-16Cs. US and Iraqi military vehicles and soldiers are shown in the foreground of a relatively confined area of destruction typical of modern precision weapons. (© Joao Silva/Pool/The New York Times/epa/Corbis)

Between February 13 and 15, 1945, UK and US bombers dropped thousands of tons of incendiary bombs to raze the German city of Dresden. As many as 600,000 people may have been killed in the area bombing raids, which destroyed more than half the city's homes in addition to industrial targets. (© Hulton-Deutsch Collection/Corbis)

F/A-18C Hornets above the USS *Ronald Reagan* (CVN 76) in the western Pacific. During 2001–02, fighters such as these projected power 800 miles [1300km] from the sea into Afghanistan. Exemplifying modern tactical flexibility, more than 80 percent of sorties against the Taliban were launched without scripted attack plans. (Lt Cmdr Tam Pham: courtesy US Navy)

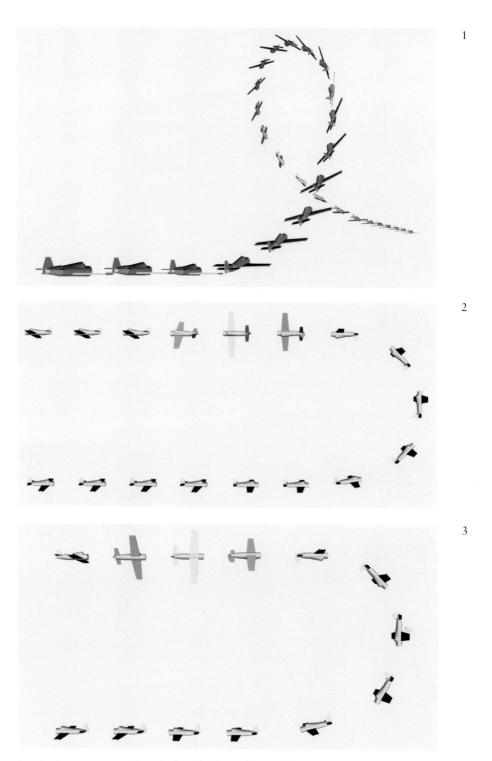

Aerobatic maneuvers, such as the barrel roll (1), the Immelmann turn (2) and the split-S (3), were standardized during World War I. Maneuvering to escape an opponent, or to gain the advantage by getting onto an enemy's tail, proved to be a crucial skill as fighter pilots discovered the aerial combat capabilities and limitations of their aircraft. (© Osprey Publishing Ltd)

On November 8, 2004, US Marines fighting in Fallujah, Iraq during Operation *Phantom Fury* call in an air strike on enemy fighting positions. A close relationship between air power and land forces is one defining characteristic of modern maneuver warfare. (Lance Cpl James J. Vooris: courtesy US Navy)

On March 26, 2003, near an Nasiriyah, Iraq, a US Marine Corps column was accidentally attacked by US Air Force A-10s. The result – 37 marines injured and several vehicles destroyed – underscored the need for better inter-service training, coordination, and identification technologies to reduce the risk of fratricide. (AFP Photo/Eric Feferberg/Getty Images)

The US Navy battleship ex-USS *Missouri* launches a Tomahawk land attack missile during Operation *Desert Storm*, 1991. Equipping the World War II-era dreadnought with cruise missiles for long-range, inland strikes is one example of the adaptive nature of modern naval warfare. (© Roger-Viollet/Topfoto)

A Royal Navy task group, including the carriers HMS *Illustrious* and HMS *Ocean*, on maneuvers in the Persian Gulf. Modern naval units of action such as this are tailored to include the vessels and capabilities necessary to accomplish a specific set of missions ranging from maritime interdiction to all-out war. (Darren Casey © Crown Copyright/MOD, www.photos.mod.uk)

Reminiscent of World War II, US marines disembark a landing craft onto an Egyptian beach during the *Bright Star* exercise. Marines practise amphibious assault landing, although they haven't made one under fire since the Korean War. Such skills could be valuable in scenarios where permission to land is denied. (Brandon A. Teeples: courtesy US Navy)

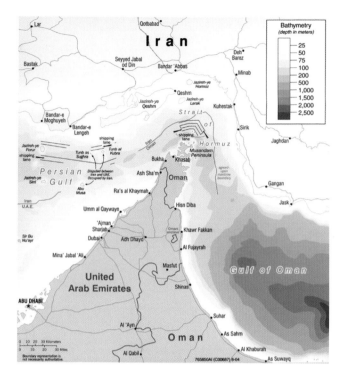

Two thirds of the world's petroleum trade passes through geographic "chokepoints," such as the Strait of Hormuz between the United Arab Emirates and Iran. Often located in regions of political instability, maintaining free flow of trade through such passages is vital to the global economy. (Courtesy University of Texas Libraries)

On October 12, 2000, the destroyer USS *Cole* was bombed by an al Qaeda-affiliated criminal group at Aden, Yemen. The attack was a good example of asymmetric warfare, whereby a determined enemy using relatively low-tech weapons may inflict crippling blows against a larger and technologically superior foe. (© Reuters/Corbis)

Weapons such as the Soviet SS-N-2 Styx and newer generations of anti-ship cruise missiles have proliferated through the world arms market. These pose a major threat to naval forces operating near to coastal launch sites (such as the Strait of Hormuz) or within range of missile-armed fast attack boats.

The 1960s-era Soviet *Osa*-class fast attack craft, armed with Styx anti-ship missiles, represented a significant naval threat. Syrian *Osa*s fought at the Battle of Latakia, October 7, 1963. Israeli naval vessels used electronic warfare technologies to jam the *Osa*s' weapon systems, and even managed to sink one of the craft. (D Beech © Corbis)

The US Navy Aegis cruiser the USS *Shiloh* launches an SM-3 missile during a test. Aegis consists of a command and decision computing system; the SPY-1D(V) radar; the Mk 41 vertical launch system; and various weapons. These elements together create a potent fleet air warfare combat system. (Courtesy US Navy)

A US Navy submarine launches a missile during a test in 1996. The Navy's 14-boat ballistic missile submarine force constitutes a major element of the US nuclear deterrent. Submarine-launched ballistic missiles may be armed with multiple thermonuclear warheads, each independently targeted against an adversary's political, military, and economic centers. (© Roger-Viollet/Topfoto)

During World War I, German soldiers attack through a cloud of tear gas. Chemical agents such as tear gas were deployed over broad areas of the battle front to drive off defenders and to obscure the movements of the attacking force. Every nation during World War I made use of chemical munitions. (©Topham Picturepoint/TopFoto)

Modern police special weapons and tactics units often employ tear gas to disperse or blunt the offensive capability of a rioting mob. As a staple, non-lethal weapon the effects of an irritant such as CS gas are usually temporary. (©TopFoto/ImageWorks)

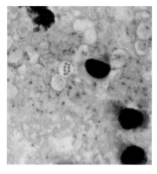 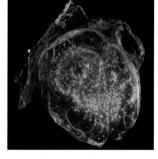 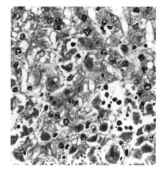

(1) Anthrax (*Bacillus anthracis*)　　(2) Small pox (*Variola vera*)　　(3) Ebola (*Filoviridae ebolavirus*)

Some micro-organisms have been made into weapons for use on the battlefield and in other venues. Lethal when inhaled, anthrax was used in the still-unsolved 2002 postal service attacks in the United States. However, the difficulty in handling, storing, and deploying biological agents somewhat diminishes their role as weapons. (Courtesy US Dept of Health and Human Services, Centers for Disease Control and Prevention)

A Kurdish victim of an Iraqi chemical bombing in 1987 displays the damage caused by blister agents to her feet, which means that she cannot walk. Blister agents such as mustard gas were used by both sides in World War I and continue to be a significant threat worldwide. (© Carlos Cazalis/Corbis)

On August 6, 1945, the American B-29 bomber, *Enola Gay*, dropped a 4,000kg (8,818lb) atomic bomb (nicknamed "Little Boy" by its creators) on the Japanese city of Hiroshima. Although only a fraction of the power of today's thermonuclear hydrogen bombs, the "Little Boy" uranium bomb destroyed half the city and killed *c.* 80,000 people. (NARA)

Gas masks, protective outer clothing, gloves, and over-boots are part of a modern soldier's standard equipment, given the global proliferation of chemical and radiological weapons capabilities. Human endurance limits significantly affect the amount of time a soldier can spend in his mission-oriented protective posture (MOPP) kit. (© Michael Macor/San Francisco Chronicle/Corbis)

of the US Air Force, the successful attack, after a lengthy and frustrating manhunt on the ground, represented the best of what modern air power could bring to the art of war. Advanced technology – in the form of satellites and UAVs, jet fighters, and precision-guided munitions – comprised a powerful, responsive, precise weapon system that had hunted its elusive target and cut him down before he was even aware of the hounds on his trail. As the US Air Force's Lieutenant General Michael W. Peterson, chief of warfighting integration, put it:

> That is exactly what happened when we went after [al-Zarqawi]. We knew he was in the area. Because we knew to expect that kind of target to pop up, we placed a continuous string of aircraft in motion. We could have picked any of them to go prosecute the target. That's what warfighting integration is all about: moving from a manual, step-by-step approach with seams and gaps, to a continuous flow seamlessly moving from sensing, to acquiring, to finishing the target.[3]

On the other hand, the bombs, however precisely guided, had killed others along with their intended target.

It may be difficult from the dead child's point of view to argue that collateral damage, even in this limited case, was kept to a minimum. In this chapter we will consider how modern air power calls for a complementary, complex, and sometimes controversial relationship between technology and human beings. We shall see how the impressive capabilities of a modern air force have evolved, and how these capabilities remain far from perfect, perhaps for the very reason that fallible human beings are, of necessity, at the center of the system.[4]

Introduction

At the turn of the 20th century, aviation pioneers like Orville and Wilbur Wright (1871–1948 and 1867–1912 respectively) and Louis Bleriot (1872–1936) had very little idea of how their newly invented flying machines would change the modern art of war. In 1909, when Bleriot stepped down from his No. XI monoplane at Dover, the warfighting significance of his flight was hardly noticed, such was the sporting excitement over his having successfully crossed the English Channel in a flimsy flying crate. Nevertheless, what his 37-minute flight had done – from a military perspective – was to render very nearly impotent the defensive barrier of the English Channel, the same barrier against which would-be invaders had broken themselves, again and again, for centuries since the time of William the Conqueror (c.1028–87). Bleriot's flight implied what would be demonstrated more conclusively in the decades to come: that aircraft could not only conquer the human limits of land and sea forces, but could also project power – directly, in the form of guns and bombs, or indirectly, in the form of air-lifted infantry, paratroops, and supplies.

During World War I many of the combatants from Europe and Asia Minor developed air corps, or groups within their armies, equipped with aircraft and staffed by trained pilots, aviation mechanics and engineers. These corps matured into distinct armed forces independent from the army chain of command, such as the Royal Air Force. Others however, held on longer to the traditional association between air power and the army. This was the case with the US Air Force, which wore a green and khaki uniform as the Army Air Force until 1947 when it became an independent service.

The most advanced modern air forces typically include both strategic aircraft (long-range bombers) and also tactical aircraft (fighter and attack planes.) As we shall see, the once hard line between these types is blurring, as heavy bombers and supersonic jet fighters begin to cross into each other's mission roles. One example of this crossover can be seen today in the skies over Afghanistan, where US strategic bombers – such as the B-1 Lancer and B-52 Stratofortress – have joined attack helicopters and fighter planes to provide tactical air support for NATO troops fighting Taliban insurgents in the mountainous terrain. Huge strategic bombers that were designed during the 1950s and 1960s to thunder into Soviet airspace carrying thermonuclear weapons now hover over a battlefield, awaiting the radio call from an infantry unit in need of a pin-point strike against an enemy stronghold.

While the role of naval air power is addressed more specifically in Chapter 6, it may be useful to note here that the air arm, as it is called in British service, or the air group, as it is the US, has long been viewed as an extension of a fleet's combat strength. Although lacking the heavy strategic bomber capabilities of a land-based air force, naval aviation has the great advantage of access. A fleet's aircraft carriers may be positioned in international waters, close to a conflict zone. From these floating bases at sea, the naval air force may reach far inland without relying on basing rights or other permission to operate, which a land-based force must have. For example, when the Turkish government refused basing rights to the US-led invasion force poised to attack Iraq in 2003, the war plans had to be rewritten, with air and land forces redeployed south to Kuwait and Saudi Arabia. Meanwhile, naval air forces already present in the Persian Gulf and the Red Sea were able to launch some of the first air strikes against Baghdad. The combat power of a US Navy aircraft carrier strike group (including its cruise missile-armed warships) and air wing may be greater than that of an adversary nation's entire air force. A modern *Nimitz*-class nuclear-powered aircraft carrier hosts a hybrid air wing of 72 tactical aircraft, including fighter/attack planes, some of which are capable of carrying as heavy a weapons load as some World War II-era bombers.

Whether on land or at sea, air forces may be organized along the traditional lines of an army's cavalry units. In place of horses, flights of three or more airplanes comprise the basic building blocks of air squadrons. In turn, the squadrons are brought together in wings, or air groups (analogous to the cavalry troop). Both land-based and naval air forces include a variety of different types of aircraft, each dedicated to different missions and support functions. While the fighters and bombers have the most glamorous roles, other planes are equally crucial to military success. Aerial tankers and logistics planes carry the life-blood of fuel and supplies, not only for the air force, but also for the army as well.

As technologies in aircraft, weapons, sensors, and other mission systems have improved, specialized aircraft have evolved to meet the requirements of a great variety of missions. There are scout and spy planes, such as the venerable high-altitude U-2, that are designed for photo reconnaissance. Other surveillance planes, such as the EP-3E Aries II, collect electronic signals intelligence that may be useful not only during a conflict, but, better still, may help influence events so that combat might be avoided altogether. An example of surveillance aircraft preventing conflict is the Cuban missile crisis in October 1962, when U-2s and other planes photographed the deployment of Russian missile sites in Cuba. Once published, the photographs forced a political confrontation that ultimately resulted in the withdrawal of the missiles and cooling of tensions that had heated with the US deployment of intermediate-range missiles at Izmir, Turkey in 1961.

Still other aircraft cross the boundary between reconnaissance and attack. Antisubmarine warfare planes such as the Nimrod are equipped with powerful sensors that allow them to detect the magnetic signature of submarines beneath the surface of the ocean. Once the maritime surveillance plane detects its target it may be able to attack, or it may help direct the weapons of other warships or aircraft against the enemy submarine.

Some planes are specialized in the art of electronic warfare. Modern high-tech weapons and sensors depend upon transmissions – such as those of radar or laser energy – to detect, track, and attack targets. Aircraft like the EA-6B Prowler fly with special equipment to jam and disrupt these signals, protecting the fighters and bombers that they escort from being attacked by air defense artillery and missiles.

In the air, squadrons of fighters and bombers are often commanded by specially trained crews aboard other planes, such as the E-3 Sentry airborne warning and control, which has a powerful radar system that is able to track many aircraft simultaneously. Because of the speed and technological complexity of modern warfare, airborne command and control has become a necessity, especially in large operations such as Iraq and Afghanistan. The E-3 acts like a flying air traffic control center, following the movements of everything in the sky over the battlefield, coordinating the flight paths of attack squadrons, and directing, or vectoring, interceptors in case enemy fighter planes appear.

In war, one advantage of an air force is that it can seize and hold the "high ground" of the sky. Nevertheless, it took time for the full potential of aviation to make itself clear to those who pioneered its military application. The experience of World War I demonstrated that to win on the battlefield, one had to get control over the sky. For example, the Imperial German Air Force, the Luftstreitkräfte of World War I, showed the destructive potential of strategic bombing in 1916 when it shadowed the skies of the UK with Zeppelins and Gotha bombers. In the 1930s, the Third Reich's Luftwaffe linked air power and land maneuver to create a new kind of warfare: *Blitzkrieg*, fast maneuvering, armored ground forces supported by tactical air strikes that broke open an enemy's defenses and quickly exploited the breaches before a counterattack could be organized.

Aerial reconnaissance – spy planes – provides other military and naval forces with information, not unlike the way a skilled boxer "reads" his opponent and counters his telegraphed punches. As American baseball legend Walter Johnson put it, "You can't hit what you can't see." Reconnaissance planes collect pictures and intercept radio transmissions, helping a friendly force stay ahead of an enemy's decision cycle.[5]

In battle, a crucial strength of air power is that it may strike where an enemy is weakest, to his flanks and rear and along his supply lines. Bombers and attack planes may blind or paralyze an enemy's military forces – by destroying his communications and command centers, smashing up airfields and roads – causing the enemy to divert his defenses from another possible point of attack.

However, for the bombers to be successful (and indeed for an army to be free to maneuver on the ground without fear of being blasted back into its foxholes), the air force's fighters must first achieve air dominance. Dominance requires that the enemy be not only overpowered, but completely denied the use of the sky. US Air Force General Joseph W. Ralston put it this way:

> We used to talk about the requirement for air superiority and spoke in terms of kill ratios – accepting US losses to kill enemy forces. Now, what we want is not air superiority, but air dominance. ... The consequence of having air dominance means that all the other things we are trying to do – at sea and on the land – are made possible because these operations are not going to be halted by opposing enemy air forces ... No US soldier has been killed by an enemy aircraft in over 40 years – and we don't intend to relinquish that advantage.[6]

To achieve this, fighters interdict the enemy's air force, either in the air or on the ground at its bases. In the pursuit business, as it was called during World War I, fighters chase and intercept enemy aircraft, destroying them in aerial combat – sometimes engaging in great pitched battles, such as the "dog fights" that became legendary during World War II. Having cleared the skies of enemy planes, the dominant air force is free to do its work, striking enemy targets and supporting the army (or the navy) maneuvering on the surface.

When working with the infantry or armored units on the battlefield, air forces provide firepower for several different kinds of missions, including deep strike (moving well forward of the line of battle to hit the enemy's army), and close air support (perhaps the most challenging type of air-to-ground mission because here is the greatest risk of accidentally hitting friendly forces – fratricide).

Reconnaissance: Scouts and Spies

In the early days of military aviation, airplanes were used for scouting. Biplanes like the Curtiss Jenny would be sent out ahead of an infantry or cavalry unit to study and report on enemy activity, or to spot for artillery. In the latter role, airplanes were carrying on a tradition that had begun in the 19th century with many armies deploying balloons at or near the front lines of a battle to help the big guns adjust their fire onto a target. Early planes carried no weapons, other than the personal arms of the pilots. At the beginning of World War I it was not unheard of for Allied and Imperial German airmen to shoot at one another with their pistols from the cockpits of their otherwise unarmed Bleriot No. XIs and Etrich Taubes. Later in the war, especially by 1917, both sides had developed much more heavily armed aircraft, such as fighters with Vickers and Spandau machine guns, and large bombers carrying high-explosive and incendiary bombs. Yet, even as the fighters and bombers have risen in prominence, reconnaissance has remained a primary role for the military airplane.

The continued reliance upon airborne reconnaissance speaks not only of the suitability of airplanes for the job, but also of the vital role that information plays in modern conflict. Today, achieving air dominance is inextricably tied to the achievement of information dominance. The most technologically advanced aircraft and weapons are useless without data and other information products that enable pilots to act, or weapons to find their targets. It may be difficult to overstate how important good data is to the modern air force, given the dependence of electronic weapon systems upon accurate information for navigation and for programming target coordinates. This dependence, as some observers have pointed out, has produced a more flexible kind of air power that is capable not only of hitting vital fixed targets – like command centers, power plants, and other infrastructure – but of finding and fixing its sights upon moving or elusive targets as well: getting closer to the "holy grail" of strikes that occur in real-time, without delays for intelligence collection, dissemination, etc. "In the three years between Yugoslavia (1999) and Afghanistan (2001), American airpower went from being effective principally against fixed targets like infrastructure to routinely devastating moving formations using real-time intelligence."[7]

Part of achieving information dominance is the development of Intelligence, Surveillance, and Reconnaissance, or ISR, capabilities that take advantage of air power's inherent high vantage point. ISR technologies include satellite-based communications systems, radar, and electro-optical (such as infra-red radar and laser) sensors. These technologies are carried as payloads aboard spy planes, spacecraft, and unmanned aerial vehicles (UAVs.) Collecting data, processing and then disseminating information is what enables the weapons delivered by the fighters and bombers actually to destroy their targets. Smart bombs are only as smart as the data with which they have been programmed. A war game hosted in 2003 at the US Army's War College at Carlisle Barracks, Pennsylvania, highlighted the importance of ISR capabilities in modern warfare. Typical of such war games post-Gulf War, the situation concerned two fictitious nations, named "Korona" and "Kartuna," whose situations were not unlike those of Kuwait and Iraq in 1991. Set in the near future, the game's conflict featured some of the technologies being developed today, including sensors capable of penetrating foliage and other camouflage to reveal hidden targets. In the game, victory went to the force that had access to and made the best use of high-quality information.

After proving themselves in World War I, reconnaissance aircraft matured during World War II, with photo-reconnaissance missions being carried out by stripped-down fighters that flew high and fast over enemy territory. The pilots of these planes took great risks, armed only with cameras in hostile airspace, with speed as their only defense. During the Cold War (1946–92), new generations of jet-powered surveillance planes evolved. These aircraft were capable of high-speed, high-altitude flights and carried advanced surveillance cameras and other technologies for aerial spying. Perhaps the most famous of the early jet spy planes was the U-2 (developed during the 1950s at the "Skunk Works" laboratory at Burbank, California), which, five decades after its first flight in 1955, is still gathering intelligence.[8]

On the airfield, the modern U-2S is a large, gracefully lined (if slightly ungainly-looking) aircraft, more than 62ft (19m) long, with an enormous wingspan of approximately 103ft (31m). It has a mission range of 3,500nm (5,633km), and may carry a payload of more than 41,000lb (18,600kg) to an operating altitude of greater than 70,000ft (21,336m), according to the US Air Force. The U-2 flies so high, and on such long missions, that its pilot must wear a full pressure suit and sealed helmet, similar to those worn by astronauts during spaceflight.

Perhaps no reconnaissance mission in history is more famous than the ill-fated flight of Captain Francis Gary Powers in 1960. Powers' U-2 was collecting photographic intelligence inside the Soviet Union. His aircraft was tracked by Soviet air defense radar and knocked out of the sky over Sverdlovsk, Russia, by an SA-2 missile.

All of my engine instruments were normal up to the time of the explosion, which I both felt and heard. I also saw an orange flash or glow when I looked out. I cannot be sure but I think the explosion was behind and to the right of the aircraft. I felt no impact of anything against the airplane itself, therefore I think the shockwave from the explosion caused the damage. I can only guess at what happened after that. I am of the opinion that the tail of the aircraft came off first, causing the nose to drop sharply resulting in the failure of both wings. The cockpit and what was left of the aircraft tumbled and finally settled into an inverted spin causing 'G' forces, which made it impossible for me to use the ejection seat. I finally got out of the aircraft at 14,000ft [4,267m] or below. I give the altitude because my parachute opened automatically and it is set to open at 14,000ft [4,267m]. It opened immediately upon my getting free of the aircraft. I was at maximum altitude, as stated in the trial, at the time of the explosion. This altitude was 68,000ft [20,726m].[9]

Soviet-made surface-to-air missiles also destroyed U-2s over China and Cuba, leading to a number of defensive upgrades and prompting the development of lower-risk assets, such as satellites and UAVs, to get the pilot out of the line of fire. Nevertheless, the U-2 has continued to prove its value as a workhorse of intelligence collection, flying more than 800 missions during Operation *Desert Storm*.[10]

Today, ISR missions are carried out by many types of manned and unmanned aircraft and spacecraft. The wet film cameras of World War I aerial reconnaissance have evolved into a new generation of digital imaging systems including thermal cameras and sensors capable of detecting and designating targets, as well as of assessing battle damage following an air strike. The U-2S's updated mission payload also includes a synthetic aperture radar, or SAR, which is a kind of radio frequency, or electromagnetic wave, sensor. SAR is able to create extremely accurate and detailed pictures or maps.

Other ISR aircraft and systems are designed for signals intelligence – or electronic eavesdropping – such as the US Navy's EP-3E Aries II. The EP-3E (derivative of the P-3C Orion maritime patrol aircraft) is a propeller-driven plane fitted with classified electronic equipment to collect radio waves and other electromagnetic transmissions that may provide valuable scraps of intelligence about a potential adversary and his military capabilities or political intentions.

Though, for obvious reasons, the EP-3E mission profile is normally secretive, one mission in 2001 made front page news out of an Aries II and its crew. On April 1, 2001, off the coast of China, two People's Liberation Army Air Force J-8 Finback fighters intercepted an EP-3E piloted by US Navy Lieutenant Shane Osborn. One of the J-8s, piloted by Wang Wei, and Osborn's EP-3E collided over the South China Sea. The impact almost immediately destroyed Wang's fighter and crippled the Aries II.

After the J-8 hit us, we snap-rolled right away [to port] and went into an inverted dive. I thought we were dead, no question! There was a sick acceptance. We were upside down for 8,000ft [2,438m] before we were able to regain any control. It was plenty of time to consider death ... Ditching the plane would kill everyone. I knew it wasn't going to hold together indefinitely. I had to find a place to land immediately.[11]

Osborn and his aircrew survived to land at Lingshui air base, on Hainan Island, China. The crew endured 11 days in captivity before being returned to the United States, along with their damaged EP-3E. According to a source in the US State Department, the Chinese government had the opportunity to make a thorough inspection of the EP-3E during the incident, including the possible disassembly and study of some of the electronic signals sensor and data processing equipment aboard.

Unmanned Aerial Vehicles (UAVs)

Increasingly, unmanned systems are replacing manned aircraft in ISR data collection missions. Since the debut of remotely piloted reconnaissance and attack drones in the 1940s and 1950s, robot aircraft have provided lower risk alternatives to piloted aircraft on some missions. A significant milestone in the history of UAV reconnaissance was the first flight of the MQ-1 Predator over the Balkans in 1995. Since that time, these drones have become major contributors to ISR missions over Afghanistan and Iraq. Predator television and thermal cameras have provided dramatic images of the battlefields in Southwest Asia. For example, during 2001–02 Predator UAVs regularly flew over the so-called no-fly zones in Iraq. These UAVs captured images of the Iraqi integrated air defense system, including missile and gun fire against coalition aircraft. The footage was used in the United Nations to justify arguments for stiffer sanctions against Saddam Hussein's government and, ultimately, as part of the case for going to war with Iraq in 2003.

Somewhat controversially, UAVs were used in Operation *Allied Force* not only to collect intelligence, but also to identify and illuminate targets for destruction. For example, the US Army's RQ-5 Hunter UAV was equipped with a laser target designator and used to spot targets for laser-guided weapons to destroy.

Some pilots at first resisted the idea of having a robot provide targeting capability. One senior US Air Force aviator from a Vicenza, Italy-based F-16 squadron that flew over Kosovo in 1999 said he would not release weapons to a target that a robot had identified. He argued that the potential for error by a machine left unacceptable uncertainty about the target's disposition. Until the UAV's target location and discrimination capabilities were matured, that particular pilot would not trust the robot to "lase" (capture) a target for weapons release. Nevertheless, in the decade since that conflict, the technology has become more convincing for many.

UAVs have evolved with great rapidity from being strictly reconnaissance assets to blurring the line between reconnaissance and attack, taking direct action in combat. For example, in Afghanistan in 2002 a Predator UAV shot an AGM-114 Hellfire missile at the vehicle of a suspected al Qaeda leader.[12] Moreover, during Operation *Anaconda* in 2002, the Predator proved its mettle as a close air support asset, using its missiles to provide suppressing fire against Taliban militia while soldiers on the ground moved to better fighting positions. "With the Hellfire, the Predator can watch a potential target for hours then, single-handedly, eliminate it without ever having to put an aircrew at risk. It's like combining the best of our reconnaissance and strike assets for a fraction of the cost and almost none of the risk."[13]

High altitude UAVs, such as the RQ-4A Global Hawk, are designed to fly enormous distances and cover large territories with their sensors. The US Air Force developed the Global Hawk to fly missions of 12,000nm (22,224km) in range, at an altitude of 65,000ft (19,812m) feet. Global Hawk's chief selling point is its ability to remain over an area for 24 hours or more, providing an unblinking eye with which to survey an area of approximately 40,000nm (74,080km) of the Earth's surface.

Steel Rain: Bombers

If artillery is the "king of battles," perhaps no other manifestation of air power is as familiar, or as feared, as the bomber. Traditionally, the bomber groups are the strategic arm of an air force, its heaviest firepower, encompassing the platforms and missions that may deliver the most decisive effects. Italian air power advocate Giulio Douhet wrote of strategic bombardment in the 1920s:

> The selection of objectives, the grouping of zones, and determining the order in which they are to be destroyed is the most difficult and delicate task in aerial warfare, constituting what may be defined as aerial strategy. Objectives vary considerably in war and the choice of them depends chiefly on the aim sought, whether the command of the air, paralyzing the enemy's army and navy, or shattering the morale of civilians behind the lines. The choice may therefore be guided by a great many considerations – defense, political, social and psychological, depending upon the conditions of the moment.[14]

During World War II, the bomber was used as another kind of artillery, with the emphasis on delivering weight or mass of fire. In crude terms, the greater the tonnage of explosive applied to the problem, the more assured the solution. Given the limited accuracy of unguided bombs the mass of fire concept made a kind of grim sense: the more bombs one dropped, the better the odds of destroying a target. Due to the technological constraints of World War II-era aircraft and weapons, the air forces of the 1940s had no choice but to take the massed fire approach to strategic bombing. One had to send a lot of aircraft to get the job done, and that meant a lot of aircrew at risk and a lot of bombs being dropped in places where civilians lived and worked. There were devastating ethical and political consequences; perhaps the most sobering example is the still-controversial fire bombing of Dresden, Germany, February 13–15, 1945, in which more than 25,000 people (most of them civilians) may have been killed.

The massed fire approach may have been deadly, but it was also inefficient. On a mission in June 1944, 47 B-29 Superfortress bombers raided the steel works at Yawata, Japan. According to a US Air Force researcher, only one bomber succeeded on the mission, hitting the factory with just one of its load of eight 500lb (227kg) bombs.

> This single 500lb [227kg] general purpose bomb represented one quarter of one percent of the 376 bombs dropped over Yawata on that mission. [In another mission,] it took 108 B-17 [Flying Fortress] bombers, crewed by 1080 airmen, dropping 648 bombs to guarantee a 96 percent chance of getting just two hits inside a 400ft by 500ft [122m by 152m] German power-generation plant.[15]

The National Museum of the US Air Force records that the maximum payload of a B-29 was 20,000lb (9,072kg), which would translate to 40 500lb (227kg) bombs. However, because of the range and fuel requirements of missions flown against the Japanese main islands, the B-29s often carried less than their maximum payload.

During World War II it also cost a great deal – in lives and resources – to get the bombers close enough to their targets to do their work. For example, the B-29s that dropped the first atomic bombs had to stage their attacks from the Marianas Islands, such as Tinian, which is approximately 1,500nm (2,778km) from Hiroshima, Japan. The campaigns to take the Marianas and the island of Iwo Jima, which is within 650nm (1,205km) of Tokyo, were vital to the Allied air force's strategic bombing operations, which between 1944 and 1945 finally brought Imperial Japan to its knees. However, the campaigns were costly in the extreme for the soldiers and marines of the amphibious assault forces that carried them out.

On June 15, 1944, US Marine Corps amphibious tractors growled up out of the sea and onto the hot beach at Saipan Island, initiating a vicious fight that cost the lives of more than 3,400 marines and US Army soldiers and 4,300 Japanese troops. The nearby island of Tinian fell after another week of fighting in which 355 Americans and more than 5,500 Japanese were killed. On July 21, US soldiers and marines stormed Guam in a operation that cost 1,350 American and 18,377 Japanese lives. And in perhaps the most dramatic moment in the bloody parade, the airfields at Iwo Jima finally fell on March 25, 1945, after a bitter 36-day brawl that killed approximately 8,000 Americans, wounded more than 19,000 others, and destroyed almost 20,000 Japanese.[16]

Once suitable airfields had been secured, the B-29s were close enough to wreak havoc on the Japanese economy and war-making industries, as well as on the civilian population. It was to be massed fire on an enormous scale. According to a lecture delivered by Dr David Rogers, a professor of geological engineering at the University of Missouri, "Virtually every city in Japan with more than 35,000 people was destroyed in area-wide bombing by B-29s between November 1944 and July 1945 ... On the night of 9–10 March 1945, 325 B-29s hit Tokyo, each carrying seven tons of incendiaries. The raid destroyed 16 square miles [41 sq km] of Tokyo and killed upwards of 115,000 Japanese ... By war's end 3,895 B-29s had been built, accounting for 29,150 combat missions."[17]

During the inter-war years of the 1920s and 1930s, engineers of the future Axis and Allied powers launched parallel programs to improve their precision bombing capabilities. These projects proceeded to focus on two essential factors: 1) the modernization of aircraft sighting systems; or 2) the development of specialized aircraft types that delivered dumb bombs more accurately.

This may be an oversimplification – better airframes vs better bomb sights – but the discussion that follows highlights two important technological vulnerabilities that spurred requirements for aircraft and weapons able to strike from greater range and with more precise effects. This discussion may provide some perspective on the development of precision-guided munitions such as the laser-guided bombs and JDAMs we have today.

An example of precision through airframe design can be seen in the development of the German Ju-87 Stuka dive bomber. Introduced in 1936, the gull-winged Ju-87 had won the Luftwaffe's dive bomber competition, and was designed expressly for precision bombing. The German air staff had deliberately foregone investment in heavy four-engine, long-range strategic bombers in favor of accuracy at the tactical level.[18] The Stuka boasted extremely strong wings and a powerful Jumo engine on an airframe able to withstand the stresses of steep dives, and strong enough for six-G (six times the force of gravity) automatic recoveries. During the Spanish Civil War, and later in the campaigns across Poland and Russia, the Stuka became a symbol of the German *Blitzkrieg*. The Stuka had limitations, however, beginning with its limited weapons-carrying capacity: either one 1,100lb (500kg) bomb under its fuselage; or one 550lb (250kg) bomb under the fuselage and four 110lb (50kg) bombs under its wings. But the important factor from the German air staff's point of view was that the Stuka could deliver its weapons with surgical precision, given a skilled pilot at the controls. The Ju-87B-1 (the model in service in 1939–40), "was to prove effective in the hands of expert pilots, who, in dives of eighty degrees to within 2,300ft (701m) from the ground, could deliver a bomb with an accuracy of less than 30yds (27m). Even average pilots could achieve a 25 percent success rate in hitting their targets, a far higher proportion than that attained in conventional, horizontal attack bombers."[19]

Nevertheless, the Stuka was to prove ill suited for some of the tasks to which it was put.[20] The Stuka had been the terror of Dunkirk, but had not fared well against the Hurricanes and Spitfires it met during the Battle of Britain (July 10–October 31, 1940). On August 18, 1940, after heavy losses, the Luftwaffe ceased flying the Stukas over the British Isles. Especially vulnerable on its slow, automatic recovery climb, the ferocious Stuka proved to be a pussy cat for pilots like Royal Australian Air Force ace Clive Caldwell, who served with No. 205 Squadron in North Africa. During a single sortie in his P-40 Tomahawk, on December 5, 1941, Caldwell sent down five Ju-87s with bursts of .303in and .50cal machine-gun fire.

> We attacked the JUs from the rear quarter. At 300yds [274m] I opened fire with all my guns at the leader of one of the rear sections of three, allowing too little deflection, and hit No. 2 and No. 3, one of which burst into flames immediately, the other going down smoking and went into flames after losing about 1,000ft [305m]. I then attacked the leader of the rear section ... from below and behind, opening fire with all guns at very close range. The enemy aircraft turned over and dived steeply ... opened fire again at close range, the enemy caught fire ... and crashed in flames. I was able to pull up under the belly of one of the rear, holding the burst until very close range. The enemy ... caught fire and dived into the ground.[21]

The Allies focused on other means of delivering precision airborne firepower. Having invested millions in the development of large, four-engine strategic bombers, the search was on for technologies that would improve the accuracy of these heavy platforms, which dropped their bombs from high altitude to minimize vulnerability to antiaircraft guns. "The US Army Air Force typically designated a radius of 1,000ft [305m] as the 'target area' aim point for the 'pickle-barrel' bombing conducted in Europe."[22] Dropping bombs into a pickle barrel – an expression coined by journalists in the 1930s – referred to a bomber's alleged (though seldom achieved) accuracy. Placing a bomb into something that looks as small as a barrel from 20,000–30,000ft (6,096–9,144m) altitude was a feat wholly reliant upon precision equipment. One such device was the top secret Norden bomb sight, developed for the US Navy and the US Army Air Force in the 1920s. Key to the Norden's success was a rudimentary computer that calculated bomb release trajectory, although this depended upon the operator's having accurately input airspeed, altitude, and other data by hand. The Norden system coupled the bombardier's optical sight with the aircraft's autopilot – an electronic device that controlled the plane's ailerons, elevator, and rudder trim. In operation, the Norden sight actually steered the plane, such as a B-17, to the aim point selected by the bombardier. However, one of the important limitations of the Norden system was that its optics would be difficult to use if the target area were invisible due to cloud cover, haze, or smoke.

The strategic bomber of today is no longer the blunt, massed fire instrument it was in the days of the B-17s and B-29s. Advanced aircraft design, targeting electronics and weapon guidance systems give modern weapons a much better chance of hitting and destroying their intended targets, from beyond the reach of air defenses. Because of its technological advantages, modern air power is increasingly protected by the shield of distance, and may act with greater assurance of destroying an intended target, without damaging the civilian homes, schools, or hospitals that may be located nearby.

The US Air Force's 509th Bomb Wing – heir to the group that dropped the atomic bombs on Hiroshima and Nagasaki, Japan in 1945 – can sortie its B-2 Spirit stealth bombers from Whiteman Air Force Base, Missouri, to fly around the world (refueling at a tanker a few times along the way), deliver a payload of 40,000lb (18,144kg) of ordnance, and return in 30–50 hours. Instead of nuclear weapons in their bomb bays, the B-2s now more frequently carry precision JDAMs and conventional air-launched cruise missiles that follow satellite data and digital map images to precise aim points on their targets. The B-2's design, a lifting body derived from experimental aircraft that were first drawn up during World War II, helps absorb and redirect enemy radar energy, making the bomber difficult to detect.

Other, more conventional bomber designs have recently been given a new lease of life with the advent of the JDAM and other precision munitions. The venerable B-52, affectionately called the Buff, or "big ugly fat fucker" by its crews, first flew in 1952. The Buff was designed as a long-range strategic bomber, capable of thermo-nuclear combat, "toe-to-toe with the Russkis!" to quote Major T.J. Kong from Stanley Kubrick's film, Dr Strangelove.[23] When retired in the second decade of the 21st century, the B-52 design will be roughly 80 years old – on the face of it, that's comparable to the US Air Force in 2007 still flying the P-26 Peashooter, although today's B-52H is more sophisticated than earlier models.

Despite its pedigree as a nuclear war horse, the B-52H has been seeing a lot of action in Central Asia as a strike and close air support platform – notably during Operation *Anaconda* (2002). A typical weapons load for the Buffs over Afghanistan included 2,000lb (907kg) JDAMs and 27 Mk 82 500lb (227kg) bombs. During *Anaconda*, the Buffs patrolled above Tora Bora, releasing JDAMs on-call, in direct support of Special Forces and other ground units.

Today's soldier, fighting with dedicated air support from B-52s and other attack planes, has only to key the microphone of his radio to bring down tons of exploding steel upon his enemy's head. The effect of a B-52 bombing raid, using even the humblest conventional munitions, is dramatic, as recounted by a soldier of the US Army's 82nd Airborne Division. Sam Ryskind, who had served in Kuwait and Saudi Arabia during Operation *Desert Storm* (1991), said he remembered feeling pity for the Iraqis, entrenched as they were then in fixed fighting positions, and being hammered into dust by B-52 bombing raids.

> As I sat in my foxhole, this bombardment was taking place eight to 12 miles [12–19km] away. These planes were flying over, non-stop. And from where I was, I couldn't see the bombs dropping, but I could feel the "boom, boom, boom-boom, boom," coming down. After a day or two of this – it was incessant – I was thinking, "If I can feel this here; what is it like to be right under it?" I could feel the deep explosions, the rumbling like a low frequency vibration, making things tremble. [The sound] wasn't coming from the air; it was the whole ground that was emitting this sound. It is extremely hard to imagine how people could endure it.[24]

Precision-Guided Munitions (PGMs)

During World War I, Imperial Germany experimented with wire-guided drones, remote-controlled unmanned aircraft loaded with explosives that were used to attack enemy ships. In World War II, the Germans matured the technology into the radio-guided "Fritz" missiles used in 1943 to sink the Italian battleship, the *Roma*. In 1944, the US Navy flew its own radio-controlled drone, a B-24 Liberator bomber packed with Torpex explosive, to attack a German airfield on Heligoland Island. Despite these sometimes successful experimental weapons, their relatively high cost, complexity, and unreliability worked against the widespread adoption of high-tech precision weapons until after World War II.

Far less costly, although less accurate, are conventional iron bombs, or "dumb bombs" as some pilots today refer to them. Essentially these weapons are unchanged from the way they were during World War II: fused artillery shells – steel cases of varying size, filled with high-explosive. The accuracy of a gravity bomb is measured by its CEP: PGMs – such as laser-guided bombs and JDAMs – have much smaller CEP circles than unguided weapons. For example, a modern general-purpose (unguided) Mk 82 500lb (227kg) bomb has a CEP of more than 328ft (100m). A laser-guided bomb cuts that error radius to less than 25ft (8m). The JDAM's satellite-assisted inertial guidance can deliver the warhead with greater precision still, to within 43ft (13m). Weapons using image correlation and high-data rate processing computers may strike within an even narrower radius, of 7ft (2m) or less.[25]

Modern PGMs first came onto the scene toward the end of the Vietnam War in 1972. US Air Force and US Navy attack jets had made many futile sorties – and lost many aircrews – against targets like the Thanh Hoa Bridge, on North

Vietnam's Song Ma River just 85nm (158km) from Hanoi. Hundreds of general-purpose bombs, and even some PGMs, such as the television-guided AGM-62 Walleye, had failed to destroy the bridge, also called the "Dragon's Jaw." On October 6, 1972, the first generation of a new breed of PGM made its debut. A group of F-4 Phantom II jets from the US Eighth Fighter Wing, the "Wolf Pack," opened Operation *Linebacker* with a mission that finally destroyed the bridge. The Phantom crews had launched 24 laser-guided bombs, including GBU-10s, to bring down the western span of the bridge, in a coordinated attack that destroyed a series of valuable highway and railroad river crossings.

The laser-guided weapons heralded another shift in the balance of power between offense and defense in aerial warfare. These bombs used seekers (an optical sensor at the front end of the bomb) to sense the direction and intensity of reflected laser light. The seeker then sent electrical signals to the bomb's control surfaces, which aerodynamically adjusted the weapon's flight to its target.

By 1975, the United States had launched more than 28,000 laser-guided bombs in Southeast Asia. According to US Air Force historian Dr. Richard P. Hallion, "17,000 of the weapons hit their aim points, a 61 percent hit rate."[26] During *Desert Storm* in 1991, however, far more unguided weapons than PGMs were used. For example, a total of 152,295 single-warhead bombs (at a total cost of almost $99 million); 57,421 cluster munitions (at a total cost of more than $328 million); contrasted with 9,271 laser-guided bombs (at a total cost of more than $282 million); and 5,255 AGM-65 Mavericks of various types, guided by infrared or other electro-optical electronics (at a total cost of almost $48 million).[27]

Like any human-designed system, there are imperfections in PGM technology. For example, laser guidance is vulnerable to jamming from inclement weather and perhaps the oldest defensive technology of all, the battlefield obscurant (such as dense smoke.) Smoke not only masks maneuvers but also foils penetration by laser range finders and target designators crucial to guiding weapons onto their targets.

Following the Gulf War, with its smoky infernos of vandalized Kuwaiti oil fields, the US Navy and US Air Force jointly developed a new guidance system that would be impervious to weather and heavy smoke. The result was the JDAM – which is a general-purpose dumb bomb fitted with a new tail section containing smart guidance electronics and, crucially, a GPS-aided inertial navigation unit. JDAM tail kits have been developed for many classes of general-purpose bombs, including 2,000lb (907kg), 1,000lb (454kg), and 500lb (227kg) bombs.

In the JDAM, known coordinate data is entered into the weapon guidance system's microprocessor. The coordinate data is communicated to the JDAM through an electronic interface with the aircraft's weapon system computer. Usually, this interface is a cable linkage attached to the wing or fuselage pylon (also called a hard point), upon which the bomb hangs. Target coordinates are checked for accuracy against signals from the GPS satellite constellation, and, thus corrected, fed into the JDAM's inertial navigation unit. The guidance unit uses electronic signals to command the bomb's control surfaces to adjust the weapon's course as it falls toward its target.

Increasingly sophisticated buried and "hardened" targets – reinforced concrete and deeply buried bunkers – have inspired the development of weapons and targeting systems capable of finding and striking the specific, hidden weaknesses of hardened structures. Such vulnerabilities may take the form of a bunker's ventilation duct, or a revetment's protected entry. Still other variants of unitary warhead weapons are designed to penetrate reinforced structures with delayed fuses, which are capable of punching through re-bar concrete or rock, detonating only after reaching the vital interior of the structure.[28]

PGMs will hit their targets or aim points, provided there are no technical flaws in the system. However, controlling those weapons are human beings, who make mistakes. In the "kill chain" – finding, fixing, tracking, targeting, engaging, and assessing – there are multiple opportunities for errors to be introduced into the system. For example, during Operation *Allied Force* (1999), in May NATO jets accidentally attacked the Chinese embassy in Belgrade, killing three and wounding 20. In that case, the targeting process had included not only several layers of the defense establishment but also the bureaucracy of the NATO alliance, according to Pentagon officials. Another NATO error occurred when aircraft struck a hospital and market in Nis, Yugoslavia, killing 15 civilians.[29]

The incidents had been the result of failures of intelligence, according to the US Department of Defense.[30] The US Air Force allegedly had outdated maps. Apparently, the only charts available showed the Chinese embassy in a different location in the city. Then-US Defense Secretary William S. Cohen described it this way:

> There were several mistakes made in identifying and locating this target. First, they failed to correctly locate the target on their maps. The Procurement Directorate was near the building they had targeted. Second, the building that they did target turned out to be the Chinese embassy, but their maps inaccurately located the embassy in a different part of Belgrade.[31]

As noted above in the section on reconnaissance, a precision strike is only as good as the information that supports it. In 2003, a US Air Force B-1 Lancer bomber attempted to strike a building in Baghdad's al Mansour district, based on rapidly processed intelligence that Saddam Hussein was at that location. Colonel (ret.) W. Patrick Lang on April 8, 2003 told the American television program, *The News Hour with Jim Lehrer*:

In fact this was a meeting which had only an hour or two of duration then ... the strike would have to take place in the time bracket in which it was estimated these people would be there. And, because of everything lining up like this, it's easy for this airplane in flight to reprogram this [GPS] guided set of bombs on the right building. And if they gave them the right coordinates and Saddam was there, the chances he's alive is [sic] not very great.[32]

The "Bone" (B-1) had dropped four bombs – 2,000lb (907kg) JDAMs – that had struck the coordinates at which they had been aimed. But Hussein had been elsewhere. The failure to kill Saddam – even though the aircraft and weapon systems had functioned as desired – underscored the Achilles heel of the precision strike: the accuracy and freshness of the information with which a weapon is programmed and a strike carried out. With greater precision in weaponry comes an equally greater demand for precise intelligence.

As the wealthier nations continue to invest in precision-strike capabilities, other more controversial weapons are likely to remain in service. The military usefulness of these weapons may outweigh their drawbacks, at least from an air force's point of view.

Cluster Bombs

One of the best examples of an equally loved and hated weapon is the venerable cluster bomb. These weapons generally are canisters that contain a number of smaller bombs, or submunitions, which are released when the weapon falls to a certain altitude or strikes the ground. Cluster bombs are area-effect weapons and not PGMs. The 1,000lb (454kg) CBU-87 cluster bomb unit is viewed by the military as an important weapon against infantry and soft-skin (non-armored) vehicles. The CBU-87 dispenses hundreds of BLU-97 (Bomb Live Unit) submunitions which are fragmenting, shaped charges with incendiary characteristics that are detonated by proximity fuse (meaning they go off when they sense objects nearby). Sometimes, not all of the submunitions released by a cluster bomb canister explode; some (perhaps 5 percent or more, according to the US Department of Defense) remain on the battlefield as a significant source of unexploded ordnance, or UXO, a hazard for bomb disposal units to address.

> The United States prides itself on the low dud rates of its munitions; however, all explosive ordnance has the potential to become UxO. Therefore, commanders and staff should plan for dud munitions and their impact on future maneuver [sic] or cleanup after hostilities are complete. The actual hazard area produced by UxO depends on the type and density ... A fire mission of 36 Multiple Launch Rocket System rockets could produce 1,159 (36x644x5 percent dud rate) UxO hazards in the target area. A B-52 dropping a full load of 45 ... CBUs (with each CBU

containing up to 650 submunitions) may produce 1,462 (650x45x5 percent dud rate) ... Scatterable mines can produce a significant amount of UxO hazards. For example, the bomb live unit [or BLU] -91 and -92/B Gator System can dispense hundreds of mines covering an average area of 200m by 650m [656ft by 2,133ft] in a matter of seconds.[33]

Scatterable mines and submunitions are equipped with self-destruct mechanisms, which may destroy the small weapons within hours or days of their release. However, the US joint armed forces explosive ordnance disposal community notes that self-destruct may fail, and thus the dud weapons become a limiting factor in the speed or combat effectiveness of the maneuvering force[34] (see Chapter 2). UXO on the battlefield may slow down or halt infantry and armor on the advance, potentially checking one of the key advantages of modern armies: the speed with which they are able to attack and then push through an opponent's lines of defense. UXO may reduce the combat power of a land force by occupying, wounding, or damaging soldiers and vehicles as they move through an area with live scatmines.

Despite some negative characteristics, cluster bombs have proven to be militarily useful as area-denial weapons – constraining an enemy's movements – and as antiarmor weapons. For example, the US Air Force successfully employed a kind of cluster munition called the sensor-fused weapons, or SFWs, which are heat-seeking bomblets.

> Each bomblet [floating down by parachute] releases ten warheads that spew out four "skeet" armor-piercing weapons that descend by parachute, scanning the battlefield with infrared sensors designed to detect armored vehicles. Upon detecting targets, these smart submunitions fire explosively formed penetrator slugs that strike tanks from above, where their armor is weakest. The 40 skeets within a single SFW can search for and engage stationary and mobile ground combat vehicles within a 30-acre area. The SFWs released from a Wind-Corrected Munitions Dispenser (WCMD) dropped by a B-52 bomber on 2 April 2003, were the first use of these munitions in combat. Consequently, by the time the 3rd Infantry Division reached the outskirts of Baghdad, only about a dozen Iraqi tanks opposed it. They were quickly dispatched in what may have been the only traditional tank encounter of the war.[35]

Nevertheless, cluster bombs have been controversial in other venues. In June 2006, Israel aroused domestic and international condemnation for its use of cluster bombs in its air and artillery campaign in Beirut. The Israel Defense Forces had intended to direct its air strikes and artillery fire against the Lebanese strongholds of Hezbollah, following the militants' kidnapping of two Israeli soldiers. However, contrary to the wording of a resolution from US Congressman E. Clay Shaw, Jr, the cluster bombs and other munitions Israel fired into Beirut did not "corrupt the rocket capabilities of Hezbollah," nor did the Israeli use of the weapons appear to have been "carefully adjusted to successfully carry out any rescue attempt to obtain the kidnapped soldiers."[36] According to an article printed in the *Washington Post*:

> The [United Nations] has estimated that Israel dropped as many as four million of the bomblets in southern Lebanon during last year's war with Hezbollah, with as many as 40 percent failing to explode on impact. Activists say children can be attracted to the unexploded weapons by their small size, shape and bright colors or shiny metal surfaces. As many as 60 percent of cluster bomb victims in Southeast Asia are children, the Cluster Munition Coalition said.[37]

The antilandmine/cluster bomb activist organization, Handicap International, claims that more than 360 million cluster munitions have been released globally and have caused more than 11,000 casualties – 98 percent of whom are civilians, according to the organization's web site.[38]

Incendiaries

Flame weapons – from the terrible WWI-era flame throwers and the development of incendiary bombs designed to set cities afire to the infamous image of a napalm-burned child fleeing an inferno during the Vietnam War – inspire controversy. The WWII horrors of Dresden, the fire bombing of London and Japanese cities remain illustrative in the discussion of the political and moral implications of such weapons. However, the military utility and legality of flame weapon are matters of ongoing debate.

The Organisation for the Prohibition of Chemical Weapons does not classify military munitions whose effects are derived primarily from "thermal energy" as chemical weapons.[39] The Convention on Certain Conventional Weapons, Protocol III, on Prohibitions or Restrictions on the Use of Incendiary Weapons, prohibits the use of incendiary weapons against civilian populations or against military targets located within concentrations of civilians.[40] So, within the boundaries of these agreements, flame weapons are not strictly banned under international law. There is little doubt of the military utility of these weapons, in terms of the physical as well as psychological impact on an enemy. However, the use of fire as a weapon can be a public relations challenge, to say the least.

Take the case of napalm, for example. It may be academic, but the US military draws a distinction between the original napalm (a WWI-era invention that used a gasoline mixture – naphthalene – jelled with a palm tree extract, hence the term "napalm") and the fill used in today's Mk 77 Mod 5 500lb firebomb, which is a mixture of jet fuel and polystyrene. According to the US Department of Defense and the Department of State, "all napalm in the US arsenal had been destroyed by 2001." Strictly speaking, this is a true statement. However, in 2003, new controversy ignited amid rumors that US forces had in fact used firebombs in Afghanistan. The Mk 77, which has similar effects to original napalm – burning fuel that is thickened to adhere to its target – was used against enemy positions in 2003, according to the DoD.

However, the distinction between "old" napalm and the Mk 77, academic or not, was enough to prompt US Army General Tommy R. Franks, then-commander, US Central Command, to answer a reporter's question in a December 2001 press conference thus, "We're not; We're not using the old napalm at Tora Bora."[41] The reporter had asked specifically about napalm, not the newer mixture delivered by the Mk 77; and Franks had not attempted to clarify the reporter's understanding of the technology.

Other fire weapons have generated similar controversy. For example, white phosphorous, or WP, munitions are often employed as battlefield markers or obscurants as their rapid oxidization produces clouds of white smoke useful in identifying enemy positions, or in preventing the enemy from detecting one's movements on the ground. As incendiaries, WP or "Willy Pete" bombs are useful for burning or melting down military equipment such as armored vehicles and artillery tubes. WP has controversially been labeled as a chemical weapon by some observers owing to the tenaciousness with which this substance burns and may remain "live" even underwater or embedded in the ground, or in a person's body cavity. According to the US Army Corps of Engineers:

> Unreacted white phosphorous will ignite when it comes in contact with air, producing flame and dense smoke. Touching unreacted white phosphorous can cause severe burns. Reacting white phosphorous can sometimes form a "skin," protecting itself from further exposure and reaction with air. Puncturing this "skin" will cause the unreacted material to ignite, producing flames and smoke.[42]

However, there remains widespread public misunderstanding about the WP technology, and a frustrating lack of educational engagement by the military on the subject. The confluence of these factors has resulted in misconceptions about the purpose and use of these weapons, and apparent errors in reporting. For example, media reports that WP was used to cause extensive casualties at Fallujah, Iraq, in Operation *Phantom Fury* (November 7–December 23, 2004) have not been substantiated by the record, although controversy persists. According to a US Army surgeon, at Fallujah there were "no casualties whatsoever from any white phosphorus in our sector."[43] The army surgeon added that the bodies found after the fighting subsided were blackened by decomposition rather than white phosphorus.

Directed Energy

Future air forces may have other unconventional weapons, including "directed energy" devices. The military uses the term "directed energy" in reference to a family of electrically-powered unconventional weapons technologies – lasers, microwave emitters and the like – that may be useful to defend against artillery shells, ballistic missiles, and enemy personnel. In the offensive role, such weapons may be used to disrupt or destroy satellite communications and surveillance, and to shoot down hostile aircraft. The points in favor of directed energy are that the technology almost eliminates the need for a fire-control solution – the mathematical plot that describes the angle or arc of a weapon's trajectory in order to ensure that it intersects with that of its target. Because lasers and other forms of directed energy move at the speed of light, there is no need to "lead" the target, as one does with shot fired at a clay pigeon, for example. Of course, some of the same limitations – environmental and tactical – apply to the use of directed energy as to the use of laser targeting devices, including safety considerations for those operating the weapon.

The intensity of a directed energy weapon may be tuned like a rheostat to achieve precise effects. For example, ground vehicle mounted microwave emitters have been developed that project a beam capable of causing intense pain at low settings, and perhaps horrific burns if dialed up to maximum power and held upon a target for a given period of time.[44] Having been exposed to a small demonstration of these devices, the author Hunter Keeter can say that the sensation is not unlike being scalded, quite suddenly, over the entirety of the skin area exposed to the beam. Some experts contend that the moral implications of directed energy weapons have not been fully explored. "Like many conventional munitions, indiscriminate use of lasers or lethal microwaves can produce widespread collateral damage and [weapon of mass destruction]-like effects similar to the conventional munitions used on Tokyo and Hamburg during World War II."[45]

Fighters: Pursuit and Attack

The fighter aircraft was born out of the need to protect vulnerable reconnaissance scouts and bombers. The B-52s and B-2s would be incapable of doing their work if fighters had not first gained and secured their access to the airspace. From the beginning – 1915, when Anthony Fokker's Eindecker E.3s, with their synchronized Spandau machine guns, were the scourge of European skies – the lethal game was on, and it didn't take long for everyone to start learning the rules. For fighters the classic contest is between pilots and airplanes, where the aerobatic capabilities and limits of the machine and its weapons make the difference between life and death.

In 1914, the combatants in Europe had just a few frontline combat aircraft: Germany had 232, France had 138, and Britain had 113. By war's end in 1918,

France had 4,500, Britain 3,300 and Germany 2,390.[46] Just as it was in the trenches below, the war in the sky over Flanders was about attrition: killing more of the enemy's aircraft than he killed of your own.

Dog Fight

For wartime fighter pilots of World Wars I and II, life could be short and violent. Despite the image of "knights of the air" jousting over the trenches, the real picture of aerial combat was about ambush, shock, and the fleeting fractions of a second within which one could slip up and die. These battles were quite properly called "dog fights," because the apparent chaos of battling aircraft resembled a pack of pit dogs tearing into each other.

On September 14, 1918, over Mars-la-Tour, France, Arthur Raymond Brooks – then a young second lieutenant with the 22nd Aero Squadron, 2nd Pursuit Group, American Expeditionary Force – won the US Distinguished Service Cross for heroism in a dog fight. Brooks, in his lone Spad XIII, *Smith IV*, had been jumped by eight Fokker DVIIs from the elite Jasta 11 unit, one of the best fighter aircraft designs of World War I. Despite the odds, by determination and aggressive skill, and not a little good luck, Brooks destroyed two enemy planes that day, fighting the Germans from 5,000ft (1,524m) nearly to the ground, and driving off the others.

> We were still at 5,000 meters, or about three miles up. The 'we' in this case referring to myself and eight red-nosed [Manfred von] Richthofen's [Jasta 11 Flying] Circus DVIIs bent on eight-to-one shots. I figured I had come to the end. I was frankly scared, but in spite of much high tension and futile yelling at the top of my voice, I calculated by nature of my training, I suppose, to get as many of the Fokkers as possible before the inevitable. Twice I tried to ram them ... one red-nosed 'night mare' came in from my right ... I had just time to dip enough to see his features before I let him have a few incendiary bullets. I turned upon another and after a short, close burst was satisfied a second had quit.[47]

While it would be an overstatement to say that the dog fight is a thing of the past, the picture is quite different today. Air combat engagements at great distances are the norm, with the loser perhaps having never seen the enemy fighter or the guided missile that has just killed him. Here again, sensor technology (specifically, radar) has played a pivotal role in the transformation. During World War II, the first radio detection and ranging, or radar, equipment came into general use. Originally designed to direct naval gunnery, and also to provide early warning for air defense, radar has evolved into a crucially important tool in aerial combat. Modern radar mounted inside the nose cone of a tactical fighter is able to track small and fast moving targets with great accuracy. In the dog fighting recounted above by Rickenbacker and Brooks, the pilot's eyes were his only means of keeping track of the enemy – a huge challenge in the case of Brooks' fight, where he put himself up against eight enemy fighters. The modern jet fighter's weapon system helps its pilot keep track of a number of targets, and prioritizes these according to their proximity or the threat they pose (if, for example, the enemy plane has illuminated the pilot's aircraft with its targeting radar).

Additionally, the command and control aircraft, noted earlier, are essentially flying radar platforms. These carry large airborne early warning (AEW) radar systems – such as that carried by the NATO E-3 Sentry, or the Royal Australian Air Force's 737-700 Wedgetail. AEW radars are capable of tracking and controlling the action of dozens of aircraft simultaneously. AEW crews identify targets and direct, or vector, the fighters to intercept them. This vectoring often occurs when the targets and fighter/interceptors are well beyond one another's own onboard sensor range. This has an effect similar to the 19th artillery spotter balloons mentioned earlier, telegraphing an artillery battery with directions how to improve its aimed fire. The airborne command and control aircraft's radar system enhances the squadron's or group's situational awareness. This improved awareness has the effect of boosting the lethality of the attacking air force, and helps fighter pilots stay a few moves ahead of their opponents, who may not have the same comprehensive picture of what is happening around them.

As fighter pilots begin more advanced stages of their training, they are taught aerobatic maneuvers, some of which have been in the "rule book" of dog fighting since the beginning of military aviation. For example, German ace Max Immelmann during World War I perfected a reversal maneuver called, appropriately, the Immelmann turn, which is still taught to pilots of the most advanced jet fighters. This maneuver, like a "wingover," requires the pilot to climb, turn until the airflow is nearly stalled from his wings and then fall through the turn to level out facing 180 degrees from his original heading. This maneuver may turn the tables on a tailing enemy, if he has allowed too much distance to open between himself and the chased pilot. Another classic maneuver is the split-S, which essentially is the inverse of the Immelmann, reversing direction from a dive rather than from a climb (see diagram in the picture section).

Whatever the maneuver, one of the oldest lessons pilots are still taught is never to fly straight and level in battle. This is a sure way to be killed, by presenting the easiest of targets to an enemy. There is a price to be paid for maneuvering, however. Climbing and turning cost valuable energy, which could prove a deadly expense in combat. To stay ahead of the enemy, a pilot not only tries to gain the advantage of height and to get on his opponent's tail; he also tries to build up more energy (moment) than his opponent. Losing too much energy in a maneuver can give the enemy the upper hand, or can lead to other fatal mistakes: stalling out, falling into a spin, or otherwise losing control of the aircraft.

Guns

Of course, information, radar sensors, and even high performance aircraft don't do the actual killing in combat. As Douhet put it:

> What determines victory in aerial warfare is fire power. Speed serves only to come to grips with the foe or to flee from him, no more ... It will be enough to keep in mind the following basic principle, the same one which governs warfare on land and sea: inflict the greatest amount of damage in the shortest possible time.[48]

The firepower of a modern fighter is spectacular. Many still carry machine guns or cannon, with some of the most common automatic weapons being much improved versions of weapons developed during World War II, firing explosive shells. Nevertheless, even with computer control and radar targeting, hitting a fast moving target like an enemy jet fighter with guns requires considerable skill. Among the most common aircraft guns used by the US Air Force and US Navy, and others, is the M61 Vulcan, a six-barrel 20mm rotary cannon.

That modern fighters in US service still carry guns is somewhat controversial, given that air combat today often takes place beyond visual range, well outside the effective range of most guns. The reason the weapons persist is that during the Vietnam War (1965–73) American air forces came to regret the missile-only design of the F-4 Phantom II fighter. This workhorse of the war, designed for both land-based and naval squadrons, carried out air-to-air fighter missions as well as air-to-ground attack missions. The later models of the Phantom had a cannon pod fitted to increase their firepower when missiles proved unreliable in close quarters fights with more agile Vietnamese MiGs. Since then, all US fighters (including the F-16 and the larger F-15, as well as the Navy's F-18 Hornet) have been designed with internal guns. However, the aerial combat record from Vietnam to the present shows that guns have not shot down as many enemy aircraft as missiles.

> F-15s and F-16s in service have 46 kills – all of them with missiles. The Air Force has had exactly two gun kills since the F-16 came on the line – both of them against helicopters shot down by the A-10's 30mm GAU-8, a gun specifically designed to kill tanks! ... [according to] Dr. Daniel L. Haulman's "Table of USAF Aerial Victories by Guns and Missiles," draft (Maxwell AFB, AL: Air Force Historical Research Agency). Even in Vietnam, missiles got 89 kills, and aerial guns only 43. In the first Gulf War [1991], guns got two helicopters, and missiles downed 33 airplanes. Missiles registered all of the kills in Kosovo [1999].[49]

Guided Missiles

The effort to develop more lethal and precise weapons for aerial combat resulted in radar and infrared, or IR, guided missiles. As is clear in the passage quoted above, the missile has fundamentally changed the character and lethality of aerial combat. It has increased the range at which a fight may occur, and has bettered the odds of destroying the target over bullets alone. For example, a typical AIM-9 Sidewinder-series IR guided missile attacks its target with a 20–40lb (9–18kg) blast-fragmenting warhead that throws a spread of supersonic, razor-sharp fragments to shred the metal, flesh, and bone of an enemy and his aircraft.

During the 1950s, homing technologies began to emerge in two basic types. The Sidewinder was among the first heat-seeking (infrared, or IR) missiles. The AIM-9 was first flown at the US Naval Ordnance Test Station China Lake, California, in 1953 and by 1958 the AIM-9B version of the weapon had been used in combat (Republic of China F-86 Sabres downed 11 Communist Chinese MiG-17 fighters with the new weapons). In combat, an IR missile's seeker will detect a target's heat source and send a warning tone to the pilot's headset. The sound is a sort of growling buzz that grows louder as the IR source becomes more visible to the missile's seeker. Once launched (the pilot announces his missile launch as "Fox two!" which is NATO radio parlance for a heat-seeking missile launch), the IR missile seeks out the heat source, usually the hot jet exhaust of a target airplane.

Other types of air-to-air missiles are radar- (radio frequency, or RF) guided. The AIM-7 Sparrow-series missiles use semi-active RF homing technology. Basically, radar guidance works by homing in on electromagnetic waves reflected from the target. When RF waves reflected from a target are read and calculated by the launching aircraft's weapon system, a missile "lock-on" is achieved.

AIM-7 missiles are semi-active radar homing, meaning the missiles follow reflected RF waves that their host aircraft's radar has emitted at the target. AIM-7s were first used in combat over Vietnam. In 1965, US Navy F-4s used Sparrows to shoot down two North Vietnamese MiG-17s. Early versions of the AIM-7 had trouble tracking maneuvering targets and fears of fratricide – that the missiles might accidentally lock on and attack a friendly plane after launch – limited the range at which the missiles could be launched. This was one of the factors that contributed to the development of a gun pod for the F-4: if one had to get in close to fire the missile safely, one might as well have a gun to shoot as well.

In combat, an aircraft using radar-guided missiles first develops a firing solution by using its radar to detect a target. Setting the radar in search mode, the aircrew sweeps the sky with RF energy. Once a target is detected, the aircrew may switch the radar to acquisition mode, narrowing the beam toward the signal reflected from the target. The reflected signal is read by the aircraft's fire-control computer – which calculates the target's range, altitude, course, and speed. In tracking mode, the radar's narrowest but most powerful beam follows the target as it maneuvers. When the radar has enough information to follow the maneuvering target, the radar has locked on. The pilot keeps his plane's nose cone (and the radar antenna beneath it) aimed at the target (usually within plus or minus 60 degrees) to maintain the lock.

In air-to-air mode with the AIM-7, the pilot's HUD displays a reticule – a small green diamond – superimposed in space over the location of the target. When the reticule lines up on the target, the missile may be manually or automatically released, at which time the aircrew will announce, "Fox one!" (NATO language for a radar-guided missile launch.) Because the electronic systems that manage radar-guided air-to-air combat are complex, some aircraft are designed to have a second crewman, called a Radar Intercept Officer (RIO), whose task is to manage the radar- and RF-guided missile weapon system, while the pilot focuses on flying the plane and shooting the IR missiles or guns at close range.

The latest versions of the Sidewinder have improved flight performance and a redesigned guidance section. The new guidance section allows the Sidewinder to be launched from "off-bore sight," meaning the missile is fired at a target that is not aligned with the host aircraft's nose or the seeker head of the missile. A helmet mounted cueing system links the pilot's field of view with his weapon system. Wearing the cueing sight on his visor, the pilot has only to turn his head and look at his target to keep the weapons lock, even if the target is no longer aligned with his weapons' IR seeker. The advantage of this system is obvious. As a dog fight progresses, an enemy may maneuver (perhaps making a split-S), reversing direction to get away. But the off-bore sight missile seeker enables a pilot to launch against the target as it passes abeam or astern, literally striking backhand blows at the enemy as he attempts to escape.

Case Study: Gulf of Sidra Incident, Libya 1989

An example of missile combat in action occurred on January 4, 1989, off the coast of Libya, when two US Navy F-14A Tomcat fighters from the USS *John F. Kennedy* (CV 67) fought two Soviet-built Libyan MiG-23 Floggers. The F-14A aircrews downed their opponents with AIM-7 and AIM-9 missiles. The following extract is from a transcript of the Navy cockpit communications during the engagement. The transcript picks up just as the MiGs and F-14As have begun to close at one another aggressively. The Tomcats' aircrews are designated "Gypsy" 207 and 204; "Closeout" is an E-2 Hawkeye AEW and command and control plane.[50]

Gypsy 207 Radar Intercept Officer: Master arm on; master arm on. [A beeping sound is heard, warning the F-14A's aircrew that the weapon system is active.]

Closeout: Ok, good light.

Gypsy 207 Pilot: Good light. [The pilot confirms that the weapon system is functioning properly.]

Gypsy 207 RIO: [The RIO is lining up his radar scope onto the target for a lock.] Ok, centering up the 'T.' Bogie has jinked [maneuvered] back into me again; 16 miles [26km]. At the center of the dot.

…

Closeout: Say [his] Angels. [Altitude, in 1,000ft (305m) increments]

Gypsy 207 RIO: Angels are at nine [9,000ft (2,743m)].

…

Gypsy 207 RIO: [As the MiG closes range, the RIO launches an AIM-7 missile] Thirteen miles. Fox one! Fox one!

Gypsy 207 Pilot: Ah, Jesus! [The pilot is heard breathing heavily into his oxygen mask.]

Gypsy 204 Pilot: Breaking right. [The MiG evades the AIM-7.]

Gypsy 207 RIO: Roger that. Ten miles. He's back on my nose. Fox one again! [The RIO launches a second AIM-7.]

…

Gypsy 207 RIO: Six miles; six miles.

Gypsy 204 RIO: Tally two; Tally two! Turning into me. [Gypsy 204 will attack the second MiG-23.]

Gypsy 207 RIO: Roger that. Five miles … Four miles.

Gypsy 207 Pilot: [One of the MiG-23s launches an AA-7 Apex radar-guided missile.] Ok, he's got a missile off.

Gypsy 204 RIO: [Gypsy 204 turns sharply to evade the MiG's missile.] Breaking right.

Gypsy 207 Pilot: [The second AIM-7 arcs across the sky and connects with the first Flogger.] Good hit! Good hit on one!

Gypsy 207 RIO: Roger that. Good kill; good kill! [The MiG falls, sputtering flames; its pilot ejects.]

Note that the first AIM-7 had been launched at 13nm (24km), and that the closest approach of the aircraft was roughly 4nm (7km). This is a bit further out than the in-your-face dog fighting of World War II. A few seconds further on in this engagement, Gypsy 204 launched an AIM-9 heat-seeking missile to destroy the second MiG-23. Although the Flogger had passed in front of Gypsy 207's weapons as well, the pilot could not launch his own AIM-9s because he did not receive a tone. His missile's seeker may have malfunctioned and failed to detect the MiG, or the target may not have presented a strong enough heat signature to Gypsy 207's IR sensor.

Intercept

Even as technology improves, one constant in air combat – which may make the difference between success or failure, life or death – is disciplined aggression. Sometimes this can lead to unexpected consequences. This was the case in an incident in 1968, when two US Air Force planes collided during a training exercise.[51]

During the Cold War, Soviet "Bear" bombers would often fly from Siberia toward US airspace, testing the responsiveness of the North American Aerospace Defense Command and the Alaskan squadrons. Not infrequently, US Air Force fighters would be launched to encounter the Russians. Sometimes, the Russian crews would shine bright lights into the Americans' cockpits or make insulting gestures. Usually the rivalry was more or less sporting, but beneath the surface, the tension of possible confrontation was very real. In a genuine attack, the bombers would be carrying thermonuclear bombs to wipe out American or Canadian cities. For their part, the fighters would be carrying live missiles, including nuclear-tipped AIM-4s, to destroy the Bears before they could penetrate more deeply into North American airspace.

To prepare for the ultimate test, the crews of Alaskan Air Command would often tangle with one another to simulate actual intercept procedures. A typical scenario would include a flight of B-57 Canberra bombers playing the role of the Russians. Interceptors, such as F-102 Delta Daggers ("Deuces"), would be scrambled from an alert base. A powerful network of ground radar stations would manage the intercept, tracking the bombers and directing the F-102s to fly a specific vector (compass heading), airspeed and rate of climb to place them in the best position from which to launch missiles against the bombers, if it came to that.

The radar controllers would direct the Deuces toward the formation of bombers coming in from the Kamchatka Peninsula: in this case in 1968, two Canberras masquerading as Bears. Each of the fighters is assigned one of the bombers. This is a one-chance, head-on contest with the opponents closing at a blistering 1,200 knots (2,222km/h). Once the intercept pass is set up, if it fails (if the fighters cannot launch their missiles on the attack run), they will rocket past the bombers and lose too much energy circling back to catch them from behind.

The F-102 pilots are waiting to close within 10,000ft (3,048m), when they will snap up to a steep climb, release their weapons, and roll away, putting the belly of their planes between them and the flash from the low-yield nuclear air-to-air missiles that will destroy the bombers. But the missiles need time to acquire the target signal from the Deuce's radar, and to count down and arm their fuses before launch.

The aircrew in the Canberras know the limits of their opponents' weapon systems and are playing for seconds. They are doing their best to put RF jamming energy on the Deuces rushing up at them, preventing the radar from locking on and arming the missiles.

In the cockpits of the F-102s, the pilots have raised their helmet visors and have put their faces down into their radar scopes. They are not looking up at the cloudy sky rushing past but are tracking the intercept by watching the glowing cathode ray tube display of their instruments. Seconds are passing and one of the Deuce pilots is trying to put his weapon system's cursor on the target image of a Canberra. But the jamming signal is too strong. The cursor will not lock onto the image, and the missile will not arm.

The pilot is trying to get his weapon system to track off the jamming signal from the Canberra, attempting to use its own electronic countermeasures against it. But the missile will not arm. Closing fast, the pilot considers his options. The doors of the F-102's missile bay have direct-fire, unguided rockets built in; these could be salvoed at close range to wreck the targeted bomber. But there will be only one pass, and it has to be lined up perfectly ...

Suddenly, the pilot looks up from his radar scope. The broad wing and engine nacelle of the Canberra covers the Deuce's windscreen. The bomber is right above him! The F-102 pilot rolls away, too close. An elevon – one of the control surfaces at the trailing edge of the Deuce's delta wing – strikes the Canberra in the roll, cutting off its wing.

The bomber rolls over, mortally wounded, and its crew ejects. The Deuce has lost its elevon, and with it, the hydraulic system has bled out under pressure. The controls are unresponsive. The fighter is rolling smoothly to the right and falling at 500 knots (926km/h).

The pilot pulls the black and yellow striped ejection seat handle, blowing open the canopy and firing a shell that drives the seat up into his spine (breaking his back, although he is unaware of it then). The ejection seat throws him free of the aircraft. The speed is too high, and the parachute canopy fails to open properly. The pilot is oscillating in the straps at 25,000ft (7,620m), drifting the long way down onto the north slope of Mt McKinley. Despite insulated clothing, the cold is almost unbearable. Once on the ground, the pain from his broken back is acute. The pilot spreads his life raft and the parachute in the trees. A rescue helicopter arrives to bring him out, along with the aircrew of the Canberra. In debriefing later, the pilot recalls:

> You are not out there intercepting passively. [The enemy] can see the ground station illumination and your [the interceptor's] weapon system. [The enemy] are going to do all kinds of things to jam you, hoping they can make the pipper dance on your screen and keep you from being able to time down your missile ... If we were shooting nukes it would be an area effect weapon. Some of the radar missiles we used, you would hope to get those right into the body of the bomber to do maximum damage to the propulsion and control surfaces. I didn't care if they crashed or just went home; the idea was to do maximum damage to the max number of targets ... In a real mission, if I knew that those guys were headed to Chicago, I would have no compunction about running into them.[52]

G-Force

As aircraft fly higher, maneuver more quickly, navigate with greater precision, and carry more lethal weapons, the human operator is becoming a liability to performance. This is the factor driving the development of Unmanned Combat Aerial Vehicles (UCAVs) that would be capable of flying higher, faster, and with greater maneuverability than a piloted jet, where the limiting factor is biology. The challenge is not only technological. There is another dimension, a line that some pilots still are unwilling to cross, where human beings cede too much authority to the machines. Through the foreseeable future, even as UCAVs and other technologies enter service, an operator will remain in the middle of the system, able to maintain some degree of moral control over the release of weapons.

The human body is capable of withstanding only so much gravitational or centrifugal force, which sets limits on the combat maneuverability of modern fighter jets. The limit is generally not greater than nine times the force of gravity, or G-force. In climbing or hard turns, the pilot experiences positive Gs, which make his body feel heavier. Too much positive G-force may cause the blood to flow away from the brain, resulting in a blackout of a few seconds, or even longer. In diving or other maneuvers that cause a sudden loss of altitude, the body feels weightless, and blood rushes upward into the brain, causing redout: unconsciousness. If this happens at low altitude or during violent maneuvering, the pilot may not have time to recover his senses and may lose all control of the plane and crash.

To prevent blackout or redout, fighter pilots often wear G-suits, specialized garments that cover the legs and midsection. The G-suit has air bladders that automatically fill with air under positive Gs, squeezing the thighs and abdomen to prevent blood from rushing into the lower extremities.

Most modern fighter planes have computer flight controls, which translate human input (through the control stick or rudder pedals) into energy that moves the plane's control surfaces. These controls limit the aircraft's range of maneuver to accommodate the human body. In fact, the wings, control surfaces, and fuselage of most fighters are capable of withstanding much higher G-loading that would kill a human being. Without the pilot in the cockpit, the machine would be capable of much more violent aerobatics. In the not too distant future, analysts predict, there may be whole squadrons of these flying robots doing battle in the skies over our cities.

Attack

As we have seen in Chapter 1, the desire for an intermediate cartridge and weapon drove the development of the modern assault rifle. In much the same way, there has been persistent demand for aircraft capable of acting as both fighter and bomber. During World War I, airplanes often were jacks of all trades, sometimes strafing and bombing trenches, sometimes attacking enemy fighters in pitched battles. Some designs were better than others at multitasking. Today, most fighter aircraft are engineered to be multirole: equally adept at dropping bombs on tanks as at intercepting and shooting down enemy formations. The GR4 Tornado, flown by the British, German, Saudi Arabian, and Italian air forces, is an example of a very successful multirole fighter/attack design.

The attack plane's role is to provide both deep strike and close air support. Often armored and heavier than nimble interceptors, the attack plane is designed to deliver devastating firepower at close range to the enemy's army, and take punishment if necessary. It may be tempting to see the pilot's perspective as altogether removed from danger, when contrasted with his infantry counterpart locked in hand-to-hand combat with the enemy. But that would be a mistake. In combat, aircrew are often in harm's way doing some of the most dangerous jobs in any of the armed forces. Few know the risks more personally than former Royal Air Force GR4 pilot John Peters, who was shot down and captured by Iraqis during the 1991 Gulf War. Here, Peters puts into perspective the fear he felt upon coming face-to-face with Iraqi soldiers after being shot down:

> From the Iraqi's point of view, he has just been bombed for 24 hours, he's lost 10 of his friends and his best man at his wedding has just tried to scrape up his own stomach before he died in his arms. Suddenly, he comes across someone like me who has just been shot down. How would you react if you were in his shoes? I might be a nice guy with two lovely kids, but so is Ahmed except he has no legs anymore and you've just killed his best friend. It's not personal but, even though people talk about political correctness, you can't remove the human aspect. What do you seriously expect them to do to someone like me? They can't kill me because they know I have some worth in intelligence terms, but they're sure going to make me aware that they're not very happy with me. And, yes, it does make you scared. It makes you s___ scared.[53]

By their nature, attack aircraft must fly lower and closer to the action – to the danger – in order to do their job. During the Vietnam War, the US Navy and US Air Force pilots who flew the versatile A-1 Skyraider – a massive tactical fighter of World War II design – regularly faced great danger in a variety of missions from strike to armed reconnaissance and search and rescue, often in close partnership with other aircraft and troops on the ground. The A-1 was ideally suited for these missions as it was a very strong airplane, capable of carrying a heavy weapons load and of surviving a great deal of battle damage. This latter point was especially important, as the tactics employed by A-1 aircrews often called for slow, low-level flight – 200 knots (370km/h) at 300ft (91m) – well within range of enemy guns.

On one search and rescue mission we located a [downed pilot] and every time we passed over him, we would run over the top of this hill. There was a lot of smoke. I could see fires burning on the ground, and then tracers shooting up at me. The bad guys were right on that hill, firing vertically at us. They [the North Vietnamese] mostly had small arms and rocket propelled grenades. I could feel it all hitting my plane, and triple-A [antiaircraft artillery] shells of some kind, rocking the wings. I got hammered pretty good. One of the RPGs knocked a big hole in my wing; I think it would have done me in if it had hit my fuselage, or one of my weapons. On the A-1 we had weapons hung all over the place, a lot of ordnance.[54]

The Kill Box

From a command and control perspective, attack planes are a blessing and a challenge. With all the sources of long-range firepower at work on today's battlefield, from naval guns to strategic bombers, the challenge is how to make sure these fires are de-conflicted and don't accidentally turn on friendly forces. Doctrine writers came up with the concept of the fire support coordination line, or FSCL, which is a line drawn on a map representing a boundary beyond which all forms of firepower were to be confined. In theory, all air, land, and naval component commanders would inform one another of their units' movements and attack plans beyond the FSCL, so the forces would avoid firing on one another as they maneuvered through the battle space toward different tactical objectives.

During the 1991 Gulf War, the US-led coalition developed another doctrine tool that sought to exploit the flexibility and varied firepower of modern attack planes (including Tornadoes, A-10 tank busters, and attack helicopters). The idea was called the "kill box," which is a three dimensional area reference that enables timely, effective coordination and control and facilitates rapid attacks. The idea was that specific missions and targets within a given box – such as Scud missile transporter-erector-launcher vehicles – could be hunted down by cooperating ground and air units. During Operation *Iraqi Freedom*, the kill box and FSCL were to synchronize air and land operations.

> According to Maj. Gen. Daniel P. Leaf, director, air component coordination element ... the "kill box/grid square method of de-conflicting fires worked well and buy-in was complete at all levels by the end of offensive operations."~ However, in the next sentence of his report, he alludes to a problem. There was, he says, "difficulty in getting some major subordinate commands to open kill boxes short of the FSCL." This observation reinforces comments, made by some [US] Air Force officers, suggesting that V (US) Corps, by refusing to open kill boxes within its area of operations but short of the FSCL, created sanctuary for Iraqi forces ... These officers have said that the decision of V (US) Corps to leave

closed kill boxes in its area of operations meant that as many as 80 percent of the [air interdiction] sorties pushed to the corps at critical stages of the fight left without engaging any targets.[55]

The story was different in southeastern Iraq, where US Marine Corps units had drawn kill boxes on their maps short of the FSCL. Apparently 80 percent of the interdiction sorties in this area "expended all of their ordnance."[56] Nevertheless, other ground units – such as the 3rd Infantry Division – reported there was less close coordination than desired between air power and the land component, sometimes leaving desired targets undamaged, and sometimes putting US troops at risk of being targeted by friendly aircraft.[57]

The kill boxes and FSCL could also be used to indicate free-fire zones, wherein any enemy activity could be struck by whatever firepower assets were available. As the 1991 campaign in Iraq reached its fiery crescendo, air power came to be personified in the images from the now infamous "highway of death." More than 2,000 vehicles were destroyed by A-10 Thunderbolt II attack jets and Apaches, which had strafed and bombed a convoy all through the night. The incident on the Abdali Road, between Kuwait and Basra, Iraq, in February 1991, was controversial. Critics charged that coalition aircraft had unnecessarily attacked a defenseless convoy. The argument – not unlike that presented by some critics of the Royal Navy's torpedoing of the Argentine cruiser, the *General Belgrano*, in 1982 – was that the targets might have been considered *hors de combat* at the time they were attacked. Army and air force pilots counter that a retreat is not a surrender, and that it is quite appropriate, under the rules of war, to attack a retreating, undefeated foe. In a 1995 interview with the US Department of Defense's *Stars & Stripes* newspaper, the US commander during the Gulf War, General H. Norman Schwarzkopf, said of the attack, "There was a great deal of military equipment on that highway, and I had given orders to all my commanders that I wanted every piece of Iraqi equipment that we possibly could destroyed."[58]

Depleted Uranium

Perhaps no exotic weapon technology has generated more controversy than the Depleted Uranium (DU) shells used in some tactical aircrafts' antiarmor cannon. The A-10 Thunderbolt II and the AH-64 Apache both use 30mm DU rounds in their guns. Because the heavy metal is both toxic and radioactive, DU shells have been the focal point of controversy, including some claims by Gulf War veterans of DU contributing to the so-called Gulf War illness.[59]

The US Department of Defense has studied DU intensively following the Gulf War, amid concerns over the exposure of soldiers and civilians to the after-effects of radioactive dust and shrapnel on the battlefield (DU radiates alpha, beta, and gamma rays which are about 60 percent the strength of rays emitted by full-strength

U-235). DU rounds are particularly effective against armored vehicles, due to the metal's mass (DU has twice the density of lead) and the tremendous release of energy that occurs as the bullets strike a target. DU metal burns on impact, even at relatively low velocities. When a DU projectile hits an armored vehicle, the shell burns, creating a hot jet of molten metal that penetrates homogeneous rolled steel and other types of armor.

> Depleted uranium was considered an attractive material for kinetic-energy penetrators for a number of reasons. Its high density (almost twice that of steel) makes it easy to produce a penetrator that delivers high momentum and kinetic energy to a small volume of target armor. Uranium is highly pyrophoric, and its impact against steel targets at velocities as low as 30 meters [98½ft] per second produces burning fragments that can ignite fuel or propellants. In addition, depleted uranium is readily available in large quantities and is considerably cheaper than alternative materials.[60]

The US Department of Energy Los Alamos National Laboratory worked with the Department of Defense to develop militarily suitable alloys of uranium, finally settling on a .75 percent solution of titanium, providing the right balance of corrosion resistance and lethal effectiveness. The alloy was first made into a weapon for the A-10's GAU-8 30mm gun, which is capable of firing 1,000–4,000 rounds in a minute, each exiting one of the GAU-8's seven barrels at more than 3,400ft/sec (1,036m/sec). At full power, the A-10's gun firing sounds like a boat's sail being torn in half by a pair of monstrous hands. The DU/Ti alloy has also been scaled up for the US Army's M1 Abrams tank's 120mm main gun, in the form of the M829-series sabot round. The consequences of a DU strike against a vehicle are spectacular, and lethal.[61]

> When a vehicle is impacted and perforated by a DU projectile, the projectile splits into small shards, many of the small shards burst into flames, and fills the insides [sic] of the vehicle with flying metal, fumes, and particulates. The bulk of a DU projectile may pass directly through the vehicle. The inside of the damaged vehicle remains contaminated with particles of DU and its oxides after the impact. In the event of a vehicular fire, the heat of the fire can cause any onboard DU ammunition to oxidize. Personnel in, on, or near (less than 50 meters [164ft]) may have exposures to DU that are greater than the general population's natural exposure by breathing it in, getting dust in their mouth, or in a wound if hit by high velocity depleted uranium shards.[62]

According to the US Department of Defense *Depleted Uranium Environmental Exposure Report*, released in August 1998, "an extensive investigation into the use of depleted uranium during the Gulf War ... finds that there is no evidence to support the claim that depleted uranium caused or is causing the undiagnosed illnesses some veterans are experiencing."[63] Nevertheless, the controversy over the use of DU weapons persists, with non-governmental organizations and other groups calling for more research and, in some cases, the banning of these munitions. Many nations use some form of DU projectiles in their weapons, including the United States, the United Kingdom, Russia, and France.[64]

Attack Helicopters

Among the ranks of attack aircraft, it would be remiss not to make some mention of the role that rotary-wing (helicopter) aviation has to play. A modern attack helicopter, such as the AH-64 Apache, generally is a two-seat aircraft, with the pilot's seat behind and above the front seat of the Co-Pilot/Gunner (CPG). The Apache's weapon system features two key sensor packages, the Target Acquisition Designation Sight (TADS) and the Pilot Night Vision System (PNVS). The TADS is capable of detecting and tracking targets, which the CPG views by looking through a thermal imaging scope. Armed with a 30mm gun firing depleted uranium rounds, and able to carry as many as 16 laser-guided missiles, the Apache is a formidable antiarmor platform whose primary mission is tank busting.

Apaches have had some prestigious roles in recent conflicts. For example, in Operation *Desert Storm*, on January 17, 1991, eight US Army Apache attack helicopters flitted across the Saudi border to blast the Iraqis' air defense radar systems with AGM-114 Hellfire missiles. That move crippled the Iraqis' ability to sense and respond, and enabled a sustained aerial bombing campaign followed by an unstoppable flanking attack by the fast-moving coalition armored force.

Nevertheless, rotary-wing aircraft remain vulnerable to even relatively low-tech air defenses (such as rifle-armed infantry), raising some controversy about whether the sun is setting on the helicopter's usefulness on battlefields where antiaircraft artillery (AAA) and rockets are becoming more commonplace. During Operation *Iraqi Freedom*, US Army and US Marine Corps attack helicopter squadrons often came under intense fire and suffered significant battle damage. For example, on March 23, 2003, a large force of approximately 30 Army Apaches moved into action around the Iraqi city of Karbala, and was driven off by enemy forces using relatively low technology – mobile phones for tactical communications, small arms (rifles and machine guns), and rocket-propelled grenades.

> The most glaring and disquieting Iraqi employment of asymmetric techniques occurred during the approach to Baghdad on 23 March 2003. Highly dispersed small Iraqi units set ambushes, using a cell phone and observer network in the cities south of Baghdad. These ambushes damaged a number of AH-64s that were conducting a corps-level, deep-shaping attack against Republican Guard divisions surrounding Baghdad.[65]

US Marine Corps AH-1W Super Cobras, also operating south of Baghdad, fared little better in some cases. According to Major General James F. Amos, commander of the 3rd Marine Aircraft Wing:

> I had 58 Cobras; I had 49 of them shot up. I hauled six of them out of the field. I didn't have any of them shot out of the sky ... but I had 49 of them shot up and ending up in various states of depot-level repair. We can't afford that. We have got to decide how we are going to do business. [The Army] has learned the lessons of Mogadishu and the lessons [the Russians learned] in Chechnya. When the Army went out with their Apaches, they sent 25 of them out and got all 25 of them shot up. We also noticed that they did not go into downtown Baghdad with their helicopters. We began to work on some procedures on how we can go in there with firepower, using [AV-8B] Harriers and [F/A-18C/D] Hornets [fixed-wing attack jets].[66]

Additionally, the threat posed by Serbian integrated air defense had been one factor preventing the use of Army Apaches in Operation *Allied Force* in 1999. Thus debate has continued over the place of rotary-wing aviation in strike and close air support, given the potential vulnerability of the platforms.

Advocates argue that the versatility of the helicopter as a platform outweighs some of the risk associated with its vulnerability. US attack helicopter units have developed new tactics to counter the asymmetric tactics witnessed at Karbala, including forming protective partnerships with fixed-wing assets, such as A-10s, and making use of the situational awareness provided by ground units and UAVs operating nearby. As a result, the attack helicopter has emerged as a potentially more flexible asset, somewhat divorced from its legacy role as a frontline tank killer, and has been pressed into service as an asset for many supporting soldiers patrolling Iraq's complex urban and political territory.

Air Defense, Electronic Countermeasures, and Stealth

As we have seen from the example of Gary Powers' U-2 being shot down by an SA-2 missile, very capable air defenses have evolved to threaten reconnaissance, bombers, and fighters as they attempt to carry out their missions. The B-17s and B-24 Liberators that bombed the Third Reich in daylight raids with their Norden bomb sights were easy marks for German antiaircraft artillery and interceptor planes. According to the US Eighth Air Force, the service lost 6,000 heavy bombers and 500 medium bombers in the European theater of the war. The Norden bomb sight and the tactics for employing it contributed to the bombers' vulnerability: evasive maneuverability was sacrificed for bombing accuracy.

On daylight raids over Europe – for self defense against German fighters – American strategic bombers flew in combat box formations, not unlike the "formed square" of 19th-century British infantry opposing Napoleon's cavalry.[67]

Like the infantry square, the bombers' combat box could be composed of hundreds of aircraft, with a lead bomber signaling the start of an attack. But there was a price to pay for the safety of numbers: each formation was required to fly straight and level while on a bombing run – the crews had to maintain spacing, heading, airspeed, and altitude to ensure maximum accuracy. For the Luftwaffe's 88mm flak batteries on the ground, this arrangement often proved ideal: allowing air defense gunners to find range, and then fire for effect as neat ranks of bombers inched by overhead. In a famous raid over the German ball-bearing factories at Schweinfurt on October 14, 1943, of 291 B-17s launched on the mission:

> The total number of B-17s lost ... was 82 of 291, 28.2 percent of the force dispatched, 60 of them with all the crews. Moreover, of 175 bombers remaining, 142 had sustained damage to a greater or lesser degree. Only 33 bombers landed unscathed, about 12 percent of the force. It was a hecatomb.[68]

German fighter planes, like the Focke-Wulf 190, had made a Roman holiday of it as well. Right through 1943–44, the "Butcher Birds," with their 13mm machine guns, 20mm cannon and 8.27in (210mm) rockets, took a high toll of the formations of Flying Fortresses and Liberators. Not that the bombers were defenseless, however. A B-17 could carry as many as 13 .50cal M2 Browning machine guns, in addition to 17,600lb (7,983kg) of bombs.[69] It could get pretty hairy for the Luftwaffe's interceptors. On February 3, 1945, in one of the largest raids of the war, the Eighth Air Force struck Berlin with 959 B-17s. Each 21-plane combat box presented a palisade of more than 273 defensive machine guns, capable of slinging more than 150,000 bullets every minute. One copper-jacketed, armor-piercing .50cal bullet had a mass of approximately 1.6oz (45,359mg). Add a few numbers together and the figures show that to break in and attack the bombers, the Focke-Wulf 190s, in theory, had to fly through an expanding storm cloud of metal weighing more than 15,015lb (6,811kg). In contrast, the Focke-Wulf 190A8 model weighed just 9,735lb (4,417kg).

Fast forward 20 years or so to the Vietnam War. The squadrons of strategic bombers had been joined by smaller cousins: jet fighter-bombers like the US Air Force F-105 Thunderchief attack jets that flew in most Southeast Asian campaigns, such as Operation *Rolling Thunder* (1965–68). The "Thuds," as they were known, were fast – capable of achieving 2 Mach, or twice the speed of sound, which is 769 mph (1,238km/h) at sea level. They could carry a heavier bomb load than the B-17. Nevertheless, the Thunderchief's design and its tactics – low-altitude flights using terrain to mask approach and attack, followed by high-speed, maneuvering escapes – proved ill suited to the situation in Vietnam (not unlike the Stukas that had ultimately failed during the Battle of Britain), when pitted against a determined and capable air defense.

The F-105 did not fare well in combat. The Thunderchief served as a fighter-bomber but was limited by its avionics designed for nuclear, not conventional, missions. Ironically, the bomb bay was used to carry a fuel tank, not bombs. At low level it was the fastest aircraft of the war, but was at a disadvantage in air-to-air combat because of its lack of maneuverability ... More than half (397) of the 753 F-105Ds and Fs built were lost in the war. Overall, the F-105 had the highest loss rate of any US aircraft operating in Southeast Asia and over North Vietnam.[70]

Surface-to-Air Missiles (SAMs)

During the Vietnam War, air defense technology introduced by the Soviet Union – together with effective jet interceptors like the MiG-17 and MiG-21, and the US government's restrictive rules of engagement – had trumped the Thunderchiefs' principal advantage of speed. In 1965, the USSR had supplied the North Vietnamese with SA-2 Guideline Surface-to-Air Missiles (SAMs), to bolster the defense of Hanoi and surrounding infrastructure, including the "Dragon's Jaw" bridge. A report from the US Air Force Air University Library, states that 617 Air Force aircraft were lost over North Vietnam, including 280 F-105s.[71]

According to a report comparing the Vietnam and Gulf Wars, from 1962–73 the United States lost a total of 8,588 aircraft across Southeast Asia, "including 2,251 fixed-wing planes, and 2,700 airmen killed in action."[72] To be more precise, AAA guns had accounted for many of the aircraft shot down rather than SAMs. However, it could be argued that the SA-2 and other SAMs had been at least indirectly responsible for the successes of the relatively low-tech AAA. The missiles' presence had altered strike aircraft tactics, requiring low-level flights that put the F-105s and other jets well within the range of 23mm and heavier antiaircraft guns.

Electronic Countermeasures (ECM)

The term Electronic Countermeasures (ECM) refers to a variety of technologies and techniques that are used to defeat an enemy's sensors and weapons. ECM includes very low-tech solutions, such as chaff – metal foil confetti scattered into the beam of an enemy's radar transmission to confuse his receiver with multiple false returns – and more advanced radar-jamming equipment, which sends out RF signals to "spoof" SAMs and RF homing air-to-air missiles. In the era of electronic weapon systems, ECM can provide a life-saving layer of defense, denying an enemy's weapons the data they need in order to lock on and strike. US Air Force doctrine spells out the importance of ECM, particularly in defeating air defense systems: "One Air Force officer estimated that ECM reduced losses by 25 percent, while a Navy officer put the figure at 80 percent."[73]

The SAM threat in Vietnam spurred development of a generation of specialized ECM, such as radar-jamming equipment that could be fitted to strike aircraft.

Specialized aircraft called "wild weasels" were created using fighters and fighter/bombers as host platforms, removing some weapon systems and replacing these with powerful jamming equipment and anti-radiation missiles, such as the AGM-45 Shrike, which homed-in upon the electromagnetic energy emissions from a SAM launch site's air defense radar.

During Operation *Desert Storm*, the US Air Force organized combat missions in strike packages, with bomber aircraft escorted by wild weasel aircraft. In 1991, 86 coalition aircraft were shot down or damaged by Iraqi air defense, including 21 during the closing week of the month-long air war.[74] Between the Gulf War in 1991 and the end of Operation *Allied Force* in 1999, a total of 13 US Air Force fixed-wing aircraft (including an F-15, four F-16s, six A-10s, an AC-130H gunship, and an F-117) were shot down, again mostly by mobile surface-to-air missile systems.

The numbers argue the case for developing dedicated aircraft and defensive systems to carry out the Suppression of Enemy Air Defense (SEAD) mission. In 1991, the wild weasels, which were then modified F-4G Phantoms, were partnered with F-16Cs to escort other strike forces into Iraq. On these missions both types of jets carried AGM-88A, a weapon similar to but more advanced than the Vietnam-era Shrike. The wild weasels' task was to tempt Iraqi air defense sites into activating their radar systems, thus giving away their locations. Once a target had given itself away, the wild weasels would use powerful radio frequency electromagnetic emissions to jam the radar and its communications equipment. The wild weasels would then fire or direct the F-16Cs to attack the site with their missiles. The AGM-88A delivered a 145lb (66kg) warhead, designed to rip apart the antenna arrays with 25,000 steel and tungsten fragments. Today, other ECM aircraft, such as the EA-6B Prowler, are equipped and armed after the model of the wild weasels. These dedicated electronic warfare planes and their successors have become essential to mounting attack or deep strike missions. A little known fact of both the 1991 and 2003 air wars over Iraq, and the 1999 war in the Balkans, is that even the so-called "stealth" fighters, the F-117 Nighthawks, required electronic warfare escort on their way into enemy territory.

Stealth

During Operation *Allied Force* (1999), electronic warfare and countermeasures became crucial elements of the air war against Serbia. The Yugoslavian military had deployed a sophisticated and integrated air defense network that took full advantage of the rough Balkan terrain. In that war, the EA-6Bs, although based on the 1960s-vintage A-6 Intruder airframe, became absolutely essential to the safety of bombers on sorties into Serbian territory. According to sources in the US Department of Defense, the vaunted stealth fighter would not launch on a mission over Serbian territory without an EA-6B escort. The same had been true during the Gulf War, where the Nighthawks had first sharpened their talons.

Stealth works because the plane's angular geometry and specialized, energy-absorbent coatings reduce the return of RF energy to an emitting radar. The radio waves are deflected away from the Nighthawk (or the B-2 bomber), and away from the receiver antenna of the enemy's radar. This gives the smallest possible return image on an enemy's scope, making the F-117 appear as background static, or as nothing at all. But nothing human-engineered is perfect. Even the most advanced self-defense technology has its imperfections, as Lieutenant Colonel Dale Zelko discovered in the Kosovo war when his F-117 became the first NATO aircraft to be shot down using old-school surface-to-air missiles. Subsequent analysis showed that the fighter had remained invisible until it opened its bomb-bay doors to release a laser-guided bomb. According to the US Air Force, the F-117 becomes more radar reflective when its geometry is altered by opening the bomb bay.[75]

> My target was in downtown Belgrade, the key C3 [command, control, and communication] facility for the entire north half of the country ... It was number one on the hit list ... I saw the missiles launch just after they punched through the bottom layer of cloud; so right after launch I picked them up on my four o'clock position. As soon as I saw them I thought, "They got me." I could tell right away. I had flown many combat missions in the -117, in *Desert Storm*, and this was my third one in *Allied Force*. I saw a lot of SAM launches and a lot of triple-A. This was the first time that I ever thought from a SAM that they got me ... The first [missile] went right over the top of the aircraft, so close that it buffeted the aircraft ... Then I re-acquired the second missile and I thought, man that is going to run right into me. If it didn't have a 200lb [90kg] warhead on it, I think it still would have harpooned the aircraft.[76]

Because of its potential vulnerability, even stealth gets an electronic warfare escort now. Building on the lessons learned from the F-117, new classes of tactical fighters, such as the F/A-22 Raptor, have stealth in their pedigree, with reduced visibility to radar and built-in countermeasures to protect against air defense and air-to-air weapons. Perhaps one of the best defenses the F/A-22 has is its supersonic "super-cruise" capability, by means of which the jet can sustain a speed of more than 1.7 Mach and dash at more than 2 Mach.

Fratricide: Blue-on-Blue

The speed with which targets may be engaged, attacks countered, and defenses re-engaged has become blindingly fast.[77] As a consequence, one persistent challenge has been the difficulty of answering the basic questions, "where am I?" "where are other friendly forces?" and, crucially, "where is the enemy?"

Nowhere is the imperative of overcoming the fog of war more clear than in the horror of fratricide: the accidental killing of one's own or friendly troops in battle.

According to Brigadier General Robert W. Cone, former commander of the US Army's National Training Center at Fort Irwin, California, the solution to the problem of fratricide will come not only through technology, but also through the development and maintenance of human awareness and skill – in other words, through training.

> We look at fratricide prevention having two critical ingredients. One is combat identification; things like identification friend or foe that the aircraft have, or some system on the ground like these thermal panels or the [infrared] bug lights that they have – something, a positive [identification] when someone decides to shoot, that they can confirm. And then the other part is really the situational awareness: Who's supposed to be over there? Who is over there?[78]

Confusion about the location of friendly forces on the battlefield is one of the close air support, or CAS, aviator's worst nightmares. Some believe that technology eventually will solve the problem, through "blue force tracking" and other projects. As a technological advancement, blue force tracking is a new generation of electronic equipment that is evolving from the legacy of Identification Friend or Foe (IFF) radio systems. As a process, blue force tracking also includes shared access – for air, land, and naval units – to a "tactical Intranet," through which navigation maps and intelligence information may be displayed. The intent is for pilots and ground unit commanders to be able to see the same display of the battle space, updated in real time, showing where the aircraft or vehicles are positioned, and where other friendly and enemy forces are located. However, the technology has not yet matured, and the pace at which offensive capabilities are evolving has made blue force tracking and combat identification challenging at best. In practice, IFF devices – old or new – by themselves are not sufficient to eliminate the risk of fratricide:

> In the 1973 Arab–Israeli War, the Soviet-trained Arab forces employed dense concentrations of surface to air missiles [SAMs] and antiaircraft artillery, or AAA, batteries with their MiGs in the same airspace. Using only their [IFF] systems to differentiate between the Israeli and Arab aircraft, they used their SAMs and AAA impressively to destroy 70 Israeli aircraft in the 19-day war (70 percent of Israel's total losses from all causes). But fratricide from these same systems cost the Arabs 60 to 90 aircraft, or 15 to 20 percent of their own total losses! We have similar potential weaknesses in our own IFF systems.[79]

Often, all-too-human failures, such as errors in visual identification, are shown to have been crucial factors in fratricide incidents. One such incident during Operation *Iraqi Freedom* involved US Air Force A-10s and an unfortunate US

Marine Corps ground unit near the southern city of an-Nasiriyah. The A-10s rolled in on a close air support mission that a subsequent Pentagon investigation found had been called by the ground force commander. The US Air National Guard pilots did not see that their targets were in fact Marine armored vehicles. According to the marine force's senior commander, the resulting fratricide – in which 10 marines were killed – was not for lack of technology:

> It was March 23. We had over 400 sets [of blue force tracking equipment], some given to us by the [US] Army, some that we procured ourselves. But blue force tracker, ladies and gentlemen, creates situational awareness on the battlefield. When my counterpart, [US Army] Gen. Wallace, in V Corps looked at his screens, it showed the same as my screens in terms of where units were. Fratricide is caused by our inability for the Air Force A-10 pilot to look at a vehicle and have an immediate recognition, friend or foe. The same is true with tanks. If a tanker, on a dusty, dark night, lines up his main gun and he can't query a target, then we aren't where we need to be with regard to the avoidance of fratricide. Blue force tracker helps tell you where units are in general design; it does not solve the problem of blue on blue, or fratricide.[80]

Other incidents have reinforced the argument that the challenge of overcoming fratricide is best addressed through a combination of technology and better training. In March 2003, US A-10s accidentally gunned a British armored column, killing Lance Corporal of Horse Matthew R. Hull and wounding others. The A-10s had not been aware of the location of the British troops, and the pilots had not reacted to British identification marks on the vehicles they attacked. Hull was killed and five of his comrades wounded after a pair of Idaho Air National Guard A-10s destroyed their Scimitar and Warrior armored vehicles. British authorities have ruled that the A-10s' attack was unlawful and criminal, based on evidence that the pilots did not follow proper procedures, and that identification markers on the UK armored vehicles were ignored.[81] A US Department of Defense inquiry cleared the A-10 pilots of wrongdoing and found that the friendly fire incident was an accident.

In the end it is sometimes difficult to pin down a single point of failure that explains why fratricide occurs. The fog of war persists, despite all of the investment in precision-strike and command, control, communication, and intelligence technologies. Human error continues to be a major factor, which training and doctrine have not yet eliminated from the tactics, techniques, and procedures of war. Each case may have very different technical, environmental, and human factors. But one thing all friendly fire incidents seem to share is the mutual grief felt by those who realize what they have done, and by the survivors of those incidents. Psychologists who have studied fratricide note that debilitating depression and other mental health problems often arise following an incident of friendly fire. Of the victims' relatives, perhaps it is remarkable that in the aftermath of the verdict at Lance Corporal Matty Hull's Oxfordshire coroner's court, Hull's widow appealed for the forgiveness of the American A-10 pilots.[82]

Poor situational awareness, and failures of technology, training, or procedure can work against aviators as well. In March 2003, as Operation *Iraqi Freedom* began with coalition air strikes on Baghdad, US Army MIM-104 Patriot missile batteries were involved in a series of own goals against coalition aircraft. An Army Patriot crew targeted and destroyed a Royal Air Force GR-4 Tornado jet, killing both crewmen aboard. Another Patriot battery automatically attacked a US Marine Corps F/A-18, having confused the Hornet with an Iraqi ballistic missile. Finally, in what very nearly was a case of double fratricide, a flight of four F-16CJs was illuminated by a Patriot battery radar. One of the F-16CJs in self defense fired an anti-radiation missile that destroyed the battery's radar, and no one was injured.

Case Study: Gunfighter Six, Iraq 1991

Given the fast pace of the modern battlefield, the technologies and procedures for targeting and releasing weapons require careful training and reliable technology to limit the chances of things going wrong. One thing technology cannot prevent, however, is gross errors in judgment on the part of humans releasing weapons against their own. One such case during Operation *Desert Storm* drives home the point. On the night of February 17, 1991, an AH-64A crew of the 1st Battalion, 1st Aviation Regiment, accidentally obliterated an M2 Bradley infantry fighting vehicle and an M113 armored personnel carrier of the US Army's 1st Infantry Division (Mechanized). The attack killed two soldiers and wounded six others. A tragic combination of technical flaws and human error led the Apache aircrew to misidentify the friendly vehicles, and fire on them with AGM-114 Hellfire missiles.

Just past 01:00am local time, the 1/1 Apaches were directed by their battalion commander – who was in the front seat of the lead gunship, call sign "Gunfighter Six," as its co-pilot/gunner, or CPG – to an incorrect set of navigation coordinates. According to an investigation by the US Army, the commander also misidentified the target vehicles as hostile, because he believed these vehicles to be located beyond the lines of US forces.[83] Also according to the Army investigation, the ground units could not transmit or receive on the UHF (Ultra High Frequency) band radio frequencies used by the Apache aircrews for command and control in the air. It is notable that the Apache battalion commander was improperly taking part in the battle as the Apache's CPG. Apparently, his qualifications on the equipment were not up to date as he is heard several times to defer to the AH-64's pilot, a junior officer, on how to operate the system.

The Apache battalion commander/CPG engaged one of the vehicles with his helicopter's 30mm cannon, but the gun jammed. A few moments later, the commander re-engaged the vehicles with two Hellfire missiles. The following is a pared-down transcript of the engagement from the AH-64's flight recorder:

Gunfighter Six CPG: Ok, you have a Bradley at [coordinates] 946245 and he's oriented north on the screen line. He's got an APC [armored personnel carrier] near him also. Then, off to his right are these two vehicles that I see and those are the vehicles at [coordinates] 915270. Your Bradley is not even looking anywhere near them. Over.

Iron Deuce Six: [the ground force commander, who had called in the Apaches to support his unit's advance across the desert] Roger. I ain't worried about that. Can you still engage those two vehicles at the 270 grid line?

Gunfighter Six CPG: Roger. I can shoot those easy; right. [The Apache aircrew see the Bradley and the M113 in their thermal sight, but they mistakenly believe these are Iraqi armored vehicles.]

...

Iron Deuce Six: I say, go ahead. Take them out.

Gunfighter Six CPG: Radar searching ... Gun jammed. [After a short, chattering burst of four or five rounds, the 30mm cannon malfunctions, but not before a few of its DU bullets smoke one of the vehicles.]

...

Gunfighter Six Pilot: All right. Go missiles.

...

Gunfighter Six CPG: Gunfighter Six is on the net. Have the two vehicles in sight. It appears one of them is, in fact, killed and I'm going to go ahead and shoot the other one now.

Iron Deuce Six: Roger. I say, go ahead. Take them out.

Gunfighter Six Pilot: De-WAS gun. [In the weapon system's computer, the pilot coaches the CPG to de-select his 30mm cannon, and select instead the AGM-114 missile.]

...

Gunfighter Six CPG: Boy, I'm going to tell you, it's hard to pull this trigger. Back me up a little bit here. Tell me – I'm firing heading 070, 3,800m [12,467ft]. So my current grid is ... Let me pull up the current grid.

...

Gunfighter Six Pilot: Switch to black hot. [After difficulty achieving a thermal sensor lock on the vehicle, the pilot coaches the CPG to switch his TADS scope to show hot targets as dark shapes against a pale background.] ... There you go. Now, do the motherfucker.

...

Gunfighter Six CPG: Ok. 070; ready.

Gunfighter Six Pilot: Ready in the back. Do him. [A Hellfire missile lances out into the darkness. With a laser projected from the TADS turret on the AH-64's nose, the CPG is tracking his weapon to the US vehicle.]

...

Gunfighter Six Pilot: Nice and steady.

Gunfighter Six CPG: I hope it's enemy.

Gunfighter Six Pilot: That's all right. Just stay on them.

Gunfighter Six CPG: Because here it comes. [The missile climbs sharply and dives into one of the vehicles. It erupts fire and burning debris, with secondary explosions from the vehicle's fuel and ammunition magazine. The inverted grayscale image is seared into the TADS scope.]

Gunfighter Six Pilot: That's one; alright.

...

Gunfighter Six CPG: Gunfighter Six. Completely destroyed the first target with the first bullet.

Gunfighter Six Pilot: Let's pick up the second one. Let's go. You got the second one.

...

Gunfighter Six CPG: Roger. I'm going to go ahead and shoot the second vehicle. It's still intact, but it's fixing to go away. [The vehicle had been struck by the burst from Gunfighter Six's 30mm gun, before it jammed.]

...

Gunfighter Six CPG: Are you lined up on it?

Gunfighter Six Pilot: Yep. Ready in the back. Let's do him. [The CPG launches a second missile and tracks it toward the remaining US vehicle.] ... On him. Looking good. This Bud's for you.

Gunfighter Six CPG: Uh-oh. [The second missile impacts.]

Gunfighter Six Pilot: That's all right. He's dead too.

...

Almost immediately after the second missile struck, a radio call came through warning that Gunfighter Six had engaged friendly forces. The call, "Check fire!" came only moments before a second gunship in the formation was about to open fire on the survivors with its 30mm gun. On the recording, one may hear the horror felt by the battalion commander and pilot, upon realizing what they had done.

Apparently, despite highly sophisticated targeting and navigation technologies, and at least some coordination with the commander, none of the players really knew with certainty where they were in relationship to one another. Neither the helicopter nor the vehicles were able to talk with one another on the same radio frequency. And adding to the stress and confusion, the Army discovered later that its own ground surveillance radar inadvertently activated the Apaches' threat warning receivers, resulting in false indications that enemy antiaircraft systems were operating in the area. The US Army and the Government Accountability Office investigated the incident in 1993 and found that human error had been the cause. As a result, the Apache battalion commander, Lieutenant Colonel Ralph Hayles, was "relieved of command for failing to exercise command and control over the Apache team by becoming personally engaged in the fighting," according to a US government report.[84]

Summary

We have seen how airpower has evolved over the last century into modern forces capable of strategic action (bombing an enemy state's economic centers, for example), as well as tactical action (getting into the thick of the fighting). We have also seen that airpower is crucial to military intelligence, with piloted and robotic aircraft now routinely playing central roles in surveillance and reconnaissance of the battle space beneath their wings. The hazards of modern combat aviation are many, from enemy fighters to antiaircraft artillery and surface-to-air missiles. Countermeasures are equally complex – electronic warfare and stealth-locking, attacker and defender, are in a high-tech arms race. In the sky, specialization has gradually given way to more general requirements as many new warplanes possess multiple abilities – fighters may dominate the sky one night and bombard an enemy's presidential palace the next. In the 21st century, air forces have perfected the art of striking at an opponent's weaknesses, particularly supply chains and infrastructure, which define his ability to make war.

But the technology of air power, impressive though it is, has limits. Precision munitions are only as accurate as the information that is programmed into their guidance computers. That information is provided by fallible human beings. Even as the scientists and engineers produce more accurate and "smart" weapons, there will always be a place for the low-tech, inexpensive solution such as that provided by an unguided bomb or a cannon shell. Like the warheads of a cluster munition, such weapons can be indiscriminate killers. And if used near friendly forces or civilians, the results can be tragic.

6

FIREPOWER AT SEA – NAVAL WEAPON SYSTEMS

More than 71 percent of the Earth's surface is covered by water. What does this mean in terms of civilization and warfare? In 2005, a study led by the University of East Anglia found that 23 percent (about 1.2 billion) of the global population lives within 54nm (100km) of the world's coastlines.[1] The US Navy prefers a far larger figure, from around 50 percent to more than 70 percent.[2] The sources seem to concur upon the fact that the population of the littoral zone – which refers to coastal regions from the shore out to 600ft (183m) of water depth – is growing rapidly, and may definitively account for more than half of all humanity by 2030. Already, according to the US National Academy of Sciences, two thirds of the world's urban centers (with populations of more than 2.5 million) are located near the coastal zone.[3]

Where there are people, there is conflict; whether for natural wealth or for control of territory, competition for increasingly scarce and valuable global resources will intensify over the course of this century. In the modern, globalized economy, more than 80 percent (by volume) of world trade moves by sea.[4] The situation has created a crucial dependency – shared alike by the developed and the developing world – upon the ocean, literally as the life's blood of global commerce.

So it could be argued that navies (perhaps even more than armies or air forces) are especially relevant forms of armed power, to ensure and defend one's access to the sea lanes of commerce, and to protect vital interests abroad, such as the sources of the goods, services and raw materials upon which national well-being depends. A former secretary of the US Navy put it this way:

> Our vital interests – those interests for which the United States is willing to fight – are at the endpoints of highways of the seas or lines of strategic approach. These endpoints lie in the world's coastal regions which coincide with the concentration of our vital interests in Europe, Asia, the Middle East, and Latin America. While representing only a small portion of the world's surface, the littorals provide homes to over three-quarters of the world's population, locations for over 80 percent of the world's capital cities, and nearly all the major marketplaces for international trade.[5]

Traditionally, navies have been bulwarks of defense against invasion or foreign exploitation of territorial resources – consider Britain's "wooden walls" under Vice Admiral Horatio, Viscount Nelson (1758–1805); and as guarantors of commerce and security – enforcing the free movement of commerce and of military power. For a seafaring nation, such as the UK or the United States – the latter with more than 90 percent of its foreign trade ocean-borne – sea power underwrites prosperity. Today, with most nations' interests distributed at least somewhat globally, not even the land-locked can discount entirely the importance of marine commerce to economic success.

Nowhere is economic inter-dependence on the sea more apparent than in a brief glance at the petroleum trade. According to the US Department of Energy, each day ocean-going tankers move more than 40 million barrels of oil – approximately two thirds of the world's oil trade. The tankers ply fixed maritime routes, passing through several geographic "chokepoints," such as the Strait of Hormuz, the Strait of Malacca, the Bab el-Mandab passage, the Suez Canal, the Bosphorus Straits, and the Panama Canal.[6] These narrow channels are located at the regions of greatest instability, and this is no coincidence. Consider what would happen to the international economic scene if one or more of these chokepoints were significantly disrupted or disabled by war, piracy or other violence.

More relevant to warfare itself is another role that navies play, building upon their inherent abilities to gain and defend access to sea lanes: navies are an effective and efficient means of projecting power. An army or an air force may depend more or less upon foreign bases for its access to the conflict zone. This host nation support requires permissions and leaves the force vulnerable to changes in the political situation (consider Turkey's denial of access to the United States Army and air forces in the build up to the 2003 invasion of Iraq). On the other hand, a navy – operating from the global commons of international waters – makes its own access. From offshore, the fleet and its air wing may hold at risk an adversary's vital interests. To be sure, there are counter-access strategies – such as sea mines – very effective at slowing down even the most technically capable navies. Nevertheless, a fleet needs no permission to transit the ocean to an area of operations; with naval aviation, and long-range weaponry now available, targets far inland may be attacked decisively – consider the case of Operation *Enduring Freedom*, or OEF, in Afghanistan (2001–02).

Within a few weeks of the September 11, 2001 attacks at New York, Virginia, and Pennsylvania, Task Force 50 in the Arabian Gulf had been assembled. At its maximum extent, the fleet assembled for OEF included six aircraft carriers, with their carrier-embarked air wings, among 59 warships from the United States, Australia, Britain, Canada, France, Italy, and Japan. On October 7, 2001, the war began with ship-launched Tomahawk cruise missiles, carrier-based strike fighters and long-range bombers (based at Diego Garcia in the Indian Ocean). The aircraft and the missiles struck the Taliban regime, with targets more than 400nm (740km) from the coast. Within six weeks, naval forces had helped project Marine and Army assaults into Afghanistan, toppling the Taliban government by November 17, 2001. US Air Force Colonel Forrest Marion clarifies this operation:

> Shortly after the horrific 11 September 2001 attacks, the United States found itself fighting a war in Central Asia for which it lacked adequate forward basing. For the first three months of Operation *Enduring Freedom* ... the dearth of forward bases required the US to rely heavily on navy assets and air force long-range bombers to deliver the vast majority of ordnance against enemy targets.[7]

Fleet Force Structure

Modern fleets are made up of varieties of warships and submarines; shore-based and carrier-based aircraft; and support vessels – including supply ships and oilers – that provide the fuel, food, ammunition, and spare parts necessary to keep the fleet in fighting shape. A navy is usually supported by a robust shore establishment that includes headquarters, bases, air stations, naval shipyards, maintenance and training centers, and depots staffed by thousands of personnel. Organized into major domestic commands, such as Atlantic Fleet and Pacific Fleet, the US Navy also has forces permanently stationed at London, UK, at Gaeta, Italy, at Yokosuka, Japan, and at Manama, Bahrain.

The US Navy's battle force includes 12 aircraft carriers; 11 carrier air wings (each with more than 70 aircraft); 12 amphibious assault ships (smaller aircraft carriers, with large marine and cargo transport capacity); 50 nuclear-powered fast attack submarines, or SSNs; 14 ballistic missile submarines – the SSBNs at the front line of America's strategic deterrent force, with their Trident II/D5 thermonuclear ballistic missiles; four nuclear-powered guided missile submarines (converted *Ohio*-class SSBNs that have capacity for as many as 154 Tomahawk missiles); and 116 surface combatants (frigates, destroyers, and cruisers).

When deployed, the principal US Navy formation is the strike group. The typical carrier strike group is centered on a 97,000-ton, 900ft (274m)-long *Nimitz*-class nuclear-powered aircraft carrier (CVN); a *Ticonderoga*-class guided missile cruiser (CG), and two *Arleigh Burke*-class guided missile destroyers (DDGs). These surface combatants are equipped with the Aegis combat system. Aegis is an integrated computer, sensor, and weapon system capable of conducting air, surface, and undersea warfare operations. The carrier strike group also includes an SSN and a fast combat support ship (AOE), with capacity for more than 177,000 barrels of fuel oil, 2,150 tons of ammunition and 750 tons of stores.

For its part, the Royal Navy's battle force is organized into two major flotillas, based at Portsmouth and Devonport. The Portsmouth Flotilla includes the aircraft carriers HMS *Ark Royal* and HMS *Illustrious*; eight guided missile destroyers; eight guided missile frigates; a fishery protection squadron of three offshore patrol vessels; and the Falkland Islands patrol ship HMS *Dumbarton Castle*. The flotilla also hosts two Mine Countermeasures (MCM) squadrons – including seven *Hunt*-class and two *Sandown*-class MCM vessels – and 14 *Archer*-class patrol boats. The Devonport Flotilla includes the helicopter carrier HMS *Ocean*; four Type 22 frigates; seven Type 23 frigates; two amphibious transport dock ships, or LPDs; seven SSNs; and a five-ship surveying squadron.

The nucleus of Britain's frontline strategic force is the Faslane Flotilla, with its four SSBNs, three SSNs and a third mine countermeasures squadron of seven MCM vessels. The Royal Navy also fits out patrol vessel squadrons at Gibraltar and Cyprus, and the 18 logistics and support vessels of the Royal Fleet Auxiliary.

Royal Navy tailored air groups, which embark aboard the three carriers, may include 24–36 aircraft – attack planes (such as those of 800 and 801 Naval Air Squadron, which operate Harrier GR9s owned by the RAF under "Joint Force Harrier"); Sea King Mk 7 airborne surveillance and area control helicopters; Chinook CH-47 transport helicopters; and Merlin HM Mk 1 antisubmarine helicopters. In joint operations with the British Army, the air group also may include Apache Longbow AH-64D attack helicopters.

Air warfare is the soul of a carrier group's combat power. When deployed, the US naval air force is typically organized as a carrier air wing, with approximately 70 aircraft, including four squadrons of strike fighters (tactical aircraft capable of conducting both air-to-air and air-to-surface combat). The fighter/attack squadrons are composed of F/A-18 Hornet series aircraft – single seat Cs, tandem Ds, and the newer E- and F-model Super Hornets. The air wing also may include an S-3B Viking surveillance and aerial refueling squadron; an EA-6B Prowler electronic warfare aircraft squadron; an E-2C Hawkeye airborne early warning squadron; and an SH-60 Seahawk utility helicopter squadron. When viewed in context with other military powers, an embarked carrier air wing compares favorably, in some cases possessing aboard a single carrier more striking power than could be mustered by another nation's entire air force.

During Operation *Enduring Freedom* the naval air force's carriers had arrived very shortly after the planning for war began. Their presence had helped to shape the conditions of the coming conflict – by providing a base afloat for theater-level command and control, communications, and intelligence capabilities – and had been able to "kick in the door" for following land and air forces.

Navy aircraft flew 7,000 strike sorties in Afghanistan, dropped 5,000 precision weapons, and were backed up by another 4,000 support missions. Eighty percent of the strike missions' targets were unknown to the pilot at aircraft launch: that's called flexibility. Naval forces also define lethality dropping 50 percent of all the precision ordnance expended in Afghanistan by hitting at least one target in 85 percent of all strike missions.[8]

Sea-based air strikes had provided some of the first blows against Afghan strongholds. However, it was up to land forces to exploit the breach. Here again, naval power provided vital access, launching the deepest amphibious operation in US Marine Corps history. The amphibious strike groups in the Arabian Gulf projected the 15th and 26th Marine Expeditionary Units (MEUs) – more than 4,400 marines – 441nm (817km) overland to seize a Taliban-held air strip and establish Forward Operating Base Rhino. From that point, US and allied land and air forces could support the assault on Kandahar.

Naval air power is also used to support other forces ashore. For example, during Operation *Telic* (2003–present), 846 Naval Air Squadron, deployed to Basra, helped transport British Army units operating in the south eastern corner of the country with their Sea King Mk 4 helicopters. One pilot recounted her duty:

> We held an Incident Response Team (IRT) at both Basrah [sic] and further North at al Amarah. This consisted of the aircrew, two medics and a team of four Airborne Reaction Force (ARF), utilized for security of the aircraft and medics at landing sites. IRT was the most intense flying of all, more often than not for a serious incident, and always time critical. We regrettably have many IRT accounts, one of which tells the story of a Sea King that got called out after a ground patrol came under contact. The Sea King arrived to pick up an army private who had his leg blown off by an RPG. Once he was in the aircraft the crewman put a headset on him to hear the medics, his initial words to the crew were, "I'm so sorry, I hope you didn't have to get out of bed for this."[9]

Strike groups also operate through two other major warfighting domains: those of surface and undersea warfare. Surface warfare has the longest tradition of any naval domain, encompassing all operations conducted on the ocean. Surface combatants, such as the US Navy's Aegis cruisers and destroyers, are designed and armed to perform a variety of tasks, from fleet escort and anti-ship combat to long-range surface strike and air defense. In an offensive role, the missions of a surface combatant are to intercept and destroy enemy combatants and merchant vessels, and to carry striking power far inland with extended range naval gunfire and guided weapons, such as the BGM-109 Tomahawk cruise missile. In a defensive role, ships equipped with Aegis, or a similar combat system, may employ their radar and guided missiles as screens against enemy aircraft. In this role, the Aegis ships deploy at a distance around the carrier and other vessels potentially vulnerable to air attack. The CGs and DDGs form a picket with their radar systems by means of which hostile traffic – including attack jets and anti-ship missiles – may be interdicted before it reaches the strike group's vital heart. Surface combatants also have sensors – sonar – and weapon systems designed to address threats from the undersea domain by enemy submarines and mines.

Undersea warfare, dominated by modern nuclear- and diesel electric-powered submarines, is a world of stealth, where silence and surprise are commodities at a premium. Modern nuclear-powered fast attack submarines, such as the *Virginia* class, armed with Mk 48 advanced capability torpedoes and equipped with powerful bow, sail, hull, and towed array sonar systems, pose a major threat to an adversary's naval and commercial shipping. Under a joint US–UK program during the 1980s, a launch canister was produced enabling submarines to launch Tomahawk missiles, adding long-range surface strike to the SSNs' mission portfolio.

A navy by nature represents deployed power, forces that are embarked on expeditions overseas, safeguarding the nation's interests and influence abroad. Because of this, navies are able to apply limited amounts of power in all domains of warfare, including ashore, by means of a marine corps: a sea-going army is capable of putting up a spirited fight while paving the way for a larger force to arrive. So the idea of expeditionary warfare, which refers chiefly to the amphibious projection of power ashore, is central to understanding the role of a modern naval force.

The US Navy's fleet includes formations devoted to amphibious warfare, called expeditionary strike groups. These groups are centered on large amphibious assault ships, an LHA or LHD (amphibious assault ship and amphibious assault ship/dock), which essentially are small aircraft carriers hauling the bulk of a Marine Expeditionary Unit (MEU) and its air wing. The typical marine air wing includes AV-8B Harrier II attack jets; CH-53E Super Stallion and CH-46D Sea Knight transport helicopters; and AH-1W Super Cobra attack helicopters. The group also includes an amphibious transport dock ship, or LPD, and a dock landing ship, or LSD, which carry the remainder of the MEU's marines as well as a number of landing craft to help disembark and ferry the unit's heavy equipment ashore. The expeditionary strike group is escorted by surface combatants, including an Aegis-equipped CG and DDG and a *Perry*-class guided missile frigate, or FFG. Like the carrier strike group, the amphibious force is shadowed by an SSN, which helps protect against enemy submarines and other threats in the coastal zone. Among those other threats is that of the sea mine, perhaps the most dangerous obstacle to operating in this zone. Sea mines have emerged from history as one of the most lethal ship killers. Approximately 77 percent of US Navy ship casualties since 1950 have been caused by mines of various types, including bottom, moored, and floating weapons.[10]

Another important aspect of naval power is the relatively modern phenomenon of Naval Special Warfare. While naval commando units have existed since World War II (1939–45), and perhaps earlier, the modern commando is much more than the "ninja" of a bygone era. Today, naval Special Forces are trained to excel at a number of activities, including combat skills. Increasingly, Special Forces are required to perform in operations other than war, especially intelligence gathering and other tasks intended to shape the conditions of a potential conflict, or to avoid it altogether.

Costs

The cost of building and maintaining a fleet is immense. For example, the average cost per ship of the US Navy's newest class of aircraft carriers, the CVN 78 *Gerald R. Ford*-class, is $10.1 billon. In its report on the US Navy's fiscal year 2008 proposed budget, the US Congressional Budget Office noted that the Navy would likely spend $20.6 billion annually on shipbuilding to construct its 313-vessel fleet as planned. Including the cost of refueling the reactors on the fleet's nuclear-powered aircraft carriers and submarines, the shipbuilding and conversion account would require $21.7 billion annually, through 2037.[11]

The shipbuilding bill is one thing; the cost of naval operations is another story altogether. The US Department of the Navy in 2007 estimated a total of nearly $30 billion could be required to "reset" the force – that is, to bring the Navy and Marine Corps back up to the materiel levels they possessed prior to the wars in Afghanistan and Iraq. The Navy department's fiscal year 2008 proposed budget also included $25.5 billion for both the Navy and the Marine Corps to cover as-yet-unfunded fiscal year 2007 war costs – including personnel, operations and maintenance, ammunition and weapons procurement, as well as other expenses. The two services requested another $20 billion for fiscal year 2008 war costs.

In the competition for resources during the Cold War (1946–92), the US Navy drew down from a fleet of 6,600 ships at the end of World War II to just 642 ships by June 1950. However, with the outbreak of the Korean War (1950–53), naval offshore mobility enjoyed a renaissance in relevance, as it had been an amphibious assault at Inchon that had helped turn the tide for the United Nations' forces.

In May 1954, Samuel P. Huntington wrote in an article for the US Naval Institute Proceedings that the key to justifying the staggering cost of maintaining a fleet was to spell out what investment in a navy bought: aircraft carriers, marine infantry and naval artillery, and sea bases. There was no need to invent a reason for the Navy, in Huntington's view. Rather, the issue was to explain what the sea services could do in support of the nation's vital interests. US Marine Corps Colonel (ret.) Robert Work, a senior naval and military analyst with the Center for Strategic and Budgetary Assessments in Washington, D.C. said the naval force's core competencies always have been expeditionary, forward-deployed, and joint-service.

> The way I look at this, this United States' naval forces have since 1783 been in an expeditionary posture, and now are coming back to their central focus. With modern naval power as part of the joint force, the nation now possesses a multi-dimensional capability, including limited numbers of forward based forces; forward deployed forces; forcible entry forces; strategic mobility – with 95 percent of the world's militarily useful sealift – logistics; global strike; global [communications]; and security capabilities.[12]

China is an example of a nation that has not traditionally valued investment in modernizing its navy. The People's Liberation Army Navy (PLAN) has built a fleet focused only on coastal defense, with little or no credible power projection capability (aside from the limited nuclear deterrent represented by its two ballistic missile submarines). Strategically, the Chinese Navy's mission is subordinate to the PLA's broader intent to offer "massive resistance" to enemy invaders. Comprised of 18 major surface combatants and more than 330 fast attack craft – such as guided missile boats – the PLAN has no aircraft carriers and relies upon a large, shore-based air wing of aging Soviet-design aircraft for striking power. The PLAN also has a submarine force, including SSNs and SSBNs, although these have yet to mature into a world-class deterrent force. The PLAN possesses amphibious warfare ships, including co-opted merchant cargo vessels, although these are not designed for long-range missions and have been focused principally on local theater contingencies – in other words, Taiwan. During the 1980s, the PLAN's leadership developed a somewhat controversial vision for expanding the Navy by building power projection capabilities into the fleet, including two aircraft carriers, which are scheduled to be completed after 2009. The PLAN also has considered expanding its expeditionary forces, although amphibious ships and infantry remain a low strategic priority for China.[13]

An assistant naval attaché with the Chinese embassy to the United States, PLAN Captain Zhang Junshe, said that his nation's intention was to develop naval capabilities that would support domestic economic growth, and not to develop power projection forces to counterbalance the US Navy's presence in the Pacific.[14] However, Zhang's research into US military and naval capabilities and the US Department of Defense's planning, programming, and budgeting process implied competitive concern. On March 29, 2007, giving testimony before the US–China Economic and Security Review Commission, Professor Andrew Erickson of the US Naval War College articulated the United States' current perception of Chinese naval expansion:

> Every surface warship launched by China in the past decade (with the possible exception of the new LPD) carries sophisticated YJ series anti ship cruise missiles. These missiles deserve a measure of respect. It is important to recall that a single, Chinese-made C-802 anti ship cruise missile, which is less capable than China's newer [missiles], disabled Israel's *Hanit Sa'ar 5*-class missile boat in 2006 and killed four sailors. Additionally, the *Houbei* class, or 2208, wave piercing catamarans (based on an Australian ferry design) are an impressive anti-surface weapons system, employing high speed (perhaps 45 knots [83km/h] or so), low observability, and two or four advanced cruise missiles. China is building dozens of these vessels at many shipyards. Although I am not an expert on surface warfare, I am told that these would be highly effective in attacking surface warships in the waters around China, but their limited endurance would not allow them to operate for extended periods at much greater distances.[15]

Essential Capabilities

Historically, western naval forces have provided three essential capabilities: as rapid reaction forces; as combat-credible forces forward; and, in time of war, as forces that may immediately shift to offensive operations – capable of penetrating an enemy's defenses, and of taking pressure off a central battle front.

Since 1989, the United States has withdrawn much of its Cold War-era global army and air force garrisons, moving most warfighting power back to the continental United States. For the US Army, this has meant reducing forward deployed forces to a Stryker armored vehicle brigade in Germany, an airborne brigade in Italy, and one heavy brigade and a rotational Stryker brigade in Korea. There will probably be some small number of residual land and air forces in Southwest Asia after campaigns in Afghanistan and Iraq stabilize. Compare this posture with the Cold War era, when the United States had three army corps in Germany, and more than 40,000 soldiers and airmen in Korea.

As combat power has shifted back to the United States, the defense establishment will rely more upon the Navy for the rapid reaction capability of its expeditionary fleet and marines. In that context, naval forces will have returned to their roots: keeping the sea lanes open, ensuring access to markets and demonstrating a credible deterrent, capable of fighting a peer competitor, should one emerge.

Ultimately, naval power projection is about being able to seize control of the entire maritime battle space – from the blue water of the open ocean, through the green water of the coastal zone, to the brown water of the riverine environment, and ashore.

Today, naval and military forces must be able to do more than just fight and win wars. Success in the global political scene requires forces that are comfortable in any operation, from peacetime crisis mitigation (such as responding to a terrorist attack or a natural disaster), to low-intensity conflict (an insurgency or a civil war), to mid-intensity conflict (a localized war), and high-intensity conflict (a regional war). Forces must be able to modulate the kind of capabilities that they apply, appropriate to a situation, including both hard and soft power, so as not to win the war and lose the peace. By training and working with non-governmental organizations and other agencies, defense forces gradually are becoming more adept at recognizing where their capabilities fit across the operational spectrum – from humanitarian aid to major theater war.

At the upper end of the operational spectrum, naval power represents perhaps the ultimate armed deterrent: by means of the aircraft carrier and its air wing, from a conventional standpoint; and also by means of the ballistic missile submarine and the submarine-launched thermonuclear missile. SSBNs, such as the US Navy's *Ohio* class, or France's *Le Triomphant* class, may deploy stealthily and remain undetected for the entirety of their patrol cycle (six months or more for US submarines). The knowledge that these platforms and weapons are out there, somewhere at sea, at all times, presents an adversary with a major problem. Without knowing where the nuclear missile boats are located, even the most credible counter strategy – such as missile interceptors, or attack submarines – is given a nearly insoluble problem: where should these defenses be deployed to ensure that they would interdict or counter the submarines' missile launch? It may be argued that the ballistic missile submarine was one of the great checks and balances of the Cold War, preventing the too-aggressive expansion of either Western or Eastern Bloc, and driving both sides inevitably toward *détente* or proxy wars – such as the Vietnam War (1965–75) – rather than risk direct confrontation.

At the lower end of the operational spectrum, which includes operations other than war, navies contribute a great deal of capability for shaping the conditions of a potential conflict before it occurs. Fleets may prevent conflict by delivering softer effects such as humanitarian aid. For example, in January 2005, after the devastating tsunami of the preceding December, the US Navy deployed the hospital ship, USNS *Mercy* (T-AH 19), as part of the relief package contributed by the United States. The *Mercy* brought 1,000 beds, 12 operating rooms, diagnostic and clinical laboratories, and 275 trained medical staff (including physicians) to the worst-hit areas of Indonesia and elsewhere, where no hospital facilities were then functioning.

In the remainder of this chapter we shall see how a navy performs in its principal operating contexts – air warfare, surface warfare, undersea warfare. We will also take a closer look at what is meant by expeditionary power projection, as well as the role of Special Forces in modern naval power.

Air Warfare

During the second decade of the 20th century, the French and British had experimented with aircraft-carrying vessels – cruisers converted to host seaplanes. It was the Japanese, however, who in 1914 had enjoyed the first wartime victories for carrier-borne naval aviation. The seaplane tender *Wakamiya* had launched a successful strike, sinking an Imperial German minelayer at Tsingtao harbor, China. During the broader siege at Tsingtao, Japanese troops had also pioneered the use of radio communication with ships at sea, to call for and direct both naval gunfire and air strikes against targets ashore.[16]

The first aircraft carrier in United States service was the USS *Langley*, converted in 1922 from the ex-collier *Jupiter*. The *Langley* boasted a 540ft (165m) wooden flight deck and could carry 55 airplanes. By 1927, the *Langley* had been joined in the battle fleet by other converted carriers, the *Saratoga* and the *Lexington*. In 1931, the US Navy commissioned its first aircraft carrier designed as such from the keel up, the USS *Ranger*.

Through the inter-war decades of the 1920s and 1930s, the world's most powerful fleets – the British, the Japanese, the Germans, and the United States – remained conservatively focused on the battleship as the proper capital vessel. These fleets measured their strength by the number of large guns they could put to sea and, truly, few weapons of the day could match the firepower of these battleships' main armament. Nevertheless, as World War II began, some key incidents highlighted the sea change that would raise naval aviation to the prominence it enjoys today.

In May 1941, the German battleship *Bismarck* was successfully engaged by Royal Navy surface and air forces off Ushant, France. 15 Fairey Swordfish torpedo planes from the HMS *Ark Royal* attacked the German battleship. The "String Bags," as the clunky old bi-planes were affectionately called by their pilots, could maneuver at very low speeds, almost on the wave tops. The air group flew too low for either the *Bismarck*'s radar or her antiaircraft battery to deflect fire down upon them. From their low perch, the Swordfish of 825 Squadron torpedoed the *Bismarck*'s rudder, slowing her enough for the Royal Navy battle force to catch up and sink her with shellfire.

Another key moment for naval air power came with the Japanese attack at US Naval Station Pearl Harbor, Hawaii, December 7, 1941. During that attack, Imperial Japanese Navy (IJN) carrier-based aircraft had torpedoed, bombed, and strafed most of the US Pacific Fleet's battleships, which had been caught – like pickles in a barrel – within the enclosed harbor.

Fortuitously, the US fleet's aircraft carriers had been away on maneuvers and thus survived the attack. The US carriers' survival proved fateful for the Japanese, who then faced the revenge of the American naval air force at the Battle of Midway (June 4–7, 1942). During the battle, US Navy dive bombers and torpedo planes – and US Army Air Force B-17s – sent to the bottom four Japanese carriers and a cruiser, blows from which the IJN never fully recovered.

> Now we come to the Battle of Midway. Pearl Harbor was just bombed. Battleship Row was damaged heavily. The Japanese navy missed the carriers. The Pacific Fleet had nothing to throw against the Japanese in the Battle of Midway with regards to the "big gun" concept. But the aircraft carriers could get there. So here come these aircraft carriers, and it's not the sea battle that everybody dreamt about. It was airplanes sinking ships; a new concept. Hence, the birth of the carrier navy.[17]

Emerging from World War II, naval aviation and the aircraft carrier had proven their dominant places as the decisive instruments of power at sea, and as a crucial element of expeditionary power projection. Currently, the US, British, and French navies are developing new classes of aircraft carriers, as developing nations, such as India and China, work on similar projects. In the United States, the newest super carrier project, the *Gerald R. Ford*, CVN 78, is now under construction at Newport News, Virginia, slated for delivery in 2015. The new class will build upon the *Nimitz* class design, powered by two nuclear reactors, with turbines turning four shafts for a transit speed of better than 30 knots (56km/h). The *Ford*-class carriers will be 1,092ft (333m) long, with flight decks 256ft (78m) wide, and will displace approximately 100,000 tons fully loaded. The CVN 78's air wing will consist of more than 75 aircraft, including F/A-18E/F Super Hornets; EA-18G electronic warfare aircraft; Marine and Navy F-35 Lightning II strike fighters; and unmanned combat aerial vehicles, or UCAVs.

The armament of the modern carrier air wing includes a wide variety of air-to-surface weapons, many of which in the US and UK fleets are precision-guided munitions, or PGMs, such as the Joint Direct Attack Munition, or JDAM; and laser-guided bomb units. These weapons were used effectively during Operation *Iraqi Freedom*. Among the naval squadrons performing deep strike and close air support missions, Marine Corps air wings added to the combat power of their comrades in ground maneuver units. US Marine Corps Major General James F. Amos, commander of the 3rd Marine Aircraft Wing in 2003 said that marine aircraft flew a total of 25,600 hours in 9,800 sorties, dropping more than 6 million lb (2.7 million kg) of ordnance, including 2,200 precision-guided munitions and 2,300 general-purpose munitions.[18]

In an anti-ship role, modern naval air power has lost none of the prowess of its World War II ancestors. During the Falklands War (March 19–June 14, 1982), Argentine air power – principally A-4 Skyhawks and Super Etendards – proved devastatingly effective against six British ships. Although in many cases the

Argentine bombs – simple, unguided weapons with apparently unreliable fuses – struck their targets without detonating, on May 21 Argentine jets armed with 500lb (227kg) and 1,000lb (454kg) bombs attacked the Type 21 frigate HMS *Ardent*, which caught fire and sank with the loss of 22 crew. On May 24, Skyhawks bombed the Type 21 Frigate HMS *Antelope*, setting off an explosion in her magazine. Ironically, the *Antelope* had been on air defense duty when she was destroyed. On May 25 the Argentines bombed the destroyer HMS *Coventry*, which went down with the loss of 19 crew. On June 8, the A-4s caught the logistics landing ship RFA *Sir Galahad* unloading troops at Bluff Cove. Two bombs hit her and exploded, killing 48 soldiers from the Welsh Guards still aboard.

Perhaps the most ferocious anti-ship weapon the Argentines brought to the Falklands War was the French-made Exocet AM-39, a supersonic, sea-skimming missile with a 364lb (165kg) high-explosive warhead. The missile may be released from aircraft, surface combatants, submarines, or land-based launchers. The Argentines typically employed Exocets from their naval Super Etendard fighters, which could launch missiles from over the horizon, and strike targets at range of 45nm (83km). The targeted ships often neither detected the Super Etendard's approach, nor had warning of being targeted by its fire-control system. In separate attacks, Exocet-armed jets sank the destroyer HMS *Sheffield*, and the commercial container ship, the MV *Atlantic Conveyor*.

> The Super Etendard's inertial navigation system and the curvature of the earth permitted the plane to remain undetected by British radar. Once the plane entered British radar coverage, the pilot identified the target quickly with his radar, programmed the flight of the Exocet, launched, and departed the area immediately, not waiting to observe whether the missile struck its target. Hence, the Exocet was advertised as the "fire and forget" missile.[19]

The destroyer HMS *Glamorgan* survived, with damage, an Exocet strike from a land-based launcher the Argentines had set up near Port Stanley, on the Falklands' main island. British air-defense capabilities in the theater consisted of shipboard surface-to-air missiles, or SAMs, such as the Seawolf, and land-based Rapier SAMs, which scored hits against the Argentine Pucara and other planes. For its part, the Royal Navy's Fleet Air Arm made a respectable showing against the Junta's air force, with Harriers scoring about one third of the total number of Argentine aircraft splashed. The balance of 109 Argentine aircraft shot down was tallied by British surface-to-air missiles and small-arms fire.[20]

Among the lessons learned from the Falklands War was the crucial importance of air-defense capability to screen fleet activity, particularly in coastal waters where navigation is more confined and vessels are in closer proximity to enemy air power. Another important lesson was the powerful effect of sea-skimming anti-ship cruise missiles, which, when launched from high speed aircraft from beyond visual range, present a huge problem for defense. Aside from electronic countermeasures (ECM) – RF transmitters and other equipment designed to jam or prevent targeting in high threat environments – there are few defenses against weapons like the Exocet and more powerful high-speed missiles developed by the former Soviet Union and China.

The US Navy has had its own experience with the Exocet. On May 17, 1987, the frigate USS *Stark* was struck by two missiles, fired by an Iraqi Mirage F-1 fighter.

> At 2109 on the night of May 17, the port bridge wing lookout sighted a glow that appeared inbound from the horizon. The seaman called, "missile inbound, missile inbound." ... The junior officer of the deck also sighted the missile just before it struck the port side of the *Stark* below the bridge at frame 110. General quarters was sounded almost simultaneously with the first hit. The JOOD then observed a second missile inbound, grabbed the 1MC [intercom] and announced, "inbound missile, port side." At 2110, the second Exocet missile hit *Stark* in the same location as the first.[21]

Only the second missile's blast-fragmentation warhead exploded upon impact with the *Stark*, heavily damaging the ship's internal structure. Both missiles' rocket motors and burning propellant caused a lethal fire – flashing to 12 million BTUs or 1400–1500°F (760–816°C) – among berthing spaces and the ship's Combat Information Center (CIC), the nerve center of a modern warship where the vessel's weapons systems are operated. The explosion of the second missile also severed the ship's fire main, which limited the crew's firefighting capabilities and contributed to flooding aboard. The crew jettisoned their ship's ammunition "to prevent cook off in the intense heat."[22] The *Stark*'s damage control and firefighting parties saved their ship, but by the time the frigate USS *Waddel* arrived to assist the next morning, 25 sailors had died.

Following the attack on the *Stark*, the US Navy began to review the technology and procedures associated with cruise missile defense. Like all *Perry*-class guided missile frigates, the *Stark* had been equipped with the SLQ-32 electronic countermeasures system. The "Slick 32," as it is known by ship crews, is designed to detect and jam enemy fire-control radar emissions.

In 1973, the Israeli Navy had been among the first to demonstrate the potential effectiveness of shipboard electronic countermeasures in combat. During the Yom Kippur War, a squadron of Israeli corvettes, led by the *Hanit* and armed with relatively short-range Gabriel missiles and 76mm guns, engaged Syrian missile boats, which were armed with Soviet-designed long-range

SS-N-2 Styx missiles. Off the Syrian port of Latakia, the Israelis made effective use of active and passive electronic countermeasures, jamming and spoofing all 52 of the missiles the Syrians launched at them. In something of an historic irony, during the 2006 conflict between Israel and the militant group Hezbollah in Lebanon, the Sa'ar 5-class corvette, INS *Hanit*, namesake of the vessel that had led the 1973 victory, was crippled by a land-launched anti-ship missile.

According to the US Navy, the *Stark*'s Slick 32 had detected Iraqi jets and the Exocets' homing signals. However, the system had not been able to jam the Mirages' targeting radar, nor the missiles. Subsequently, the Navy added an active jamming system to the Slick 32 equipment. The *Stark* had also possessed the Mk 33 Rapid Blooming Offboard Chaff launcher, which was capable of dispensing metallic confetti to obscure the ship's radar return image and confuse an enemy's targeting radar or RF-homing missile. However, caught by surprise, the *Stark*'s automatic defenses had not responded to the threat.

Countermeasures against anti-ship missiles also include a family of specialized gun and missile weapon systems, designed to be the last line of defense should ECM fail to avert an attack. The US Navy and 16 other nations have adapted versions of the Phalanx Close-In Weapon System (CIWS), which is a shipboard, radar-directed, 20mm rotary gun system designed to blast missiles and other airborne threats at close range. The CIWS's weapon essentially is the same as the aircraft-mounted M61 Gatling gun, firing a blistering 3,000–4,500 rounds per minute. The Phalanx's computer-controlled radar uses a closed-loop tracking algorithm to automatically locate and lock onto a target, directing the gun's stream of armor-piercing discarding-sabot bullets against it. At maximum rate of fire, the CIWS sounds like the roar of an un-muffled diesel engine's exhaust.

Many vessels, including the US Navy's amphibious assault and landing ships, are equipped with the RIM-116 Rolling Airframe Missile (RAM), which is derived from the Army Stinger manportable air-defense system. RAM, a joint development between the US and German navies, is designed to intercept maneuvering anti-ship missiles.

Shipboard countermeasures and self-defense weapons are tools of last resort, however. Far preferable to a ship commander is the ability to engage threats far beyond their lethal range. Among the most sophisticated anti-air warfare systems in any fleet is the Aegis Combat System. Installed aboard the US Navy's *Ticonderoga*-class CGs and *Arleigh Burke*-class DDGs, Aegis is also deployed aboard various vessels of the Spanish, Norwegian, Australian, Japanese, and South Korean navies.

At its heart, Aegis is a powerful computer command and decision system, linked to key sensors including the AN/SPY-1D radar. Aegis processes target identification and tracking information for the ship's fire-control system, which in turn launches missiles and directs fire from the ship's main battery. Aegis is capable of simultaneously tracking more than 100 targets at greater than 100nm (185km) range. The SPY-1D is a phased array radar system with both surface and air search capabilities. The radar's distinctive, fixed antennas are electronically scanned and pulsed to emit electromagnetic energy in specific directions, rather than being mechanically steered, like rotating antennas.

The SPY-1D is being modernized to discern targets in the cluttered airspace over coastal waters. Further improvements add image resolution, processing capacity, and speed to track and cue the interception of ballistic missiles. With several successful intercepts having been demonstrated over the last few years, sea-based missile defense has been one of the few success stories in the Pentagon's multibillion dollar missile defense programs portfolio.

Aegis is able to attack surface, air, and undersea targets with missiles launched from CGs' and DDGs' Mk 41 Vertical Launch System (VLS). The VLS includes a variable number of launch cells, embedded in the ship's deck, hosting as many as 90 missiles aboard a CG. In the air-defense mission, the VLS fires Standard Missiles (SMs), which actively home in on their targets using radar.

For all its capability, however, Aegis carries a large price tag. In 2002, the US Navy estimated that the total development and production cost of the Aegis weapon system was more than $40 billion.[23] That staggering figure includes decades of systems engineering, design and development, as well as the purchase of many "ship sets" of equipment, but not the cost of the ships themselves. The first DDG-51-class ship was developed and built in 1985 for approximately $2.4 billion (adjusted to fiscal year 2007 dollars). The US built 62 DDG 51-class ships between 1985 and 2005, at an average cost of $1.1 billion (again, adjusted to fiscal year 2007 dollars).

Aegis also has been at the center of some controversy. On July 3, 1988 the Aegis cruiser USS *Vincennes* shot down an Iranian Airbus, Flight 655, killing 290 passengers and crew. The crew on watch in the *Vincennes'* CIC that morning had misinterpreted the data displayed by Aegis, resulting in a false identification of the Airbus A300 as a hostile F-14.

> Both the International Civil Aviation Organization report and that undertaken by the United States attribute the mistake to tension on board the *Vincennes* and the conviction among the crew that the ship could be attacked that day. This led a technician so to misread the information on his computer screen that he believed the opposite of what it was indicating. The mistake occurred in circumstances that did not amount to a full-scale conflict, so one can only assume that in intensive armed conflict such mistakes will be more frequent. Close ranges and a rapid approach of a hostile contact make tension particularly acute.[24]

On the Flight Deck[25]

While operational conditions often expose sailors, marines, and aircrew to the dangers of combat, the industrial environment aboard a modern carrier presents risks of its own. Aboard ship, personnel must develop and maintain a high level of technical proficiency, analogous to the materiel readiness condition of their ships, aircraft, and mission systems. Underway, crews maintain near-constant training and work "evolutions" to hone their skills and promote safety.

There are perhaps few working environments as potentially dangerous as those of an aircraft carrier. The US Navy Safety Center notes that while perhaps as many as 90 percent of major mishaps are related to human error, nevertheless, the shipboard environment is an inherently dangerous one. Quite apart from the hazards associated with combat training and operations, sailors and marines must navigate the ever-present shipboard risks of fire, flood and accidents with heavy equipment.

An American nuclear-powered aircraft carrier's flight deck is a particularly hazardous place where a moment's inattention may result in catastrophe. Underway, the carrier's flight deck crew are nearly constantly engaged in "flight ops," launching or recovering aircraft. These operations involve a large number of personnel moving across 4.5 acres (18,211sq m) of deck area. The topside crew wear standardized and color-coded protective clothing, including a "cranial," or flight deck helmet, which is a close-fitting cloth cap reinforced at the brow and at the back of the skull by plastic plates. In addition to the cranial, crewmen wear goggles and hearing protection – absolutely essential during long duty hours amid more than 145 decibels of constant jet noise. As an aside, that decibel count is analogous to a gunshot, and is about 25 decibels above the human threshold of pain.[26] Crewmen also wear steel-toed boots and gloves, color-coded shirts and Mk 1 "float coats." The colors designate one's duty assignment on the flight deck. For example, blue shirts handle the aircraft while on the flight deck, or on the carrier's four massive elevators that bring planes up onto the flight deck from the hangar deck below. Red shirts are trained in rescue, fire fighting and explosive ordnance disposal – crucial in the event of a crash, or an accident on the flight deck involving weapons. Red shirts also load and unload weapons from the aircraft preparing to launch on missions. Purple shirts, or "grapes," handle aircraft fueling and de-fueling. Green shirts include aircraft-maintenance crewmen. Brown shirts, usually seen draped with their jet's steel tie-down chains, are the plane captains. The brown shirts are responsible for the general condition of their planes, and often view the aircraft as belonging to them and merely loaned to pilots for the duration of their missions.

Yellow shirts work for the carrier's "air boss," and supervise the handling, launch, and recovery of all embarked aircraft. The air boss supervises and directs primary flight-control, "pri-fly," which is a station located in the carrier's superstructure, or "island," overlooking the flight deck. Though outranked by the ship's captain, and flag officer, should an admiral be aboard, the air boss is a supreme authority during flight ops. His yellow shirts are trained to manage some of the most potentially dangerous tasks on the carrier, including the catapult officer, or "shooter," who is stationed toward the bow, directing the safe operation of the ship's massive, steam-powered launch system.

To have some idea of the forces involved in a catapult launch, a typical F/A-18's combat-loaded takeoff weight is 40,000lb (18,144kg), requiring 178,000N (Newtons) to get into the air (a Newton is a unit of measurement for the force required to accelerate a body with a mass of 1kg at rate of $1m/s^2$.) To launch this aircraft, the catapult must thrust the Hornet from the flight deck with force at least equal to its mass, or more than 256ft/sec (78m/sec). During a typical launch, the steam catapult's shuttle, attached to the plane's nose gear, travels a 309ft (94m) rail embedded into the flight deck. The catapult shuttle is impelled by a steam piston that exerts a constant force of more than 106ft/sec squared (almost 33m/sec squared), for just under 2.5 seconds, to put the fighter into the air. The pilot feels more than 3Gs at launch, and as he goes over the bow, his jet's engines are at full "military power," the maximum throttle setting, blasting off right over the heads of the catapult officer and his crew.

Another yellow shirt, the arresting gear officer, stationed toward the stern, manages the operation of the carrier's recovery equipment, which includes the Mk 7, Mod 3 shipboard arresting gear. This system is capable of stopping a 54,000lb (25,000kg) aircraft in less than 350ft (107m).[27] The arresting gear includes four cross-deck pendants, which are the 1⅜in (3.5cm) thick steel cables that traverse the after section of the flight deck. On landing, an aircraft's tail hook is to catch one of the pendants, drawing tension from an arresting engine below deck. The engine includes a massive hydraulic ram that gradually absorbs the energy from the aircraft's landing. Following an arrested landing, a 400psi compressed air charge retracts the cable, drawing back across the flight deck.

During launch and recovery, the flight deck crew must be continually aware of their and their comrades' positions and actions, and those of the aircraft and other heavy equipment moving about the relatively crowded area. Crewmen wearing white coded float coats are responsible for the safety of the men and women working in close proximity to aircraft, heavy equipment, and weapons. The basic rules of flight deck safety include an admonishment to "avoid walking in front of jet intakes or behind jet exhaust, especially if you aren't sure whether the aircraft's engines are turning. This is very important at night."[28] That warning was underscored by one well-known incident in which a crewman was sucked through the air intake of an ES-3A Shadow electronic reconnaissance aircraft. The incident was recounted by the Shadow's pilot, Lieutenant Marc Shuford:

> As a second cruise pilot flying the ES-3A aboard the USS *Enterprise*, I had seen a lot of unusual things happen on the flight deck. I had seen people blown overboard, into equipment, and into each other enough times to have a healthy respect for what a turning engine can do if you don't stay clear. [While waiting for the signal to launch,] one of the catapult crewmen had walked right in front of my engine and had been sucked in ... The 19 year-old crewman had been pulled completely off his feet and into the intake. He had put his hand out to stop the rest of his body from going in and his hand was mangled ... I went down and visited with him in medical ... I will never forget the look on that poor guy's face as he stared in shock at the nub that remained where his right hand had been.[29]

Surface Warfare

During World War II, particularly in the Pacific, there were many gun battles between cruisers and battleships, smashing each other to pieces with volleys of armor-piercing shells the size of automobiles. And yet, of the warships still on active service in the US Navy, the venerable sail frigate USS *Constitution* has the distinction of being one of the last actually to have defeated an enemy with naval gunfire.[30] Once the only option, the modern surface combatant's main battery – of radar-directed 76mm or 5in weapons – is now just one of many options a skipper has at his disposal.

For example, the commanding officer of the guided missile frigate USS *Nicholas*, Commander Dennis G. Morral, recounted an action in 1991, involving his ship's gun and its SH-60 Light Airborne Multipurpose System (LAMPS) helicopters. At the start of Operation *Desert Storm*, the *Nicholas* was at sea with several Kuwaiti naval vessels, including the fast attack missile craft *Istiqlal* and *Al Sanbouk*. The squadron had maneuvered close to the Iraqi-held Dorra Oil Field, and launched a helicopter to reconnoiter the area. Unexpectedly, the helicopter came under fire from heavy weapons aboard the oil platforms. The squadron withdrew. Commander Morral during an interview in 1991 said:

> I asked at that time that we be allowed to go back up there with just my *Nicholas* and the *Istiqlal*, which was the most capable of the two fast patrol boats, and engage and eliminate the enemy forces on these platforms ... The following day I was given permission to do that ... Under the cover of darkness, then, the *Nicholas* and the *Istiqlal* [were] in total EMCON [emissions control], meaning that they had nothing radiating at all.[31]

Stealthily, the two ships returned to the platform, approaching from the south, and the *Nicholas* launched her LAMPS helicopter. Also aboard was a US Army air detachment, with its OH-58 Kiowa helicopter, armed with AGM-114 Hellfire missiles. The helicopters and the ships' main battery had the advantage of greater range than the weapons the crews expected to find on the Iraqi-held platforms. The OH-58 launched the first surprise volley: three Hellfire missiles against the Iraqis' fortified positions. Fire from the *Nicholas*' 76mm and the *Istiqlal*'s 40mm guns finished off the antiaircraft emplacements on the platforms.

> All three of the missiles were direct hits on the bunkers. And I have to say, in retrospect, the weapon of choice against a well-fortified sandbagged bunker ... is in fact the Hellfire missile. We picked the two [bunkers] on the side that we thought were the most heavily fortified. We thought, perhaps, those were where the radios and the officers, if there were any, were going to be manning. In fact that was the case. We were a little concerned that if we gave them too much time they would have the ability to radio back to about 40 miles [64km] north where the enemy forces were and then we would be faced with an F-1 Mirage or an Exocet missile.[32]

Even in the era of precision-guided missiles, naval gunfire still is an attractive option for the relatively low cost of its ammunition, and its relatively high rate of fire. It may not look as glamorous as a sail frigate's broadside of cannon, but the modern naval gun is more than capable of overwhelming a target with rapid shellfire. In the land attack role, the long-retired *Iowa*-class battleships' 16in, 50cal Mk 7 rifles[33] have pride of place as being among the heaviest naval gunfire support weapons ever to put to sea. These huge guns fired two basic types of ammunition, including 1,900lb (862kg) high-explosive and 2,700lb (1225kg) armor-piercing rounds, capable of penetrating the armor equivalent of 30ft (9m) of concrete. The gun could reach out to hit targets 23nm (42km) away.

Typical of the *Iowa*-class battleships, the USS *Missouri* was 887ft (270m) long, with a beam of 108ft (33m), drew 28ft (8.5m) of water and displaced 45,000 tons. During World War II, her main battery included nine 16in guns, with 20 additional 5in guns. When decommissioned on March 31, 1992, the *Missouri* was the last battleship on active service. The "Mighty Mo'" had used her guns during the bitter fight for Iwo Jima (February–March 1945), and had bombarded Okinawa (March 24 and May 27, 1945). On August 29, 1945, the *Missouri* had steamed into Tokyo Bay to host the formal ceremony announcing the Japanese surrender. On January 17, 1991, having been fitted out with new armored box launchers above her No. 3 16in gun turret, the *Missouri* fired 28 Tomahawk cruise missiles during Operation *Desert Storm*.

During World War II, and until the last battleship was decommissioned in the 1990s, amphibious troops depended upon the battleships' 16in guns to batter entrenched or fortified enemy fighting positions. *Iowa*-class battleships could fire 90 rounds of 16in and 450 rounds of 5in shells within 5 minutes, the equivalent of 12–16 sorties of attack aircraft, at a sustained rate of fire of approximately one round per gun tube, per minute, according to US Army Captain Michael P. Ley, a student of naval gunfire support.[34] Naval gunfire support missions made use of naval artillery to augment the field artillery of troops maneuvering ashore. Some sailors, marines and soldiers are specialized in the discipline of air and naval gunfire liaison, or ANGLICO.

In the US Marine Corps, ANGLICO companies – dating to the Spanish–American War (1898) and earlier – are small units whose task is to secure a location ashore with good lines of sight onto enemy positions. The ANGLICO units use radio or other signaling technologies to adjust the fire of ships' main batteries, or aircraft, to clear a path through enemy defenses from the beach inland.

With the decommissioning of the battleships, the US fleets' remaining naval artillery largely consists of the 5in, .54cal Mk 45 guns aboard CGs and DDGs. These weapons fire a 69lb (31kg) shell 13nm (24km). The Navy is developing a heavier gun – the 155mm Advanced Gun System, with precision-guided ammunition – for a new class of destroyers, but until these arrive, the service is working to improve the range and lethality of legacy ammunition.

For example, at the US Naval Surface Warfare Center's facility at Dahlgren, Virginia, engineers are developing a series of rocket-propelled, GPS/inertial navigation unit-guided artillery rounds, based on decades of army and naval research during the 1960s and 1970s. If proved suitable, such projects could add programmable, precision accuracy to rounds capable of reaching out 40–50nm (74–93km) from a 5in gun. Standard 5in projectiles have a maximum range of about 24km (13nm). Other projects are developing technologies for 155mm guns and precision-guided ammunition to arm a new generation of surface combatants, such as the DDG 1000 destroyer. If this platform and its weapons are successful, they would provide naval gunfire capable of striking targets at 83nm (154km) range.[35]

Nevertheless, critics have pointed out that with the decommissioning of the battleships, the limited number of guns and the types of warships available for naval gunfire support missions today are inadequate to meet the expeditionary maneuver force's requirements.

> Despite ... improvements, the 5in. weapon still does not fulfill the requirements of modern naval gunfire support ... The use of ... expensive lightly protected ships can best be demonstrated by a [naval gunfire support] mission in Lebanon [1983] when the USS *Ticonderoga*, a $1 billion cruiser ... was called on to provide [naval

gunfire support] with her two 5in. weapons. The ship is lightly armored and is not designed to withstand either numerous cruise missile or 122mm [4.8in] artillery hits. Had the Syrians and militia used these weapons on her, the navy would have been forced to leave the [naval gunfire support] mission to its one armored ship [at that time still in commission], the [battleship] USS *New Jersey*. In a future conflict with a foe having the capability of Syria, Iran or Libya, using such expensive, lightly protected ships, equipped with relatively short-range guns may force the navy to limit its [naval gunfire support]. Additionally, any confrontation with a power that has a viable naval and air threat could force the navy to devote its limited assets to higher-priority missions.[36]

Some zealots continue to argue in favor of bringing back the battleship with its big guns, yet this idea is a non-starter with the US Navy's leadership. The costs of modernizing and maintaining the great dreadnoughts are prohibitive. In a fleet that is actively seeking ways to reduce – through automation and other means – the cost and risks associated with manpower aboard its warships, there is little room for another ship that requires a complement of 2,800 sailors.

Electric Weapons

So the fleet must find other ways to meet naval gunfire support and deep strike requirements. The US Navy is looking beyond conventional guns and ammunition to consider new ways of harnessing the immense amount of electrical power that will be generated by the prime movers of next-generation warships. At Dahlgren's weapons laboratory in 2006, the Navy restarted its electromagnetic rail gun efforts using some of the original hardware from the US Department of Defense's "Brilliant Pebbles" missile-defense project from the 1960s and 1970s.

The rail gun system demonstrator at Dahlgren is being used to validate performance parameters established by the Office of Naval Research, to demonstrate the ability to launch 44lb (20kg) projectiles to a range of 200nm (370km) – comparable to the Marine Corps' naval surface fire support requirements, as outlined in *Ship to Objective Maneuver*.[37] To meet the full fire support objective, a rail gun would have to sustain a rate of fire of a half dozen rounds per minute. Additionally, the system would have to be robust enough to fire 1,000 shots before launch rail replacement, a tall order when one considers that the electromagnetic gun expends 32 megajoules with each shot, enough energy to generate high heat between the launch rails and the projectile, or its sabot. In experiments to date, the high temperature and friction have significantly ablated many of the metals and ceramic structures from which the demonstration gun's rails have been made.

If its technology can be proven operationally suitable and effective, one advantage of the rail gun will be that its hypersonic projectiles don't need explosives to deliver lethal force to a target. The kinetic energy of the round's impact would be enough to destroy an armored vehicle, or to penetrate a structure. Without explosive fill, the projectiles become much less hazardous to handle aboard ship. The rail gun also permits launch power to be fine-tuned. Instead of a one-shock fits all launch force, the rail may deliver different effects by launching projectiles at lower or higher power settings. One operational benefit of this may be the ability to precisely direct multiple-round, simultaneous impact projectiles – a technique used by artillery batteries, whereby several shells are fired at intervals and varying trajectories, so that all fall onto the target at the same time, providing no warning or opportunity for escape.

Cruise Missiles

While naval artillery may enjoy a renaissance with the arrival of new precision-strike munitions and advanced technologies like the rail gun, missile weapons have been developed to meet the lion's share of the surface warfare mission set, including anti-ship and long-range precision strike. Many of the world's less sophisticated navies have developed weapons that trump some of the advantages enjoyed by more costly, capital ships. The missile-armed fast attack craft is a powerful adversary, especially in the crowded and confused coastal zone where targets may blend into non-combatant traffic.

The danger from anti-ship missiles is obvious, with the Falklands War and the USS *Stark* incident fresh in mind. Other examples underscore the fearsome reputation of anti-ship cruise missiles. In October 1967, at the end of the Six Day War, the Egyptians fired four SS-N-2 Styx missiles at the Israeli destroyer, *Eilat*. One officer recounted his ship's crisis:

> The captain was pointing out the buildings in Port Said that we viewed through our binoculars when we saw the launch from the harbor. Earlier, he had witnessed test firings of our own Gabriel missiles, and so correctly decided that what we saw meant that a missile was headed our way. It turned out to be the first of four Styx radar-guided missiles launched at the *Eilat*. He immediately sounded the alarm, called for battle stations, and turned the ship in order to present the smallest target to the incoming missiles. In about a minute most of the crew were at their stations and I could hear the chatter of our machine guns firing at the inbound missiles. But it wasn't enough.[38]

Two of the missiles struck the ship, cutting main power and severely damaging the hull. The ship went down in the Red Sea. Forty-seven of *Eilat*'s crew died in the attack, or in the water after, many suffering injuries all too characteristic of modern naval warfare.

"Immersion blast exposure" is an additional cause of injury and death among waterborne survivors ... Of the 32 *Eilat* sailors rescued after the explosion, most suffered significant injuries of gas-filled abdominal viscera, as well as pulmonary injuries, without any external signs of bruising or injury. Most required emergency surgery. These survivors had experienced "immersion blast injury," a phenomenon rarely seen in peacetime, but long documented in military medical history. During World War II, repeated dive-bombing and torpedo attacks on ships often left the majority of a ship's company in the water after a direct hit. On those occasions where a depth charge, mine, or torpedo exploded near swimming survivors, grave danger to life existed from water blast, and death frequently occurred.[39]

The BGM-109 Tomahawk Land Attack Missile (TLAM) has added a new dimension of deep-strike capability to the surface fleet. The missile is driven by a F107-WR-402 turbofan engine. The TLAM's guidance system is able to find its target using a technology called Digital Scene Matching Area Correlation (DSMAC), which compares the landscape visible to the missile's camera with a digital map image stored in its memory. Also, the missile may use its GPS-assisted inertial navigation system.

The US fleet's destroyers and cruisers, as well as US nuclear-powered fast attack submarines carry Tomahawks loaded in vertical launch system canisters. The Royal Navy's *Swiftsure-* and *Trafalgar*-class attack submarines also have TLAM-launch capability.

TLAMs sounded the opening notes of Operation *Desert Storm*, and came up for an encore on March 20, 2003, at the start of Operation *Iraqi Freedom*. The cruisers USS *Cowpens* and USS *Bunker Hill*, the destroyers USS *Donald Cook* and USS *Milius*, and the SSNs USS *Cheyenne* and USS *Montpelier* launched hundreds of TLAMs in the opening salvo of the war. During Operation *Allied Force* (1999), as NATO forces moved against Serbian units in Kosovo, two TLAMs struck a Yugoslav Ministry of Interior (MUP) police headquarters building in Pristina, destroying two floors of the building with their 700lb (318kg) warheads but leaving the rest – and the other structures nearby – relatively unscathed.[40]

The only other target that was in the urban area was the Pristina MUP regional headquarters. It was attacked near the stadium after midnight when the stadium and the arena were not inhabited. And it was destroyed, and in fact the collateral damage was limited primarily to, I think, some broken windows, except at the designated aim point.[41]

Forward Presence

Surface combatants act as ambassadors of their nation. However, forward presence also exposes ships and crews to threats including political violence such as terrorism. On October 12, 2000, the destroyer USS *Cole* was visiting Aden, Yemen, when it was attacked by al Qaeda-affiliated suicide bombers. The attackers had approached the *Cole* disguised as a contract garbage scow, offering the crew service while in port. The scow carried explosives, which detonated amidships alongside the *Cole*, blowing a 40ft (12m) hole in the ship's side, killing 17 sailors and causing more than $150 million in damage. In addition to penetrating the hull, the explosion had compressed steel decks together, literally crushing sailors in between. According to the US Naval Medical Center, Portsmouth, Virginia, 39 sailors survived with a variety of conditions, including predominately lower extremity injuries, orthopedic injuries, open fractures, and infection. In the days after the attack, then-Secretary of Defense William R. Cohen was defiant: "We have an obligation to be forward deployed as we are today. We cannot shrink back ... I can see no alternative but for us to remain active and engaged in world affairs as we are today."[42]

The *Cole*, whose keel had been broken in the blast, was repaired at the Ingalls shipyard at Pascagoula, Mississippi, and returned to active service in 2002. Improvised explosive devices, which have become infamous and deadly on land in Iraq, remain a serious threat for naval vessels in unsecured ports. Partly in response to this threat, as well as in support of renewed emphasis on expeditionary operations, the US Navy established an acquisition program office focused on force protection capabilities. Working with the US Navy's Explosive Ordnance Disposal (EOD) and naval special warfare acquisition offices, the force protection program provides tools and capabilities designed to prevent future incidents such as the *Cole* attack.

For example, the US Navy's EOD program maintains marine mammal systems (comprised of specially trained Atlantic bottlenose dolphins and California sea lions) that are capable of sensing and locating mines and other undersea objects, as well as divers intruding in restricted areas. As sentries guarding sensitive areas such as the exclusion zones around warships at anchor or in port, the animals are unrivalled in their abilities to detect and home in on underwater sound and motion. Even in the murkiest conditions, with zero visibility, the mammals may use echo-location or their sense of smell to find a human swimmer. Once they have located a diver, the animals approach with a specially designed restraint (held in their jaws or attached to a harness), which they may fasten to the diver's arm or leg. The restraint is attached by pressing it against the diver's body or limbs, causing a spring activated clamp to close and lock (very similar to the location markers used by the animals to identify mines or other objects). The clamp is buoyant and includes an electronic beacon. The beacon emits a signal to a security team patrolling in a boat nearby. The team may use the signal to track, locate and arrest the intruder.

Fire!

Damage control and fire fighting are fundamental skills sets all sailors must master. Few crisis events aboard ship are as dangerous as fire. Crews are drilled continually in fire prevention and mitigation techniques, as well as escape. Seawater pumps and hoses, chemical foam extinguishers, and flame-retardant clothing are standard equipment, kept stored in the fire fighting and Damage Control (DC) lockers located throughout a ship.

With aviation fuel, weapons and other hazardous materials aboard, the modern warship poses multiple potential fire hazards. In 1965, off North Vietnam, the aircraft carrier USS *Forrestal* suffered perhaps the worst fire disaster aboard an American warship since World War II, one which cost the lives of 134 crewmen and caused more than $72 million in damage to the ship. At 10:52am local time, July 29, 1965, an A-4 Skyhawk on the flight deck accidentally launched one of its 127mm Zuni rockets, which hit the fuel tank of another A-4. The blast also ruptured the fuel tank of a third aircraft.

> The burning fuel quickly spread to the after portion of the flight deck, pushed by thirty-two knots [59km/h] of wind and the exhaust of several jets positioned ahead of the stricken aircraft ... Many of the high capacity foam and firefighting hoses on the port [left] side of the flight deck were engulfed in flames and unusable. A 1,000lb [454kg] bomb fell from A-4 number 405 when it was struck by the rocket, and rolled into a pool of burning jet fuel.[43]

Less than two minutes later the bomb exploded, instantly killing 27 men as they fought the flames. Another bomb detonated and set off a chain of explosions that spread the fire down three decks into the *Forrestal*'s aft section. The fire was fueled by 40,000 gallons (151kl) of JP5 fuel from the stricken jets. This and the weapons cooking off in the blaze killed another 107 sailors sleeping in aft berthing areas, or on duty in other compartments.

Surface combatants, such as DDGs, also have flight decks – small helicopter pads near the stern. Here too vigilance against fire is crucial, as is shown in this account by pilot Lieutenant Commander Michael Stoll, of the armed helicopter detachment aboard the destroyer USS *Bulkeley*, February 2004.

> Early one dark morning in February, our carrier strike group was only a few hours away from conducting a high-speed transit of the Bab el Mandeb strait. My

[helicopter squadron light] detachment on board *Bulkeley* had been tasked to fly one of our two SH-60B helicopters on an armed escort in support of the transit ... We had discovered a problem with the hydraulic system that downed the aircraft for flight.[44]

As the crew worked to get the second helicopter ready as a replacement, a sailor ran to the group. He announced that there was smoke in the recovery assist securing and traversing control room, adjacent to the Landing Safety Officer (LSO) station, starboard, or to the right, of the flight deck. The casualty report was passed via the ship's intercom:

"White smoke is reported in ... RAST [recovery assistance securing and traversing systems] machinery room and LSO shack. Away the at-sea fire party. Provide from repair [locker] three. This is not a drill." ... The [source of the fire had been] rags ... soaked in various chemicals, including hydraulic fluid and restroom cleaner, earlier in the day ... A chemical reaction between the strong oxidizer in the restroom cleaner and the alkaline, petroleum-based hydraulic fluid apparently generated enough heat to ignite the pile of rags. It didn't take long for white smoke to fill the RAST machinery room. The smoke then spread to the LSO shack via the air feed between the two spaces. It took only nine minutes to extinguish the fire from initial detection, but it took another hour to ensure both spaces were de-smoked and safe to enter.[45]

Other than a flight deck, the most dangerous places for fire to break out aboard ship include the spaces housing the ship's main propulsion and electrical power generation systems. The risk is heightened by the presence of fuel, the close confines of the engineering compartment on many ships, and the high levels of heat and noise, which may interfere with rescue efforts in the event that a crewman becomes trapped. In a fire, once a compartment becomes filled with smoke, the atmosphere may be just as deadly as the flames themselves. On May 8, 1985, the US Coast Guard high endurance cutter *Chase* (WHEC 718) endured an explosive fire in her engine compartment. One crewman became trapped in the space, unable to escape as the intense fire and smoke had blocked the compartment's only exit. The trapped crewman died in the fire, according to a citation for heroism awarded to Petty Officer Randall Rogers, who had braved the flames in an attempt to rescue his shipmate.[46]

Undersea Warfare
Strictly speaking, the first true submarines – colloquially called *boats*, not ships, vessels designed to live out their entire service lives undersea independent of atmosphere – are products of the nuclear age. The purists would argue that diesel

electric-, gasoline- or – hearkening back to the Confederate torpedo boat, CSS *Hunley* – manually-powered subs of earlier periods in history are more properly classed as submersibles. These vessels are air-breathing, and must surface or at least raise a snorkel to feed oxygen to their propulsion plants.

For a nuclear submarine, propulsion is motivated by a reactor, which boils water to move a steam turbine, which turns the boat's screw or impels its propulsor. The nuclear reactor requires no air to function, nor fuel, until the more than 30-year life of its radioactive core is exhausted. For these boats, the only factor limiting the time they may remain submerged is the human crew itself, who must be resupplied and relieved at some point. The first nuclear-powered submarine was launched on January 21, 1954, christened the USS *Nautilus* (SSN 571).

The purists notwithstanding, since its operational debut with the German and British fleets during World War I, the submarine has evolved into one of the most feared platforms at sea. One has only to look at the war record of the German U-Boat squadrons operating off North America during the "happy time" in 1942, to get the picture. During the early phase of the Battle of the Atlantic, Allied merchant shipping ferrying supplies from the United States to Britain and the Soviet Union suffered appalling losses from the torpedoes and guns of the Kriegsmarine's wolf pack.

> During 1939–1940 the Royal Navy held its own against the submarine menace in the Atlantic but, beginning in 1941, their merchant ship losses began to grow. For example, one night in April 1941 a Nazi wolf pack sank 10 of 22 ships in one slow trans-Atlantic convoy. From the beginning the Allies had relied upon the battle-tested tactics of merchant convoys to shepherd vessels between the coastal waters of North America and England. They found in 1941, however, that even with warship escorts, they could not drive off or sink all the U-boats prowling the Atlantic.[47]

Some of the most advanced submarine designs in service worldwide are diesel-electric boats produced by Germany and Holland. These submarines are very capable and may remain submerged for long periods of time. Because of its relatively small size, compared with the United States' nuclear-powered fast attack boats, the modern diesel electric submarine may prowl the shallow coastal waters, posing a major threat to amphibious landing and logistics support operations.

In 1982, during the Falklands War, the super-quiet nuclear submarine demonstrated its prowess. On May 2, 1982, HMS *Conqueror* attacked the Argentine cruiser *General Belgrano* with two Mk 8 torpedoes. The incident was somewhat controversial as the attack drowned 360 Argentines. One point of view held that the *Belgrano* had been outside the limits of the conflict zone around the islands and should therefore have been considered *hors de combat*. Nevertheless, the British high command viewed the *Belgrano*'s presence as a significant threat to the embattled Royal Navy-led expeditionary force. To date, the *Conqueror* has the fame of being the only nuclear submarine on active service to have sunk an enemy warship with her torpedoes.

The most modern nuclear-powered fast attack submarines, the US Navy's *Virginia* class, have evolved from several decades of development, going back to Admiral Hyman G. Rickover's (1900–86) early vision of what the "nuclear navy" would become.

Having discussed the heavy cost for modern carriers and Aegis surface combatants, it remains to note the staggering costs of acquiring and maintaining a credible nuclear fast attack submarine force. The lead ship costs for the USS *Virginia* are estimated at more than $2.7 billion.[48] It is not entirely clear how many *Virginia*-class boats the US Navy will acquire; however, its strategic fleet force structure plan calls for approximately 50 submarines in service through 2036 (although not all of them *Virginia*-class boats). The Navy's plan also indicates that by 2036 approximately 20–30 would be "improved" *Virginia*-class boats. So what does the taxpayer get for spending the equivalent of the gross domestic product of Bangladesh (roughly $65 billion) buying 30 *Virginia*-class subs?

More than 370ft (113m) in length, with a beam of approximately 33ft (10m), the *Virginia* displaces approximately 8,000 tons. Her combat power is resident in a 12-cell vertical launch system, for Tomahawk and other missile weapons. Four torpedo tubes will be able to launch Mk 48 advanced-capability torpedoes and Tomahawk missiles, as can the *Virginia*'s antecedents, the *Los Angeles-* and *Seawolf*-class submarines.

The *Virginia*'s conning tower includes a new "photonic" mast, in place of a traditional periscope. The mast does not penetrate the *Virginia*'s hull, and may be safer than a periscope, allowing the boat to dive to greater pressure depths than earlier designs with many through-hull fittings. Sensors include bow-conformal and flank wide-aperture sonar arrays, and towed arrays – long cables (up to 1nm [2km]) equipped with hydrophones (basically the same technology as the common telephone handset) that are trailed behind a submarine or surface ship. The towed cable can be deployed to different depths and ocean thermal layers, which have varying acoustic properties. Towed arrays collect acoustic data and transmit this to signal processing equipment within the host vessel. They complement the acoustic signal resolution and range of the submarine's integral sonar systems, allowing the vessel's automated processing station to resolve and triangulate on contacts using sophisticated algorithms that improve upon the human sonar operator's interpretive skills.

The *Virginia*s will be among the most powerful intelligence collection assets the Navy can deploy in the coastal zone, as these boats will be able to collect and process intelligence information across the sea bed as well as on shore. The *Virginia* class will also host and operate unmanned underwater vehicles (UUVs) to extend the submarine's sensor reach remotely into areas where the boat may be at greater risk – from mines, or from an adversary's undersea detection systems. The boats will also be able to deploy with a Special Operations Force detachment for expeditionary missions. The SOF sailors or soldiers would deploy through one of two lock-out trunks, aft of the *Virginia*'s sail, which are connected to a mini-sub or other clandestine vehicle.

The other aspect of the submarine service is the strategic deterrent patrol boats, SSBNs or "boomers," which carry thermonuclear missiles. These vessels are designed to deploy in relative secrecy, often remaining out of public view for the entirety of their six-month patrol voyages. These weapons of the Cold War were designed, as noted previously, to present an indefensible trump card in the event that diplomacy or other measures on land had worn thin. If history is any indication, the SSBN and other weapons of its type served their purpose, helping to end the Cold War without either side resorting to un-winnable nuclear confrontation. According to one sailor who had served on nuclear submarines during the Vietnam War era:

> I hear some people compare the danger of duty aboard an SSBN with the danger faced by a soldier or marine in the field, in Vietnam. Well, I won't argue with them about whether the soldier had it tougher; I know it was hard duty. But if the soldier does his job, [in a fight with the enemy] a few people die. If I did my job right [launching missiles in the event of a nuclear war], then tens of millions of people would die. Don't tell me that's not a hard thing ... But I would do it, and I would have expected any submarine sailor on my watch to do the same.[49]

With the end of the Cold War, the US Navy is finding new ways to keep its SSBN force relevant. The service has converted four of its 18 SSBNs into so-called SSGNs, a designation that refers to guided missile capabilities. The Navy had experimented with SSGNs during the 1960s under the Regulus missile program, which produced the USS *Halibut* (SSGN 587) and the Regulus I nuclear-tipped cruise missile.

The $3.8 billion SSGN program converts four *Ohio*-class boomers – the *Ohio*, *Florida*, *Michigan*, and *Georgia* – which had been slated for de-commission under the US-Soviet START II treaty. The four SSGNs have specialized launchers capable of loading 154 Tomahawk missiles. Additionally, the huge boomers provide ample space to host a company-sized team of 60 Special Operations Forces (SOF). The SSGN in effect will become a submerged platform for SOF mission planning, deployment, and command and control. Commander David Duryea, the *Florida*'s commanding officer, said during a January 25, 2003 test event at the Navy's Atlantic Undersea Test and Evaluation Center deep water range, off the Bahamas:[50]

> I would argue that this is a good value for the taxpayers; there are 25 good years left in [the *Florida*] and as you walk around the ship you will see that it is well-maintained and is in good shape. This ship could operate as a member of a battle group, working for a fleet commander, or work as an independent operator ... without support from the outside. We can gather information and send it to the battle group commander or we can use [that information] ourselves in our own decisions if we are operating independently.[51]

The test event was called *Giant Shadow*, and included a series of experiments designed to invigorate "outside the box" thinking in the submarine force. A good example of this occurred during World War II, when US Navy Commander Gene Fluckey's submarine, the USS *Barb*, demonstrated its potential as a strike platform. In 1944 Fluckey had Pearl Harbor Naval Shipyard weld an army rocket launcher to the *Barb*'s weather deck, bringing land-attack capability to his boat. On patrol, Fluckey would cruise into Japanese territory, surface, and shoot rockets at targets ashore. According to Captain William Toti, assistant chief of staff for requirements for Commander, Naval Submarine Forces and director of the *Giant Shadow* experiment:

> A lot of the things we are doing here [in *Giant Shadow* and in the SSGN program] are not even as bold as some of the things Fluckey did ... It is that kind of boldness that we need to bring back ... It is impossible to be sure about the future; what we can be sure about is the volume and payload capacity [of the SSGN design] makes this flexible ... As we develop new payloads they will be able to be incorporated into the SSGN with very little difficulty.[52]

From a design perspective the biggest challenge for industry involved in the SSGN project has been working with future flexibility, according to Alan Blay, the Electric Boat Corporation's attack weapon systems integration team leader.

> What we have to do is make sure that the platform we put out there is flexible enough to allow more than just Tomahawk, more than just UUVs; that's the biggest challenge. That is one of the biggest things that we [in industry and the Navy] have tried to address as we have worked together doing the integration of the weapon system: making sure that we are flexible enough for the future.[53]

In 1999 the US Defense Advanced Research Projects Agency launched a submarine sensors and payloads study under which two industry consortia were to develop concepts for expanding the kinds of technological capabilities that submarines could carry and employ. To date, the crucial constraint for the capabilities of the submarine has been the size of its apertures to the sea. In most US attack submarines, this limit is the standard 21in (53cm) torpedo tube. Thus any weapons or vehicles the submarine's crew wishes to launch must be designed to fit within this size tube. With larger ship-to-ocean interfaces, such as those offered by removing the ballistic missiles from the 87in (221cm) inside diameter missile tubes of the SSBN class, a window of opportunity is opened for other payloads, and therefore other missions.

The SSGN concept still needs to prove the limits of its operational utility as a complement to the Navy's existing submarine fleet. The Navy's first nuclear-powered aircraft carrier, USS *Enterprise*, remains in service today with new, vastly more powerful aircraft – carrying very different payloads – in comparison with the population of its flight deck after commissioning in 1961. According to Toti, "'Big E' still has the knife in her teeth; she is still carrying the fight to the enemy better than almost anything else. SSGN could be like that; these boats could be the aircraft carriers for SOF ... for unmanned systems too. Certainly the SSGN is going to be like the aircraft carrier for strike weapons."[54]

Other experiments aboard the *Florida* included the first D5 missile tube launch of a large UUV, which swam by night to a designated landing area, providing ammunition and supply for a SOF team deployed ashore. During the next two decades the Navy will put its four SSGNs through their paces, building on what the *Barb*'s Commander Fluckey had started in 1944 when he chalked the first victory silhouettes of blasted Japanese locomotives onto his boat's sail.

Aboard a Nuclear-Powered Fast Attack Submarine

On March 7, 2000, the USS *Miami* (SSN 755), having earned in battle the moniker "Big Gun of the Fleet," in the Middle East and the Balkans, calls at Port Canaveral, Florida, on her way home to US Naval Submarine Base, Groton, Connecticut. The boat's commanding officer, Commander James P. Ransom III, welcomes a few guests aboard for an afternoon underway, conducting missile drills while running at periscope depth off Cape Kennedy.

The submarine navy is a very different world from the surface, aviation, or shore-side communities of the service. For example, once aboard the *Miami* it becomes obvious there isn't a single navy-issue black shoe to be seen on anyone's foot. The crew's dozen officers and 115 enlisted men all wear trainers of one type or another, all non-regulation: one of the few comforts afforded the crew, whose duty is long and trying on patrol. Another perk is food. The submarine service enjoys some of the best cookery in the fleet, prepared by experienced chefs. In the officers' wardroom aboard the *Miami*, the cook serves an excellent lunch of chicken, rice, and soup.[55]

On the bridge, which is a partially enclosed platform atop the submarine's sail, a few observers enjoy the ride, standing braced against the periscope and other masts. Departing the pier at Port Canaveral, the *Miami* is escorted by a harbor patrol craft to the limit of the narrow approach channel, beyond which the submarine's way is free and clear to navigate. During the long surface cruise toward deep water, the *Miami* passes close to the Cape Canaveral Air Force Station and the NASA Launch Operations Center on Merritt Island, where the space shuttle is put into orbit. Ahead, early spring clouds break up the sunlight on the Atlantic. There is traffic on the sea lanes, and Commander Ransom orders his radar operator and the bridge watch officer to run drills, identifying and tracking surface targets for handoff to sonar. The watch officer tallies his contacts with a grease pencil on the Perspex windscreen of the bridge enclosure, noting their range bearing and speed as communicated by the radar operator.

Below, in the submarine's control room – where the boat's steering, periscope, sensor, and weapons control stations are located – it's all business. Some newer SSNs are arrayed like a science fiction film set. The USS *Seawolf*, for example, one of a class of three high-speed, extremely stealthy attack submarines, is all black enamel and chrome inside, dark steel grid flooring and instrument panels that light the glistening cave of its control center with an impressionistic spray of amber, red, green, yellow, and white lights. The *Miami*'s command center is more prosaic: a crowded, gray metal room with various control stations distributed about, a small navigation chart table, the periscope column and a ladder well up the sail to the bridge.

As it turns out, almost everything one has seen in the films (*Run Silent, Run Deep*; *Das Boot*) about the procedure of diving a submarine is true. Still, there is something unnerving about watching the crew very professionally go about the business of scuttling their $1 billion, 360ft (110m) long, 7,000-ton vessel, especially while one is standing aboard.

Commanding officer [CO] (Cmdr Ransom): I am satisfied that we have reached the dive point and have sufficient water to dive the ship. Officer of the deck, are you ready to submerge the ship?
Officer of the deck [OOD]: Yes, sir.
CO: Very well, submerge the ship to periscope depth.
OOD: Periscope depth, aye sir. Dive, submerge the ship, six zero feet.
Diving officer [DO]: Submerge the ship, six zero feet, aye. Chief of the watch, on the 1MC [The 1MC is the boat's intercom.], "Dive, dive." Sound two blasts of the dive alarm. "Dive, dive."

Chief of the watch [COW]: On the 1MC, "Dive, dive." Sound two blasts of the dive alarm. "Dive, dive." Aye. [The chief of the watch keys a microphone that looks like a chunky police radio's handset, announcing:] Dive! Dive! [He turns a knob by the 1MC speaker overhead, and sounds two horn blasts, a bit like strangled, mechanical whalesong, throughout the boat.]

OOD: [Through the periscope, the officer of the deck observes the surface, and the ballast tank valves opening toward the bow and toward the stern, venting air and taking on water to dive the boat.] Venting forward ... Venting aft.

COW: Dive! Dive!

DO: [The diving officer stands beside a helmsmen, who is seated at the ship's steering controls, in what looks not unlike the cockpit of a commercial airplane. The helmsman monitors the boat's angle of descent as registered on a bubble level above his steering yoke. The diving officer counts off the depth of the boat, measured in feet of water above the keel.] Three zero feet ... Three two ... Three four ...

OOD: Deck's awash.

DO: Three six feet ... Three eight ... Four zero feet ... Four two ... Four four ... Four six ... Four eight ...

OOD: Sonar, Con, monitor the forward ... correction, aft main ballast tank vent.

Sonar: [On the 1MC] Con, Sonar: monitor aft main ballast tank vent, aye.

DO: Five zero feet ...

DO: All vents shut, officer of the deck; straight board [The diving officer indicates that all valves to the ballast tanks are closed and the submarine has ceased taking water.].

OOD: Very well, dive.

DO: Five two ...

And so on, until there is 60ft (18m) of water above the *Miami*'s keel. At periscope depth, the on-watch crew focuses on the tasks of submerged maneuvering. The sonar department monitors targets acquired by radar while on the surface, these having been logged and mapped, so that the sonar operators may make regular reports to the captain on their disposition relative to the submarine.

Once having arrived at a suitable spot – well away from surface traffic and other hazards – the *Miami* prepares to conduct missile drills, simulating the preparation, programming, launch, and reset from the boat's Tomahawk weapon control system.

OOD: [On the 1MC] Man battle stations! [The officer of the deck sounds an alarm that sounds like a fire bell: "Clang-clang-clang ... !" Twenty-five pulses, to get everyone moving.]

Sonar: Sir, no contacts to report.

CO: Very well ... Chief of the watch, over the 1MC, "Man battle stations for cruise missile launch."

COW: Man battle stations for cruise missile launch, aye sir. [On the 1MC] Man battle stations for cruise missile launch!

CO: ... We will be shooting from tubes one two and three. Carry on ... [56]

In the control room, there is little to see: men manning consoles that monitor the status of the missiles and the launch tubes. The action is forward, in the *Miami*'s torpedo room, beneath the crew berthing spaces. During an actual wartime launch, the weapons handlers would maneuver the 4,000lb (1,814kg) Tomahawk missile-launch canisters into position for loading into the *Miami*'s torpedo tubes. The procedure makes use of heavy overhead hoists and tackle to support the massive weapons while the men align the missiles with a framework of rails and rollers that is positioned at a torpedo tube's massive, bronze inner door. The missile drill simulates programming a weapon with target coordinates, preparing the canister for torpedo tube launch, loading, and releasing the weapon (actually just a "water slug," thrust from the flooded tube with a charge of compressed air). Back in the control room, this sounds like a knock on the 3in (7.62cm) thick steel hull.

The *Miami* had earned her *nom de guerre* as the fleet's big gun by becoming the first SSN to empty her vertical launch and torpedo tubes of all missiles, reload, and shoot her magazine empty again a few weeks later, in two separate conflicts during the same patrol. In 1998, the *Miami* was with the USS *Enterprise* carrier battle group in the Arabian Gulf at the start of Operation *Desert Fox*, a series of punitive air raids against Iraq. The *Miami* launched all 12 missiles from her vertical launch tubes and emptied her torpedo hold of Tomahawks.

Early in 1999, the *Miami* was at La Maddalena naval base, Sardinia, and became the first SSN ever reloaded with Tomahawks by a forward-deployed submarine tender, the USS *Simon Lake* (AS 33). Between March and April 1999, the *Miami* fired her Tomahawks again, this time from the Adriatic Sea as part of the NATO task force confronting Serbia over the Kosovo crisis, Operation *Allied Force/Noble Anvil*. An officer from the *Miami*'s crew, Lieutenant (jg) Alexander Barbera, wrote of his experience:

Since no one knew what a missile launch would be like, each of us was amazed at the way it felt when the first vertical missile was away. The ship reacted strongly to the force of each round being launched – a sound and shake that could be heard and felt anywhere onboard. The crew's reaction was best captured in the words of Lieutenant Tim Miklus, the senior-most junior officer on board at the time. Looking through the periscope at the missile emerging from the water to begin its journey, he could only exclaim, 'Oh-my-God! We just shot a real missile!'[57]

The Naval Expeditionary Force

Amphibious power projection – the ability to host, deploy and support land forces from warships at sea – has long been a featured attribute of the world's most powerful fleets. In a marked contrast with the blue water, open ocean emphasis of World War II and the Cold War, today's expeditionary naval force is developing more specialized capabilities for projecting and sustaining power ashore, dominating the green water of the coastal zone, and operating successfully in the brown water of the riverine and inland waterway environments.

Mine Warfare

The task of dominating the waters of the coastal zone alone is a major challenge. These waters are congested, difficult to navigate, and present complex threats. Among the coast zone's most dangerous threats is the sea mine. In a mined area, ships cannot maneuver freely and the fleet's ability to project and sustain power ashore is jeopardized.

Swedish engineer Immanuel Nobel (1801–72) first perfected one of the earliest forms of the modern naval mine, which comprised submerged casks filled with black gunpowder. Nobel sold his invention to Russia, to protect the harbor of St Petersburg from British and French attack during the Crimean War (1854). Today, naval mines come in a variety of forms, including surface and near-surface floating and tethered mines; moored mines (anchored, hovering in the water column at various depths); and proud (unburied) or buried bottom mines.

During World War II, naval mines were effectively and extensively used in both Asian and European theaters, countering the naval mobility of Axis and Allied forces alike. While many nations then (and now) used surface mine layers to deploy their weapons, the United States and others also made successful use of aircraft to deploy mines, particularly against the Japanese.

> In the Pacific, aircraft accounted for 86 percent (21,389) of the 24,876 mines deployed against Japan. Allied mining efforts sank or damaged 961 vessels (over two million tons of shipping) representing nearly a quarter of the pre-war strength of the Japanese Merchant Marine. Mine-laying B-29s (in addition to their land attack missions) sank or damaged over 1.2 million tons of shipping in the last five months of the war through the deployment of 57 percent of the 21,389 Allied aerial mines laid. The Japanese later conceded that B-29 mining was so effective that it eventually starved the country – and shortened the war.[58]

In 1972, US Navy planes deployed mines off the coast of Vietnam. These weapons effectively blockaded military supply and commercial traffic to and from North Vietnam's crucial Haiphong harbor.[59]

Current US air-deployed mines are called "Quickstrike," designating a series of munitions that are converted from general-purpose bombs. The series includes the Mk 65 2,000lb (907kg); Mk 62 500lb (227kg); and Mk 63 and Mk 64 1,000lb (454kg). When released, these weapons deploy an aero-structure to retard their descent, and come to rest on the sea bed, armed and waiting for a ship to pass over. Other types of mines are deployed from submarines, traveling a preprogrammed course and distance before coming to rest or anchoring on the sea bed. Upon detection of a target vessel, the mine may activate and launch its warhead, which attacks the target in much the same way as a self-propelled torpedo.

Less sophisticated mines – including the classic, World War I-style knobbly floating spheres – remain in service. Despite their obsolescent technology, these weapons are a significant threat to naval and civilian shipping. In 1988, the crew of the frigate USS *Samuel B. Roberts* learned just how dangerous old-school floating mines can be. According to a record by the US Navy Historical Center:

> While steaming 55nm [89km] northeast of Qatar on 14 April 1988 ... lookouts onboard [the] guided missile frigate *Samuel B. Roberts* (FFG 58) spotted three mines ahead. Going to general quarters, the ship soon struck a fourth mine that exploded and blew a 6.4m (21ft) hole in her port side near frame 276, injuring 10 sailors, and inflicting "considerable damage to the hull, deckhouse and foundation structures, essentially breaking the ship's back." Herculean damage control efforts by the crew, however, saved the ship. Over the next 10 days, coalition mine countermeasures vessels located eight additional mines, examination of which left little doubt as to their Iranian origins.[60]

The sea mine is not to be taken lightly. It may be useful to recall that water is not compressible, so when an even partly submerged mine detonates, its shock wave displaces a mass of water like a battering ram at its target. The result – as several ships other than the *Roberts* could attest – can be devastating.

Since 1950, more US Navy vessels have suffered damage from mines than from any other form of attack. During Operation *Desert Storm*, Iraq laid more than 1,150 mines across the approaches to Kuwait and to Iraq's al Faw peninsula, according to the US Navy. The move countered US plans for an amphibious assault on Kuwait. As a bonus for the Iraqis, the amphibious helicopter landing platform USS *Tripoli* and the cruiser USS *Princeton* struck mines in the area and were severely damaged. The *Tripoli* blew a 20x16ft (6x4.8m) hole in her hull, while the *Princeton* set off a 375lb (170kg) bottom mine that put her out of commission.

One grim advantage of the naval mine is that it provides a good return on investment. For example, the mine that the *Samuel B. Roberts* struck, resulting in $96 million in repairs, had cost the Iranian Navy $1,500. The Iraqi mine that caused *Tripoli* $3.5 million worth of damage was worth about the same price. Even the more sophisticated mines may seem like bargains compared to the results they can achieve. The Italian-made Manta magnetic, acoustic influence mine that caused $24 million worth of damage to the *Princeton* had cost Saddam Hussein just $10,000.

As naval mines have matured, some have been engineered with advanced capabilities – including more sensitive and discriminating magnetic field and pressure sensors, and algorithms that count the tonnage and number of vessels passing by. These mines are able to remain unarmed, and nearly undetectable, until a certain set of preprogrammed criteria has been met. The challenge is acute for a fleet's mine countermeasures, or MCM, squadrons, as such weapons may be lying in wait, camouflaged and undetected by sonar and magnetic-influence hunting and sweep gear. An MCM squadron may clear a sea lane – a "Q route"– and declare it safe for traffic, having missed the stealthiest mines, which then arm and detonate only upon detection of a larger warship, such as an aircraft carrier. This is one good reason the strike group tends to stage its operations from relatively far out to sea, away from the most dangerous threats closer to shore.

Most fleets include at least some MCM capability, often aboard specialized wooden or composite-hulled ships whose task it is to hunt and sweep for the wide variety of mines available on the arms market today. The US Navy's MCM force includes 14 MCM-1-class and 12 MHC-51-class ships, based at Manama, Bahrain, Sasebo, Japan, and San Diego, California. Two airborne MCM squadrons – HM-14 in Norfolk, Virginia, and HM-15 in Corpus Christi, Texas – are equipped with a total of 32 MH-53E helicopters. The MH-53Es tow a variety of minesweeping gear, including mechanical, acoustic, and magnetic-influence minesweeping systems, and side-scan sonar. The MCM force also includes the divers and "marine mammal systems" (bottlenosed dolphins and California sea lions)[61] of San Diego, California-based Naval Special Clearance Team One, with eight deployable explosive ordnance disposal detachments.

Mine hunting is the act of using sonar or magnetic field detection equipment to locate mines or mine-like objects (apparently, one would be surprised how many derelict refrigerators litter the sea bed). Mines will be defeated by precision munitions with specialized warheads – 2,000lb (907kg) JDAMs, or other weapons that will release thousands of darts to kill mines through chemical interaction, explosives, or kinetic energy alone. In the latter case, the darts strike a mine, either destroying it outright or causing it to detonate, thus helping to clear a lane for an assault landing force. Out beyond the very shallow water zone, autonomous neutralization vehicles (underwater robots that carry remote-controlled explosive charges) will make kamikaze attacks on mines floating in the water or lurking at the bottom. Hunting for and disposing of mines can be a dangerous job, particularly for the MCM vessel crews, explosive ordnance disposal divers and marine mammals that support these operations within the boundaries of an active minefield.

The US Navy, in partnership with Britain, Germany, and others, is investing in a new generation of MCM technologies that promises greater efficiency and effectiveness through automation, remote operation, and improved safety by removing the man and the mammal from the minefield. Perhaps more importantly to the success of a naval and military enterprise, the new MCM systems also promise speed: a crucial factor when operational timelines may depend on expeditionary forces gaining access to target areas in order to exploit breaches in an enemy's defense that may have been opened by air power or naval surface fire support.

The American defense establishment's strategic vision is to develop sea, air, and land forces that are capable of expeditionary operations which can influence events ashore within ten days (shape the battle space, as it were); swiftly defeat an enemy in combat within 30 days; and within a further 30 days reconstitute the force to the level of readiness attained prior to the beginning of the operation. This so-called 10-30-30 plan remains somewhat of an elusive goal. Nevertheless, the pace of combat during the opening phases of Operation *Iraqi Freedom* is an indication of the direction in which the US Department of Defense is headed.

For the Navy's MCM squadrons, the 10-30-30 plan means lighting a fire under almost every aspect of their mission portfolio. Now the job has to get done within ten days for the expeditionary force to stay on schedule. The problem can be broken down into three inter-related parts: time, area, and risk. The Navy uses a probabilistic approach to mine warfare, using sensors (magnetic or acoustic) with a given probability to detect mine-like contacts. The risk is measured in terms of residual mines; those that may remain after a hunting/sweeping squadron has moved through the area. The MCM squadron can step up the pace of its efforts, but increased speed also increases risk. Despite the US Department of Defense's huge budgets, the Navy cannot afford to acquire the number of MCM ships that would be necessary to accomplish the ten-day MCM mission the "old-fashioned way" – "mowing the lawn" by patrolling with towed sensors across a huge ocean area. One answer may be to look to offboard sensors to extend the reach of the manned vessels and aircraft working the minefield: doing more with less.[62]

The Navy divides the mine warfare mission set into zones: from deep water (>200ft/>61m), through shallow water (40–200ft/12–61m), to very shallow water (10–40ft/3–12m), and the surf zone/beach landing zone (0–10ft/0–3m).

The Navy is developing technologies to address the specific requirements of each zone. In future, the mine warfare mission set will not necessarily include legacy MCM vessels. Instead, the missions will be conducted from standoff range by interlinked networks of manned platforms; autonomous surface and undersea vehicles with sophisticated behavioral algorithms; and deployable sensors and neutralization weapons.

Remote sensing from satellites, surveillance aircraft, and unmanned aerial vehicles, or UAVs, will provide persistent awareness of the movements of mine weapon stockpiles ashore, preparations to load mines aboard military and civilian vessels, and the movement of potential minelayers at sea. Undersea surveillance systems will detect the movement of enemy submarines, which can potentially carry mines. Notably, an undersea sensor network isn't only a mine warfare issue. It would also be beneficial to the antisubmarine warfare, surface warfare, and air warfare communities. Sensors in the water, coupled with overhead ISR capabilities, all contribute to building the intelligence picture that supports many types of missions.[63]

Another way the Navy plans to use technology to defeat the mine threat is through the development of geospatial databases, with GPS-enabled ships, autonomous vehicles, and aircraft contributing information to a stored search grid, which could be used in future to reduce the time it takes to acquire and neutralize naval mines. By collecting environmental data – such as that provided by synthetic aperture sonar imagery of the sea bed,[64] with detail comparable to the digital maps collected by space shuttle missions – the Navy could gather a precise data library of natural and manmade features and clutter on the seabed in important coastal regions. Mine hunting or sweep vehicles could compare the archived data with new information collected by their sensors in real time, to rapidly discriminate changes within the environment, such as a new mine-like object appearing amid the piles of discarded refrigerators.

The Return of the Brown Water Navy

In 2006, the US Navy created a new organization, called Expeditionary Combat Command, dedicated to coastal and inland waterway operations. The missions of this command include maritime interception (stopping and searching vessels suspected of carrying illegal or dangerous cargos), force protection, and explosive ordnance disposal (two specialties that have gained importance in the wake of the October 2000 bombing of the USS *Cole*). The new command has commissioned Riverine Force, which includes Riverine Group, or RIVGRU, One, and Riverine Squadron, or RIVRON, One, at Norfolk, Virginia.

To flesh out Riverine Force, the Navy has absorbed the US Marine Corps' small boat company – formerly based at Camp Lejeune, North Carolina – with its inventory of 17 riverine assault craft, 135ft (41m) boats capable of 40 knots

(74km/h) and 200nm (322km) range; and 65 riverine raiding craft, 18ft (5.4m) boats capable of 25 knots (43km/h) and 70nm (113km) range. The Navy's plan is to equip three RIVRONs with as many as 36 small combatant craft for river patrol and maneuver.

What is interesting about the resurrection of a riverine fighting force in the regular Navy fleet is that it recalls the somewhat experimental formations – joint Army and Navy – that had been developed during the Vietnam War, and were perhaps too quickly abandoned during subsequent decades. By re-establishing professionalism in riverine warfare, the service is making the change from blue water to green and brown a permanent part of its culture.

After 1966, the Navy and Army realized that operations in Southeast Asia, particularly in and around the vital Mekong Delta region, required joint amphibious capability that went far beyond traditional sealift, transport, and assault landing. To operate in places like the Rung Sat Special Zone, south of Saigon, a new kind of force had to be created – one that worked, lived, and fought in the permanently waterlogged mangrove forests of the region in enemy-held territory.

The result was the "Mobile Riverine Force," or Task Force 117. This group included sailors, soldiers from the 9th Infantry Division, and South Vietnamese marines. For vessels, the task force had an unusual assortment of specialized and heavily armed craft, some having more firepower than tanks.

For example, the force had a small patrol craft, similar to the commercially derived motorboats used today by naval inshore boat units, for force protection (policing a port where larger naval ships are moored), reconnaissance, and waterway patrol. Vietnam-era patrol craft included the River Patrol Boat (PBR) and Assault Support Patrol Boat (ASPB). These were not unlike the PT boats of World War II fame. The PBRs and ASPBs were armed, often interchangeably, with a variety of weapons, including .50cal heavy machine guns, 40mm grenade launchers, and 60mm mortars. The ASPBs also carried two 20mm cannon.

But the world of the Mekong Delta proved to be an extremely hazardous and difficult place to navigate and in which to fight. Attack could come from any quarter, and disabling hits meant certain death as the crippled craft would then be exposed to close-range fire from all sides. An Army report on the riverine force in Vietnam highlighted both the dangers and the successes of the flexible firepower that the Navy and land force units brought to the fight.

On two occasions, river assault craft came under particularly heavy and well-aimed enemy fire from the river banks. On 24 February, units of River Assault Division 131 received combined rocket and automatic weapons fire from both banks of the Song Ba Lai at a position three miles [4.8km] northeast of Ben Tre. Six craft were hit and slightly damaged; eleven US sailors were wounded. Again, on 27 February, units of River Assault Division 112 came under heavy rocket, recoilless rifle, and automatic weapons fire from both banks of the Song Ba Lai at a position four miles [6.4km] northeast of Ben Tye. In this attack there were twelve US Navy sailors wounded and five of the river assault craft received hits causing minor damage.[65]

As a consequence, the Navy began to experiment with new kinds of craft, specially designed with armor and weapons capable of fending off the most determined assaults. The three basic types were the monitor, armored troop carrier, and command and control boats. The monitor was developed from a World War II-style landing craft, equipped with armor and heavy weapons – machine guns, grenade launchers, mortars, and two 105mm howitzers or two heavy flame throwers – to provide assault and covering fire for the infantry embarking and disembarking the armored troop carriers. The command and control boats were specialized versions of the troop carrier, with radios and other equipment to support a command staff during extended operations. The joint service task force began to develop new tactics that exploited the capabilities of the new craft in support for maneuvering infantry.

> The tricky tides were known, and the boat commanders knew when and how far up a stream they could go to provide support. The infantry commanders maneuvered their troops across the rice paddies carefully, alert for booby traps and ambushes. Just in advance of lead elements, artillery delivered white phosphorus rounds which exploded 200ft [61m] above the ground. Constantly re-adjusted, this marking fire insured that rapid and accurate artillery fire could be placed on the ground in front of the US troops when they were engaged with the enemy. The navy moved up close to the infantry positions to add the fire of the monitor's [heavy weapons] ... and maintained direct fire.[66]

Many of the lessons learned during the Vietnam War's riverine operations are informing the kinds of craft and capabilities the Navy is developing for its present and future RIVGRU and RIVRONs. Rear Admiral Donald Bullard, commander of Naval Expeditionary Combatant Command, stated in January 2007 that the squadrons would require several types of craft, working with aviation and land units, to develop a fully rounded set of capabilities. Riverine squadrons will be comprised of vessels that are scalable, multimission, and armored – capable of performing the same basic missions that Task Force 117 had carried out in Vietnam, namely transport, fire support and command and control.

The Marine Expeditionary Unit (MEU)
Expeditionary power projection requires more than riverine force capabilities, however. US Marine Corps infantry units are at the spearhead of projecting

naval combat power ashore. The marines are organized around a basic formation called the Marine Air-Ground Task Force (MAGTF). This in turn is scalable and made up of a ground combat element, an air combat element, and a combat support element. The ground combat element of a MAGTF includes infantry, artillery, and armored vehicles. A typical air combat element includes both fixed-wing aircraft, such as the AV-8B Harrier II fighter, and rotary-wing aircraft, such as the AH-1W Super Cobra, with its 20mm gun and rockets. The combat service support element provides supply, maintenance, engineering, medical and other support services. The MAGTF that typically deploys with a Navy expeditionary strike group is called a Marine Expeditionary Unit, or MEU, and includes approximately 2,200 marines. The MEU is able to disembark and operate ashore for approximately 15 days before requiring resupply. On extended deployments and during war, these relatively small versions of the MAGTF have to be creative about accomplishing their missions and supporting themselves as well as possible in the field.

The 26 MEU (Special Operations Capable) was one such unit that deployed to Afghanistan at the leading edge of the war against the Taliban in 2001–02. An infantry platoon sergeant recorded his experiences in an instructional guide for marines and other personnel deploying to Afghanistan:

> Our purpose near Khowst was to conduct a raid on cave complexes located near there. The raid was supposed to last under 10 hours from insertion to extraction; however, it lasted 10 days. In those 10 days we gathered much of our intelligence information. We also proved that marine units could and did survive, fight, and prevail without re-supply. Because we had no re-supply, we had to live off the land (a 10 hour raid means you carry very little gear). We seized an abandoned terror training facility and found livestock and grain. We soon began making corn bread, pop corn, and other types of food. After a couple days we had chicken, lamb, and steak. We found water in cisterns and in natural springs in the wadi. We purified the water in 19l (5 gallon) jugs.[67]

Later, during Operation *Iraqi Freedom*/Operation *Telic*, marine expeditionary forces demonstrated that while the typical role for marine infantry and armored forces is not to sustain the heavy fighting that some army units are designed for, the sea-soldiers nevertheless bring a highly motivated, pugilistic attitude to the fight. Lieutenant General James T. Conway, commanding general of I Marine Expeditionary Force during two tours in Iraq, said his Marines' objective was to get into trouble. "Our job was to pick a fight with everybody who would pay attention to us and make them think we were the main attack ... We manage the level of violence. If we take fire, we immediately achieve fire superiority and then we govern the de-escalation; we don't let the [enemy] do that."[68]

Aside from fighting spirit, one of the more impressive aspects of the Navy/Marine operational symbiosis is the ability of naval forces to accomplish significant logistical feats that more conventional forces found at best challenging during the war in Iraq. These feats are achieved by effectively managing a network of capabilities that includes high-capacity strategic sealift, operational lift from the expeditionary strike group's amphibious ships, and (the secret weapon) a Maritime Prepositioning Force (MPF). The MPF is made up of cargo ships organized into squadrons that are deployed forward to locations around the world, especially near potential conflict zones, such as the choke points of globalized trade discussed in the introduction to this chapter. The MPF squadrons are loaded with heavy equipment – aircraft, tanks, ammunition – that is kept in a combat-ready state at all times. If a crisis occurs, the first marines on scene, usually a MEU, may go ashore to join, or close, with the equipment offloaded from MPF ships and become the leading element for a much larger combat force to follow. According to Conway:

> [In Iraq] we closed ... in about 45 days a force of 60,000 marines: a feat of strategic agility that left our army commanders in awe ... We deployed almost 41,000 Marines in that 45-day period via strategic lift ... One of our proudest achievements had to do with the maritime prepositioning squadrons. The navy estimated it would take about 22 days based on ports and pier space available, to offload two squadrons. We thought we could do it in 18 [days]. In fact we did it in 16 [days].[69]

Naval Special Warfare

The US Navy's Sea, Air, Land (SeAL) teams are among the world's finest special operations forces, or SOF. Working together with partners in the UK Special Air Service, or the US Army's Green Berets, SeALs were able to accomplish some feats that more conventional forces found difficult.

For example, during the push to Baghdad in 2003, a force of more than 30 AH-64 helicopters was forced back from the line of engagement after scoring hits on three Iraqi tanks. During the same period of time, special operations forces had deployed a 12-man Operational Detachment Alpha (ODA) team in western Iraq. The team had been linked to airborne sensors and weapons. The relationship between the clandestine ground unit and strike aircraft produced a kill capability totally different from the massive Apache force, and the ODA team killed 14 tanks in its sector. One senior US Navy official put it this way: "This is what the revolution is about. It is about changing from an attrition warfare concept to a concept enabled by pervasive knowledge, created by sensors, married with persistent precision strike. That changes fundamentally the way of warfare." [70]

The lethal side of warfare is only part of the story about special operations, however. A US Navy SeAL and former platoon commander noted that some operational commanders still don't know quite what to do with SOF units when they have them. Special operations forces often end up being used like personal tools; sometimes employed in the "right" way, and sometimes in a more backward way. SeAL teams and other special units don't have the resources to be on the front line all the time. It is a misconception that SOF, while highly trained, experienced and motivated, are some kind of "shock troops." That is the role of a marine corps and army. What SOF are best suited for is the deep mission, shaping the conditions of the conflict before, during and after the fight is over. SOF have always had forward thinkers that have asked, what will the force be capable of doing tomorrow? That question has initiated many capabilities that have become part of the conventional forces' tool kit: high-altitude airborne operations, fast roping from helicopters, training and equipping allied forces, etc. Meanwhile, SOF have moved on to find their next new set of competencies, including an emerging concept for hybrid operations.

In the future, SOF may be used not only for direct action, but as part of a package that blends the skill sets of intelligence officers with shooters, with explosive ordnance disposal specialists, with diplomats and others. With this diverse portfolio of skills, the hybrid SOF team will be more responsive to whatever operational requirements emerge.

For example, a mission may arise that requires immediate action. A commander is assigned, who then assembles his team with elements that are on station, or relatively close to his area. On the mission, the ad hoc team is controlled and fed information, able then to exploit that intelligence instantly to achieve a mission objective, and in turn to feed information back into the system. The result, the SeAL commander said, would be an organization capable of "continuous, instant self-healing task formation and execution."[71]

Summary

Watching films of the Battle of Midway or the invasion of France in 1944 may provide a seemingly romantic glimpse into the nature of naval combat and the culture of life at sea. That culture is in fact quite hazardous during peacetime, and can be the setting for horrific violence in combat, as we have seen. For the men and women who serve aboard the world's battle fleets, there is danger in the industrial surroundings and heavy machinery aboard their ships. There is the challenge of working in the unforgiving environment of the sea itself. At war, these platforms – whether carriers launching air strikes or surface combatants firing missiles – become hives of activity, with safety a continuous challenge for everyone. And if the ship is hit, as with the *Sir Galahad* and the *Cole*, the cost in lives can be high.

Fighting through these risks, a symbiosis has developed between the crews and their ships, and the weapons systems they operate aboard. Unlike an army or an air force, which may have access to communications and support infrastructures ashore, a ship's crew must rely entirely on its self-contained support. Computers, wireless communications, fuel, food, ammunition, spare parts, fire fighting equipment, medical care – all of these must come from the ship. This self-reliance has led navies to adopt weapons systems that are capable not only of independent action but also of acting as modules or links in a broader chain of warfighting technology that may include an entire fleet action. Thus navies have always shared with their sister services on land and in the air an appreciation for the multiplying effects of teamwork: the fact that many human minds applied to a problem may yield the best solution. And there is a naval arsenal ready just off shore with which to put that solution into action.

7

SHADOW THREAT – CHEMICAL, BIOLOGICAL, RADIOLOGICAL AND NUCLEAR (CBRN) WEAPONS

There is perhaps no greater nightmare than the prospect of an attack by chemical, biological, radiological, poisons and nuclear weapons (collectively known as CBRN threats, or "weapons of mass destruction," WMD). These technologies have evolved as logical consequences of the ancient competition between offense and defense, between arms and armor. If the question in weapons development and warfare has been how to find an ultimate advantage, a form of attack against which there is no countermeasure, then, in many ways, CBRN technologies provide the darkest possible final solution. In response the military has sought to develop sophisticated detection devices, protective clothing, and environmental purification capabilities to ensure that at least some significant percentage of a force hit by CBRN attack can not only survive, but continue to fight in the contaminated environment. However, few of these systems have been tested in actual combat, and neither have the tactics, techniques, and procedures for their use been put under pressure by a real WMD attack.

On the other hand, some of the weapons in the CBRN family have seen operational use. In April 1915, Imperial German Army engineers released chlorine gas against French troops near Ypres, causing 13,000 casualties and marking the first militarily relevant use of chemical agents. Seventy years later, at the end of the Iran–Iraq War (1980–88), the list of casualties caused by chemical weapons (mustard gas, chlorine, and nerve agents) included 100,000 soldiers and civilians treated for effects.[1]

Almost as quickly as the djinn escaped the bottle, the civilized world has spent much of the last century diffidently trying to stuff it back in, with limited success. The Brussels Convention of 1874, the Geneva Protocol of 1925, and, later, the Chemical Weapons Convention (CWC) had all banned the development, production, and use of chemical weapons in war. The CWC went into force on April 29, 1997, and as of April 2007 had accumulated 182 parties, according to the Arms Control Association.[2] Nations who have not signed up to the CWC include Egypt, Iraq, North Korea, and Syria.

The somewhat more challenging science and handling procedures associated with biological weaponry have been, to date, limiting factors in its use. Fortunately, biological cultures generally tend to have limited shelf lives and must be handled carefully and delivered under strict conditions to guarantee their survival and lethality, and also to ensure the safety of those handling the pathogens. Like chemical agents, military-grade germs are governed by international law. The Biological Weapons Convention, or BWC, entered into force in 1975. The treaty bans the development and use of microbial and other pathogens other than for peaceful medical purposes. As of October 2006, the BWC had 155 parties and 16 signatories. Yet, while the military use of biological materials has largely been ruled out, there is little to stop a determined aggressor from using the technology for criminal purposes. Some toxins have long enough shelf lives to be attractive for use in improvised weapons. For example, from October–November 2001, the US Centers for Disease Control & Prevention responded to a series of anthrax infections in Florida, New Jersey, New York, Missouri, Washington, D.C., and three US embassies overseas. "Because the bacteria can persist for long periods of time as a spore and can be prepared in a powdered formulation, *B. anthracis* has been considered a serious biological threat, with potential use as a military or terrorist weapon."[3]

Radiological poisons – such as waste medical isotopes, spent nuclear reactor fuel, and the components of demilitarized nuclear weapons – compose a unique part of the CBRN threat, though their dubious lethality – aside from the conventional explosives' heat and blast – makes these far less likely to be efficient as weapons of mass destruction than the fear of radioactivity may imply. The radiological, or "dirty," bomb is significant not so much for its direct lethality, but for the relative ease with which its material components could be assembled, in contrast with the resources and level of expertise required to produce a nuclear weapon. Constructed from ordinary high explosives and some form of radioactive material, the dirty bomb has greater psychological than real effects. In reality, such weapons are a poor man's version of the atom bomb in name only, as the blast and radiation effects are thousands of times less potent than even the weakest fission or fusion devices. Nevertheless, the dirty bomb may be attractive to some attackers seeking to deny an opponent access to an area – such as shutting down a stock exchange in order to damage an enemy's economy – pending costly and time-consuming cleanup. According to the US Nuclear Regulatory Commission:

> Since September 11, 2001, terrorist arrests and prosecutions overseas have revealed that individuals associated with al-Qaeda planned to acquire materials for a [radioactive dispersal device]. In 2004, British authorities arrested a British national, Dhiren Barot, and several associates on various charges, including conspiring to commit public nuisance by the use of radioactive materials. [4]

The grim threat of nuclear Armageddon, the grandfather of all post-modern WMD, somewhat diminished in the public imagination since the end of the Cold War in 1992, nevertheless remains significant. Toward the end of the Cold

War-era, arms control regimes, such as the Strategic Arms Reduction Treaty II (1992), required the bi-lateral demilitarization and disposal of some classes of nuclear weapons and delivery systems (including a number of fleet ballistic missile submarines). The treaties helped reduce the threat of direct nuclear confrontation between the United States and the Soviet Union. Yet, despite treaty limitations, former adversaries on both sides still maintain large stockpiles of high-yield atomic and thermonuclear weapons. The national defense strategies of these nuclear powers also still include operational scenarios for atomic warfare, and likely target sets among nations with whom, ostensibly, there is *détente*.

Another worrying development is the prospect of further proliferation of nuclear weaponry, with several "new" nations – India and Pakistan among them – having joined the ranks of nations possessing at least limited nuclear warfighting capability within the last couple of decades. Another issue is whether old Cold War weapons stockpiles, particularly those of the former Soviet states, are secure from theft. As the Soviet Union has transformed into the Russian Federation and a number of newly independent states have emerged in Central Asia, some analysts warn of the probability that some amount of fissile material, or perhaps even fully functional weapons, may fall through the rusting security fence around the former Soviet weapons complex.

Bi-lateral programs between the United States and Russia, such as "cooperative threat reduction," were established to support the implementation of arms limitation treaties. These efforts included reciprocal on-site specialists and inspection teams trading presence at United States and former Soviet military nuclear facilities. Through cooperative threat reduction, the United States has provided funding and technical support to Russia for boosting security at some facilities, but according to officials involved in the inspection process security improvements have been made for only about 300 tons of nuclear weapons materiel; another 300 tons remain exposed to deterioration as environmental hazards, or possible theft. According to William E. Hoehn, head of the Washington, D.C. office of the Russian American Nuclear Security Advisory, "It only takes kilograms, handfuls of kilograms, to make a nuclear device, and so there's an enormous urgency to get this job done at a more rapid pace ... There's been a lot of blowback from the [Congress] on this subject, and it's caught a lot of attention inside the administration."[5]

The possible consequences of a large-scale CBRN attack, military or criminal, are almost unthinkable – a target city devastated to such an extent that the destruction at "ground zero" in New York after September 11, 2001 would seem light by contrast. However, an important question remains over how likely such an attack really is. From a military perspective, there are many circumstances wherein the use of non-lethal chemical weapons (such as tear gas), and even tactical nuclear weapons (perhaps to generate electromagnetic pulse to disrupt an enemy's command, control, and communications systems) becomes plausible, even rational, if somewhat extreme. However, there is perhaps no militarily significant role for biological weapons in the modern battle space, and the outright revulsion and horror caused by these has rightly binned them from the modern arsenal. Nevertheless, the assessment is very different from a criminal or ideological point of view, where a combatant may perceive the use of biological or other WMD as a way to maximize casualties and thereby the visibility of his cause. From the perspective of non-state actors and criminals, CBRN technologies become the ultimate asymmetric advantage against a larger and more technologically capable adversary.

Chemical Weapons

The Canadian Defence Forces' research and development organization identifies seven broad classes of chemical weapons – tear, choking, blister, blood, nerve, vomiting and incapacitating agents – each with unique effects.[6] Germany may have been the first nation to employ chemical weapons in battle, but was not the last to do so. By the end of World War I every major combatant had developed and used their own version of these chemicals.

Perhaps the most familiar class of chemical weapon is the non-lethal family of "tear gas" weapons often used by police and military units to disperse violent mobs. Tear gas causes irritation of the skin, some respiratory discomfort and, just as it says on the tin, watering of the eyes. A standard formula is (2-chlorophenyl)methylenepropanedinitrile, commonly known as CS riot control agent. In the US military, almost every recruit passes through a diluted CS gas event during basic training, to drive home the point that upon a battlefield alert of "Gas! Gas! Gas!" the soldier should waste no time donning his respirator mask and other protective clothing and equipment. Exposure to CS may have various effects, including coughing, headache, dizziness, nausea, and vomiting. The agent causes severe sensations of burning and watering of the eyes, and irritation of the mucous membranes of the nasal passages and throat. Germany's use of chemicals such as tear gas in World War I met with mixed success. In 1915, German artillery attacked the Russian line using 6in (15cm) howitzer shells filled with xylyl bromide, a form of tear gas. Unexpectedly, the cold weather prevented the tear gas from forming, leaving the German infantry who followed the barrage to face a nasty surprise:

> On 31 January 1915, over 18,000 shells were fired at Russian positions at Bolimov. German officers, confident that their new weapon would neutralize the enemy positions, were surprised when their attack was repulsed with severe casualties. The shelling had had little or no effect on the Russians because cold temperatures had prevented vaporization of the xylyl bromide.[7]

Some chemicals are specifically designed to cause maximum discomfort without necessarily being lethal. The objective of using these agents is to render victims unable to resist other forms of attack, such as an infantry advance. Vomiting agents, such as diphenylarsinous cyanide, or DC, irritate the mucous membranes of the eyes, nose and throat, resulting in severe headache and nausea, and violent vomiting. Incapacitating agents, such as 3-Quinuclidinyl benzilate, or BZ, are engineered to cause psychomimetic effects, including long-lasting (approximately 8 hours) hallucinations. BZ attacks the victim's nervous system's ability to control the body's organs, including the cardiovascular system, the respiratory system, the gastrointestinal tract, and skin, and in high doses may be fatal.

Choking Agents

Among lethal chemical weapons are those that use chlorine or phosgene gas to affect the victim's respiratory system and cause debilitating chemical burns to the mucous membranes of lung and bronchial tissues. Today, one of the challenges in controlling the proliferation of these chemical agents is that both chlorine and phosgene have legitimate use in many industrial processes, and so may be obtained with relative ease. The Germans used chlorine most infamously at Ypres, France, in 1915.

> By the end of World War I, Germany, France and the United Kingdom had all used chlorine gas. Not very efficient and in low concentrations, it was observed that even rudimentary protection would prevent a soldier from succumbing to its full effects. Its use, however, was still enough to cause "gas hysteria" during an attack.[8]

Symptoms of phosgene intoxication include eye irritation, tearing and clouding of the corneas; burning in the nose and throat, and coughing. There may be a latent period between exposure and the appearance of symptoms.

Blister Agents

Some chemicals have been engineered to cause maximum casualties through tissue damage and systemic trauma. Among the most heinous are the vesicants, or blister agents, including (2-chloroethenyl)arsonous dichloride, also called Lewisite, and Bis(2-chloroethyl)sulfide, commonly called mustard gas. According to the US Army's Center for Health Promotion and Preventive Medicine:

> [Lewisite] is a blister agent, a toxic lung irritant, absorbed in tissues, and a systemic poison. When inhaled in high concentrations, it may be fatal in as short a time as 10 minutes. Lewisite is not detoxified by the body. Common routes of entry into the body include ocular, percutaneous, and inhalation.[9]

On July 26, 1917, the Germans released *Gelbkreuz* (the official designation for mustard gas) at Ypres, France. The result was devastating – 20,000 Allied casualties.[10] Sulfur mustard agents, still available today, have a faintly sweet, not unpleasant odor, which belies the horrific effects these may have when absorbed by human tissues. According to the US National Institutes of Health, inhalation of the gas or its penetration of the skin (often without irritation), may result in delayed effects 2–24 hours later:

> [Mustard] is corrosive to skin and lung tissue resulting in skin blisters and hemoptysis. A lethal dose is about 1.5tsp or enough to cover about 25 percent of the body surface area. Mustard is an alkylating agent that disrupts cell function by reacting with DNA and other macromolecules. The eyes, skin, and respiratory tract are most commonly affected by mustard poisoning. High doses also damage the hematopoietic, gastrointestinal, and central nervous systems. Death is usually caused by pulmonary injury, immunosuppression, and secondary infections. Most casualties recover completely after treatment of first and second degree burns. Victims who have lost vision should be reassured that it is temporary.[11]

Blood Agents

The horror show goes on. Blood agents, such as hydrogen cyanide (also known as AC agent) attack an enzyme called cytochrome oxidase, and prevent oxygen from reaching the body's cells. The effects appear quickly, causing central nervous system depression, convulsions, and respiratory arrest.

Hydrogen cyanide is the same chemical as the German Zyklon B, which the Nazi regime used to implement its "final solution" during the Holocaust. The Soviets and the Japanese also used hydrogen cyanide, with the Japanese allegedly testing the chemical on the Chinese. Others have made use of cyanide in a variety of applications:

> The United States issued cyanide pills (L pills) to its intelligence agents during World War II to be ingested in the event of capture. Unfortunately, when taken in pill form, hydrogen cyanide produces painful death-throes, which may last for several minutes ... [Reports from the] 1980s suggest that hydrogen cyanide was used by the Syrian government against an uprising in Hama, Syria, in an Iraqi military attack on the Kurdish town of Halabja, Iraq, in 1988, and in Shahabad, Iran, during the Iran-Iraq War.[12]

Nerve Agents

Truly terrifying are the nerve agents, such as S-(2-diisopropylaminoethyl) methylphosphonothiolate, also called VX. Such compounds are almost 100 percent fatal, and military medical researchers have no definitive data on low-dose survival rates.

All the nerve agents cause their toxic effects by preventing the proper operation of the chemical that acts as the body's 'off switch' for glands and muscles. Without an 'off switch,' the glands and muscles are constantly being stimulated. They may tire and no longer be able to sustain breathing function.[13]

Before the invasion of 2003, Iraq was known to have possessed and to have used chemical weapons – during the 1980–88 war with Iran and, later, during police actions against rebellious tribes within Iraq. The United States, the Soviet Union, Libya, and France are all known to have chemical weapon stockpiles. The technology may have proliferated to a further 24 nations, according to the US Army. The United States' stockpile of mustard and VX agents is slowly being destroyed, chiefly at an incineration plant on remote Johnston Atoll in the middle of the Pacific Ocean.

On the modern battlefield chemical agents, such as those noted above, are comparatively rare, but the US Army believes that should an attack occur it is most likely to be in the form of mustard or nerve agent. As reported by the United Nations, the eight-year Iran–Iraq war saw large amounts of these weapons brought to bear. Iraq reportedly used more than 19,000 chemical bombs, more than 54,000 chemical artillery shells, and 27,000 chemical rockets in 1983–88, including mustard and nerve agents.[14] That record helped strengthen the US government's argument in favor of going to war against Iraq in 2003, as it was able to claim that Saddam Hussein remained committed to reconstituting its chemical weapon programs as soon as Western sanctions could be lifted. As it turned out in 2003, the invading coalition forces found no credible cache of CBRN weaponry, nor any sophisticated efforts toward building a stockpile. According to the CIA, Iraq's chemical weapons program apparently had never recovered from the blows it took during Operation *Desert Storm* (1991).[15]

That the fear of CBRN weaponry in the hands of someone like Saddam Hussein had been such a convincing part of the argument for war speaks volumes about the visceral response these weapons engender in the public and official imaginations. One has only to consider the sarin gas attack on the Tokyo subway in 1995 to realize how shocking even a small-scale chemical attack can be. The Aum Shin Rikyo, or "supreme truth" cult, under its charismatic leader Shoko Asahara, had released sarin nerve agent on the train during rush hour, killing 12 and hospitalizing more than 5,000 others. During the subsequent investigation, the Japanese police learned that the cult had acquired enough chemical elements to engineer much more sarin, possibly for larger-scale attacks, and a helicopter, presumably for airborne delivery.

During 2007, some among the insurgents in Iraq fighting US, Iraqi government, and coalition forces have begun using chlorine gas in terror attacks, injuring many. Early attacks left some injuries but few fatalities, due to the somewhat finicky nature of the agent and its means of delivery. Apparently, the explosives in the first bombs were too powerful, and had made the chlorine less effective. More recently, these devices have become deadlier.

> On 23 March, Iraqi police in Ramadi alertly intercepted a suicide bomber driving a cargo truck filled with 5,000 gallons [19kl] of chlorine and two tons of explosives. On 28 March, another two chlorine truck bombs were engaged and detonated outside the Fallujah military operations center, injuring 14 US troops and 57 Iraqis.[16]

The problems posed by chemical weapons are issues not only for the soldiers and police who may confront their intentional use, but also for the population (military and civilian) that may become inadvertently exposed. For example, during Operation *Desert Storm*, coalition aircraft attacked several sites that were found to harbor stockpiles of chemical weapons and production materials. Subsequently, as cases of the so-called Gulf War illness came to light, veterans and other stakeholders began to question whether the air strikes against Iraqi chemical storage facilities could have released agents in sufficient quantities to affect the health of soldiers operating near the affected areas.

An analysis of 17 air strikes between January 19 and February 24, 1991 found that "bombing definitely released mustard agent" during February, although not within close proximity to regular forces, or Special Operations Forces units operating inside Iraq during the period. The bottom line from the US Department of Defense was that there was no clear link between the inadvertent release of chemical agents through bombing and the symptoms of Gulf War illness.[17]

Incidents such as the Tokyo subway attack show that all one really needs in order to develop chemical weapons is knowledge of chemistry, laboratory skill and facilities, and access to chemical components. As noted above, many of the precursor chemicals used to develop weapons are in fact commercially available and found in many industries. For example, the chemicals used to develop mustard gas are also found in the paper, plastics, pharmaceuticals, and cosmetics industries. Precursor chemicals for VX and other nerve agents are commonly found in insecticide and paint solvent manufacturing. Monitoring the world market for these chemicals, and determining to what purpose they are being put after purchase, is the ultimate hunt for a needle in a haystack.

Biological Weapons

The Center for Nonproliferation Studies at Monterey, California, reports that many countries may have some level of research into biological warfare agents, although only China, Egypt, and Iran are likely to have developed an offensive capability. Nevertheless, it is difficult to imagine the battlefield utility of "germ warfare" unless the objective is to create mass effects among a population, and there are much more effective and efficient tools for achieving that goal. Perhaps because of this uncertainty, most governments have long given up spending on ambitious programs for developing biological weapons.

What is perhaps more worrisome is the prospect that, as with some chemical weapons, one need only have a little expertise and some starter materials to begin the process of manufacturing a biological weapon outside the control of international law. Biological weapons technologies may be classed in two broad categories, those containing bacteria pathogens, and those that are derived from viruses. Bacteria-based weapons may make use of relatively common organisms, such as anthrax. The symptoms of an anthrax infection are not unlike those of an influenza infection, including high fever and chills, sore throat and coughing, fatigue and muscle aches, vomiting, and diarrhea.

In October 2001, a series of letters containing threatening notes and anthrax spores were used to carry out a series of attacks in the eastern United States and at US missions in Lithuania, Peru, and Russia. The letters were sent to targets in government, the media and business. Of the 22 cases of anthrax identified October 4–November 20, 2001, five cases out of the 11 that received the infection by inhalation were fatal. To date, the origin of the letters remains a mystery and no arrests have been made, strengthening the assessment put forth by the Centers for Disease Control and Prevention that biological weapons used in terror attacks lend themselves to more secretive forms of delivery (as contrasted with a chlorine bomb, for example).

> In contrast, attacks with biological agents are more likely to be covert. They present different challenges and require an additional dimension of emergency planning that involves the public health infrastructure. Covert dissemination of a biological agent in a public place will not have an immediate impact because of the delay between exposure and onset of illness (i.e., the incubation period). Consequently, the first casualties of a covert attack probably will be identified by physicians or other primary health-care providers.[18]

Viral weapons could, theoretically, be developed from small pox, hemorrhagic fever, or other exotic horrors, although these organisms are extremely dangerous to handle and difficult to culture and store safely. These difficulties tend to limit the usefulness of viruses for either military or terror weapons, as the desired effects (causing casualties, or drawing attention to a cause) may be achieved more economically in other ways. Consider Ebola, a hemorrhagic fever known to be fatal in 50–90 percent of clinical cases. The virus incubates from 2 to 21 days, leading to a sudden onset of disease. Later stage symptoms include inflammation of the eyes, painful skin rash, swelling in the genitals, and, just as it says on the tin, severe hemorrhaging – from the eyes, ears, nose, and the upper and lower gastrointestinal tract. Seizures, coma, and death typically follow.

The last major outbreak of Ebola Zaire, a particularly virulent strain, occurred 2001–02 in the border region between Gabon and the Republic of the Congo. Of the 122 people infected, 96 (79 percent) died. A subsequent outbreak in the Republic of the Congo, April 25–June 16, 2005, killed nine of 12 confirmed cases.[19] Needless to say, the challenge of making a weapon out of a wildfire like Ebola or similar organisms is supreme. Success would require sophisticated and well-equipped laboratory facilities, such as those possessed by the United States. Even with the best resources, the risk of accidental infection or destruction of the organism upon delivery makes the whole gamble seem naïve. Delivering a lethal virus of this type in a truly robust, weapons-grade form would require more resources than most wealthy states possess, let alone criminal or militant organizations. "It would be extremely difficult for 'terrorist' groups to either obtain cultures of filoviruses or work with them without killing themselves. Any 'terrorist' attempting to use Marburg or Ebola would almost certainly have to be an extremely well-trained and equipped scientist."[20]

Radiological Weapons

The point of a dirty bomb is not the immediate effect of its blast, which may be no more powerful than the conventional explosives of which it is composed. What makes the dirty bomb potentially dangerous is the incorporation of radioactive material, which the blast scatters to contaminate an area. Once the bomb has detonated, the health effects on persons exposed to radioactive debris are variable according to the radioactive intensity of the source material; whether it releases alpha, beta, or gamma rays; the victim's proximity to and time spent within the effective radius of the weapon and its debris. Generally speaking, the level of radiation released by the explosion may not be sufficient to kill or immediately poison people in the area. However, the public perception of contamination is such that the terror effect could be significant. Nevertheless, some experts downplay the threat posed by dirty bombs, by comparing the technology's limited effects with those of a true nuclear weapon:

> A dirty bomb is not a nuclear weapon. A nuclear bomb creates an explosion that is millions of times more powerful than that of a dirty bomb. The cloud of radiation from a nuclear bomb could spread tens to hundreds of square miles, whereas a dirty bomb's radiation could be dispersed within a few blocks or miles of the explosion. A dirty bomb is not a 'Weapon of Mass Destruction' but a 'Weapon of Mass Disruption,' where contamination and anxiety are the terrorists' major objectives.[21]

As radioactive materials decay (the measure of the rate of decay is the substance's half-life), they release ionizing radiation. The forms of radiation include alpha, beta, and neutron particles, and gamma electromagnetic waves. Alpha articles are positively charged, incapable of penetrating clothing or skin, but damaging once inside the body. Beta particles are negatively charged and capable of penetrating the skin and eyes. Neutron particles have no charge and are slightly more penetrating, although they may be stopped by concrete. Gamma radiation is very dangerous and takes the form of high energy, deeply penetrating waves.

Radioactive materials that could be used in dirty bombs are possessed by hospitals (for imaging technologies and radiological therapies), academic laboratories, and industrial facilities (such as power plants). Securing these sources from possible theft has become a priority since September 11, 2001. In the United States, the Nuclear Regulatory Commission has tightened licensing restrictions for the storage and use of radioactive materials. The commission says it has also strengthened regulations compelling owners of radioactive materials to report immediately any loss or theft. However, the record shows that some limited loss of material has already occurred, reported or not. Regardless of bureaucratic measures in place, the theft of even small amounts of radio-isotopes points toward the potential for the loss of more significant amounts of these materials.

Fear of negative health effects – including cancers and birth defects – from exposure to radiation fuels the deep-rooted mythology of the evils of radioactivity, even though no criminal attacks with nuclear or radiological weapons have ever been carried out. Nevertheless, since the Three Mile Island incident in 1979 at Middletown, Pennsylvania, and the disaster in 1986 at Chernobyl, Ukraine, the public has felt a profound disquiet about the prospect of accidental releases of radiation. On April 26, 1986, the Chernobyl nuclear reactor core melted down, releasing a radioactive cloud that contaminated a broad area of eastern and western Europe, resulting in US$ tens of billions in damage, particularly to the agricultural sectors of many nations' economies. Studies into the long-term health effects of Chernobyl continue, both in the affected area and among the unfortunate soldiers from the Russian Army who were assigned to clean up.[22]

More recent events have driven home the fear of radiation for Londoners who watched with the world as the drama unfolded around the death of ex-Soviet intelligence officer, Alexander Litvinenko. Litvinenko was killed by poisoning, having somehow ingested a small but slowly lethal amount of Polonium-210, an extremely radioactive substance that emits tissue-damaging alpha waves.

Nuclear Weapons[23]

Perhaps the most enduring symbol of the Cold War is the nuclear weapon, emblem of the days when giant stockpiles of hydrogen bombs faced off, waiting for the moment that never came. Nuclear weapons have evolved dramatically in terms of range, precision targeting, delivery system and warhead yield when compared with the atomic bombs "Little Boy" and "Fat Man," of the Hiroshima and Nagasaki bombings, August 1945.

The 12.5-kiloton weapon released by the *Enola Gay's* crew over Hiroshima, August 6, 1945, erased much of the city and killed 140,000. The 22-kiloton weapon released by the *Bock's Car's* crew over Nagasaki, August 9, killed 70,000. The Emperor of Japan surrendered six days later. Horrifying and effective as they were, the weapons used against Japan – the former drawing power from enriched uranium, and the latter from plutonium – were minor league compared to some of the monsters in the arsenal today.

Nuclear weapons technology generally falls into two basic types. On the one hand there is the fission reaction, which releases a great deal of energy from splitting atomic nuclei. On the other hand, there is the fusion reaction, the process that powers the sun, a compression of atomic nuclei to create a single, heavier nucleus, releasing a great deal of energy in the process. Fusion weapons, also called thermonuclear weapons, or H-bombs, have energy yields of 15–58 megatons, many times more powerful than the Hiroshima and Nagasaki bombs.

Early on, the Russians had the largest number of high-yield weapons. Toward the end of the Cold War, as delivery systems had expanded from manned bombers to long-range Intercontinental Ballistic Missiles (ICBMs), the United States flexed its strength in the guidance systems and payload capability of its weapons. For example, the Multiple, Independently targeted Re-entry Vehicles (MIRV) technology of the Minuteman ICBM program put several individually targeted warheads on the same missile, allowing the weapon to hit several dispersed targets or concentrate its yield on one.

> The yield of the Minuteman III MIRV ... as of the early 1970s ... approximated 170 kilotons, substantially less than the Minuteman I's 1.2 megaton yield. (Nevertheless, one Minuteman MIRV warhead would have had over eight times the yield of the ... weapon dropped on Hiroshima, thus, collateral damage would still be extensive).[24]

Such powerful weapons were developed to deter an opponent of equal or greater military might. Today, more than a decade after the end of the Cold War, and well into the "post-9/11 era," what is the relevance of these strategic monoliths of East-West confrontation? After 1991, the US Air Force and other services began a precipitous contraction of their strategic forces. All B-1, B-2, and B-52 bombers were taken off strategic alert and freed for conventional strike missions, such as those carried out over Afghanistan in 2001. Land-based nuclear weapons were withdrawn from Europe, just as nuclear weapons were removed from the Navy's surface squadrons. The number of strategic ballistic missile submarines, or SSBNs, was drawn down from 18 to 14, with four boats recycled as SSGNs (fitted out to launch conventional Tomahawk cruise missiles and host more than 60 Special Operations Forces). Additionally, the land-based ICBM force has been gutted, decreasing from 1,054 ICBMs at nine bases during the Cold War to a force of 450 missiles at three bases today. The Titan II, Minuteman II, and Peacekeeper ICBMs are all museum pieces now. The Moscow Treaty of 2002 further reduces the stockpile to between 1,700 and 2,200 nuclear warheads by December 31, 2012.

Nevertheless, the argument remains, why spend the money maintaining any nuclear forces in an era where there are no more Soviet Unions or Maoist Chinese to confront? The British recently debated the issue, having addressed the question whether to modernize the nation's Trident SSBNs. After a fierce debate in the House of Commons in March 2007, the Labour government finally obtained support for its proposed $40 billion plan to recapitalize the Royal Navy's fleet of ballistic missile submarines. During the debate, outgoing Prime Minister Tony Blair said: "I think that [the modernization] is essential for our security in an uncertain world. ... I believe it is important that we recognise that, although it is impossible to predict the future, the one thing ... that is certain, is the unpredictability of it."[25]

For some the deterrent effect of a nuclear force loses value with the demise of monolithic adversaries. For others, the weight brought by a credible nuclear deterrent may underwrite respect and independence of action in an increasingly dangerous and globalized economy. As the superpowers' stockpiles are reduced, the proliferation of nuclear weapons technologies seems to be on the rise.

Proliferation

CBRN weapons technologies, as well as the technologies of delivery systems such as ballistic and cruise missiles, are on the move worldwide, enabled in no small measure by the exponential growth of information on the internet and a robust overt and black market arms trade. Many states and non-state actors interested in acquiring the capabilities of WMD are masking their activity by making use of the dual nature of precursor chemicals and equipment, according to George J. Tenet, former director of the CIA.[26] Many nations and multinational corporations also produce materials and technologies that could directly or indirectly be applied to the proliferation of chemical and biological weapons. The Center for Nonproliferation Studies, Monterey, California, has named China, Egypt, Iran, Iraq, Israel, Libya, North Korea, Russia, Sudan, and Syria as significant proliferators of chemical and biological weapons capabilities.

Chem-bio materials are available and there is clear evidence of terrorists being interested in obtaining these materials. This supply-demand dynamic could easily be played out at biological research institutions in the [former Soviet Union]. If security is poor or lacking (as many suspect) at these institutions, they would be vulnerable to theft of pathogens, toxins, and other material of potential use by criminals, other countries, or terrorists. Most important, after theft, it would be easy for the perpetrator to hide and transport seed cultures of organisms that could be directly used in biological weapons or to produce toxins.[27]

Compounding the challenge of interdicting the movement of weapons precursor materials is the fact that chemicals and laboratory equipment of potential military use also often have legitimate applications. Many precursor agents are found in industries that could be important to a region's economic development, such as paper mills, agricultural chemicals and insecticides, and the plastics industries. Nevertheless, tracking these agents and the weapons that may be derived from them is important as the CIA has assessed that there is significant risk of confronting WMD in the hands of non-state actors in the near future.[28]

The spread of nuclear materials may be mitigated somewhat by the cooperative regimes that have been in place since the end of the Cold War, whereby Russia and the West are working together to ensure stockpile security. Nevertheless, the risk of a weapon being sold into the black market is heightened by the lack of oversight and coordination in monitoring all arms transfers through the former Soviet Union, according to Tenet. In addition, the acquisition of nuclear weapons by India, Pakistan, and now, possibly, North Korea may create additional supplies of weapons and components for sale. Meanwhile, North Korea remains a significant exporter of ballistic missiles and missile production equipment. Russia continues to assist Iran in developing nuclear fuel enrichment technologies that could be used to develop a weapons program. In addition, Chinese corporations have sold chemicals and missile technologies – including ballistic missiles and anti-ship cruise missiles – to Iran, Pakistan, and others.

Missile Technology

Latter-day versions of the German V-2 rockets developed at Peenemunde, today's short and intermediate range ballistic missiles, such as the Scud – capable of reaching targets 3,438 miles (5,533km) distant – have become the AK-47s of the third world's strategic forces. More capable missiles, designed to hit targets at ranges greater than 3,438 miles, include those classed as ICBMs. To date, the ICBM, along with the submarine-launched ballistic missile, has been the purview of the superpowers. The nations who possess ICBMs today are essentially the same ones who squared off during the Cold War: China, France, Russia, the UK, and the United States.

Building an ICBM is an effort that requires the most advanced rocket engineering. Several nations have expressed desire for this capability and are doggedly developing indigenous missile programs to evolve toward ICBMs, including Iran, India, North Korea and Pakistan. However, other interested parties may one day be able to skip the step-by-step evolutionary progression in technology. With foreign help, some may be able to buy their way toward more advanced weapons capability.

China today has one ICBM system in service and several long-range missile prototypes in development. One type – the CSS-4, or DF-5 – would be capable of hitting every city in the United States when operational. China's attitude toward its strategic capability was perhaps best expressed in 1996 when it ran what Washington and Taipei perceived as hostile military exercises in the Taiwan Straits. When the US Navy deployed a battle group in a show of force, a Chinese general remarked that the United States would be ill advised to exchange Los Angeles for Taipei. As a major manufacturer of other missile technologies, including types similar to the Russian Scud-series, as well as cruise missiles, China has a record of trading in arms much as do the nations of the West. For example, Chinese assistance has been critical to the ballistic missile development programs of India, Iran, and Pakistan.

Belarus, Kazakhstan, and Ukraine are among 15 states now occupying former Soviet territory, each with residual strategic and tactical forces, including Scuds and other missiles. Russia has consolidated its grip on the former Soviet nuclear weapons complex, but is still attempting to bring under control a massive stockpile that dwarfs that of any other nuclear-armed nation on earth. Russia also owns and is developing several classes of ballistic and cruise missiles, including the ubiquitous SS 1B Scud, which can be equipped with conventional or WMD payloads.

France and the UK, as manufacturers of a variety of missile technologies, including the Exocet, have contributed to the spread of small-scale delivery systems that could be modified to carry CBRN warheads. America itself has played a significant role in spreading missile technology world-wide. One example is the Hughes/Loral scandal of 1998, involving the illegal transfer of missile technology to China.[29]

Iran has five ballistic missile systems deployed in its arsenal and is developing three others. The nation has benefited from Chinese, Russian, Pakistani, and North Korean assistance in its weapons program, although the level of effort spent on acquiring CBRN capabilities remains unclear. Iran has demonstrated its Shihab-3, a medium-range theater ballistic missile capable of hitting a target within 808 miles (1,300km). The missile could be a stepping stone to long-range capability. The leadership of Iran has announced its goal of possessing long-range missiles as a way of exerting greater influence in the region.

For its part, North Korea has said it will continue to manufacture and sell ballistic missiles, and will work to develop longer-range missiles for its own use. The communist nation played a significant role in Pakistan's nuclear secret-selling scandal centered on A.Q. Khan, founder of Pakistan's nuclear weapons complex. Certainly, without North Korean aid, the Pakistanis and Iranians would not be as far along with their missile arsenals or atomic energy programs. Pyongyang has tested two missile systems of potential strategic importance – the Nodong and Taepo-dong. The Nodong is capable of reaching targets within 702nm (1,300km), including most of Japan. The Taepo-dong is an intermediate-range, 1,890nm (3,500km) missile. North Korea created controversy with missile tests in 1998 and again in 2003, which launched rockets over Japanese territorial waters.

Washington and Pyongyang agreed in 1994 to limit North Korea's development of nuclear arms in return for US aid to build a nuclear-electric reactor. However, underground research and development indicating a possible nuclear weapon detonation, coupled with new missile technology, has raised the bar for negotiations between the two nations.

With regard to nuclear-armed India and Pakistan, while it may seem unlikely that the dispute over Kashmir would erupt into nuclear war, the possibility is real. India has been working on long-range ballistic missiles, spun-off technology from its space launch program. India's Agni rocket is a medium-range missile undergoing tests and nearing the stage of full deployment. India also has Scuds and several other domestically produced ballistic missiles. Pakistan's Ghauri medium-range missile is the result of long-term cooperation with North Korea. Pakistan has also benefited from its reciprocal relationship with Iran; both have shared missile technology with one another. China and Russia have both played roles in the development of India's and Pakistan's missile arsenals. The United States, too, has aided them by sharing inspection techniques, information which allowed the Indians better to conceal their nuclear testing program.

CBRN Countermeasures

Defeating the threat posed by CBRN weapons may take many forms, including the collection and management of intelligence information that may support efforts to avert a pending attack, and direct action, or interdiction. Among the world's intelligence communities, missions to locate, find, fix, track, and analyze a potential adversary's CBRN capabilities have been given added emphasis. As the public fear of enduring a WMD terror attack has grown, the sense of urgency among intelligence officers as they grapple with the broad scope of the problem has also increased. One major challenge that is only now gradually being overcome is the linguistic and cultural barrier encountered by US and other nations' intelligence services attempting to operate in areas of the world only recently open to Westerners. These areas, including much of Central Asia, are also the training grounds for al Qaeda and other militant groups, and are proximate to potential targets for obtaining WMD technologies (such as the decaying former Soviet stockpile).

Intelligence alone is insufficient. Detailed knowledge must be coupled with forces capable of direct action, including conventional military, naval, and air power, as well as the highly skilled and motivated members of the Special Operations Force. For example, cued by intelligence service reports in 1998, the US Navy launched Tomahawk cruise missiles to destroy the al-Shifa chemical plant at Khartoum, Sudan, which was believed to have been producing a precursor chemical for VX nerve agent.[30] Another example, albeit one of mixed success, is the infamous "Scud hunt" of Operation *Desert Storm*, when air force planes and special forces, including British Special Air Service teams, operated inside Iraq on seek and destroy missions against Saddam Hussein's Scud missile transporter-erector-launcher (TEL) vehicles. The Iraqis launched more than 80 Scuds during the war, approximately half of them aimed at Israel. Despite the Scud hunting mission's relative failure to destroy TELs and missiles, the fact that the coalition forces were carrying it out helped prevent Israel from retaliating against Iraq – a move that would have put some Arab members of the coalition in an awkward position politically, finding themselves fighting on the side of their traditional enemy.

> Arab reaction to a retaliatory strike by Israel against Iraqi Scud sites remains speculative. Moderate states, including Saudi Arabia, might have condoned an Israeli strike. Other, more radical nations such as Syria might have immediately pulled out of the coalition. Western officials, including General [H. Norman] Schwarzkopf, were concerned that Israeli intervention, even in defense of their own territory, could splinter the fragile coalition against Iraq. Observers deemed it quite unlikely that Arabs would help Israelis kill other Arabs.[31]

Although the anticipated gas attack never happened in 1991, soldiers would nevertheless rush into their protective kit when the warning sirens indicating an inbound Scud sounded. Having learned the lessons of World War I, protective clothing and equipment against exposure in a CBRN-contaminated environment is standard issue. The US military calls its highest level of protection Mission Oriented Protection Posture Four, or MOPP-4, which includes the M17A2 mask – designed to protect the wearer from chemical agents and biological pathogens. It also features a drinking tube to allow a fully kitted soldier to maintain his isolation from the environment while drinking from his canteen. The M17A2 is usually worn with a battle dress over-garment, a hood, chemically protective gloves and over-boots. The over-garment – worn for 24 hours in a contaminated area, and then replaced – is impregnated with charcoal and other features that improve its resistance to penetration by chemical or biological weapons. The full protection kit restricts movement, and the mask narrows the wearer's field of view. Above all, however, the MOPP coveralls and equipment are uncomfortably hot, especially in desert conditions. In addition to protective clothing, soldiers are issued personal decontamination kits in case of accidental exposure to liquid agents on the skin. The kits include applicator pads and packets of powdered, activated resins that absorb and neutralize liquid chemical agents on the skin.

Ships are designed to protect their entire crews in a contamination-free environment. For example, a modern warship's heating, ventilation, and air conditioning atmosphere controls are a closed loop system that generates positive outward pressure throughout the ship (note the breeze continually blowing outward as a hatch is opened). This pressure prevents air penetration by chemical, biological, or radiological plumes, as well as repelling nuclear fallout. Additionally, the surfaces of the ship, both exterior and interior, are accessible to sprinkler systems that may share double duty as a fire fighting and decontamination wash-down system. Topside, the seawater and detergent wash-down can remove any CBRN contamination that the sea spray itself doesn't eliminate. Electronic equipment to detect the presence of contaminants may also be fitted to some warships, operating in areas where there are known CBRN threats.

On the home front, few civilians find themselves out and about with their MOPP-4 kit tucked away in the shopping cart, just in case. If efforts to prevent a domestic attack fail, then a mitigation plan that involves a robust response from national and local government, as well as from non-government disaster relief organizations, should be in place. In the United States, several agencies including the Department of Defense, the Department of Homeland Security, and the Department of Health and Human Services have worked together to develop mitigation strategies by modeling how they would interoperate in the event of a CBRN attack. If the somewhat disorganized effort to respond to Hurricane Katrina in 2005 is any indication, however, there is a great deal of ground to cover in preparing the federal agencies to work more closely with state and local counterparts. Another major challenge, also hinted at by the Katrina disaster relief operations, is the possibility of a CBRN attack that could overwhelm regional medical response capabilities by filling hospitals beyond capacity and by presenting operational challenges – toxic agents, radioactivity, etc – for which the non-federal agencies, such as local police and fire brigades, are ill equipped.

Missile Defense

Direct action may also include, as something of a last resort, interdicting a CBRN-tipped ballistic missile after launch, while it is boosting to altitude, or during the terminal phase of its attack. In any context, missile defense is a chancy game of shooting a rocket at the incoming warhead, similar to the principle of antiaircraft surface-to-air missiles. The principle behind this sort of defense is the "hit-to-kill" interception. Hit-to-kill means the defending missile has no explosive warhead, but rather aims to strike its target – such as a Scud – at high velocity, using kinetic energy to wreck the target at high altitude.

One obvious problem with this concept is that debris from the impact may rain down over the Scud's intended target, as happened in Israel during some MIM-104 Patriot–Scud interceptions. The US Department of Defense says this problem can be managed, but recognizes that the consequences could be serious, especially if the incoming missile carries a chemical agent that could linger in the atmosphere and remain dangerous while settling to earth. A safer place to knock down an enemy missile would be over its own launch site, or out in space (for the long-range ICBMs) before it releases its re-entry vehicle and warhead. Interceptions at these areas would limit collateral damage to friendly populations.

Depending upon the sophistication of the ballistic missile, the interceptor rocket may have to overcome countermeasures, as has been shown in several high-profile test failures of the developmental US ground-based midcourse element of the National Missile Defense system during the 1990s. Sophisticated ballistic missiles will release a number of objects in addition to their warhead(s), to confuse enemy tracking radar with multiple images of the re-entry vehicle. Powerful radar and electro-optical/infrared sensors have been developed to overcome this challenge, and discriminate the real warhead amongst lighter or less dense clutter.

Of the ballistic missile defenses that have been most successful in testing to date, the US Navy's Aegis-based Ballistic Missile Defense (BMD) system has pride of place. On April 27, 2007, Aegis BMD completed its 27th successful test interception since 2001. The concept makes use of the fleet's guided missile cruisers and destroyers, equipped with powerful radar and SM-3 standard missiles. Aegis BMD is designed to tackle the threat from ballistic missiles in the littorals, over areas comparable to that covered by Army Patriot missile batteries during Operation *Desert Storm* and Operation *Iraqi Freedom*. Naval mobility makes the Aegis system attractive, because unlike land-based interceptors the ships underway in international waters require no permission to establish an operating base.

Summary

There can be little doubt that the horror inspired by CBRN technologies is a genuine force in the modern imagination. 49 nations readily supported the invasion of Iraq in 2003, even without general UN agreement, based largely on the argument (now apparently proved exaggerated) that Saddam Hussein's government was armed with WMD, such is the fear aroused by these weapons. The possibility that WMD could be sold into the hands of criminals who might use them in a terrorist attack such as the Aum Shin Rikyo's in Tokyo is every government's worst nightmare.

Perhaps the saving grace (although an inappropriate word) of CBRN weapons technologies is inherent in their design: that they represent the unthinkable extremes of war or violence, and that to use (or even to handle) them would present significant risks to the attacker. This is certainly the case in the world of bio weapons, where the more lethal bacteria and viruses are difficult to contain and transport safely, and for which great precautions must be taken to ensure they arrive at their target still viable. In other words, it's no good stuffing an artillery shell with disease cultures as they would probably be destroyed when the shell bursts. Chemical and radiological weapons are a different story, with raw materials much more easily obtained and handled. The most lethal of these nevertheless also require careful handling. In the case of radiological weapons, the danger is perhaps blunted slightly by the limitations of the conventional explosive that may be used to deliver the radioactive material.

There has never been an adequate defense against genuine nuclear weapons, especially as the warheads and ballistic missiles that deliver them have become increasingly sophisticated and accurate. However, this lack of defense is probably the reason that the tide of mutually assured destruction that carried the West and the Soviet Union through the Cold War did not result in Armageddon, as any use of nuclear weaponry would have rebounded on the head of either party. We have almost become unconscious of the fact that out there in silos beneath the plains of the midwestern United States, across Russia, and in submarines cruising beneath the Pacific Ocean, there is enough power to rival the sun. Perhaps we have also grown accustomed to trusting the professionalism and training of the men and women with their hands on the controls of these weapons.

CONCLUSION

If we have learnt one thing from our study of modern weaponry, it is that any weapon is only as smart as the person with his finger on the trigger, whether that trigger is real or metaphorical. You can automate everything to the hilt, but even in the sterile environment of a modern command center someone, at some point, must sit down, gnaw anxiously on the end of a pencil, and decide whether to "unleash hell," and where. Avoiding the temptation to focus exclusively on the technology (the capabilities of the weapons) has forced us to wrestle instead with a big, frequently controversial topic – how do human limitations influence what weaponry can do?

That said, we have also rediscovered the blindingly obvious point that some weapons are much, much better than others. Think of the Kalashnikov, removed from months of entombment in African river mud, rattling though a full magazine of ammunition without a hitch, compared to the SA80A1 with its melting stock and bits dropping off. And when its comes to radiological devices, dirty bombs, here might be a case of hype exceeding reality – nasty as these sound, their bark really may be worse than their bite. Focusing on the human factor never implies that the technology is less important. Technology must, as far as possible, attempt to compensate for human failings, whether those failings are in the diligence in cleaning a gun or in the targeting of a submarine-launched cruise missile.

The problem technology faces, however, is that warfare always exists on many levels. On the one hand, there are still plenty of conflicts fought with all the subtlety of World War I trench battles, with armies basically hacking it out with each other at close ranges with AKs and cannon bolted to the flatbed of Toyota pickups. On the other hand, there is the hyper-sophistication of modern air and naval combat systems, with multibillion dollar technologies networked together in huge computerized war systems. But all too often these extremes of warfare mingle. US soldiers in Iraq, for instance, may be part of the most advanced army in human history, with the capability to call in wrecking air and artillery strikes in minutes, but much of their work takes place at a cruel grass roots level, where they must make terribly human decisions such as whether to open fire on a speeding minicab potentially full of civilians who actually just want to put distance between them and an awful experience. Even combat pilots, at the cutting edge of military personnel in terms of technology, must wrestle with their humanity. For a pilot who releases a JDAM, what assumptions has he made to be sure that the weapon is going to hit its target? Is the target in fact what he believes it is? What are the consequences if he is wrong?

We have seen how information is a crucial common element involved in every weapons system. The life of the explosive ordnance disposal technician depends on information – he needs to know what he is up against if he is to face a weapon that could vaporize him if he makes the wrong decision. The captain of a nuclear-powered fast attack submarine who is preparing to launch Tomahawk missiles against a target hundreds of miles away needs all the justificatory information at his fingertips if he is possibly to avoid troubled nights as an old man. Faith in information underwrites faith in the performance and accuracy of the weapon system itself.

With regard to the targets, both intended and those caught in the crossfire, we have hopefully never forgotten the lethal impact of weapon technologies. It is sobering to realize that while the era of precision warfare is truly with us, civilians still make up the largest percentage of casualties in any war. One other fact that governments of all persuasions must understand is that the effect of a weapon is a beginning as much as it is an end – the target may be destroyed, but those who survive the impact of that weapon will go on to make their own contribution to the conflict, based on their response to the violent experience. With a significant portion of the world either at war or drawn into violence at some point during the last decade, the relevance of weaponry to the everyday experience of millions has, unfortunately, made itself all too clear. The bottom line is that while this is ostensibly a book about guns, tanks, and dirty bombs, it is really a book about people.

ENDNOTES

Introduction

1. Thanks for this information go to Dr Amer Hameed, senior lecturer at the Defence Academy of the United Kingdom.

Chapter 1: Hand-Held War – Small Arms

1. See Martin L. Fackler MD, "Stockton – the Facts" (2000), http://www.cs.cmu.edu/afs/cs/usr/wbardwel/public/nfalist/fl_aw_report2.txt

2. Peter S. Kindsvatter, *American Soldiers – Ground Combat in the World Wars, Korea, and Vietnam* (Lawrence, KS: Kansas University Press, 2003), p.223. Kindsvatter is quoting from George Wilson, *If You Survive* (New York: Ivy Books, 1987), p.111.

3. See Ian Hogg and John Weeks, *Military Small Arms of the Twentieth Century* (London: Arms & Armor Press, 1991), p.209.

4. Gene Weingarten, "Spray It, Don't Say It," *Washington Post* (October 16, 2005).

5. Peter Taylor, "Six Days That Shook Britain," *The Guardian* (July 24, 2002), www.guardian.co.uk/Archive/Article/0,4273,4467433,00.html

6. For example, the British Home Office Research Study 298, *Gun Crime: the market in and use of illegal firearms* (Home Office Research, Development and Statistics Directorate, December 2006) was based on interviews with 80 offenders convicted for crimes under the Firearms Act. The report noted that: "Technical expertise regarding firearms appears to be the exception rather than the rule – only a very few of the 80 interviewees volunteered any depth of technical knowledge, notably including the two former cadets and one former soldier."

7. Interview with Chris McNab (July 9, 2006).

8. Mark Baker, *Nam* (London: Abacus, 1981), p.104.

9. Firearms Tactical Institute, "Shotgun Home Defense Ammunition," Tactical Briefs 10 (October 1998), www.firearmstactical.com/briefs10.htm

10. Leroy Thompson, *Hostage Rescue Manual* (London: Greenhill Books, 2001), p.91.

11. D. F. Allsop and M. A. Toomey, *Small Arms – General Design* (London: Brassey's, 1999), p.1.

12. James Dunnigan, "The Weight, Again (Infantry Still Carry Too Much)," www.strategypage.com (July 16, 2005).

13. Rachel K. Evans, "Upper body fatiguing exercise and shooting performance," *Military Medicine* (June 2003), http://findarticles.com/p/articles/mi_qa3912/is_200306/ai_n9247111

14. Globalsecurity.org, "The Infantryman's Combat Load" (1985), www.globalsecurity.org/military/library/report/1985/IDC.htm

15. Dick Culver, "The M16 Saga" (1999–2000), www.jouster.com

16. Ibid.

17. As an example, Allsop & Toomey (p.64) note: "During the SA80 trials it was also found that firing between 300 and 360 rounds at any rate above 60 rounds per minute, heated the barrel so that a 'cook off' was almost inevitable on ceasing fire with a round in the chamber, within 30s, or even quicker."

18. James Meek, "Off Target," *The Guardian* (October 10, 2002), www.guardian.co.uk/g2/story/0,,808713,00.html

19. Ibid.

20. The Light Support Weapon is a version of the SA80 with a longer and heavier barrel and intended as a light machine gun, although on that count it is inadequate in almost every respect, hence the British Army has moved to acquire the Belgian Minimi as the core of its squad firepower.

21. See Lewis Page, *Lions, Donkeys and Dinosaurs – Waste and Blundering in the Armed Forces* (London: Heinemann, 2006), p.22.

22. Ibid., p.23.

23. *Hansard* (Westminster, UK, July 15, 2002), column 12, www.publications.parliament.co.uk

24. The ITDU report mentioned above cited tests of the SA80A2 producing Mean Round Between Failure incidents of an incredible 6,745 rounds, against the 99 of the original SA80.

25. N.W.A, "Straight Outta Compton" (Priority Records, 1989).

26. *Jackie Brown*, dir. Quentin Tarantino (Miramax, 1997).

27. Interview with Chris McNab (July 2006).

28. Abdel Fatau Musah and Robert Castle, "Eastern Europe's Arsenal on the Loose: managing light weapons flows to conflict zones," Occasional Papers on International Security Issues, IANSA, 26 (May 1998), http://www.iansa.org/documents/development/eeurope_arsenal.htm

29. Catherine Philp, "Children killed as US troops fire on van at roadblock," *The Times* (November 22, 2005), www.timesonline.co.uk/tol/news/world/iraq/articles592700.ece

30. Baker, *Nam*, p.85.

31. Bruce Bergum and I. Charles Klein, "A Survey and Analysis of Vigilance Research," Human Resources Research Organization Report 8 (November 1961).

32. Anthony Swofford, *Jarhead – A Marine's Chronicle of the Gulf War* (London: Scribner, 2003), p.123.

33. S.L.A. Marshall, *Men Against Fire – The Problem of Battle Command in Future War* (New York: William Morrow, 1947).

34. See John Whiteclay Chambers, II, "S.L.A. Marshall's *Men Against Fire*: new evidence regarding fire ratios," *Parameters* (Carlisle, PA: Autumn 2003), http://carlisle-www.army.mil/usawc/Parameters/03autumn/chambers.pdf

35. Harold P. Leinbaugh and John D. Campbell, *The Men of Company K: The Autobiography of a World War II Rifle Company* (New York: Bantam, 1991).

36. Joanna Bourke, *An Intimate History of Killing – Face-to-face Killing in Twentieth-Century Warfare* (London: Granta, 1999), p.74.

37. Hugh McManners, *The Scars of War* (London: HarperCollins, 1993), p.168.

38. Ibid., p.254.

39. Jason Burke, " 'Run or you will die.' The soldiers did not go and they died," *The Guardian* (June 26, 2003), www.guardian.co.uk/international/story/0,,985171,00.htm

40. Statement by Dr Stephen Biddle, Associate Professor of National Security Studies, US Army War College, Strategic Studies Institute, before the Committee on Armed Services, US House of Representatives, First Session, 108th Congress, "On Operation *Iraqi Freedom*: outside perspectives" (Washington, D.C., October 21, 2003).

41. Rex Applegate, *Kill or Get Killed* (Boulder, CO: Paladin Press, 1976).

42. Public Record Office, SOE Syllabus, "Weapon Training," I.5 (January 1944).

43. James Dees et al., "An Experimental Review of Basic Combat Rifle Marksmanship: marksman phase I," HumRRO Technical Report 71–74 (March 1971).

44. Peter Watson, *War on the Mind – The Military Uses and Abuses of Psychology* (London: Hutchinson & Co., 1978), p.57.

45. Sean Rayment, "Trigger happy US troops will 'keep us in Iraq for years'," *Daily Telegraph* (May 15, 2005), www.telegraph.co.uk/news/main.jhtml?xml=/news/2005/05/15/wirq15.xml

46. Evan Wright, *Generation Kill* (London: Corgi, 2004), p.199.

47. Lt Col Dean Mengel, "Ammunition Shortages Experienced in Operation *Iraqi Freedom* – Causes and Solutions" (US Army War College, 2005), www.strategicstudiesinstitute.army.mil/pdffiles/ksil75.pdf

48. One important point about tracers is that as the chemical element burns away the bullet loses mass, so its trajectory will drop more quickly than ball rounds. When firing over long ranges the machine-gunner will have to compensate for this effect by aiming slightly higher than the impact point of the tracers.

49. Declaration of St Petersburg, November 29, 1868.

50. International Peace Conference, "Declaration on the Use of Bullets which Expand or Flatten Easily in the Human Body" (The Hague, The Netherlands, July 29, 1899.)

51. John Steele, "Police Used 'Dum Dum' Bullets to Kill de Menezes," *Daily Telegraph* (November 16, 2005), www.telegraph.co.uk/news/main.jhtml?xml=/news/2005/11/16/nmenez16.xml

52. BBC, "Outrage at Menezes Bullet Report" (November 16, 2005), http://news.bbc.co.uk/1/hi/uk_news/4443082.stm

53. Steele, "'Dum Dum' Bullets."

54. Martin L. Fackler, "Gunshot Wound Review," *Annals of Emergency Medicine*, 28:2 (August 1996), pp.194–203.

55. In his article "Wound Ballistics and Soft-Tissue Wound Treatment," written in 1995, Fackler notes that "modern textbooks of surgery recommend extensive excision of tissue when wounds are presumed to have been caused by "high

velocity" missiles, whereas they recommend little or no excision if the wound was presumed to have been caused by a "low velocity" projectile." See *Techniques in Orthopaedics*, 10:3 (1995), pp.163–70.

56. "7.62mm versus 5.56mm – Does NATO really need two standard rifle calibers?," Command and Staff College report (1986), www.globalsecurity.org/military/library/report/1986/MVT.htm. Note, though, that the report also stated that: "These comparisons, however, do not consider the fact that the SS109 uses a semi-armor piercing, steel-cored projectile, while the 7.62mm ball uses a relatively soft anti-personnel, lead-cored projectile. A semi-armor piercing 7.62mm caliber projectile, using second-generation technology like the SS109, would easily outperform the smaller SS109 projectile in penetration tests at all ranges."

57. Philip Katcher, *Armies of the Vietnam War 1962–75* (London: Osprey, 1980), p.18.

58. See Martin L. Fackler, "Wounding Patterns of Military Rifle Bullets," *International Defense Review*, 1 (1989), pp.59–64.

59. CSC, "7.62mm versus 5.56mm."

60. Urey W. Patrick and John C. Hall, *In Defense of Self and Others ... Issues, Facts & Fallacies – the Realities of Law Enforcement's Use of Deadly Force* (Durham, NC: Carolina Academic Press, 2005), pp.62–63.

61. Ibid., pp.63–64. The quoted list is taken from K. Newgard MD, "The Physiological Effects of Handgun Bullets," *Wound Ballistics Review*, Journal of the International Wound Ballistics Association, 1:3 (Fall 1992).

62. Firearms Tactical Institute, "The Myth of Energy Transfer," Tactical Briefs 3 (March 15, 1998), www.firearmstactical.com/briefs3.htm

63. Dave Spaulding, "What Really Happens in a Gunfight," *Guns and Ammo Handguns* (2006), www.handgunsmag.com/tactics_training/what_happens_gunfight/

64. Clint Smith, "Communicate, Move, Shoot" (June 2006), www.policeone.com/writers/columnists/PoliceMagazine/articles/77200/

65. Patrick and Hall, *In Defense*, pp.108–09.

Chapter 2: Perfect Destruction – Explosives

1. See A. Bailey and S.G. Murray, *Explosives, Propellants & Pyrotechnics* (London: Brassey's, 1989), p.2.

2. Globalsecurity.org, "Explosives" (2006), www.globalsecurity.org/military/systems/munitions/explosives.htm

3. See US federal regulation 18 USC. § 845(a)(5); 27 C.F.R.§ 55.141(b).

4. The device actually consisted of three separate pipe bombs detonated as one, with nails packed around them to produce a lethal fragmentation effect.

5. See US Department of Justice report at http://www.usdoj.gov/oig/special/9704a/09kikumu.htm

6. Globalsecurity.org, "Explosives."

ENDNOTES

7.   Bailey and Murray, *Explosives*, p.6.

8.   Maureen Rushton, "The Canary Girls of Chilwell," *Nottingham Family History Society Journal* (April 2001), http://www.nottsfhs.org.uk/society/journals/apr01.htm

9.   Madonna Tribe News, www.madonnatribe.com/news. It is worth noting that Explosia, the company that produces Semtex, is at the time of writing taking out legal action against Madonna for misuse of its trademark.

10. Explosia a.s., www.explosia.cz/en/?show=semtex

11. Arie Farnam, "Czechs Try to Cap Plastic Explosive Sales," *Christian Science Monitor* (February 26, 2002), www.csmonitor.com/2002/0226/p07s02-woeu.html

12. Peter Taylor, *Brits – The War against the IRA* (London: Bloomsbury, 2001), p.296.

13. Globalsecurity.org, "Explosives."

14. Explosia a.s., "Brief History of Plastic Explosive Semtex," http://www.explosia.cz/en/?show=semtex

15. US Navy Surface Warfare Center, "Warheads Primer," Explosives and Energetics Division (Indian Head, MD).

16. Thomas L. Norman, "Building Security Design Considerations: the effects of bomb blasts," *Best Practices*, American Institute of Architects (January 2004), pp.1–2, http://develop2.aim.org/siteobjects/files/17-07-13.pdf

17. US Navy Surface Warfare Center, "Warheads Primer."

18. Defense Intelligence Agency, "Fuel-Air and Enhanced-Blast Explosive Technology – Foreign" (April 1993).

19. See Vladimir Odintsov, "Fragmentation Missile Warheads: development potentials," *Military Parade* (July–August 1998), http://milparade.udm.ru/28/060.htm

20. Thomas L. Norman, "Building Security Design Considerations", p.1.

21. A rigorous and disturbing paper on the physiological effects of bomb explosions, based on the analysis of bomb victims in Israel, is by Yoram Kluger, "Bomb Explosions in Acts of Terrorism – Detonation, Wound Ballistics, Triage and Medical Concerns," *Israel Medical Association Journal*, 5 (April 2003), pp.235–40, http://www.ima.org.il/imaj/ar03ap-1.pdf

22. S.G. Mellor and G.J. Cooper, "Analysis of 828 Servicemen Killed or Injured by Explosion in Northern Ireland 1970-84: the hostile action casualty system," *The British Journal of Surgery*, 76:10 (October 1989), pp.1006–10, www.bjs.co.uk

23. Kluger, "Bomb Explosions," p.238.

24. Ibid., p.235.

25. Field report, US Marine Corps Systems Command Liaison Team, Central Iraq (April 20–25, 2003), http://www.sftt.org/PDF/article05122003a.pdf

26. US Army Technical Center for Explosives Safety, *USATCES Explosives Safety Bulletin*, 13:2 (March 2002).

27. "Army Explosives Mishaps: human error during training is most common scenario," *Ground Warrior* (Winter 2002), http://findarticles.com/p/articles/mi_m0PAD/is_2002_Winter/ai_104681792

28. US Department of Defense, United States Code, Title 10, Chapter 141, Section 2389.

29. Neil Gibson and Rupert Pengelley, "Insensitive Munitions Make the Military Less Accident Prone," *Jane's Defence Weekly* (September 21, 2005), www.janes.com/defence/land_forces/news/idr/idr050921_2_n.shtml

30. Egmont Kock and Bernard Rix, "A Review of Police Trials of CS Aerosol Incapacitants," Police Research Series Paper 21 (London: Police Research Group, 1996), http://www.homeoffice.gov.uk

31. Interview (2006).

32. Evan Wright, *Generation Kill* (London: Corgi, 2004), p.331.

33. Landmines sown in World War II still pose a serious problem to some nations. Poland, for example, has 241,090,000 sq m (624,420,233 sq km) of territory known to contain mines and unexploded ordnance, and in 2001 alone 3,842 mines, along with 45,322 other munitions, were cleared. Figures from Human Rights Watch, *Landmine Monitor Report* (2002), http://www.icbl.org/lm/2002/

34. Figures from International Campaign to Ban Landmines, www.icbl.org

35. Norman Youngblood, *The Development of Mine Warfare* (Westport, CT: Praeger Security International, 2006), p.162.

36. Article 7 Report, Form F and Annex 4 (April 22, 2005).

37. International Campaign to Ban Landmines, "Bosnia and Herzegovina Country Study," *Landmine Monitor* (2006), www.icbl.org/lm/2006/bih.html#Heading69

38. Hugh McManners, *The Scars of War* (London: HarperCollins, 1993), p.165.

39. Human Rights Watch, "Backgrounder: antivehicle mines with sensitive fuzes or antihandling devices" (February 25, 2002), p.10.

40. US Government Accountability Office, *Military Operations – Information on US Use of Land Mines in the Persian Gulf War*, GAO-02-1003 (Washington, D.C.: September 2002).

41. Ibid., p.9.

42. Ibid., p.10.

43. Ibid., pp.27–28.

44. US Army Technical Center for Explosives Safety, *Report of Findings for Study of Ammunition Dud and Low Order Detonation Rate* (McAlester, OK: July 2000).

45. US Government Accountability Office, *Military Operations*, p.29.

46. Ibid., p.33.

47. Ibid., pp.33–34.

48. Ibid., p.26.

49. Maki K. Habib, "Mine Clearance Techniques and Technologies for Effective Humanitarian Demining," *Journal of Mine Action*, 6.1 (April 2002), http://maic.jmu.edu/JOURNAL/6.1/features/habib/habib.htm

50. Peter A. Schoeck, "The Demining of Farmland: cost/benefit analysis and quality control," *Journal of Mine Action*, 4:3, http://maic.jmu.edu/Journal/4.3/features/Farmlands/farmland.htm

51. Note that "bombmaker" here need not solely imply an insurgent. IEDs have been constructed by conventional military forces since the American Civil War, typically in the form of booby traps to interdict advancing enemy forces.

52. Bronislav V. Matseevich, "Selected Technologies and Procedures Intended to Restrict Unauthorized Access to Explosives," from *High Impact Terrorism – Proceedings of a Russian-American Workshop*, Committee for Confronting Terrorism in Russia (Washington, D.C.: National Academies Press, 2002), pp.165–70.

53. Ronald L. Simmons, "Terrorism: Explosives Threat," in *High Impact Terrorism*, pp.171–80.

54. Interview with Chris McNab (March 22, 2007).

55. Bruce Hoffman, "The Logic of Suicide Terrorism," *The Atlantic Monthly* (June 2003), www.theatlantic.com/doc/200306/hoffman

56. See Dr Robert J. Bunker and John P. Sullivan, "Suicide Bombings in Operation *Iraqi Freedom*," Association of the United States Army, The Institute of Land Warfare, No.46W (Arlington, VA: September 2004).

57. Hoffman, "Logic."

58. Much of the following information on IED cell structure comes from Greg Grant's excellent article "The IED Marketplace in Iraq," *Defense News* (August 3, 2005).

59. Ibid.

60. Hoffman, "Logic."

61. Interview (April 2, 2007).

Chapter 3: Mechanized Muscle – Battlefield Armor

1. Paul Hornback, "The Wheel vs. Track Dilemma," *Armor* (March–April 1998), www.fas.org/man/dod-101/sys/land/docs/2wheels98.pdf

2. Ken Tout, "Lessons of War: the tank crew in battle," transcript of DRAC Briefing Day speech (November 27, 1986).

3. Ibid.

4. Vorvolakos Nicolaos, "The Psychology of the Tank Crew," presentation at the Greek Army Armor and Training Center (Greece, June 1984).

5. Ben Shephard, *A War of Nerves – Soldiers and Psychiatrists 1914–1994* (London: Jonathan Cape, 2000), p.183.

6. Richard Holmes, *Dusty Warriors – Modern Soldiers at War* (London: Harper Press, 2006), p.270.

7. Ibid., p.241.

8. Ken Tout, "Lessons of War."

9. Jason Conroy with Ron Martz, *Heavy Metal – A Tank Company's Battle to Baghdad* (Dulles, VA: Potomac Books, 2005), p.33.

10. Jorg Sandmann, "Health Disturbances of German Battle Tank Officers: results of an interview with 64 commanding officers

of a tank battalion," *Military Medicine* (September 2003),
http://findarticles.com/p/articles/mi_qa3912/is_200309/ai_n9256099/pg_1

11. "Tank Gunner Performance and Hearing Impairment," *Army Research, Development and Acquisition Bulletin* (1990).

12. Ashley John, "The Hot HMMWV Becomes a Little Cooler," *RDECom Magazine* (November 2004), www.rdecom.army.mil/rdemagazine/200411/itf_HMMWV.html

13. Department of Military and Veteran Affairs, State Safety Office, *M1 Abrams Tank Safety Guide* (Anneville, PA), www.dmva.state.pa.us/paarng_sso/lib/paarng_sso/safety_guides/sg4.doc

14. Rupert Smith, *The Utility of Force – The Art of War in the Modern World* (London: Penguin, 2005), p.1.

15. Ibid., p.2.

16. Quotation taken from Simon Dunstan, *The Yom Kippur War 1973 (2)* (Oxford: Osprey, 2003), p.56.

17. Stan Morse (ed.), *Gulf Air War Debrief* (London: Aerospace Publishing Ltd, 1991), p.173.

18. J. Michael Gilmore, CBO Testimony, "The Army's Future Combat Systems Program," before the Subcommittee on Tactical Air and Land Forces, Committee on Armed Services, US House of Representatives (Washington, D.C.: April 4, 2006), p.2.

19. Federation of American Scientists, Military Analysis Network, "Arjun," www.fas.org/man/dod-101/sys/land/row/arjun.htm

20. House Report 106-371 – *Making Appropriations For The Department Of Defense For The Fiscal Year Ending September 30, 2000, And For Other Purposes.*

21. Bruce I. Gudmundsson, *On Armor* (Westport, CT: Praeger, 2004), p.175.

22. Elizabeth Book, "Pentagon Needs Accurate Accounting of Fuel," *National Defense* (March 2002), www.nationaldefensemagazine.org/issues/2002/Mar/Pentagon_Needs.htm

23. James Dunnigan, *How to Make War* (New York: HarperCollins, 2003), p.67.

24. Major J.G. Pierre Lamontagne, CD, Master of Defence Studies, *Are the Days of the Main Battle Tank Over?*, Canadian Forces College (Toronto, Ontario: 2006).

25. Quotation taken from George Forty, *Tank Aces – From Blitzkrieg to the Gulf War* (Stroud, UK: Sutton Publishing, 1997), p.117.

26. Gudmundsson, *On Armor*, p.174.

27. Michael Smith, "Army Leak Reveals Shortage of Guns," *The Times* (May 6, 2007), http://www.timesonline.co.uk/tol/news/uk/article1752368.ece

28. Michael Green and Greg Stewart, *M1 Abrams at War* (St Paul, MN: Zenith Press, 2005), p.60.

29. Ibid., p.77.

30. Conroy, *Heavy Metal*, pp.8–9.

31. Steve Rodan, "Israel's Military Debates Use of Flechette Round," *Jane's Defence Weekly* (May 22, 2001), www.janes.com/defence/land_forces/news/jdw/jdw010522_2_n_shtml

32. Supreme Court of Israel, HCJ 8990/02 "Physicians for Human Rights/The Palestinian Center for Human Rights vs Doron Almog (OC Southern Command)/The State of Israel (The Minister of Defense)" (April 27, 2003).

33. Dunnigan, *How to Make War*, p.99.

34. Scott Boston, "Toward a Protected Future Force," *Parameters* (Carlisle, PA: Winter 2004–05), pp.55–70, p.60; http://carlisle-www.army.mil/usawe/Parameters/04winter/boston.htm

35. Captain Neil Prakash in interview with John McCool (October 20, 2006); from Kendall D. Gott (ed.), *Eyewitness to War, Volume II – The US Army in Operation Al Faj, an Oral History* (Fort Leavenworth, KS: Combat Studies Institute Press, 2006), p.159.

36. Greg Grant, "Army reset bill hits $9 billion," *Army Times* (February 20, 2006), http://www.armytimes.com/legacy/new/0-ARMYPAPER-1526955.php

37. See Thomas E. Bowen, *Emergency War Surgery* (Desert Publications/US Army, 2004).

38. Interview (2006).

39. Clay Wilson, *Improvised Explosive Devices (IEDs) in Iraq: effects and countermeasures*, CRS report for Congress (February 10, 2006), p.2.

40. Kris Osborn, "Army Officials Tout Success of Reactive Armor," *Army Times* (April 16, 2007), www.armytimes.com/news/2007/04/defense_reactive_armor_070413/

41. As interviewed by Scott R. Gourley, "Javelin," *Army* (June 2006), http://findarticles.com/p/articles/mi_qa3723/is_200606/ai_n17177002

42. Lester W. Grau, "Russian-manufactured Armored Vehicle Vulnerability in Urban Combat: the Chechnya experience," *Red Thrust Star* (January 1997), www.fas.org/man/dod-101/sys/land/row/rusav.htm

43. Timothy L. Thomas, "The Battle of Grozny: deadly classroom for urban combat," *Parameters* (Carlisle, PA: Summer 1999), pp.87–102, http://carlisle-www.army.mil/usawc/Parameters/99summer/thomas.htm

44. Press Conference, Kuwait (December 8, 2004).

45. Program aired on December 16, 2004, http://edition.cnn.com

46. Robert H. Reid and Anne Flaherty, "Stryker Losses in Iraq Raise Questions," AP release (May 13, 2007), www.washingtonpost.com

47. TM C/3-15 Infantry, Task Force 1-64 Armor, Operation *Iraqi Freedom* After Action Review Comments (April 24, 2003).

48. John Gordon IV and Bruce R. Pirnie, " 'Everybody Wanted Tanks': heavy forces in Operation *Iraqi Freedom*," *Joint Force Quarterly* (October 2005), www.dtic.mil/doctrine/jel/jfq_pubs/1539.pdf

Chapter 4: Death from a Distance – Artillery

1. Guy Sajer, *The Forgotten Soldier* (London: Sphere, 1977), p.395.

2. Peter Watson, *War on the Mind – The Military Uses and Abuses of Psychology* (London: Hutchinson & Co., 1978), p.215.

3. Ibid., p.215.

4. Ibid., p.216.

5. Theresa Y. Schulz, "Troops Returning with Alarming Rates of Hearing Loss," *Hearing Health* (Fall 2004), p.19.

6. Lt A. Alfands to Lord Northcliffe, Northcliffe Papers, British Library.

7. Arie Shlosberg and Rael D. Strous, "Long-Term Follow-Up (32 Years) of PTSD in Israeli Yom Kippur War Veterans," *The Journal of Nervous and Mental Disease*, 193:10 (October 2005), pp.693–96, www.jonmd.com

8. Kendall D. Gott (ed.), *Eyewitness to War, Volume II – The US Army in Operation Al Faj, an Oral History* (Fort Leavenworth, KS: Combat Studies Institute Press, 2006), p.115.

9. Fred Majdalany, *The Monastery* (London: Houghton, 1946); excerpt taken from Desmond Flower and James Reeves (eds), *The War 1939–1945 – A Documentary History* (Cambridge, MA: Da Capo Press, 1997), p.691.

10. Chris Bellamy, *Red God of War – Soviet Artillery and Rocket Forces* (London: Brassey's, 1986), p.1.

11. James Dunnigan, *How to Make War* (New York: HarperCollins, 2003), p.101.

12. Les Roberts, Ridyah Lafta, Richard Garfield, et al., "Mortality Before and After the 2003 Invasion of Iraq: cluster sample survey," *The Lancet*, 364 (9448) (October 29, 2004), pp.1857–64. The best source for authoritative analysis of the Iraq war body count is to be found with the Iraq Body Count organization. Their data and findings are displayed at www.iraqbodycount.net

13. For a compact study of modern SP guns systems, see Eric H. Biass and Terry J. Gander, "Self-Propelled Artillery – Autoloading and 52 are the Trend," *Armada International*, 4 (2003), pp.43–54.

14. Scuds were also used extensively in Afghanistan from October 1988, from when the Soviet-backed Democratic Republic of Afghanistan (DRA) launched a total of 2,000 Scuds against Mujahideen targets, with limited effect on the insurgents' capabilities.

15. George N. Lewis, Steve Fetter, and Lisbeth Gronlund, "Casualties and Damage from Scud Attacks in the 1991 Gulf War," Defense and Arms Control Studies Program working paper (March 1993).

16. John Witherow and Aidan Sullivan, *The Sunday Times War in the Gulf* (London: Sidgwick and Jackson, 1991), p.94.

17. Statement of Professor Theodore Postol, US House of Representatives Committee on Government Operations (Washington, D.C.: April 7, 1992).

18. US Government Accountability Office, Report to Congressional Requesters, "Operation *Desert Storm* – Data Does Not Exist to Conclusively Say How Well Patriot Performed" (Washington, D.C.: September 22, 1992).

ENDNOTES

19. For a good overview of the Missile Wars debate, plus links to primary source documents, see Alexander Simon's article "The Patriot Missile: Performance in the Gulf War Reviewed" (July 15, 1996), www.cdi.org/issues/bmd/Patriot.html

20. Note that some analysts dispute Hezballah's possession of the longer-range systems, or at least their ability to use them at these ranges.

21. Dr Uzi Rubin, "Hizballah's Rocket Campaign Against Northern Israel: a preliminary report," Jerusalem Center for Public Affairs, 6:10 (August 31, 2006), www.jcpa.org

22. J. Riley Durant, "Excalibur Unitary PGM Down Range in Iraq," *FA Journal* (July–August 2005), p.3, http://findarticles.com/p/articles/mi_mOIAU/is_4_10/ai_n15966222

23. For a useful discussion of Excalibur vs the SDB, see "Excalibur Gets Closer and More Expensive," www.strategypage.com/htmw/htart/articles/20060417.aspx

24. For example, an article by Walter L. Williams on the Russian Krasnopol laser-guided projectile noted that "Reportedly India fired between 500,000 and 700,000 medium-caliber [conventional] artillery projectiles in the recent fighting in the Kargil Region. In spite of these vast expenditures, many of the insurgent positions still had to be assaulted and destroyed by Indian infantry soldiers." (Williams, "Krasnopol: a laser guided projectile," *FA Journal* (September–October 2002), pp.30–33.

25. "Third Infantry Division (Mechanized) After Action Report – Operation *Iraqi Freedom*" (2003), p.56. The full report can be found at www.globalsecurity.org/military/library/report/2003/3id-aar-jul03.pdf

26. Paul Rogers, "The Myth of the Clean War – and its Real Motive" (March 13, 2003), www.openDemocracy.net

27. Witherow and Sullivan, *War in the Gulf*, p.155.

28. "First Look at Israel's Use of Cluster Munitions in Lebanon in July–August 2006," Briefing Prepared for the 15th Session of the Convention on Conventional Weapons (CCW) Group of Governmental Experts, delivered by Steve Goose, Director of Human Rights Watch Arms Division (Geneva, Switzerland, August 30, 2006).

29. Jefferson D. Reynolds, "Collateral Damage on the 21st Century Battlefield: enemy exploitation of the law of armed conflict, and the struggle for a moral high ground," *Air Force Law Review* (Winter 2005), http://findarticles.com/p/articles/mi_m6007/is_56/ai_n14700122

30. The US Army's Field Manual (FM) 3-60 states: "DANGER CLOSE is included in the method of engagement when the target is (rounds will impact) within 600 meters of friendly troops for mortar and artillery, 750 meters for naval guns 5-inch and smaller, and 1,000 meters for naval guns larger than 5-inch. For naval 16-inch ICM, danger close is 2,000 meters."

31. Phillip Coleman, *Cannon Fodder – Growing Up for Vietnam* (Vietnam War Library, 1987). The entire text of this book is, at the time of writing, published online by The Vietnam War Library at http://members.aol.com/warlib/cf.htm

32. Col Kenneth K. Steinweg, "Dealing Realistically With Fratricide," *Parameters* (Spring 1995), pp.4–29, http://www.carlisle-www.army.mil/usawc/Parameters/1995/steinweg.htm

33. Gott, *Eyewitness to War, Volume II*, pp.13–14.

34. Eric H. Biass and Ian Kemp, "Future Combat Systems – Complete Guide," *Armada International*, 2 (2006), p.1, http://findarticles.com/p/articles/mi_hb3031/is_200604/ai_n18935112

35. See Ian Kemp, "The British Future Rapid Effects System," in "Future Combat Systems – Complete Guide," *Armada International*, 2 (2006).

36. Lewis Page, *Lions, Donkeys and Dinosaurs – Waste and Blundering in the Armed Forces* (London: Heinemann, 2006), p.70.

37. Steven Sliwa, "Artillery and Maneuver – Relevance and Reality," *Field Artillery* (March–April 2005), p.3.

38. Global War on Terrorism, Occasional Paper 4, "Field Artillery in Military Operations Other Than War – An Overview of the US Experience" (Fort Leavenworth, KS: Combat Studies Institute Press, 2004), p.37.

39. Ibid., p.40 and p.41.

40. Gott, *Eyewitness to War, Volume II*, p.102.

Chapter 5: Power from Above – Military Aviation

1. Gen John D.W. Corley, *Winning the Global War on Terrorism*, US Air Force pamphlet, the Pentagon (Arlington, VA: August 14, 2006).

2. Brig Gen William J. Rew, 57th Wing commander, quoted by Keith Rogers, "Reactivation Creates Wing for Remotely Controlled Planes," *Las Vegas Review-Journal* (May 3, 2007).

3. Lt Gen Michael W. Peterson, quoted by Staff Sgt C. Todd Lopez, "Warfighting Integration Reduces Inaccuracy, Inefficiency," *Air Force Print News* (June 19, 2006), http://www.safxc.af.mil/news/story.asp?id=123047772

4. Karl Ludwig von Bertalanffy, "An Outline of General System Theory," *British Journal of the Philosophy of Science*, 1 (August 1950), pp.134–65.

5. Maj Shannon Sullivan, "Air Power Against Chaos," *Air & Space Power Journal*, US Air Force Air University (Maxwell Air Force Base, AL: June 1, 1998), http://www.airpower.maxwell.af.mil/airchronicles/cc/sullivan.html

6. Gen Joseph W. Ralston, vice chairman of the Joint Chiefs of Staff, before the research and development and military procurement panels of the Committee on National Security, US House of Representatives (Washington, D.C.: June 27, 1996).

7. Nader Elhefnawy, "Four Myths about Space Power," *Parameters* (Spring 2003), pp.124–32, http://carlisle-www.army.mil/usawc/Parameters/03spring/elhefnaw.pdf

8. US Air Force Public Affairs, "Air Force announces Quadrennial Defense Review and Fiscal Year 2007 Budget Highlights" (February 2, 2006), http://www.af.mil/pressreleases/release.asp?id=123016013

9. Capt Francis G. Powers, letter from prison in Moscow to the editor of the *New York Times* (September 18, 1960).

10. Source: US Defense Intelligence Agency, Arlington, VA.

11. Jim Turnbull, "Lt. Shane Osborn: looking at a miracle,"
    Naval Aviation News (September–October 2003), pp.20–28,
    http://www.history.navy.mil/nan/backissues/2000s/2003/so03/osborn.pdf

12. George J. Tenet, before the National Commission on Terrorist Attacks upon
    the United States, the US National Archives and Records Administration
    (Washington, D.C.: March 24, 2004).

13. Capt Rob Kinerson, an MQ-1 pilot with the 11th Reconnaissance
    Squadron, Nellis Air Force Base, NV, as quoted by Capt Russell Parker,
    "The Predators' War," *Airman* (December 2002),
    http://www.af.mil/news/airman/1202/aerial.html

14. Giulio Douhet (trans. Dino Ferrari), *Command of the Air*
    (1921; trans. 1942 ed.), US Air Force History and Museums Program
    (Washington, D.C.: 1998).

15. Dr Richard P. Hallion, "Precision Weapons, Power Projection, and the Revolution
    in Military Affairs," US Air Force Air Armament Center (Eglin Air Force Base:
    May 1999).

16. Source: US Navy Historical Center, Washington Navy Yard, Washington, D.C.

17. J. David Rogers, "The Race to Build the Atomic Bomb," Sigma Xi
    Distinguished Lecture Series, (University of Missouri, 2001),
    http://web.umr.edu/~rogersda/american&military_history/AtomBombLectureNotes.pdf

18. Cajus Bekker (trans. Frank Ziegler), *The Luftwaffe War Diaries* (New York:
    Ballantine Books, 1969).

19. Lt Col Earle Lund, "The Battle of Britain: a German perspective," US Air Force
    Air University (Maxwell Air Force Base, AL: January 24, 1996),
    http://www.au.af.mil/au/awc/awcgate/ww2/batlbrit.pdf

20. US Army Air Defence Artillery School, "History of Air Defense Weapon Systems,"
    (Fort Bliss, TX: September 1985),
    http://www.globalsecurity.org/military/library/policy/army/accp/ad0699/index.html

21. George Dragicevic, "Clive 'Killer' Caldwell: Stuka party," *World War II Ace
    Stories* (1969), http://www.elknet.pl/acestory/caldw/caldw.htm

22. Lund, "The Battle of Britain."

23. Stanley Kubrick, *Dr. Strangelove or: How I Learned to Stop Worrying and Love
    the Bomb* (Hawk Films Ltd, 1964).

24. From an interview with Spec Samuel A. Ryskind, of the 2nd Brigade,
    82nd Airborne Division, on his experience in Iraq during Operation *Desert Storm*
    (Washington D.C.: April 15, 2007).

25. Maj Collin T. Ireton, "Filling the Stealth Gap and Enhancing Global Strike Task
    Force Operations," *Air and Space Power Journal*, US Air Force Air University
    (Maxwell Air Force Base, AL: Fall 2006),
    http://www.airpower.maxwell.af.mil/airchronicles/apj/apj06/fal06/ireton.html

26. Richard P. Hallion, "Air Power in Peripheral Conflicts: the cases of Korea
    and Vietnam."

27. US Government Accountability Office, "Cost and Performance of the Aircraft and Munitions of *Desert Storm*," *Operation Desert Storm: Evaluation of the Air Campaign* GAO/NSIAD-97-134 (Washington, D.C.: June 12, 1997), pp.162–93, http://www.gao.gov/archive/1997/ns97134.pdf

28. US ADUSD (Precision Engagement) John Wilcox at the Precision Strike Association, Winter Roundtable (Arlington, VA: February 1, 2007).

29. BBC World, "Nato Bombs Hit Hospital" (May 7, 1999) http://news.bbc.co.uk/2/hi/europe/337989.stm

30. CNN, "Nato Bombing Continues; US Blames Bad Maps for Embassy Strike" (May 9, 1999), http://www.cnn.com/WORLD/europe/9905/09/kosovo.02/

31. William S. Cohen, on the 1999 Chinese embassy bombing, Department of Defense news briefing, the Pentagon (Arlington, VA: May 10, 1999), http://www.defenselink.mil/transcripts/transcript.aspx?transcriptid=536

32. Ray Suarez, et al., "Targeting Saddam," *Online News Hour* (April 2003), http://www.pbs.org/newshour/bb/middle_east/jan-june03/saddam_04-08.html

33. US Army Training and Doctrine Command, "UxO: multi-Service tactics, techniques and procedures for unexploded explosive ordnance operations" (August 16, 2005), https://atiam.train.army.mil/soldierPortal/atia/adlsc/view/public/9610-1/fm/3-100.38/TOC.htm

34. Ibid.

35. Andrew F. Krepinevich, "Operation *Iraqi Freedom*: a first-blush assessment," Center for Strategic and Budgetary Assessments (Washington, D.C.: 2003), http://www.csbaonline.org/4Publications/PubLibrary/R.20030916.Operation_Iraqi_Fr/R.20030916.Operation_Iraqi_Fr.pdf

36. US House of Representatives, "Resolution Condemning the Recent Attacks Against the State of Israel," *H. RES. 923* (Washington, D.C.: July 18, 2006), http://thomas.loc.gov/cgi-bin/bdquery/z?d109:HE00923

37. Doug Mellgren, "48 Nations Gather to Fight Cluster Bombs," *The Associated Press* (February 22, 2007), http://www.washingtonpost.com/wp-dyn/content/article/2007/02/22/AR2007022200722.html

38. Handicap International, http://www.handicap-international.org.uk/page_347.php

39. See http://www.opcw.org/index.html for an overview of internationally recognized chemical weapons.

40. Geneva, October 10, 1980.

41. Gen. Tommy Franks and Air Vice Marshall G.E. "JOC" Stirrup, British Coalition Contingent Commander, US Central Command operations briefing (Tampa, FL: December 14, 2001).

42. "Frequently Asked Questions (FAQs) About the Former Five Points Outlying Field," US Army Corps of Engineers (Fort Worth District: April 2002), http://www.swf.usace.army.mil/pubdata/FUDS/5points/documents/040802FactSheet.pdf

43. Maj Dr Lisa DeWitt, a surgeon with Task Force 2-2 during Operation Phantom Fury, as quoted in Kendall D. Gott, (gen. ed.,) *Eyewitness to War: the U.S. Army in Operation Al Fajr*, (Ft. Leavenworth, KS: US Army Combat Studies Institute

Press, April 23, 2006).

44. US Department of Defense Joint Non-Lethal Weapons Program, US Marine Corps Base (Quantico, VA: February 22, 2007), https://www.jnlwp.com/ActiveDenialSystem.asp

45. Lt Col John P. Geis II, "Directed Energy Weapons on the Battlefield: a new vision for 2025," US Air Force Air University (Maxwell Air Force Base, AL: April 2003), http://handle.dtic.mil/100.2/ADA463429

46. *The Aerodrome: Aces and Aircraft of WWI*, http://www.theaerodrome.com/aircraft/statistics.php

47. From an oral history memoir of 2nd Lt Arthur Raymond Brooks, a pilot with the 22nd Aero Squadron, 22nd Pursuit Group, US Army Air Service, American Expeditionary Force, Smithsonian Institution National Air and Space Museum, (Washington, D.C.).

48. Giulio Douhet (trans. Dino Ferrari), *Command of the Air*.

49. Dr David R. Mets, "Boydmania," *Air & Space Power Journal*, 28:3, Air University Library (Maxwell Air Force Base, AL: Fall 2004).

50. An audio recording of this engagement is available at http://www.flight-level.com/dogfight/dogfight.html

51. From an interview (May 2007) with the author's father, Col (ret.) Jack E. Keeter, Jr, on his experience as an F-102 interceptor pilot based at Anchorage, Alaska.

52. Ibid.

53. John Peters, from an interview with Roo Media (January 4, 1989), http://www.roo-media.com/RAF%20Magazine%20003%20Interview%20-%20John%20Peters%20-%20041004%20Submitted%20Text.doc

54. From an interview (May 2007) with the author's father, Col (ret.) Jack E. Keeter, Jr, on his experience fighting in Laos and Vietnam as a pilot with the US Air Force's 1st Special Operations Squadron, Nakhon Phanom Royal Thai Air Base, 1970–1971.

55. Maj James W. MacGregor, "Bringing the Box into Doctrine: joint doctrine and the kill box," School of Advanced Military Studies, US Army Command and General Staff College (Fort Leavenworth, KS: May 26, 2004), p.22, http://handle.dtic.mil/100.2/ADA429320

56. Ibid.

57. Ibid.

58. Joseph Giordono, "US Troops Revisit Scene of Deadly Gulf War Barrage," *Stars & Stripes Sunday Magazine* (February 23, 2003), http://www.estripes.com/article.asp?section=126&article=14772&archive=true

59. US Department of Defense, "Environmental Exposure Report: depleted uranium in the Gulf," the Pentagon (Arlington, VA: July 31, 1998), http://www.gulflink.osd.mil/du/

60. Donald J. Sandstrom, "Armor, Anti-Armor," *Los Alamos Science*, Los Alamos National Laboratory (New Mexico, Summer 1989), pp.36–50, http://library.lanl.gov/cgi-bin/getfile?00326856.pdf

61. For a more detailed discussion of tank gunnery, see Chapter 3.

62. "Depleted Uranium – Individual," *Just the Facts*, no.65-050-0503, US Army Center for Health Promotion and Preventive Medicine (Aberdeen Proving Ground, MD), http://chppm-www.apgea.army.mil/doem

63. Bernard Roster, *Environmental Exposure Report: Depleted uranium in the Gulf* (II), ref. 2000179-0000002, ver. 2.0, US Department of Defense (Arlington, VA: December 13, 2000), http://www.gulflink.osd.mil.du_ii

64. US Army, *Advice on the Implications of Depleted Uranium (DU) on the Battlefield*, Training Support Package TA-031-DUAT-003, Directorate of Training Development, US Army Chemical School (Fort McLellan, AL: November 15, 1999).

65. Maj Robert M. Cassidy, "The Renaissance of the Attack Helicopter in the Close Fight," *Military Review* (July–August 2003), http://usacac.army.mil/CAC/milreview/English/JulAug03/JulAug03/cassidy.pdf

66. From an interview with Maj Gen James F. Amos, commander of the 3rd Marine Aircraft Wing (September 2003).

67. Maj Mark K. Wells, "The Human Element and Air Combat: some Napoleonic comparisons," *Airpower Journal* (Spring 1988), http://www.airpower.maxwell.af.mil/airchronicles/apj/apj88/spr88/wells.html

68. William R. Emerson, "Operation Pointblank: a tale of bombers and fighters," US Air Force A. Harmon Memorial Lecture No.4, US Air Force Academy (Colorado Springs, CO: 1962), http://www.usafa.af.mil/df/dfh/docs/Harmon04.doc

69. Source: National Museum of the US Air Force, Wright Patterson Air Force Base, Ohio, http://www.nationalmuseum.af.mil/factsheets/factsheet.asp?id=798

70. Kenneth P. Werrell, "Did USAF Technology Fail in Vietnam? Three Case Studies," *Air Power Journal* (Spring 1998), http://www.airpower.maxwell.af.mil/airchronicles/apj/apj98/spr98/werrell.html

71. Michael McCrea, "US Navy, Marine Corps, and Air Force Fixed-Wing Aircraft Losses and Damage in Southeast Asia (1962–1973)," Center for Naval Analyses (Alexandria, VA: August 1976)

72. Jeffrey Record and W. Andrew Terrill, "Iraq and Vietnam: differences, similarities and insights," US Army Strategic Studies Institute (May 2004), p.11, http://www.strategicstudiesinstitute.army.mil/pdffiles/PUB377.pdf

73. US Air Force, "Electronic Warfare," Doctrine Document 2-5.1, 5, the Pentagon (Washington, D.C.: November 2002), http://www.dtic.mil/doctrine/jel/service_pubs/afd2_5_1.pdf

74. US Government Accountability Office, *Operation Desert Storm: Evaluation of the Air Campaign*.

75. Tech Sgt Mark Kinkade, "The First Shot," *Airman Magazine* (July 2003), http://www.af.mil/news/airman/0703/air.html

76. Lt Col Dale Zelko, recorded during a speech at Hill Air Force Base, Utah, http://www.standard.net/pods

77. Gen Israel Tal, as referenced in Lt Col Robert S. Fairweather, Jr, "A New Model for Land Warfare: the firepower dominance concept," *Air University Review*,

US Air Force Air University (Maxwell Air Force Base, AL: November–December 1980), http://www.airpower.maxwell.af.mil/airchronicles/aureview/1980/nov-dec/fairweather.html

78.   Brig Gen Robert W. Cone, "Joint Lessons Learned from Operation *Iraqi Freedom*," US Department of Defense briefing, the Pentagon (Arlington, VA: October 2, 2003), http://www.defenselink.mil/transcripts/transcript.aspx?transcriptid=3531

79.   Maj Michael L. Straight, "Preparing for Theater Air Defense as an Air-Land Team," *Airpower Journal*, US Air Force Air University (Maxwell Air Force Base, AL: Spring 1991), http://www.airpower.maxwell.af.mil/airchronicles/apj/apj91/spr91/2spr91.htm

80.   US Marine Corps Lt Gen James T. Conway, commanding general, First Marine Expeditionary Force, Department of Defense news briefing, the Pentagon (Arlington, VA: September 9, 2003), http://www.defenselink.mil/transcripts/transcript.aspx?transcriptid=3147

81.   United Kingdom Ministry of Defence, *Board of Inquiry Report into the Death of the Late 25035018 Lance Corporal of Horse Matthew Richard Hull, the Blues and Royals (Royal Guards and First Dragoons) Household Cavalry Regiment, British Army* (May 22, 2004), http://www.mod.uk/NR/rdonlyres/887DE696-1DB9-4512-AF8E-2ECFED455356/0/boi_lcpl_hull.pdf

82.   Finlo Rohrer, "How Does it Feel to Kill a Comrade?" *BBC News Magazine* (March 20, 2007), http://news.bbc.co.uk/2/hi/uk_news/magazine/6468391.stm

83.   US Government Accountability Office, *Operation Desert Storm: Apache Helicopter Fratricide Incident* GAO-OSI-93-4 (Washington, D.C.: June 30, 1993).

84.   Ibid.

Chapter 6: Firepower at Sea – Naval Weapon Systems

1.   W. Neil Adger, et al., "Social-Ecological Resilience to Coastal Disasters," *Science*, 309:5737 (August 12, 2005), pp.1036–39, http://www.sciencemag.org/cgi/content/short/309/5737/1036

2.   College of Sciences, Department of Ocean, Earth and Atmospheric Sciences, Old Dominion University (Virginia Beach, VA).

3.   US National Academy of Sciences, *Oil in the Sea III: Inputs, Fates and Effects* (Washington, D.C., 2002), http://www.nap.edu/books/0309084385/html

4.   Rose M. Likins, "Building Capacity through Cooperation," *US Naval War College Review*, 59:1, US Naval War College (Newport, RI: January 1, 2006).

5.   John J. Dalton, et al., "Forward … from the Sea," US Navy, the Pentagon (Arlington, VA: September 19, 1995), http://www.dtic.mil/jv2010/navy/b014.pdf

6.   Energy Information Administration, US Department of Energy (Washington, D.C.) http://www.eia.doe.gov/emeu/cabs/World_Oil_Transit_Chokepoints/Background.html

7.   Forrest L. Marion, "Building USAF 'Expeditionary Bases' for Operation *Enduring Freedom* – Afghanistan, 2001–2002," *Air & Space Power Journal*, US Air Force Air University (Maxwell Air Force Base, AL: November 18, 2005), http://www.airpower.au.af.mil/airchronicles/cc/marion.html

8. Rear Adm Joseph J. Krol, Jr, assistant deputy chief of naval operations, before the special oversight panel on terrorism, the Committee on Armed Services, US House of Representatives (Washington, D.C.: June 28, 2002), http://commdocs.house.gov/committees/security/has179240b.000/has179240b_0f.htm

9. Lt Bridget Compain, Royal Navy, "Baptism by Fire," Fleet Air Arm Officers' Association (London), http://fleetairarmoa.org/pages/images_pages/page66.htm

10. US Navy Program Executive Officer, Littoral and Mine Warfare, Washington Navy Yard, Washington, D.C.; and Commander, Mine Warfare Command, Corpus Christi, TX.

11. US Congressional Budget Office, "Resource Implications of the Navy's Fiscal Year 2008 Shipbuilding Plan," (Washington, D.C.: March 23, 2007), http://www.cbo.gov/ftpdoc.cfm?index=7903&type=1

12. From an interview with Col (USMC ret.) Robert Work (Washington, D.C.: May 21, 2007).

13. Peter Jensen, "Strategic Implications of Chinese Naval Expansion," US Army War College (Carlisle Barracks, PA: 2000), http://handle.dtic.mil/100.2/ADA378255

14. From a series of three meetings (and two very fine Chinese dinners) with PLAN Capt Zhang Junshe (Arlington, VA and Washington, D.C.: Spring 2001).

15. Dr Andrew S. Erickson, "China's Military Modernization and its Impact on the United States and the Asia-Pacific," China Maritime Studies Institute, the US Naval War College (Newport, RI: March 29, 2007).

16. Timothy D. Saxon, "Anglo-Japanese Naval Cooperation, 1914–1918," *Naval War College Review*, 53:1, US Naval War College (Newport, RI: Winter 2000), pp. 2–7.

17. Lt Cmdr Anthony Kapuschansky, training officer USS *Dwight D. Eisenhower* (CVN 69), as quoted by Journalist 1st Class Mike Kramer, "*Ike* Pays Tribute to Midway's Legacy," *Navy Newsstand* (June 12, 2002), http://www.news.navy.mil/search/display.asp?story_id=2031

18. From an interview with Maj Gen James F. Amos, commanding general of the 3rd Marine Aircraft Wing (San Diego, CA: September 2003).

19. Dr Robert W. Duffner, "Conflict in the South Atlantic: the Impact of Air Power," *Air University Review*, 35, US Air Force Air University (Maxwell Air Force Base, AL: March–April 1984), pp. 78–87.

20. Ibid.

21. US Navy Damage Control Museum, Naval Sea Systems Command, http://www.dcfp.navy.mil/mc/museum/STARK/*Stark*3.htm

22. Ibid.

23. *US Navy Vision, Presence, Power* (2002), http://www.chinfo.navy.mil/navpalib/policy/vision/vis02/top-v02.html

24. Louise Doswald-Beck, "Implementation of International Humanitarian Law in Future Wars," *Naval War College Review*, 52:1 (Winter 1999).

25. Just getting to the flight deck can be a harrowing experience. For example, on July 30, 2002, during the first operational deployment of the US Navy's F/A-18E

Super Hornet fighters aboard the USS *Abraham Lincoln* (CVN 72), the author had the good luck to transit aboard what nearly became the "flaming COD." Twenty or so minutes after take-off from Naval Air Station North Island, near San Diego, and well past the "feet wet" line, the C-2 Greyhound turboprop carrier onboard delivery aircraft began to fill with smoke. After a few minutes of well mannered and business-like attempts to allay fears and bring the situation under control, the aircrew decided the best course of action to clear the atmosphere would be to open the large cargo bay door in the plane's empennage. Now, on the COD, passengers sit facing the rear of the aircraft, to lessen the jolt of arrested landings aboard the carrier. So in the case at hand, the first thing everyone aboard saw, reassuringly, as the smoke began to clear, was a bird's eye view of the Pacific Ocean, with the coast of California a not-so-reassuring gray line on the horizon.

26. Fenella Saunders, "Dulcet Dunes," *American Scientist Online* (November–December 2006), http://www.americanscientist.org/template/AssetDetail/assetid/54096;jsessionid=baa9

27. Source: Defense Supply Center, Richmond, VA.

28. *Flight Deck Awareness: A Basic Guide*, US Naval Safety Center (Norfolk, VA: 2003), p.16, http://www.safetycenter.navy.mil/media/downloads/FlghtDckAware_CV_03.pdf

29. Lt Marc Shuford, "Watch Out for the New C-40," US Navy Safety Center (Norfolk, VA), http://www.safetycenter.navy.mil/MEDIA/mech/vault/articles/0081.htm

30. On August 19, 1812, the USS *Constitution* engaged and crippled the Royal Navy frigate HMS *Guerriere*, off Nova Scotia. "Old Ironsides" would go on to chalk up eight more victories, and astonishingly is still listed as "active, on commission" in the Naval Vessel Registry, the oldest warship on active service in any fleet.

31. Maj Robert K. Wright, Jr, "Oral History Interview: Cmdr Dennis G. Morral Captain, USS. *Nicholas* (FFG 47)," US Army Center of Military History (Washington, D.C.: February 13, 1991), http://www.army.mil/cmh-pg/documents/swa/dsit/DSIT007.htm

32. Ibid.

33. Note: in artillery and naval guns, the term "caliber" often refers to the length of the gun expressed in relation to its bore diameter. Thus the *Iowa*-class battleships' 16/50 guns are 20m (800in) long.

34. Capt Michael P. Ley, "Naval Gun Fire Support, What We Need to Understand," *Field Artillery*, US Army Artillery School (Fort Sill, OK: February 1988), pp. 39–42, http://sill-www.army.mil/famag/1988/FEB_1988/FEB_1988_FULL_EDITION.pdf

35. US Navy Office of Naval Research, Arlington, VA.

36. Ibid.

37. Paul van Riper, "Ship-To-Objective Maneuver," NWC2011, US Naval War College (Newport, RI: July 25, 1997).

38. Lt Yitzhak Zoran, Israeli Navy, "In Their Own Words #6: Eleven Stories for Veterans Day," (April 2001), http://edefense.blogspot.com/2005/11/in-their-own-words-6-eleven-stories.html

39. Capt Arthur M. Smith, "Stretching the Limits of Naval Self-Sufficiency: Medical Implications of War at Sea," *Navy Medicine*, 86:6 (1995).

40. Video footage of the strike is available at http://www.globalsecurity.org/intell/library/imint/images/990330b.mpeg

41. Rear Adm Thomas R. Wilson, US Department of Defense Joint Staff, during a briefing at the Pentagon (Arlington, VA, April 8, 1999), http://www.defenselink.mil/transcripts/transcript.aspx?transcriptid=577

42. Hunter Keeter, "Cohen: despite *Cole* attack, US Military must remain forward deployed," *Defense Daily*, (October 31, 2000).

43. Lt Cmdr Henry P. Stewart, "The Impact of the USS *Forrestal*'s 1967 Fire on US Navy Shipboard Damage Control," US Army Command and General Staff College (Fort Leavenworth, KS: 2004).

44. Lt Cmdr Michael Stoll, "Fire in the RAST Machinery Room!" US Naval Safety Center (Norfolk, VA), http://www.safetycenter.navy.mil/Afloat/articles/surface/rastfire.htm

45. Ibid.

46. From Machinery Technician First Class Randall W. Rogers, US Coast Guard, medal award citation, http://www.uscg.mil/history/awards/CGMedal_Citations_R_S.html

47. John M. Lindley, "A History of Sea-Air Aviation: wings over the ocean Part 12," *Naval Aviation News* (July 1978), p.38, http://www.history.navy.mil/download/w-part%2012.pdf

48. US Congressional Budget Office, "Resource Implications of the Navy's Fiscal Year 2008 Shipbuilding Plan," (Washington, D.C.: March 23, 2007), http://www.cbo.gov/ftpdoc.cfm?index=7903&type=1

49. Interview with a former chief petty officer in the US Navy submarine service who served aboard ballistic missile submarines (Alexandria, VA: 2007).

50. From a series of interviews aboard the USS *Florida* and the AUTEC range support ship USNS *Mary Sears* off the Commonwealth of the Bahamas (January 25, 2003).

51. Ibid.

52. Ibid.

53. Ibid.

54. Ibid.

55. During another, longer-duration embarkation aboard a strategic ballistic missile submarine, the author Hunter Keeter had the excellent luck to arrive on "pizza night" in the wardroom, catered by an enlisted cook who was training for a US Department of Defense-wide chefs' competition in New Orleans.

56. From Hunter Keeter's embarkation aboard the USS *Miami* (SSN 755), March 7, 2000.

57. Lt (jg) Alexander Barbara, "The 'Big Gun's' Two-Theater TLAM Tally," *Undersea Warfare*, 2:2 (Winter 1999), p. 14, http://www.navy.mil/navydata/cno/n87/usw/issue_6/bigguns.html

58. Maj Roy Walker and Capt Larry Ridolfi, "Airpower's Role in Maritime Operations," *Air & Space Power Journal*, https://www.airpower.maxwell.af.mil/airchronicles/cc/ridolfi.html

59. Ibid.

60. From the *Dictionary of American Naval Fighting Ships*, http://www.history.navy.mil/danfs/e4/enterprise-viiif.htm

61. The effectiveness of marine mammals at locating and marking underwater objects, such as mines, is remarkable. However, it is interesting to note that their navy handlers apparently find that keeping the creatures focused on the task at flipper, as it were, and not on having sexual intercourse with one another, is no mean feat. It would seem that whenever two or more are brought together (regardless of gender, age, or any other distinction between them), these highly trained and skilled animals waste little time.

62. US Navy Expeditionary Warfare Directorate (N75), the Pentagon (Arlington, VA).

63. Ibid.

64. Synthetic aperture sonar marries powerful sound transmitters and receivers with sophisticated acoustic data processors to draw extremely detailed (very nearly photographic) images of the water column and the sea bed. These images clearly show in relief many objects that lie on the bottom or are buried beneath it, including mines.

65. Maj Gen William B. Fulton, "Vietnam Studies: riverine operations 1966–1969," US Army, Center for Military History, Pub 90-18 (Washington, D.C.: 1973), http://www.army.mil/cmh/books/Vietnam/riverine/index.htm

66. Ibid.

67. US Marine Corps Institute, *Afghanistan: an introduction to the country and people*, US Marine Barracks (Washington, D.C.: 2005), http://www.osi.andrews.af.mil/shared/media/document/AFD-061113-070.pdf

68. From a conference on Operation *Iraqi Freedom*, hosted at US Marine Corps Base (Quantico, VA: Fall 2003)

69. Ibid.

70. From a series of interviews with active duty and reserve SeAL team members and leadership (Washington, D.C. and Arlington, VA: 2002–2007).

71. Ibid.

Chapter 7: Shadow Threat – Chemical, Biological, Radiological and Nuclear (CBRN) Weapons

1. Shahriar Khateri, "Statistical Views on Late Complications of Chemical Weapons in Iranian Chemical Weapon Victims," Organization for Veterans Affairs, Tehran Dept of Health and Treatment (Tehran, Iran: September 2001).

2. The Arms Control Association, http://www.armscontrol.org/factsheets/cwcsig.asp

3. Thomas V. Inglesby et al., "Anthrax as a Biological Weapon," *Journal of the American Medical Association*, 281:18 (May 12, 1999), pp. 1735–45, http://jama.ama-assn.org/cgi/content/full/281/18/1735

4. US Nuclear Regulatory Commission, "Backgrounder on Dirty Bombs" (Washington, D.C.: June 12, 2007), http://www.nrc.gov/reading-rm/doc-collections/fact-sheets/dirty-bombs-bg.html

5. "US–Russia Pact Aimed at Nuclear Terrorism," *Washington Post* (February 24, 2005).

6. P.A. D'Agostino and C.L. Chenier, "Analysis of Chemical Warfare Agents," *TR 2006-022*, Defence R&D Centre Suffield (Canada: March 2006).

7. Maj Charles E. Heller, "Chemical Warfare in World War I: the American experience, 1917–1918," Institute of Combat Studies, US Army Command and General Staff College (Fort Leavenworth, KS: September 1984), http://www-cgsc.army.mil/carl/resources/csi/Heller/HELLER.asp

8. Defense Treaty Inspection Readiness Program, http://dtirp.dtra.mil/CBW/references/agents/AgentsCW_choking.cfm

9. Kenneth E. Williams, "Detailed Facts About Blister Agent Lewisite (L)," US Army Center for Health Promotion and Preventive Medicine (Aberdeen Proving Ground, MD), http://chppm-www.apgea.army.mil/dts/docs/detlew.pdf

10. US Army Medical Research Institute of Chemical Defence, *Medical Management of Chemical Casualties Handbook* (Aberdeen Proving Ground, MD: July, 2000), http://www.gmha.org/bioterrorism/usamricd/Yellow_Book_2000.pdf

11. "From Haz-Map Occupational Exposure to Hazardous Agents," US National Library of Medicine (Bethesda, MD: March 2007), http://hazmap.nlm.nih.gov/cgi-bin/hazmap_generic?tbl=TblAgents&id=1450

12. Defense Treaty Inspection Readiness Program.

13. US Centers for Disease Control and Prevention, "Facts About VX," Department of Health and Human Services (Washington, D.C.: February 22, 2006), http://www.bt.cdc.gov/agent/vx/basics/facts.asp

14. Central Intelligence Agency, "Iraq's Chemical Warfare Program," vol. 3, *DCI Special Advisor Report on Iraq's WMD* (September 30, 2004), https://www.cia.gov/library/reports/general-reports-1/iraq_wmd_2004/index.html

15. Ibid.

16. From a US Department of Defense news briefing with Maj Gen Michael Barbero, the Pentagon (Arlington, VA: March 30, 2007), http://www.defenselink.mil/transcripts/transcript.aspx?transcriptid=3921

17. William Winkenwerder, Jr, "Case Narrative Chemical Warfare Agent Release at Muhammadiyat Ammunition Storage Site: final report," US Department of Defense, the Pentagon (Arlington, VA: April 4, 2002), http://www.gulflink.osd.mil/muhammadiyat_ii/

18. Ali S. Khan et al., "Biological and Chemical Terrorism: strategic plan for preparedness and response," US Centers for Disease Control and Prevention, Department of Health and Human Services (Washington, D.C.: April 21, 2000), http://www.au.af.mil/au/awc/awcgate/cdc/rr4904a1.htm

19. Sources: the World Health Organization; the US Centers for Disease Control and Prevention; and the National Institutes of Health

20. Milton Leitenberg, "Assessing the Biological Weapons and Bioterrorism Threat," Strategic Studies Institute, US Army War College (Carlisle, PA: December 2005), p.115, http://www.strategicstudiesinstitute.army.mil/pdffiles/pub639.pdf

21. US Nuclear Regulatory Commission, "Security Spotlight: securing materials" (Washington, D.C.), http://www.nrc.gov/reading-rm/doc-collections/fact-sheets/security-spotlight/materials.html

22. Arnie Heller, "Researchers Determine Chernobyl Liquidators' Exposure," *Science & Technology Review*, Lawrence Livermore National Laboratory, US Department of Energy (CA: September 1999), http://www.llnl.gov/str/Jones.html

23. Duck and Cover! The Cold War produced some interesting material, but perhaps nothing to top the grimly black comedy (all the better for the earnest attempt at being serious public service announcements) of the 1950s-era public safety films that coached a naïve population in how to survive the unpleasant possibility of thermonuclear *Ragnarok*. The best of the lot was the 1951 classic, *Duck and Cover!*, produced by the Federal Civil Defense Administration. In the film, jolly Bert the Turtle shows all the boys and girls what to do when they hear an air raid alarm, or notice the flash from an H-bomb bursting nearby. Laugh or cry; see the film, courtesy of the US State Department: http://usinfo.state.gov/journals/itps/0305/ijpe/fullversion.htm

24. Daniel Buchonnet, "MIRV: a brief history of minuteman and multiple reentry vehicles," Lawrence Livermore Laboratory, US Department of Energy (CA: February 1976).

25. BBC, "Trident Plan Wins Commons Support" (March 15, 2007), http://news.bbc.co.uk/1/hi/uk_politics/6448173.stm

26. George J. Tenet, "Director of Central Intelligence Worldwide Threat Briefing 2002: converging dangers in a post 9/11 world," before the Armed Services Committee, US Senate (Washington, D.C.: March 19, 2002), https://www.cia.gov/news-information/speeches-testimony/2002/dci_speech_02062002.html

27. Amy Sands, "Deconstructing the Chem-Bio Threat," before the Committee on Foreign Relations, US Senate (Washington, D.C.: March 19, 2002), http://cns.miis.edu/pubs/reports/asands.htm

28. George J. Tenet, "Director of Central Intelligence Worldwide Threat Briefing 2002."

29. Shirley A. Kan, "China: possible missile technology transfers from US Satellite export policy – actions and chronology," Congressional Research Service (Washington, D.C.: January 11, 2002), http://www.au.af.mil/au/awc/awcgate/crs/98-485.pdf

30. Michael Barletta, "Chemical Weapons in the Sudan, Allegations and Evidence," *The Non Proliferation Review*, Center for Nonproliferation Studies (Monterey, CA: Fall 1998)

31. Maj David E. Snodgrass, "Attacking the Theater Mobile Ballistic
     Missile Threat," School of Advanced Air Power Studies, US Air Force
     Air University (Maxwell Air Force Base, AL: June 1993), p.4,
     http://www.au.af.mil/au/aul/aupress/SAAS_Theses/Snodgrass/snodgrass.pdf

BIBLIOGRAPHY

A note on sources

This is not an exhaustive bibliography; for further details of websites, articles and reports please see the relevant endnotes.

Allsop, D. F. and Toomey, M. A., *Small Arms – General Design* (London: Brassey's, 1999)

Applegate, Rex, *Kill or Get Killed* (Boulder, CO: Paladin Press, 1976)

Bailey, A. and Murray, S.G., *Explosives, Propellants & Pyrotechnics* (London: Brassey's, 1989)

Baker, Mark, *Nam* (London: Abacus, 1981)

Bekker, Cajus (trans. Frank Ziegler), *The Luftwaffe War Diaries* (New York: Ballantine Books, 1969)

Bellamy, Chris, *Red God of War – Soviet Artillery and Rocket Forces* (London: Brassey's, 1986)

Bergum, Bruce and Charles Klein, I., "A Survey and Analysis of Vigilance Research," HumRRO Research Report 8 (November, 1961)

Bourke, Joanna, *An Intimate History of Killing – Face-to-face Killing in Twentieth-century Warfare* (London: Granta, 1999)

Bowen, Thomas E., *Emergency War Surgery* (Desert Publications/US Army, 2004)

Bowman, Steven R., *Chemical Weapons Convention: Issues for Congress*, Library of Congress (Washington, D.C.: 2000), http://fpc.state.gov/documents/organization/16592.pdf

Conroy, Jason with Martz, Ron, *Heavy Metal – A Tank Company's Battle to Baghdad* (Dulles, VA: Potomac Books, 2005)

Dees, James et al., "An Experimental Review of Basic Combat Rifle Marksmanship: Marksman Phase I," HumRRO Technical Report 71–74 (March 1971)

Douhet, Giulio (trans. Dino Ferrari), *Command of the Air* (US Air Force History and Museums Program, Washington, D.C.: 1998), https://www.airforcehistory.hq. af.mil/Publications/fulltext/command_of_the_air.pdf

Dunnigan, James, *How to Make War* (New York: HarperCollins, 2003)

Dunstan, Simon, *The Yom Kippur War 1973 (2)* (Oxford: Osprey, 2003)

Flower, Desmond and James Reeves (eds), *The War 1939–1945 – A Documentary History* (Cambridge, MA: Da Capo Press, 1997)

Forty, George, *Tank Aces – From Blitzkrieg to the Gulf War* (Stroud, UK: Sutton Publishing, 1997)

Fulton, William B., "Vietnam Studies: riverine operations 1966–1969," US Army, Center for Military History, Pub 90-18 (Washington, D.C.: 1973), http://www.army.mil/cmh/books/Vietnam/riverine/index.htm

Gott, Kendall D. (ed.), *Eyewitness to War, Volume II – The US Army in Operation Al Faj, an Oral History* (Fort Leavenworth, KS: Combat Studies Institute Press, 2006)

Green, Michael and Greg Stewart, *M1 Abrams at War* (St Paul, MN: Zenith Press, 2005)

Gudmundsson, Bruce I., *On Armor* (Westport, CT: Praeger, 2004)

Hogg, Ian and Weeks, John, *Military Small Arms of the Twentieth Century* (London: Arms & Armor Press, 1991)

Holmes, Richard, *Dusty Warriors – Modern Soldiers at War* (London: Harper Press, 2006)

Katcher, Philip, *Armies of the Vietnam War 1962–75* (London: Osprey, 1980)

Kindsvatter, Peter S., *American Soldiers – Ground Combat in the World Wars, Korea, and Vietnam* (Lawrence, KS: Kansas University Press, 2003)

Kubrick, Stanley, *Dr Strangelove or: How I Learned to Stop Worrying and Love the Bomb* (Hawk Films Ltd, 1964)

Leinbaugh, Harold P. and John D. Campbell, *The Men of Company K: The Autobiography of a World War II Rifle Company* (New York: Bantam, 1991)

Mahan, Alfred Thayer, *The Influence of Sea Power upon History 1660–1783* (orig. ed. 1890) (New York: Dover Publications, 1987)

Majdalany, Fred, *The Monastery* (London: Houghton, 1946)

Marshall, S.L.A., *Men Against Fire – The Problem of Battle Command in Future War* (New York: William Morrow, 1947)

McManners, Hugh, *The Scars of War* (London: HarperCollins, 1993)

Morse, Stan (ed.), *Gulf Air War Debrief* (London: Aerospace Publishing Ltd, 1991)

Page, Lewis, *Lions, Donkeys and Dinosaurs – Waste and Blundering in the Armed Forces* (London: Heinemann, 2006)

Patrick, Urey W. and Hall, John C., *In Defense of Self and Others ... Issues, Facts & Fallacies – the Realities of Law Enforcement's Use of Deadly Force* (Durham, NC: Carolina Academic Press, 2005)

Perret, Geoffrey, *Winged Victory: The Army Air Forces in World War II* (New York: Random House, 1993)

Rickenbacker, Edward, *Fighting the Flying Circus* (New York: Stokes Co., 1919)

Sajer, Guy, *The Forgotten Soldier* (London: Sphere, 1977)

Shephard, Ben, *A War of Nerves – Soldiers and Psychiatrists 1914–1994* (London: Jonathan Cape, 2000)

Schneider, Barry R. and Davis, Jim A., (eds), *The War Next Time: Countering Rogue States and Terrorists Armed with Chemical and Biological Weapons*, US Air Force, Counterproliferation Center (Maxwell Air Force Base, AL: 2004)

Smith, Rupert, *The Utility of Force – The Art of War in the Modern World* (London: Penguin, 2005)

Swofford, Anthony, *Jarhead – A Marine's Chronicle of the Gulf War* (London: Scribner, 2003)

BIBLIOGRAPHY

Taylor, Peter, *Brits – The War against the IRA* (London: Bloomsbury, 2001)

Thompson, Leroy, *Hostage Rescue Manual* (London: Greenhill Books, 2001)

Watson, Peter, *War on the Mind – The Military Uses and Abuses of Psychology* (London: Hutchinson & Co., 1978)

Wilson, George, *If You Survive* (New York: Ivy Books, 1987)

Witherow, John and Sullivan, Aidan, *The Sunday Times War in the Gulf* (London: Sidgwick & Jackson, 1991)

Wright, Evan, *Generation Kill* (London: Corgi, 2004)

Youngblood, Norman, *The Development of Mine Warfare* (Westport, CT: Praeger Security International, 2006)

GLOSSARY OF ABBREVIATIONS

1MC	a ship's or submarine's public address system
AAA	antiaircraft artillery
ADAM	area-denial antipersonnel mine
AEW	airborne early warning
AFATDF	advanced field artillery tactical data system
AFV	armored fighting vehicle
AGM	air-to-ground missile
AHD	antihandling device
AIM	air intercept missile *also* area impact munition
ANGLICO	air and naval gunfire liaison
AOE	fast combat support ship
AP	Associated Press
APC	armored personnel carrier
APS	active projection system
APERS-T	antipersonnel – tracer
APFSDS-T	armor-piercing fin-stabilized discarding-sabot tracer
APM	antipersonnel mine
ARF	airborne reaction force
ASPB	assault support patrol boat
ATACMS	Army Tactical Missile System
ATF	Bureau of Alcohol, Tobacco, and Firearms
ATGM	antitank guided missile
ATRL	antitank rocket launcher
AVM	antivehicle mine
BAe	British Aerospace
BCT	brigade combat team
BFM	battle field mission
BLU	bomb live unit (a submunition)
BMD	ballistic missile defence
BMG	Browning machine gun
BRT	brigade reconnaissance team
BTU	British thermal unit
BWC	Biological Weapons Convention
CAS	close air support
CBRN	chemical, biological, radiological, and nuclear
CBU	cluster bomb unit
CEP	circular error probable
CG	guided missile cruiser
CIA	Central Intelligence Agency
CIC	combat information centre
CITV	commander's independent thermal viewer
CIWS	close-in weapon system
CLU	command launch unit
CMS	Conventional Munitions Systems, Inc.
CPG	co-pilot/gunner
CVN	nuclear-powered aircraft carrier
CWC	Chemical Weapons Convention
DARPA	Defense Advanced Research Projects Agency
DC	damage control
DDG	guided missile destroyer
DDNP	diazodinitrophenol
DIME	dense inert metal explosive
DoD	Department of Defense (US)
DPICM	dual-purpose improved conventional munition
DSMAC	digital scene matching area correlation
DU	depleted uranium
ECM	electronic countermeasures
EFP	explosively formed penetrator
EOD	explosive ordnance disposal
ERA	explosive reactive armour
ERGM	extended range guided munition
FA	field artillery
FAE	fuel-air explosives
FBI	Federal Bureau of Investigation
FCS	Future Combat System *also* fire-control system
FDC	fire direction center
FFG	guided missile frigate
F-Kill	firepower kill
FLM	focused lethality munition
FMJ	full metal jacket
FO	forward observer
FRES	future rapid effects system
FSAP	full spectrum active protection
FSCL	fire support coordination line
FSO	fire support officer
FTU	Firearms Training Unit
FY	fiscal year
G gravity	(as in G-force and G-suit)
GAO	Government Accountability Office
GBU	guided bomb unit
GPMG	general-purpose machine gun
GPS	global positioning system *also* gunner's primary sight
GPSE	gunner's primary sight extension
GSR	General Staff Requirement
G/VLLD	ground/vehicular laser locator designator

HBX	high brissance explosive		MCD	missile countermeasure device
HE	high-explosive		MCLC	mine clearing line charge
HEAT	high-explosive antitank		MCLOS	manual command to line of sight
HEAT-MP-T	high-explosive antitank multipurpose tracer		MCM	mine countermeasures
			MCS	mounted combat system
HESH	high-explosive squash head		MEU	marine expeditionary unit
HMG	heavy machine gun		MiG	Mikoyan-Gurevich (Russian aircraft designers)
HMTD	hexamethylene triperoxide diamine			
HMMWV	Humvee		MIRV	multiple, independently targeted re-entry vehicles
HOUNDS	high order unbelievably nasty destructive series			
			M-Kill	mobility kill
HUD	head up display		MLRS	multiple launch rocket system
IAC	Israeli Armored Corps		MMG	medium machine gun
ICBL	International Committee to Ban Landmines		MoD	Ministry of Defence (UK)
			MOOTW	military operations other than war
ICBM	intercontinental ballistic missile		MOPMS	modular pack mine system
ICM	improved conventional munition		MOPP	mission oriented protective posture
ICV	infantry combat vehicle			
IDF	Israel Defence Forces		MPAT	multipurpose antitank
IED	improvised explosive device		MPF	maritime prepositioning force
IFF	identification friend or foe		MRAP	mine resistant ambush protected
IFV	infantry fighting vehicle		MRSI	multiple round simultaneous impact
IIS	Iraqi Intelligence Service			
IMR	improved military rifle		MUP	Yugoslav Ministry of Defense
IJN	Imperial Japanese Navy		NASA	National Aeronautics and Space Administration
IM	insensitive munitions			
INS	Israeli Navy Ship		NATO	North Atlantic Treaty Organization
IPB	intelligence preparation of the battlefield			
			NBC	nuclear, biological, chemical
IR	infrared		NCO	non-commissioned officer
IRA	Irish Republican Army		NLOS	non line-of-sight
IRT	incident response team		NTC	National Training Center
ISR	intelligence, surveillance, and reconnaissance		NVA	North Vietnamese Army
			ODA	operational detachment alpha (a Special Forces A-team)
ITDU	Infantry Trials and Development Unit			
			OEF	Operation *Enduring Freedom* (Afghanistan 2001–02)
JDAM	joint direct attack munition			
KE	kinetic energy		OICW	objective individual combat weapon
K-Kill	catastrophic kill			
LAMPS	light airborne multipurpose system		OSS	Office of Strategic Services
LAW	light antitank weapon		PAC	Patriot advanced capability
LHA	amphibious assault ship		PBR	river patrol boat
LHD	amphibious assault ship (dock)		PBX	polymer bonded explosive
LPD	amphibious transport ship (dock)		PETN	pentaerythritol tetranitrate
LMG	light machine gun		PGK	precision guidance kit
LSD	landing ship (dock)		PGM	precision-guided munition
LSO	landing safety officer		PoA	point of aim
LSW	light support weapon		PoI	point of impact
MACV	Military Assistance Command, Vietnam		PLA	People's Liberation Army
			PLAN	People's Liberation Army Navy
MAG	Mitrailleuse d'Appui Général (GPMG)		PLO	Palestine Liberation Organization
			PNVS	pilot night vision system
MAGTF	marine air-ground task force		PTSD	post-traumatic stress disorder
MBT	main battle tank		PWRR	Princess of Wales' Royal Regiment

RAAM	remote antiarmor munition
RAM	rolling airframe missile
RAP	rocket-assisted projectile
RAR	Rhodesian African Rifles
RAST	recovery assistance securing and traversing systems (on surface ships' flight decks)
RDX	cyclotrimethylenetrinitramine
RF	radio frequency
RHA	rolled homogenous armour
RIO	radar intercept officer
RIVGRU	riverine group
RIVRON	riverine squadron
RoE	rules of engagement
RPG	rocket-propelled grenade
RSAF	Royal Small Arms Factory
SADARM	sense and destroy armor
SAM	surface-to-air missile
SAR	synthetic aperture radar
SAW	squad automatic weapon
SDB	small diameter bomb
SEAD	suppression of enemy air defense
SeAL	sea, air, land (US Navy Special Forces)
SEP	System Enhancement Program (for M1 Abrams tank)
SFW	sensor-fused weapon
SLR	self-loading rifle
SM	standard missile
SMAW	shoulder-launched multipurpose assault weapon
SOE	Special Operations Executive
SOF	Special Operations Forces
SP	self-propelled
SSBN	nuclear-powered ballistic missile submarine

SSGN	nuclear-powered guided missile submarine
SSN	nuclear-powered fast attack submarine
SUSAT	sight unit, small arms, trilux
SWAT	Special Weapons and Tactics
TADS	target acquisition and designation sight
TATP	triacetone peroxide
TBM	tactical ballistic missile
TC	tank commander
TEL	transporter-erector-launcher
TIS	thermal imaging sight
TLAM	Tomahawk land attack missile
TNT	Trinitrotoluene
TOW	tube-launched, optically tracked, wire-guided missile
UAV	unmanned aerial vehicle
UAH	up-armored Humvee
UCAV	unmanned combat aerial vehicle
UHF	ultra high frequency
USNS	United States naval ship (used to designate non-combatant navy vessels)
UUV	unmanned underwater vehicle
UXO	unexploded ordnance
VBIED	vehicle-borne IED
VCP	vehicle checkpoint
VLS	vertical launch system
WAAPM	wide area antipersonnel mine
WCMD	wind corrected munitions dispenser
WMD	weapons of mass destruction
WP	white phosphorus munition

INDEX

INDEX